Pilgrims Through Space and Time

Pilgrims Through Space and Time

Trends and Patterns in Scientific and Utopian Fiction

By J. O. Bailey

Foreword to the Reprint Edition

by Thomas D. Clareson

GREENWOOD PRESS, PUBLISHERS
WESTPORT, CONNECTICUT

The Library of Congress has catalogued this publication as follows:

Library of Congress Cataloging in Publication Data

Bailey, James Osler, 1903-
   Pilgrims through space and time.

   Bibliography: p.
   1. Science fiction—History and criticism.
2. Science fiction—Bibliography. I. Title.
[PN3448.S45B27 1972]   809.3'876   76-38126
ISBN 0-8371-6323-4

Originally published in 1947
by Argus Books, Inc., New York

Reprinted with the permission
of James Osler Bailey

First Greenwood Reprinting 1972

Library of Congress Catalogue Card Number 76-38126

ISBN 0-8371-6323-4

Printed in the United States of America

CONTENTS

PART I

THROUGH TIME

PART II

AND SPACE ANATOMIZED

Foreword

The reissue of J. O. Bailey's *Pilgrims Through Space and Time* is welcome. It has been a collector's item, too long out of print. It is an indispensable book to the student and teacher of science fiction, for no other study has provided so comprehensive an account of the emergence of the genre. It is, in short, at this time *the* intellectual and literary history of the development of science fiction from its origins in seventeenth and eighteenth century literature— amid the utopias and imaginary voyages— to the Second World War. Although Professor Bailey examines individual titles, such as those of Olaf Stapledon, published as late as 1945, he quite correctly gives his chief emphasis to the crucial period between 1870 and 1915, essentially the generation of Verne, Wells, and their contemporaries who responded to the visions arising from the so-called "new" science and technology.

Pilgrims Through Space and Time is not definitive, nor in view of its original date of publication (1947) could it be. Some aficionados of the specialized sf magazines have suggested that the book does not give sufficient attention to those magazines. That it does not give them more attention arises from a complex of circumstances involving its writing and publication. Professor Bailey has told me that *Pilgrims* grew out of a study of Wells and his contemporaries, for which he limited himself to fiction published in book form. (Amusingly, when I was recently compiling an annotated bibliography of sf criticism for *Extrapolation,* I found in the *Saturday Review of Literature* during the thirties a note requesting titles of "scientific romances," signed J. O. B.) With the patience of Job, he searched a basically unexplored field and acquired the fine representative bibliography on which he based *Pilgrims.* In 1939 he offered the manuscript to Ben Abramson, who accepted it, but the Second World War, with its shortages, delayed arrangements. Thus the book gained its final form only after the war when Abramson asked him to add a chapter sampling the later fiction, including the magazines, and when, as the text shows, Professor Bailey thought of the tradition of the scientific romance in the context of the dawning Atomic Age.

So a detailed history of the magazines during the so-called "classic" period—the forties and fifties when Asimov, Heinlein, Bradbury, and Clarke, among others, shaped the genre in terms of their own visions—remains to be written, as does that of the "New Wave" of the sixties. But if *Pilgrims Through Space and Time* seems to slight the specialist magazines, it accomplished something far more significant. (I think of the young girl at the World Science Fiction Convention in Boston in 1971 who asked quite seriously, "Oh, was there science fiction written before 1960?") Professor Bailey has shown that science fiction is the latest development in a continuing literary tradition which may be traced at least to the Renaissance and the medieval travel books, and that it is *not* an isolated literary phenomenon of the twentieth century.

His was truly a pioneer venture, the first full-scale academic study devoted to the genre as a whole. Moreover, it was written at the height of that period in which both fiction and criticism dwelt almost exclusively with the "realistic," everyday social scene and with the Proustian depths of the average man. The decade of the depression and the rise of Hitler was too concerned with the urgencies of here-and-now to give careful attention to "fantasies" and "American fairy tales," the latter label given sf by a British critic in a cursory review in a popular British magazine. In *The Supernatural in Modern English Fiction* (1917), for example, Dorothy Scarborough had given a chapter to Wells, but she did not know, finally, what to say of the scientific romances. Thus, despite very infrequent articles in the popular journals by such men as Edward Shanks and Bernard DeVoto, *Pilgrims Through Space and Time* marks the beginning of any serious consideration of science fiction either as a literary form or as a vehicle of ideas. No student or teacher of sf can meaningfully evaluate any phase or period without turning to *Pilgrims* as the foundation to which to refer, from which to build. Professor Bailey gave some of the basic motifs their lasting names. In a field in which devotees still delight in bickering over definitions, he stated the basic parameters of the genre:

> The touchstone for scientific fiction, then, is that it describes an imaginary invention or discovery in the natural sciences. The most serious pieces of this fiction arise from speculation about what may happen if science makes an extraordinary discovery. The romance is an attempt to anticipate this discovery and its impact upon society, and to foresee how mankind may adjust to the new condition. Naturally, the resulting narrative is often utopian, or satiric from a utopian viewpoint.

Change the final phrasing to the term dystopia; place a bit more emphasis, perhaps, upon the ideas of impact and adjustment rather than upon the discovery itself: his definition points to the core of science fiction now fully as well as it did when he first wrote it. He could not foresee, of course, as none of us could, either the rise of an antiscientific feeling or the insistence that the techniques of realistic-naturalistic fiction be applied to the genre. That is to say, he could not foresee those forces giving shape to the dystopian mood and the "New Wave" which have given contemporary science fiction its particular flavoring during the past ten or fifteen years.

Perhaps the final significance of *Pilgrims* lies in the area of intellectual history. Professor Bailey's description and analysis capture the broad, complex outlines of the initial vision that the new science and technology afforded writers of fiction. They dreamed of man, guided by reason and employing the potential of science, bringing about a far, far better world than that of the late nineteenth and early twentieth centuries. "Utopia," explained Bailey, "formerly found in a perfect land, now began to appear in a future time. Utopia is shifted from a place to be found to a condition to be achieved." While the idiom of that early vision, with its devotion to science and technology, may no longer be viable for many individuals, the hope lying behind that dream is very much with us.

Then, too, writing in 1945 in the aftermath of Hiroshima, Professor Bailey sounded very much like a contemporary futurist: "Scientific fiction offers many answers, some of them strange. Yet in a present confused beyond fantasy, we may ponder what hints for our journey into a strange future may be gathered from scientific romances."

When the Science Fiction Research Association (SFRA), an international group of individuals from the academic and "popular" sf communities, was founded in 1970, the Executive Committee decided that each year some recognition should be given for outstanding scholarship in the field. The first award in 1970 went to Professor Bailey; moreover, it was designated "The Pilgrim Award" to emphasize the importance of his book.

The reissue of *Pilgrims Through Space and Time* is, indeed, welcome.

Thomas D. Clareson

Cape May, N. J.
January, 1972

Preface

The military phase of World War II was brought to a startling conclusion by the use of the atomic bomb not only to wipe out two cities, but to threaten the annihilation of a people. The existence of this bomb and the inevitable spread of the secret of its manufacture brings us now, abruptly, into a new era, the Atomic Age, on whose threshold we stand chattering the ancient formulas of Babel.

Most of the war was fought with machines of unprecedented and constantly magnified power for destroying not only troops, but vast factories, city blocks, and even whole cities caught in a shower of bombs and rockets. Then the use of atomic power outmoded these small-time horrors. The notice served to Japan that the entire nation might be incinerated was also notice to the world that the same fate may befall any nation, in a matter of a few hours, a few minutes, or a blinding flash. In fact, the scientists who created the bomb have warned members of the United States Senate that atomic bombs of sufficient size—we could not expect moderation in a national death-struggle—might ignite the nitrogen of the atmosphere. Perhaps sun-bathers on the beaches of Mars would be relaxed by their new ocean of melted polar-cap, warmed by their new, near-by sun.

And yet, machinery is not destructive; atomic power is harmless unless guided by human folly. Machines and atomic force alter only the magnitude of man's own power, to be wielded for either construction or destruction. For this reason, the new era may be either one that makes use of the resources of the world for the unprecedented welfare of all men, or, on the other hand, a restless truce before the end of the world.

Because the Machine Age is a new phenomenon, and the Atomic Age is even newer, the important question for statesmanship today is: How can new imagination, foresight, and long-range planning adjust world-policy to the new scale? We must not bring World War III to the military phase. Even if, by the exercise of moderation unheard of in all history, the throwers of bombs should avoid setting the nitrogen of the atmosphere ablaze, there could be only one victor state, itself devastated, in a devastated world. The tangled path before statesmen today would, I think, seem an open road in comparison with the leavings of atomic terror: men of greed and prey hardened to ultimate brutality, armies without nations or homes ravaging the villages and the ruins of cities. To avoid this World War III and at the same time to establish Permanent World Peace I, the statesmen of the world need wisdom of a deep, new texture, broadly based on the understanding of all human problems. They need wisdom such as the world has never yet observed in councils of state.

Scientific fiction, the subject of this book, does not provide all this wisdom, but it may be one among many sources of suggestion. For many years, this fiction has been busy with imaginative treatments of the coming, and now present, Machine Age; lately, it has even told imaginative stories of how man might learn to live with the terrible secret of atomic power, and how he might use this power to make life abundant in a new way. Some of this fiction has dealt thoughtfully with concrete instances of startling new discoveries in science, their impact upon man's life, and the various possible readjustments to them. It is only fiction, but it may have graphic value now that we have got to anticipate a course of events in what is essentially a realm of sheer, unpredictable fiction, the future. Insofar as statesmen today need facts, fiction has nothing to offer, but insofar as we all need to bring to the consideration of certain new facts, such as atomic power, every scrap of foresight we can find, many pieces of this fiction are worth review.

Pilgrims Through Space and Time is descriptive and analytical. It describes a large number of scientific romances, arranged in somewhat chronological order, and then presents an analysis of ideas found running through these romances in a conventional pattern. Many ideas in these books are really childish. On the other hand, some ideas that seem at first fantastic may be of value as we face a world rendered fantastic by the incredible radio, the inconceivable fact of relativity, and the ghastly power of sub-atomic physics.

For example, let us consider one suggestion that writers of scientific fiction have made over and over again until it is a conventional feature. The idea of Salomon's House, a research University as the effective brain of the State, was suggested in Sir Francis Bacon's scientific-utopian fiction, *The New Atlantis*.

Scores of writers of scientific fiction have followed Bacon in suggesting a University to furnish guiding-principles for the World-State.

Does this idea suggest anything to us—can it, in a world redundant with colleges in every hamlet? Why, we have hundreds of universities! Or have we? Have we anywhere Salomon's House to provide the unprecedented wisdom our statesmen need in their predicament?

Let me take the liberty that a Preface affords an author to draw a picture of a modern Salomon's House. I do not invent this picture at all, or any part of it; I piece it together from the romances examined in this book.

Salomon's House in the University of the World. Its function is to serve as a permanent brain-trust for mankind, by collecting, assimilating, analyzing, understanding, and providing the data and the conclusions necessary for wise guidance in all governmental, social, cultural, and scientific policies. It is, of course, concerned with the learning, especially the wisdom, of the past; it is concerned with new-search in all sciences; but, unlike other universities, its primary function is to serve the world in a permanent advisory capacity.

Its colleges are graduate schools and research centers in the humanities, the sciences, and the social sciences; but the purpose of research is to provide data and background for "prosearch." The professors in each college, and in each chair, are the world's greatest specialists in their fields—each field a cloister of renowned historians, physicians, physicists, etc.—and every professor is paid enough that he can work unmolested by want and the gestures of private industry. The heads of every college, and certainly all members of the governing board of the University, are not, however, specialists, but "generalists," men of broad learning, ample wisdom, competent to co-ordinate data from many specialized fields.

There are students, of course, perhaps 30,000 of them. But they do not resemble the rah-rah boys of other colleges. The World University has no truck with fraternities or sororities, football orgies, or course-credits in snap courses. There is enough elementary education elsewhere in the world. The equivalent of the usual American A. B. degree is the minimum prerequisite for enrollment as a student in the University. The best brains from the lands called China, Arabia, Brazil, Russia, and the United States, and from all other parts of the world, are selected, tested, re-selected, and finally admitted on probation, and on salary, to the World University. There, investigating the wisdom of the world in books (including useful works from all libraries, on microfilm at least) and in the laboratory, living in an international colony of the intellectually elite, they use eight or ten years to prepare themselves for their gigantic task. Many of these students are absorbed as fellows and finally as professors in the University. Others go to spark the intellectual life of the countless elementary colleges. Others become statesmen or counsellers to statesmen. Some return home to guide the future equivalents of State Departments, Research Institutions, Public Forums, etc., in their native lands; others become writers, lecturers, commentators— sowers of the seed of a new wisdom necessary in a new age. The world thus enters for the first time seriously upon the task of educating its most alert, liberal, and humane minds for the profound responsibility of making the future.

In effect, this University renders obsolete the thinking that underlies piece-meal settlements, national jockeyings, spheres of influence, agreements about the open-secret of the atomic bomb, national conscriptions, multi-ocean navies, etc. It costs the whole world somewhat less than one middle-sized navy.

Such is the simple essence of a proposal repeatedly made in scientific fiction, varied in details from book to book: Let us marshal the brains we have, think the best we can, and act (where action is dangerous) only in accordance with the best wisdom this world affords.

* * * * *

Many people have given me advice and help in writing this book. Mr. Ben Abramson of The Argus Book Shop allowed me to use a bibliography he had spent some years collecting. Others, among them the late Dr. Miles J. Breuer, the late Mr. H. P. Lovecraft, Professor A. B. DeMille, Mr. Forrest Ackerman, Mr. H. C. Koenig, and Mr. Langley Searles, provided me with titles of scientific romances, generously expressed their ideas of scientific fiction and its place in literature, and helped me in other ways. I take this means of publishing my gratitude to them all. Among my colleagues in the University of North Carolina, I am especially grateful to Dr. John Booker, Dr. Dougald MacMillan, Dr. Howard Jones (now of Harvard), and Dr. George Coffman.

J. O. Bailey.

Chapel Hill, N. C.
December, 1945.

"We were making the future," he said, "and hardly any of us troubled to think what future we were making. And here it is!"

—WELLS, *When the Sleeper Wakes.*

PART I

Through Time

CHAPTER ONE

Staff and Scrip

ON THE NIGHT OF October 30, 1938, Mr. Orson Welles broadcast over the Columbia system a "news-story" of an invasion from Mars. The broadcast was presented as fiction, preceded and followed by the normal routines of the studio. Yet the next morning headlines described a wave of hysteria over the United States. This hysteria had been prepared by the romances of Jules Verne, H. G. Wells, and their followers, which had described space ships and invasions from Mars, just as they had foretold the airplane and the radio. They had made these fancies look so much like science, and scientific invention had so justified some of them, that naturally many people believed the invasion from Mars to be real. The hysteria testifies that scientific romances are widely read and are, perhaps, a factor in shaping popular thought.

World War II and its fantastic climax as the first bomb fell on Hiroshima have realized other prophecies in scientific fiction. But the wave of apprehension cannot this time be calmed with assurances that the radio was only fooling. Possession of the bomb by the United Nations alone does not solve the problem: destruction of Japanese cyclotrons so far used in medical research seems a gesture of rage rather than a permanent preventive; the scientists who made the bomb say that the only "secret" concerns processes of manufacture that physicists anywhere may duplicate. Victory does not seem yet to have brought either victors or vanquished the feeling that by-gones may be by-gones and we are done with war forever. Yet it is only trite to say that civilization cannot afford, perhaps cannot survive, World War III.

In scientific fiction, atomic bombs left Paris a smoking crater as early as Wells's *The World Set Free* in 1914. With more optimism than most of us feel in the ideological wasteland of our time, Wells had the characters of his romance work out a rational solution, stop their foolish war, and even use atomic power to contribute immeasurably to the welfare of all mankind. This and many other pieces of scientific fiction have attempted seriously to foresee the new world science is constantly forcing us to face; they have attempted seriously to suggest ways we may adjust our thought, our lagging culture, and our statesmanship to face it with wisdom. There may be in these romances some suggestions of value to us today.

It is time that this body of literature, often considered a curious and childish by-way, is defined, presented in some historical survey, sampled, and analyzed to see what its major patterns and ideas may be.

Nearly everybody knows what it is in a general way; everybody has heard the terms "novels of science," "fantascience," "scientifiction," and "science-fiction." Looking farther into the past than recent romances, I am using "scientific fiction" to describe the familiar, boyhood thrillers of Jules Verne; the romances of H. G. Wells written with a more adult reality; the disturbing cosmic histories of Olaf Stapledon; and also some of the pieces displayed on the newsstands for the past twenty years in lurid magazines, *Amazing* and *Astounding Stories.* Definition is needed only to exclude from the present study some related kinds of romance.

A piece of scientific fiction is a narrative of an imaginary invention or discovery in the natural sciences and consequent adventures and experiences. The invention must be imaginary at the time the romance is written, an imaginary airplane, space-flier, radio, rocket, atomic bomb, or death-ray. The discovery may take place in the interior of the earth, on the moon, on Mars, within the atom, in the future, in the prehistoric past, or in a dimension beyond the third; it may be a surgical, mathematical, or chemical discovery. It must be a scientific discovery—something that the author at least rationalizes as possible to science.

On every side, scientific fiction overlaps other kinds. Any piece of realism may describe science and scientists, as Lewis's *Arrowsmith* does. Any romance may express the utopian dream of a better world. Many novels today reflect some impact of Darwinism and relativity. The most fantastic tale of terror may exhibit its scientific formulas. In these phases scientific fiction overflows into other classes of literature.

Certain types that resemble scientific fiction may be excluded. The realistic novel that interprets character in the light of scientific fact, such as Huxley's *Point Counter Point*, does not belong to this group. The utopia or satire concerned solely with human nature and social polity is not included; hence I am ignoring Plato's *Republic*, but noticing that More's *Utopia* describes a wonderful machine, the incubator. I am excluding the imaginary voyage that has only geographic interest and fiction of the super-natural and weird unless its phenomena are "scientifically" ex-plained—as Poe's "M. Valdemar" purports to be the experiment of a medical student. I do not include fiction describing an actual invention; the imaginary tank of Wells's "The Land Ironclads" is, of course, not the same thing as a tank realistically described in 1946. There is a thin line between the pseudo-scientific and the scientific, but I am omitting most stories of the occult and psychic —though some astral bodies engage in adventures that concern the natural sciences. For instance, Kepler's *Somnium* is a dream, but is also the first attempt in fiction to describe the moon as scientists viewed it.

The touchstone for scientific fiction, then, is that it describes an imaginary invention or discovery in the natural sciences. The more serious pieces of this fiction arise from speculation about what may happen if science makes an extraordinary discovery. The romance is an attempt to anticipate this discovery and its impact upon society, and to foresee how mankind may adjust to the new condition. Naturally, the resulting narrative is often utopian, or satiric from a utopian viewpoint.

In scientific-utopian fiction, a man from the actual world ad-ventures into a world in which many ills of the real world have been corrected. The hero gradually learns how the new world is better adjusted, better managed, and happier than the old one; the writer looks forward from the actual. The utopistic satire, on the other hand, presents the actual world from the point of view of a utopian citizen who looks backward to the actual. The older utopias described imaginary voyages to strange places, but since the principle of evolution was established, utopias have generally described voyages into future times when the race has improved and men have adjusted themselves to the conditions of the future. If men have not well adjusted themselves, the result is satire: the degenerated future stands for wrong ten-dencies in the present.

The method followed in serious scientific fiction is either to predict that what will happen tomorrow is what has begun to happen today, or to predict that causes operative in the past to produce certain results will be operative in the future to produce similar results. Inventions of the nineteenth century produced the Machine Age in the twentieth; the airplane implemented World

War II. Now we have the secret of atomic power. What Atomic Age will it produce?

Scientific fiction offers many answers, some of them strange. Yet in a present confused beyond fantasy, we may ponder what hints for our journey into a strange future may be gathered from scientific romances. The hysteria when Orson Welles broadcast and the way we understood immediately the nature of the atomic bomb indicate that the fancies of scientific fiction have indeed made some impression on popular thought. Perhaps the people of the world, through this fiction made familiar with the idea of a World State and other utopian adjustments, are more ready for leadership into a good Atomic Age than our statesmen suppose.

CHAPTER TWO

And Forth We Ride

Scientific Fiction Before 1817

As SCIENCE HAS DEVELOPED, on the one hand it has replaced the belief in magic with belief in law, but on the other hand it has seemed to the popular imagination a modern kind of magic. Imaginative romances of what science may achieve have multiplied with the advance of science. The present chapter presents the earliest of these romances and traces their development up to 1817.

The stories are classified according to the kind of invention or discovery they present. Those that describe airships are classed together; so are those that describe a trip to the moon. One moon-voyage may be utopian, another satiric, and a third sheer adventure. But in each the imaginary discovery is the world of the moon, and that discovery governs the classification. Naturally, a book placed in one classification may overlap into others, but I have tried to select the main adventure and to place each narrative with others most like it.

A. *The Wonderful Machine*

Bishop John Wilkins, one of the founders of the Royal Society, published in 1641 *Mercury; or the Secret and Swift Messenger*. Though it is a tract rather than a romance, it explores the possibilities of invention in the manner of scientific fiction. "A flying Chariot" — that is, an airplane — would be so useful that "imagination itself cannot conceive any more useful." Wilkins thinks of the phonograph, "a trunk or hollow pipe, that . . . shall preserve the voice entirely for certain hours or days," but doubts whether it can be invented. He suggests a code for communicating by means of

bells, muskets, and other noise-makers, and foreshadows the telegraph in describing how men may communicate through walls by
using "magneticall vertues." These speculations by a founder of the
Royal Society show that science began very early to look forward
to an age of mechanical wonders.

Science was beginning experimentation in the seventeenth and
eighteenth centuries, during an age of geographical exploration. Narratives of voyages were popular, and so were narratives of imaginary
voyages.   Sometimes these romances included speculations about
scientific invention. Robert Paltock's *Peter Wilkins* (1751) tells the
story of a traveller who is shipwrecked off the coast of Africa and
then drawn into a strong current flowing to the south. After a trip
through a great cavern, he emerges upon a lake. On its shores live
a primitive people with wings. He marries a winged woman, who
bears him winged children. He teaches these people the use of fire-
arms for conquest of a neighboring tribe, and for this contribution
is offered the throne, but he prefers, on the death of his wife, to
return to England. The method of flying in this romance is natural,
rather than mechanical, but the story suggests a stage of transition
to the romance of invention.

Tales of flying by mechanical means followed immediately upon
the invention of the balloon by the Montgolfier brothers in 1783.
The Montgolfiers' balloon was far from dirigible. *The Aerostatic
Spy* (anonymous, 1785), however, describes balloons that can be
steered. The Preface states that "there can be little Reason to doubt"
steering apparatus will be invented, to herald "a new Aera in the
History of Science."   In the story a shipwrecked traveller escapes
from an island by making a balloon of animal skins, putting a stove
in it to heat the air, and sailing away. Landed in Africa, he leaves
his balloon, but returns to find it filled with "inflammable air" and
tugging at the ropes. Off again, he comes upon Amiel, "inhabitant
of the upper air" and donor of the strange gas. The traveller and
Amiel fly around the world, perform feats of magic, and engage in
discussion of many topics, including the future of aeronautics.

B. *The Wonderful Journey*

1. On the Earth.

Most of the numerous imaginary voyages of the seventeenth and
eighteenth centuries contain little of interest to science, but sometimes the traveller discovers a people who have machines that
anticipate inventions.

Tiphaigne de la Roche in *Giphantia* (1760-61) tells the story of
a traveller who wanders into a desert across the border from Guinea.

There a spirit materializes before his eyes and becomes his host, to describe to him the civilization of this spirit-world. These "people" keep in one-way communication with the outside world through mechanisms that suggest the telephone, radio, and television. The telephone system is made of "imperceptible" pipes led from every section of the earth. A globe so amplifies the weak vibrations in the pipes that they can be heard. A dial selects the conversation to be amplified. The traveller is able to see events in all parts of the world through a mirror to which images are "remitted" from sending stations operated by invisible spirits. He is also shown pictures of past events, and a system of picture-making that clearly anticipates photography is described. A light-sensitive substance is smeared over canvas, exposed, and put to "harden and dry" in a dark chamber. Dehydrated foods and drinks are described; certain "salts" dropped into water change it into wine, and other "salts" change a tasteless base into meat. Finally the traveller departs through an underground way that leads through the center of the earth, observes earthquakes generated in the conflict of fire and water, and emerges on his native shore.

2. Into the Earth

The whole adventure of Nicholas Klimius, in Baron Holberg's *Journey to the World Under-Ground* (in English, 1742), takes place in the hollow interior of the earth. Through a cavern Klimius falls into the earth, to find there a sun surrounded by planets. He becomes a satellite for three days, eating bread from his pockets and observing the "true laws of Motion" that carry the crumbs around him in regular orbits. A great bird draws him to the planet Nazar, inhabited by trees with human heads and short feet for creeping over the ground. In Nazar, Klimius finds, human conventions are generally inverted: men of wealth are despised, a person of quick apprehension is considered stupid, and inventors are placed in halters to be hanged unless their inventions prove beneficial. None the less, the nation has many mechanical devices, such as ships propelled by clock-work. Among the Junipers on Nazar, males do housework and engage in prostitution. In Mutak, sick people are jailed and criminals are given physic. Carried by a bird to the firmament (the inner surface of the earth), Klimius finds a civilization of monkeys. For teaching them the use of gunpowder and aiding in a conquest, he is made emperor, but when the enemy acquires gunpowder too, he flees down a cavern that leads to the surface of the earth.

Though this story is largely satiric in purpose, we note the theory that the earth is hollow, the Newtonian physics, self-propelling ships, and biological surmises.

3. To Other Planets

By the time Holberg described Klimius's visit to the planets inside the earth, the imaginary voyage to other planets, especially the moon, was well established. A number of Greek philosophers fancied the moon to be inhabited, but classic literature offers no voyages to the planets until Lucian of Samosata in the second century, A. D., wrote two stories of trips to the moon.

In Lucian's *Icaromenippus*, Menippus, angered in a quarrel with philosophers about the shape of the earth, determines to fly to the moon to view the earth from that orb. Remembering the story of Icarus, he cuts a wing from a vulture and another from an eagle, straps them on, learns to fly, and departs for the moon. From the moon, he sees that the earth is plainly round. In accordance with suggestions in classic myths, he finds spirits on the moon, especially Empedocles, who teaches him how to sharpen his sight so as to discern the most minute events on earth: grave philosophers engaging in immoral actions, earthly crises, perjuries, treasons, and murders. Still not content, he flies upward past the sun to Heaven, where he is admitted to the presence of Zeus. But the gods, disliking his boldness, take his wings from him and send him back to earth.

Lucian's *True History* is more elaborate. It begins as an Odyssey: from the Pillars of Hercules a ship sails to discover "the limits of the ocean and the people who might dwell beyond it." A waterspout hurls the vessel into the air, and the wind carries it to the moon, an inhabited and cultivated land. When the travellers arrive, Endymion, king of the moon, is at war with Phaeton, king of the sun, concerning the colonization of the planet Jupiter. Their troops are such as Horse-vultures, Salad-wings (birds fledged with herbs), and Flea-archers (archers astride giant fleas). The description of life on the moon seems pure fantasy: in old age, men do not die, but dissolve into smoke; food consists of fumes; drink is air compressed till it exudes dew; by looking down a well, lunar inhabitants can see events on earth. Finally, the travellers sail away through the air past the sun, to land on the ocean.

After Lucian, the theme rested for thirteen hundred years. Then, in Ariosto's *Orlando Furioso* (1532; translated into English during the reign of Elizabeth) Astolpho, in search of Orlando's lost wits, goes to the moon in the chariot that had received Elijah, drawn by flaming horses. He finds the moon to be a "rich champaign" filled with cities and towns. All things lost on earth are there: vows, prayers, courtiers' gifts to princes, forgotten poems, and, in a flask, Orlando's lost wits.

With the rise of astronomy after Copernicus, voyages to the moon included more science. The first trip to the moon to make use of science was Johann Kepler's *Somnium* (posthumously published in Latin, 1634). In 1610, Galileo had published *Sidereus Nuncius* describing vividly the new universe revealed by the telescope. He described the moon as we know it to be, a world of mountains and chasms and contrasts of blinding light and total shadow. This description, Kepler's own knowledge of astronomy, and the events of his life form the background for Kepler's *Somnium*. The story is told as a tale dreamed when the author was reading and fell asleep. In the tale, Duracotus is the son of Fiolxhilda, suspected of witchcraft because of her night-long observations of the moon. Duracotus becomes for five years an apprentice to the astronomer Tycho Brahe. Returning home filled with astronomical knowledge, he is amazed to find that his mother knows as much about the moon as Tycho Brahe. She finally confides that she is in league with the "daemons of Levania," inhabitants of the moon, and that she has visited the moon. One evening Duracotus is taken with his mother to the moon, by supernatural means.

But when they reach the moon, the story becomes a means of describing conditions on the moon as the telescope had revealed them. Galileo had denied water and atmosphere on the moon, but Kepler supposes water and air may exist there. Lunar geography, climatology, and biology are in accordance with observation and the laws known to Kepler. The moon is divided into two zones, Subvolva and Privolva. One zone is frozen in interplanetary cold; on the other the sunlight is blinding, the air parching hot. Mountains are higher, valleys deeper, than on the earth. Serpentine monsters of tremendous size and grotesque shapes bask in the sunlight, and shelter in caverns. The life-span of vegetation is a fortnight, while the sun shines. Kepler, that is, imagined conditions on the moon that accorded with what he had seen in the telescope. Physical features of the moon resemble those in Wells's *First Men in the Moon,* where mention is made of Kepler's lunar world.

Kepler's book is in Latin. The first narrative of a trip to the moon written in English is Bishop Francis Godwin's *The Man in the Moone* (1638). Domingo Gonsales, the narrator, cast on St. Helena, trains swan-like birds called "gansas" to pull him through the air on a raft. Fleeing on his raft from brigands, he is amazed that his gansas strike straight upward, mounting higher and higher. Half a century before Newton's principles of gravitation were announced, Godwin described Gonsales's experience with a diminishing gravitational attraction. He meditates that things do not "sinke toward the Center of the Earth, as their naturall place," but are "drawen by a secret property of the Globe . . . in like sort as the Loadstone draweth Iron." Between the earth and the moon, Gonsales rests in gravitational equilibrium, but he is held (without the

effort of his gansas) on a direct line—that is, he follows the moon
as it circles the earth, which turns under him like a "huge Mathe-
maticall Globe." Gradually, as he approaches the moon, the earth is
more like a moon, the moon more like a world. There is no thinning
of the air.

Arrived on the moon after twelve days, he finds most of the
moon to be ocean. Though vegetation and animals are strange, the
land areas are inhabited by a race of men twice as high as men on
earth. Colors are curious and indescribable. Gravitational pull is
slight; Lunarians travel by leaping into the air and fanning themselves along. Lunar days and nights are a fortnight long. Thus far,
the story follows scientific observation with some faithfulness.

But here it abandons science and becomes utopistic. Gonsales
is sent to visit the prince, who sets him to learning the language —
a kind of singing. Lunarians are without disease and are remarkably virtuous. The prince gives Gonsales some jewels with magic
powers, and he departs with his restless gansas, to land safely in
China.

Influenced by Kepler and, in his edition of 1640, by Bishop Godwin, the scientist Bishop John Wilkins wrote a book to examine
whether the moon is inhabited and whether travel to it is possible,
A Discourse Concerning a New World (Book I, 1638, the third
edition including Book II, 1640). The book presents fourteen propo-
sitions in Book I and ten in Book II, to the general effect that the
moon may be inhabited and that man may learn how to journey
there. Wilkins argues that his opinion contradicts no principle of
reason or faith, that some modern scientists believe there may be a
world in the moon, that the spots on the moon represent water, that
there are mountains, valleys, and plains on the moon, that there is
air about the moon, that probably the moon is inhabited though perhaps not by men, and that perhaps men may find some conveyance
to the moon. He expresses the opinion that men will some day learn
the art of flying, and then they will plant colonies on the moon. Wilkins knew the distance to the moon, but he supposed a flying machine could go there in 180 days.

From the science in the fiction of Kepler and Godwin and the
tract of Wilkins, we might expect moon-voyages hereafter to be increasingly scientific, but they are not always so. Cyrano de Bergerac
was partly interested in science, but largely in amusing his readers
and in satirizing manners. Though drawing material from Lucian
and Godwin, Cyrano apparently neither understood the science of
his day nor bothered to rely upon it. Cyrano's *Voyages to the Moon
and the Sun* exhibit not only fantastic methods of interplanetary
travel, but also many quasi-scientific ideas that are absurd.

In *The Moon* (in English, 1659), the narrator determines to

Frontispiece from Bishop Godwin's *The Man in the Moone*

prove whether the moon is inhabited. He flies by carrying bottles of dew, sucked up by the sun, but lands in Canada. There he argues droll quasi-science with the governor, such as that the earth turns with the impact of sunbeams. In a second machine, driven by a spring, he crashes; sportive soldiers send him up again with rockets, but he is finally drawn to the moon as it "drew" the beef-marrow he had rubbed on his bruises. On the moon, he lands on the Tree of Life in the Garden of Eden, and finds there Adam, Eve, Enoch, Elijah, and Saint John. Enoch had arrived by catching smoke in vessels held under his arms, Elijah by repeatedly tossing up a load-stone and being drawn to it in an iron chariot. Outside the Garden are four-legged men and spirits. Lunarians speak in musical tones, go naked, eat by breathing fumes of food, and shoot game with a powder-and-shot composition that kills, plucks, roasts, and seasons. At the king's court, the narrator meets Godwin's Gonsales. There is much discussion of quasi-science—why pumps lift water, whether plants have sensuous life. There are fantastic inventions: glow-worms light houses, transparent balls imprison the sun's rays, machines recite the contents of books. Finally, the Devil brings the narrator back to earth.

Put into prison for sorcery in *The Sun* (in English, 1687) he escapes in a machine made of concave glasses to focus the sun's rays and thus to create a current of air that lifts the machine — and is drawn to the sun. On the sun he finds civilized birds who put him on trial because he is a loathsome human being. He meets Campanella and is discussing utopias with him at the point where the story breaks off.

Treated here in the barest plot-outline, Cyrano's *Voyages* are extremely fecund in ideas: scientific, quasi-scientific, and satiric. From Cyrano, Swift took many of his devices.

Gabriel Daniel's *A Voyage to the World of Cartesius* (in English, 1694), makes use of a trip to the moon, and then to the third Heaven, or space beyond the universe, as a means of defending Cartesian theories. The narrator learns that the spirit of Descartes is to be found in the third Heaven. To talk with him, the narrator is disembodied (by taking a pinch of snuff), and with a friend and a priest he sets out to find Descartes. Visiting the moon, they find lunar geography somewhat like that of the earth and the moon inhabited by spirits, among them Socrates, Aristotle, and Plato. Going from the moon deep into the "Indefinite Spaces," they find Descartes. With him they discuss science: axioms, the experimental method, the nature of a vacuum, gravity, etc. Descartes sets forth his principles, and to prove the "True Philosophy" offers to create a universe. He "chalks out" a portion of space, divides the matter in it into equal, small parts, and sets the parts into agitation in vortices around fixed centers. The travellers observe Descartes create a solar system and listen to his explanation of light, matter, gravity, and motion. Then the narrator's soul returns to the earth and re-enters his body. He is now ready to confute all who doubt Cartesianism.

David Russen's *Iter Lunare; or, A Voyage to the Moon* (1703) is likewise a philosophical examination, but of Godwin's and Cyrano's fiction in relation to the science of the time. It is an extended book-review that points out how the fiction fails to accord with science. Russen supposes there may be inhabitants on the moon, but doubts whether there is air between the earth and the moon; he supposes men may learn to fly by "application of wings to their Bodies," but would soon fall for "lassitude." He argues against any kind of spring to propel an airplane, for the spring would simply turn the machine over and over. But a giant spring, based on a mountain, might shoot a man to the moon — with some danger of missing it. Russen takes Cyrano's fantastic methods seriously, and painstakingly shows that they would not work.

Robert Paltock's *John Daniel* (1751) is closer in mood to Kepler and Godwin than to Cyrano. Shipwrecked on a desert island with a girl whom he "marries," John Daniel establishes, within thirty years, a patriarchal society of children and grandchildren (the children intermarry, like those of Adam and Eve). One eccentric son, Jacob, refuses to set up a home, but, alone in the mountains, experiments with plane-surfaces and finally produces a flying-machine. It is a platform to which wings (or planes) are attached; levers like those on a railway hand-car flap the wings. John and Jacob mount the platform and pump, and soon find themselves flying through space. Suddenly the machine wavers and throws them off-balance; when the confusion is over, they descend to the "earth." Looking up, they are amazed at the tremendous size of the "moon." The country they land in is mountainous; copper-colored people live there in deep caverns and worship the sun. Days and nights are enormously long. Finally John and Jacob escape from this strange place, but again their machine bowls over, and they descend as rapidly as they can. Landing in a wild country, they find amphibious creatures, intelligent children of an exiled English woman and a sea-serpent. The eldest of these creatures, a "philosopher," explains to John that the behavior of the flying machine was a *bouleversement* at the point of gravitational equilibrium between the earth and the moon, and that John and Jacob had visited the moon. This romance not only tells a good story, but presents, for 1751, a first-rate flying machine and a convincing *bouleversement*. The scenery of the moon is not without scientific interest.

Voltaire's *Micromegas* (1752) makes two important advances

beyond the romances already examined. Voltaire reverses the voyage from the earth to a planet and describes the visit of inhabitants of other planets to the earth. He contributes to the satiric pattern the cosmic point of view, that is, the judgment of the standards of men on earth as creatures with rational, but radically different, standards might judge them. Cyrano had suggested this judgment when his traveller was put on trial by creatures of the sun; Swift had given his king of Brobdingnag a similar (though earth-bound) perspective. Voltaire brings to earth Micromegas, from the solar system of Sirius, and a companion from the planet Saturn, and these creatures judge men according to standards set up on planets from which the earth seems only a pin-point.

Micromegas, using his superior knowledge of cosmic laws, travels from world to world as a bird hops from bough to bough, riding sometimes on a comet, sometimes on forces of attraction and repulsion in beams of light. He is a giant eight leagues high; his companion from Saturn is somewhat smaller. The Saturnian is a limited creature, with only seventy-two senses; Micromegas has a thousand. Though they have learned that all things in the universe are relative, that life may pulse in even the most out-of-the-way corners, they suppose the earth to be altogether uninhabited until by accident the Saturnian glimpses men through a diamond that acts as a microscope. After some difficulty, Micromegas and his companion converse with men. They learn about such things, for instance, as the Russo-Turkish war, a struggle about a lump of clay no bigger than Micromegas's heel. Thousands of throats will be cut out to see whether the clay shall belong to someone called Sultan or someone called Caesar, neither of whom has ever seen the clay; very few of the animals cutting each other's throats have seen Sultan or Caesar. When men, explaining their religion, state that all the stars were made for the pleasure of man, the visitors are choked with "inextinguishable laughter."

The satire in Aratus's (*pseud.*) *A Voyage to the Moon* (1793) is more limited. The invention of the balloon (1783) naturally suggested the use of a balloon for flying to the moon. Currents of air carry Aratus's traveller to the moon in "seventeen days, six hours, two minutes, and three seconds." He lands on an island resembling England, peopled by snakes that walk upright and speak English. The rest of the book caricatures English social and political life in describing the civilization of the snakes. The Great Snake (the king) is "a most eminent debauchee, an everlasting drinker, intolerably proud, insolent, cruel, and ignorant."

Like Kepler, George Fowler doubtless knew too much science to suppose that any available means could take a man to the moon. In his *A Flight to the Moon* (1813) the traveller, Randalthus, is simply taken to the moon by an angel, during a vision. But, even though the journey is a vision, Randalthus feels the effect of gravitation and the *bouleversement* at the "line balancing the attraction of the earth and the moon." He finds the moon a world much like the earth, inhabited by people of a golden cast. They have an idyllic society; they speak sentimentally ornate English; they are ignorant of science. Randalthus teaches them, speaking of the earth's atmosphere, which "becomes more and more rarefied the higher you advance," eclipses, the motions and habitability of the planets — surely inhabited, as nature causes even a clod of dirt to swarm with life— social life on earth, the geography of the earth, which spins before their eyes in illustration, the history of various nations, the vileness of slavery (the book was published in Baltimore), the formation of the earth, and fossil bones. In this pre-Darwinian period, he wonders where the great saurians have gone; he mentions sea-shells found on mountain tops and wonders how they got there; he discusses the cyclic theory of the rise and fall of civilizations; and he reflects upon the eventual fate of the earth when the sun's force shall be spent and the last man alive shall shed his streaming tears. Departing from the moon, Randalthus visits Mercury and then the sun, inhabited beneath its heated crust by departed souls from other planets. The book is not satire, but a vehicle for expressing Fowler's scientific theories, which were advanced ones for 1813.

Thomas Erskine's *Armata* (1816-17) returns to satire. To provide a setting for his story, Erskine invented a planet. His traveller discovers a twin-world attached to the earth at the South Pole. His ship is swept into one of two rock-bound channels (the other flowing in the opposite direction) and borne for seventy thousand miles by an irresistible current. The narrator is cast up on an island, Armata, that is a counterpart of England. Morven, his host, tells the story of Armata — that is, of England — and its problems of overproduction, wars, pauperism, crime, and the like. Customs are similar, but different in accent at points Erskine wishes to satirize. For instance, the steam engine had been invented in England; in Armata a substance has been discovered that gives momentum to engines, but there is fear that it may be wrongly used. If suppressed it will "unhinge a world for its freedom." The language used suggests a double meaning: both a physical force and Reason. The narrator returns to earth by way of the second channel.

Several possibilities for the story of a trip to other planets were explored in these stories before 1817. The satire with which Lucian began deepened and became more philosophical in the eighteenth century, especially in Voltaire's story; the scientific integrity contributed by Kepler was now in, now out of, the stories. Efforts to make

the means for voyaging to the moon scientifically credible had only
relative success, and the dream remained a common device.

4. Into the Future

The historical romance of the future is rare before the nineteenth
century. But the year 1763 produced Samuel Madden's *The Reign
of George VI, 1900-1925*. It is not scientific fiction, for it foresees
none of the advancement of science and the industrial revolution, but
it offers an early example of a type later developed as scientific fiction. Summarizing history from 1763 to 1900, the author describes
the growth of Russia, as it devours Poland, the Crimea, and the
Scandinavian countries and becomes the bully of the world, and the
ominous growth of France. In 1900, the Russians invade England;
defense is impeded by fifth-column work in the form of widespread
bribery. For effective action, King George VI makes himself dictator, attacks the invading Russians, and defeats them by land and
sea. Then France attacks England, but George VI vigorously invades France, via Dunkirk and Calais. By 1902, England has defeated both Russia and France. The defeated nations then, leaving
England alone, attack and demolish Germany. To help Germany,
George VI sends an expeditionary force to Flanders and is advancing toward victory when Spain attacks. The English in America
(loyal to England) wrest Mexico from Spain, and by 1920 the war
is over. George VI, crowned King of France, completes his glorious
reign with the spread of the arts, English law, and the English language through his vast realm. There is no suggestion that life in
1925 differs in any radical way from life in 1763.

C. *Utopias and Satires*

A piece of scientific fiction describes an imaginary invention or
discovery in science; the story then narrates the effect of this discovery. When the discovery alters human life, the writer's interest
is often chiefly in this effect. Naturally some utopias and utopistic
satires, presenting human life as it may be altered, describe discoveries that alter it — and to this extent are scientific fiction.

Except for a suggestion of eugenic mating in Plato's *Republic*,
I have not found scientific material in utopias before More's *Utopia*
(1515-16; in English, 1551). But More's citizens of Utopia are
students of the stars; they have faith in the laws of nature; and they
insure having healthy families by exhibiting bride and groom naked,
but properly chaperoned, to one another before marriage. They possess an imaginary machine, an incubator for hatching chickens.

An early utopia of importance to science is Bacon's *New Atlantis* (1627). Its publication was slightly preceded, however, by

the appearance of Andreae's *Christianopolis* (1619) and Campanella's *The City of the Sun* (1623). Perhaps these works influenced *The New Atlantis;* certainly they anticipated some of the science in it.

In *Christianopolis* a traveller shipwrecked near the South Pole finds an island on which there is an ideal Christian community. The city is well laid-out on a rectangular plan; arches over the walks shelter citizens from the weather. Without money except for foreign commerce, the city is communal; food and work are distributed according to needs and abilities. State laboratories foster experiments in "metals, minerals, vegetables, and even the life of animals," and all this experimentation is "for the use of the human race and in the interests of health." Water-supply and sewage-disposal systems have been perfected; there is running water in every house. There are other laboratories for pharmacy, anatomy, biology, painting, and mathematics. Youths are educated in science through visual education (paintings) as well as in the laboratory.

In Campanella's *City of the Sun* a sea-captain describes a city in central Asia ruled by a "Metaphysician," with the assistance of magistrates for Power, Wisdom, and Love. The magistrate for Wisdom is in charge of arts, mechanics, sciences, and education. Inside the walls around the city are painted representations to teach science: mathematics (with verses to explain the problems), geology (precious stones, minerals, and metals), geography, botany (including undersea life), birds, animals, and mechanical arts. Water-filtration and sewage-disposal systems are described. Among inventions are wagons fitted with sails which are "borne along by the wind even when it is contrary, by the marvellous contrivance of wheels within wheels" and "rafts and triremes, which go over the waters without rowers or the force of the wind, but by a marvellous contrivance." Chosen "explorers and ambassadors" are sent over the earth to collect new knowledge.

The magistrate for Love sees that citizens mate according to eugenic principles. Physiology, especially preventive dieting and exercise, is highly developed. The physicians know a secret for "renovating life after about the seventieth year."

If Bacon knew these books, he had little more to do than develop what he found. The central feature of *The New Atlantis* is the College of Salomon's House for research in science by experimental methods. It was founded about 1900 years before the time of the story by a wise prince, Salomona, and developed into the chief ornament and support of a prosperous state. Jealous of their civilization, the people of New Atlantis have not shared it with others, yet "spies" go out regularly to bring in knowledge "of the sciences, arts, manufactures, and inventions of all the world." They experiment with "all coagulations, indurations, refrigerations, and conservations of bodies," with the production of artificial metals, and with curing diseases and prolonging life. They have learned to create life of a low kind: worms, serpents, and flies. On great towers, they study meteorology. In botany, they practise grafting and plant-breeding to improve species. They have airplanes, submarines, and "trunks and pipes" for carrying sound. Inventors are highly honored, and their models are preserved in state museums. — "The rest was not perfected" at Bacon's death.

Bacon's *New Atlantis* helped to inspire the founding and to guide the early researches of the Royal Society.

But the Royal Society did not immediately create utopia. The eighteenth century in general was a period that produced satire, rather than utopias. Jonathan Swift's *Gulliver's Travels* (1726) ridicules the Royal Society. Its science, especially such as the grave account of the equilibrative and propulsive principles of Laputa, is ironic; experimenters in the natural sciences are satirized as absent-minded fools busy with idiotic inventions: to extract sunlight from cucumbers, to calcine ice into gunpowder, to build houses by beginning at the roof, and to test colors by feeling and smelling. Yet, in spite of this view of science, Swift describes men with the objectivity of a scientific report. Following Cyrano de Bergerac, Swift places man on trial among the lower animals and finds him lowest of all.

With the renewal of the romantic impulse, utopias began to appear again, in a new locale. Utopia, formerly found in a perfect land, now began to appear in a future time. Utopia is shifted from a place to be found to a condition to be achieved.

The first utopian fiction published in America (Philadelphia, 1795) was Louis Sébastien Mercier's *Memoirs of the Year Two Thousand Five Hundred* (in English, 1771). In it a sleeper goes to sleep in old Paris, but awakens in the Paris of 2500. A host takes him to see such wonders of the modern city as its wide streets governed by traffic policemen and lighted by street lamps. At every corner fountains flow; the neat houses have gardens on their flat roofs. The Bastille has vanished. Now education, the host says, no longer is concerned with the classics, but with "useful knowledge." In religion the "first communion" is a ceremony of looking through a telescope at the stars and then through a microscope. The host takes the narrator to a public museum displaying the natural sciences, especially the Chain of Being; he discourses upon the gradation of species and upon nature's effort "to the formation of man," though, of course, he says nothing of mutation from species to species. Among inventions are malleable glass, the mirror of Archimedes, the Egyptian art of embalming, the machine by which Egyptians raised their obelisks, inextinguishable lamps, an "optical cabinet" with shifting scenes, and a machine for imitating the human voice. Animal breeding has doubled the size of animals. Medicine has learned "the secret of dissolving the stone," a cure for phthisis, and a "happy specific" for syphilis. As government and social life are similarly advanced, the sleeper is unhappy to wake in old Paris.

Mercier's utopia laid in the future set a pattern followed in the nineteenth century.

D. *The "Gothic" Romance*

One other forerunner of the scientific fiction of the nineteenth century is the "Gothic" novel, which formed a curious union with science in *Frankenstein.*

"Gothic" fiction is generally spoken of as beginning with Walpole's *The Castle of Otranto* (1764), a tale of ghostly visitation. Beckford's *Vathek* (in English, 1786) adorned the tale with material suggestive of *The Arabian Nights,* Apuleius's *Golden Ass,* and necromancy. In such romances as Charlotte Dacre's *Zofloya* (1806), the "Gothic" novel continued to pick up scraps of science, Satanic and otherwise. The villain is a Moorish student of chemistry who dabbles in his laboratory with spells, incantations, and poisons; he is a hypnotist who uses his powers for evil purposes. This line of development reached a climax in *Frankenstein.*

CHAPTER THREE

Down Alph the Sacred River

Scientific Fiction, 1817-1870

MARY SHELLEY'S INTENTION in writing *Frankenstein* was to write a tale of terror. As the Shelleys, Lord Byron, and Dr. Polidori were reading *Fantasmagoriana,* tales of the dead, Byron suggested that they each write a ghost story. Mary Shelley set herself to write something to "awaken thrilling horror." At first she had no ideas, but after an evening during which Byron and Shelley talked of Dr. Erasmus Darwin's researches into the nature of life, Mary Shelley, going sleepless to bed, suddenly saw, as in a vision, "the hideous phantasm of a man stretched out, and then, on the working of some powerful engine, show signs of life." This idea includes imaginary science and is made more thrilling for this reason. The next morning she announced that she had thought of a story.

A. *The "Gothic" Romance*

1. Frankenstein

In her Preface, Mary Shelley stated that she did not wish *Frankenstein* (1817) to be considered a story of the supernatural. This repudiation of the supernatural as a basis for her tale places the romance on another basis, the power of science to perform wonders.

Though Frankenstein, a medical student at the University of

Ingolstadt, continues an early interest in the "metaphysical," he considers it "in its highest sense, the physical secrets of the world." His professors tell him that alchemy or the elixir-of-life is a "chimera," but Frankenstein labors to find the secret of life by studying anatomy, especially the processes of death. He finds the secret, and then doubles his toil to make application of it. With materials from the "unhallowed damps of the grave" he manages to put pieces of flesh together in the shape of a man and then to infuse his creation with a spark of life. The spark glimmers, an eyeball rolls, and with a convulsive motion the monster comes to life.

Frankenstein flees from it in horror, but the monster has both natural goodness and a mind as blank as that of a new-born child. Its natural goodness, however, is soured by the revulsion it meets on every side; it comes to hate its creator and to demand of him a mate. Refused, the monster slays Frankenstein's bride, and then Frankenstein turns pursuer. The monster flees across ice in the north, and Frankenstein himself dies of exhaustion.

The result of this fusion of "Gothic" materials and science was not only to bring the tale of horror clearly into the stream of scientific fiction, but also to provide for it a more credible basis. Tales of terror continue to be written, but today their locale is frequently the laboratory.

At the same time, Poe and his disciple Jules Verne, during the period 1817-1870, developed the traditional themes of the wonderful machine and the wonderful journey with more up-to-date science. One kind of scientific fiction, however, is not as abundant in this period as it is later. The full development of the scientific utopia had to wait for the industrial revolution to foreshadow the Machine Age and for the theory of evolution.

2. Alchemy

a. The elixir-of-life

Balzac's "Elixir of Life" (1830) subordinates the laboratory aspect of *Frankenstein*, yet continues the theme of the creation of life. Bartolommeo Belvidero, accumulating a fortune by the age of sixty and then devoting himself to scientific studies, has discovered the elixir-of-life. Dying, he requests his wastrel son, Don Juan, to rub the elixir upon his body. When a drop of the liquid on the eye of the corpse causes it to gleam bright and young, Don Juan grinds out the eye and grimly hides the elixir away. Himself dying after a life of dissipation, Don Juan requests his son to rub his corpse with the elixir. This more dutiful son attempts to do so, but spills the elixir in fright when the revivified right arm reaches up to choke

him. The head of Don Juan continues to live, and the Don himself
is about to be canonized for a saint. During the ceremony, however,
the head breaks from the withered neck and bites viciously into the
brain of the officiating priest. Besides its ghastly narrative, the
story is an allegory of selfishness that defeats its own ends.

In Hawthorne's story of the elixir-of-youth, "Dr. Heidegger's
Experiment" (1837), the story of "Gothic" science is merely a vehicle for allegory; the half-magic, half-scientific materials of the
story are only stage properties. Dr. Heidegger is a scientist, but he
got his elixir from the fountain of youth. Four old friends, profli-
gate in their youth but grave with age, are called in to drink the
elixir. They shed not only age, but gravity; the effects wear off, and
they are again decrepit.

Bulwer-Lytton's *Zanoni* (1842), an allegory attacking the mechanistic interpretation of life, makes use not only of the elixir-of-life,
but also of the occult "science" of the Rosicrucians and the theme
of a Chaldean alive through many centuries. Zanoni, the ever-young
Chaldean, is loved by Viola, who bears him a child. Glyndon, Zanoni's friend, desirous of learning the "science" that will yield him
everlasting life, studies under Mejnour, but is unable to face the
terrible "watcher on the threshold." This monster from some outer
plane of existence appears to Glyndon when he tastes a forbidden
liquor. Finally, Glyndon, Viola, and Zanoni are caught up in the
Reign of Terror in Paris and lose their lives in it.

The character Mejnour, a symbol for "Contemplation of the actual—SCIENCE," in attacking laboratory science and defending the
occult, declares that the lore of his ancient order is not magic, but
medicine rightly understood. Even passages attacking orthodox science and defending cabalism use footnote references to geologists to
support their view of the cosmos. Mejnour has some knowledge of
a mysterious "all-pervading and invisible fluid resembling electricity,
yet distinct from the known operations of that mysterious agency."
It foreshadows the "vril" of Bulwer-Lytton's later novel, *The Coming Race.*

Edgar Allan Poe, master of the tale of terror, made facetious
use of the theme of the elixir-of-life. In "Some Words with a
Mummy" (1845) an application of the "Voltaic pile" to a mummy
in the City Museum causes the mummy to kick Dr. Ponnonner out
the window. The mummy says he has never died; the Egyptians
used the embalming principle to hold "animal functions" in "perpetual abeyance," so that they could live in installments, sleep a few
hundred years, and then wake to see what has happened.

In *A Strange Story* (1861) Bulwer-Lytton continues his attack
upon orthodox science. The materialist, Dr. Fenwick, is gradually
brought around, through a series of marvelous events, to a belief

in soul, odic force, and the Rosicrucian world of spirits. Against Fenwick, as antagonist, stands the hero Margrave, a "young" man who is very old and who possesses the elixir-of-life as well as many other secrets of the East. Margrave exerts much of his influence by means of a magic wand that contains a tiny wire and that seems to be a means for "collecting" force and vitality from the unseen. The book reaches its climax in a scene in Australia in which Margrave, aided by Fenwick, calls up the malignant spirits of the immaterial world.

In both *Zanoni* and *A Strange Story*, Bulwer-Lytton was attempting to defend wisdom beyond that of science, and yet to use the knowledge of science to support this defense. He was interested in the supernatural, the unexplained phenomena of electricity, and whatever elixir, gas, or force might constitute the vital principle.

A facetious use of the theme of perpetual life is made in About's *The Man with the Broken Ear* (1862; in English, 1867). It is the story of a desiccated man who, when properly soaked, returns to animation. Leon Renault, returning from Russia, brings to his father, a professor of physics and chemistry, a mummy embalmed by Professor Meiser of Dantzic, who has followed up the "researches of Leeuwenhoeck, Baker, Needham, Fontana, and Spallanzani, on the revivification of animals" and is one of the "fathers of modern biology." The mummy is a French colonel of Napeolonic vintage, perfectly preserved except that one ear is broken off. A condemned spy, the colonel had been used for research purposes, subjected to vacuum, dry-cold, and baking at a temperature to remove water from his flesh, but not to disintegrate it. When the mummy is soaked and steamed, he starts from his torpor shouting, "Vive l'Empereur." The rest of the story is a narrative of his efforts to adjust himself to the new France and to get an inheritance that had grown by compound interest during his desiccation. Like Poe's "Some Words with a Mummy," the story simply uses an old theme, given a quasi-scientific explanation, to tell an amusing tale.

As the search for the elixir-of-life continues in later fiction, the elixir is found less often connected with the occult, more often in chemical formulas.

b.   The transmutation of metals

Balzac's *The Quest of the Absolute* (1834) describes the efforts of Balthazar Claes to transmute metals. A visiting Polish soldier tells Claes, rich and happily married, that diamonds have been made in the laboratory and argues that it is possible to find an "absolute" substance, the basic element from which other elements can be made. Fascinated with the idea, Claes begins to experiment; believing himself always just a hair's breadth from the great discovery, he drives his researches (involving the use of gold and silver in large quantities) on and on, to the utter ruin of his fortune and family. The book implies that this research, or perhaps any intellectual interest that moves a man to sacrifice human associations, is madness.

Poe's short story in the form of a magazine article, "Von Kempelen and His Discovery" (1848), describes Von Kempelen's success in the transmutation of lead into gold. The "article" assumes that everyone has marked Von Kempelen's sudden rise to riches; the author of the article has met Von Kempelen, knows the "facts," and sets them forth. Invading Von Kempelen's rooms because they suspect him of forgery, police find a glowing furnace, crucibles, tubes, and an unknown substance mixed with antimony. Under the bed they find a box of "brass" that turns out to be purest gold. Chemists have not yet been able to analyze the unknown substance, but that gold can be made in the laboratory is evident. This discovery, says Poe, should halt the gold-rush to California.

3.   Mesmerism

Poe's "The Facts in the Case of M. Valdemar" (1845) was likewise presented as a magazine article. Its basis is mesmerism, in 1845 widely regarded as a science. Like *Frankenstein,* the story is in mood a tale of terror, but in plot the laboratory experiment of a medical student. Dying of consumption, Ernest Valdemar allows himself, for the purposes of science, to be mesmerized at the moment of death. Mesmerism chains the soul of Valdemar to his rigid, dead body; the mesmerized soul causes the tongue to move in speech; decay is arrested for seven months. When the mesmerist releases the soul, the forces of decay operate "within the space of a single minute" to leave the body "a nearly liquid mass of loathsome, of detestable putrescence." The experiment is described in medical language through which suggestions of corruption and the charnel house are woven to produce a "Gothic" horror.

4.   Other "Gothic" Sciences

Other varieties of "Gothic" science appear in nineteenth-century fiction.

Hawthorne used pseudo-chemistry for purposes of allegory in "The Birth Mark" (1846). The chemist Aylmer marries a beautiful woman. She seems to him perfect except for a tiny mole on her cheek, and wishing her altogether perfect, he prepares a potion to remove the mole. The mole dims with each dose, but as he gives her constantly stronger potions, she weakens and dies. Aylmer's laboratory of giant furnaces, bubbling retorts, and shaggy-dwarf assistant is, however, more medieval in tone than scientific.

Invisible presences in fiction before the nineteenth century were usually ghosts. These ghosts are replaced in scientific fiction by natural creatures or men who are or become, like glass or jellyfish, perfectly transparent. Between medieval ghost-stories and Wells's famous *The Invisible Man* are a number of stories that progressively advance toward Wells's treatment. One of them is Fitz-James O'Brien's "What Was It? A Mystery" (1859). In this story a "something" attacks the narrator in his boarding house; nothing is visible. The narrator and a Dr. Hammond capture the creature and tie it with ropes—which seem to wrap the air. It has weight; it rumples the bed on which it is laid. The creature refuses food and drink, dies and is buried. A plaster cast of it, now on exhibit in a "well-known museum," reveals an ugly dwarf. Dr. Hammond, who does not believe in the supernatural, says the creature is constituted of cells like those of glass, but not so coarse, so that it is totally invisible. The setting for this story is, far from the haunted castle of older "Gothic" fiction, a boarding house on Bleecker Street, New York.

Oliver Wendell Holmes, a professor of anatomy and physiology in Harvard University, certainly placed no credence in birthmarks and pre-natal influences on the mind of the embryo. But to illustrate the doctrine that the sins of the parent are visited on the child, he produced *Elsie Venner* (1861). Elsie Venner's mother was bitten by a rattlesnake, and the story tells how this bite causes Elsie to be born with a rattlesnake necklace for a birth-mark, with eyes that glisten like a snake's, and with a dual nature, partaking of the life of the snake. She dies as the birthmark fades away. The grave village physician who attends Elsie in her last illness explains the birth-mark and Elsie's duality of nature to be an "accidental principle" which he had hoped would pass away.

5. Crime and Detection

One field into which "Gothic" fiction branched with popular success was that of stories of crime and detection. The dark Montoni of *The Mysteries of Udolpho,* the handsome introvert of "Byronic" tales, moody and intellectual, underwent only meretricious changes in becoming the drug-taking, art-collecting, eccentric genius of modern detective fiction. In one of the changes, engineered by Edgar Allan Poe, he acquired remarkable powers of ratiocination; in another he acquired a knowledge of science and a laboratory technique.

With Poe's "The Gold Bug" and "Murders in the Rue Morgue"

the detective story took the direction it has since continued. Even in these early stories science plays a rôle, though a small one. In "The Gold Bug" (1845), for instance, it is Legrand's knowledge of chemistry that enables him to grasp the significance of the suddenly-appearing skull. "Zaffre, digested in *aqua regia*," Legrand lectures, "and diluted with four times its weight of water, is sometimes employed." This lecture on the chemistry, physics, biology, and psychology of crime has continued to the present day.

The detective story advanced with the work of Wilkie Collins. His *The Moonstone* (1868) is a complicated tale regarding the disappearance of a diamond. It includes much of the paraphernalia of the "Gothic," such as Hindu jugglers and hypnotists, but its solution rests upon a "medical" theory that the words uttered by a man in delirium are revelations of the truth from the subconscious. Collins proves the solution worked out from words in delirium by employing the "medical" theory that a man placed in a former condition will repeat a former action. An experiment is performed: Franklin Blake, suspected of the theft, is given an opiate while in a highly nervous state, to reproduce his condition on the night the diamond disappeared. In his sleep Blake gets up and steal the glass "diamond" substituted for the original. Such medical theory is akin to that of *Elsie Venner*, but against the background of crime, hypnotism, and Indian fakirs belonging to the "Gothic" strain in the novel, it emerges as a relatively scientific means of solving the mystery and foreshadows the methods of detectives Craig Kennedy and Dr. Thorndyke in twentieth-century fiction.

6. World-Catastrophe

Besides the theme of *Frankenstein,* Mary Shelley introduced another theme of importance in scientific fiction, that of world-catastrophe and the awful loneliness of the last man alive. Daniel Defoe and Charles Brockden Brown had described horrible plagues; Percy Shelley had foretold a future of democracy and brotherhood; and Byron had written the poem "Darkness" to offer a vision of the end of the world. Combining these materials, Mary Shelley produced *The Last Man* (1825), a tale of the twenty-first century (2073-2100), describing first the abdication of the last king of England, then the sweep of a great plague across the world, and finally the despair of the last man alive.

Lionel Verney is the "last man." His father is a favorite courtier of the last king who, seeing his people's desire for a democracy, abdicates. Democracy works well; in London, canals, aqueducts, bridges, stately buildings are in construction; poverty is almost abolished; labor is lightened of its heaviest burdens;

"machines existed to supply with facility every want of the population." Lionel travels in a balloon whose "feathered vans" cleave the "unopposing atmosphere" and are guided by a "plumed steerage, and the slender mechanism of the wings." Then the plague comes. It sweeps over the East, strikes in America, and by 2094 has transformed London into a pest-house; by 2096 London is deserted, and its remnant of population has fled to the mountains of Switzerland. Of all the people in the world, Lionel alone passes through the sickness and survives. He wanders from city to city, from house to house, from room to room. The goods of the world are his, but everywhere there is decay; bread is blue and moldy, cheese is a heap of dust, utensils are covered with cobwebs and myriads of dead flies. On New Year's Day, 2100, he ascends St. Peter's and carves the date on the topmost stone.

As a picture of the future, *The Last Man* fails to realize the industrial revolution. The mood of the book is "Gothic"; there is little science in it. Steamboats are employed, and men travel in dirigible balloons, but in other ways life at the close of the twenty-first century is much like that of the 1820's. There are machines, but no Machine Age. Yet as anticipation of a recurrent pattern in scientific fiction, *The Last Man* is a more important book than *Frankenstein.* World-catastrophe, the collapse of society, and the "last man" theme are common in twentieth-century fiction.

This theme of world-catastrophe as well as the theme of the plague ("The Masque of the Red Death") appealed to Edgar Allan Poe. His treatment of it in "The Conversation of Eiros and Charmion" (1839) is brief, but prophetic of later scientific fiction. The story reports the conversation in Aidenn of two souls, Charmion, long dead, and Eiros, recently arrived. Eiros, telling of the calamity that overwhelms the world when a comet collides with it, describes the approach of the comet, disregard of it because scientists said it was a tenuous body, and then terror as heat from it affects the atmosphere and spurs vegetation to tropical luxuriance. The percentage of oxygen in the atmosphere increases; delirium possesses all men's minds. As the nucleus of the comet touches the atmosphere of the earth, there is a blinding flash, and the air bursts into flame. This destruction of the earth by collision with a comet or a planet is common in scientific fiction today.

These "Gothic" themes have somewhat deepened the emotional possibilities of scientific fiction; the use of science has, in return, strenghtened the basis of the tale of terror. The streams merge. Alph the sacred river, bound for a sunless sea, is diverted to a wider ocean. Ghosts, elixirs, and mesmerisms lose their thrill, but there is ample material for the tale of terror in the theory of evolution and the atomic bomb.

Meanwhile, scientific fiction continued its progress in invention of machines and in discovery of strange worlds.

B. *The Wonderful Machine*

The Frankenstein's monster of the Machine Age is the mechanical man first in fiction and lately on exhibit at the New York World's Fair. Edgar Allan Poe's first description of a wonderful machine is a magazine article, "Maelzel's Chess Player" (1835), carefully debunking a mechanical chess-player on exhibition in Richmond. The hoax had deceived Richmond crowds. Poe pointed out exactly how a man in the machine could avoid exposure by shifting his position. Later automaton-chess-players in scientific fiction are not described as hoaxes.

Having uncovered a hoax, Poe later created one by publishing a story commonly known as "The Balloon-Hoax," but first published in the New York *Sun,* April 13, 1844, as a news-story, "Astounding News by Express, *via* Norfolk! The Atlantic Crossed in Three Days." It purports to be an account of the crossing of the Atlantic in a dirigible balloon. Carrying eight passengers, the balloon travels from London to Fort Moultrie, S. C., in seventy-five hours. After a detailed account of unsuccessful means to guide a balloon with vanes and propellers, the article describes the successful mechanism, a spring-operated screw in a hollow brass tube. The article promises its readers "additional information either on Monday or in the course of the next day, at farthest." It aroused the same kind of belief as Mr. Orson Welles's broadcast of 1938.

Poe's facetious satire, "The Thousand-and-Second Tale of Scheherazade" (1845), does not describe imaginary machines, but actual machines viewed as magic. Sinbad the Sailor, from *The Arabian Nights,* goes to the seashore to begin another voyage. There he sees a monster (a steamship) on whose iron body swarm "men-vermin." The men-vermin capture him and take him around the world, where he views many incredible machines, such as "a huge horse whose bones were iron and whose blood was boiling water," balloons, the Voltaic pile, and the calculating machine. Modern inventions surpass all the magic Sinbad had seen in his career.

One of the finest stories of invention before Verne began writing is Fitz-James O'Brien's "The Diamond Lens" (1858). The story gains emotional depth from a "Gothic" strain, for the hero learns how to manufacture the "universal lens" through a spiritualistic seance and commits a murder to get the necessary diamond. But the core of the story is the lens and the strange world it reveals. The narrator is sent to New York to study medicine, but fascinated by microscopes, he spends his tuition for lenses and does not go near the medical college. His discoveries enthrall him; he is, for instance, able to overturn accepted theories about the *Volvox globator*. Yearning for the perfect lens, he visits a medium to call up the spirit of Leeuwenhoek. The spirit tells him that the universal lens may be made from a diamond of one hundred and forty carats, subjected to electro-magnetic currents until its atoms re-arrange themselves. The narrator commits murder to get such a diamond and labors for months in electrifying, grinding, and polishing it. When the lens is completed, he looks into a single atom of water and beholds a world. In it lives a beautiful girl, whom he names Animula and with whom he falls in love. Day after day he observes her till he sees her one day in agony: the last atom of his water is evaporating. He falls into a swoon and afterwards is accounted mad. The materials used in this story foreshadow a great deal in later fiction.

And now we come to Jules Verne, the widely popular "father" of scientific fiction whose stories were in 1872 given the highest praise of even the conservative *Académie Française*. Yet his imaginary inventions and discoveries were not bold ones. Because he described many imaginary machines that were invented shortly afterwards, Verne has been called a prophet. He was, no doubt. But he limited his inventions, for the most part, to machines on which scientists were at the time experimenting. He saw that mechanical progress was in acceleration, that flying, submarine travel, and electric lights were just around the corner. When he described an invention not just around the corner (as he did, for instance, in the story of a trip to the moon), he wrote in a style to make fun of the whole thing. He only touched upon the social significance of his inventions. His importance, that is, his immense popularity in every nation and the impetus he gave to scientific fiction, is due rather to the use he made of invention as a means to a new kind of geographic story, voyage of wonders, and exuberant adventure.

Verne had not thrilled the world as either lawyer or playwright; he found out what would thrill it when he published "A Drama in the Air" in a family journal in 1850. It presents no imaginary invention, but rather tells about a balloon ascension in which a fanatic, with the history of balloon ascensions and of catastrophies at his tongue's end, gets into the car and wrests control from the balloonist. The balloon travels an erratic course;

the madman, to rise even higher, cuts the car loose and clings to the ropes; he falls, but the balloonist is saved when the anchor rope catches on the seashore. The recital of balloon history and catastrophes is encyclopedic; the action is breath-taking. Verne, finding a method, a pace, and an audience, stumbled upon the material that made him famous.

His first full-length romance thirteen years later followed up this early success. *Five Weeks in a Balloon* (1863) describes no startlingly new invention, but instead a new and adventurous use for the balloon in exploring Africa. Verne experiments with a somewhat fantastic device for guiding the balloon, the inflation or deflation of the gas bag by an apparatus in the car, to make the balloon rise or fall into the current of air blowing in the desired direction. But most of the story is geographic adventure, discussion of ballooning, and hair-breadth escapes. The story opens, in a manner typical of Verne, with the scientific world agog at the proposal of Dr. Ferguson to explore Africa by balloon. Scientists squabble, newspapers argue, even missionary journals participate; but the intrepid scientist Ferguson, loyal servant Joe, and young Dick Kennedy make ready to go. Verne measures every cubic inch of balloon space, weighs every ounce of baggage. The balloon sets off across Africa from Zanzibar; it moors in trees by night; apes attack the balloon; later natives attack it. The voyagers speculate about the day when civilization shall penetrate Africa and the greatest kingdom of the world will rise from its treasures. Threatened by natives at night, Dr. Ferguson sets up an electric arc light; they rescue a missionary from torture by savages; condors attack them over Lake Tchad; Joe falls out of the balloon. Just as the balloon is sinking to the ground, its gas exhausted, and savages are closing in, French soldiers arrive. The record of the exploration is now in the archives of the Geographical Society.

Verne's famous *Twenty Thousand Leagues Under the Sea* (1870) is bolder in its inventions. The narrative is chiefly a panorama of undersea geography, but the sea-bottoms are explored in a wonderful machine, Captain Nemo's submarine, the *Nautilus*. The store of information is inexhaustible on every topic that comes to mind in a tour of the world under the oceans: coral islands, octopuses, icebergs, pearls, the buried Atlantis, geological changes, the Atlantic cable, and what not.

The submarine is the property of the misanthrope, Captain Nemo. M. Aronnax, a French scientist in New York, is appointed by the United States' government to accompany the *Abraham Lincoln* in search for a "monster" preying on shipping, and the body of the story is M. Aronnax's record of his experiences.

M. Aronnax falls overboard and is picked up by Captain Nemo and held prisoner-at-large in the submarine. The submarine is lighted by incandescent electric lights; its motive power is electricity; its stoves and even its clocks are electric. Oxygen is supplied by chemical reactions; the food is the finest the sea can afford—even cigars are made of a sea-weed that yields nicotine. The submarine has a splendid library and a museum of undersea specimens.

The submarine makes a voyage around the world, including a trip to the South Pole, a pre-canal trip through the Isthmus of Suez through an uncharted tunnel, and a voyage to submerged Atlantis. M. Aronnax observes everything; Captain Nemo is an encyclopedia of information; and they explain to one another and to the simple harpooner, Ned Land, everything they see. They go hunting on the ocean-bed in diving suits, shooting electrically charged bullets (inside breakable glass globes) from compressed-air guns; their path is lighted by flashlights. They find Spanish galleons, examine a forest of petrified trees, visit the heart of a volcano through an undersea tunnel, assist whales in a battle against cachalots, and smack their lips over the flavors of whale's milk. In short, the book is a catalog of wonders, but the wonders of nineteenth-century nature-study rather than the comparatively tame (because incredible) grotesques of earlier imaginary voyages.

Captain Nemo, who cultivates huge pearls by tampering with oysters and is already fabulously wealthy, devotes his fortune to a vague revolutionary cause, grimly sinks ships, and afterwards weeps before a picture of his wife. Fearful, though fascinated, M. Aronnax escapes near the coast of Norway.

C. *The Wonderful Journey*

1. On the Earth

In *Twenty Thousand Leagues Under the Sea* Verne sends the *Nautilus* to the South Pole. A little earlier he had devoted an entire romance to polar exploration. *Captain Hatteras* (1865) describes the discovery of the North Pole. The interest of this book is chiefly geographic; Verne does not include imaginary inventions, and his description of polar geography is taken from what was known of it at the time. The tale is told chiefly as the adventures of Doctor Clawbonny aboard the English brig *Forward*. These adventures include mutiny, fights with whales, sledding journeys across the ice, and the discovery of an American exploring party frozen to death except for one man. The explorers find an active volcano at the Pole itself; Captain Hatteras goes mad at the successful achievement of his life-long am-

bition; and on the return, Doctor Clawbonny presents a memorial
to the Royal Geographical Society establishing the discovery of
the North Pole on June 11, 1861.

Verne's *In Search of the Castaways* (1870) employs an ingenious device to enable Lord Glenarvon to circle the earth on
the thirty-seventh parallel, crossing South America, Australia, and
New Zealand. Lord Glenarvon and his party encounter an earthquake in the Andes, an attack by wolves on the pampas, a flood,
treachery among Australian criminals, a shipwreck on the New
Zealand coast, and capture by cannibals. The tale is made of
exciting adventure in pursuit of a mystery and careful description
of the earth's geography, peoples, and customs on the thirty-
seventh parallel.

2. Into the Earth

Tales of imaginary voyages to the interior of the earth were
greatly influenced by a theory set forth by Captain John Cleves
Symmes of Ohio. In 1818, Captain Symmes issued a circular to
institutions of learning in Europe and America stating that the
earth is hollow and open at the poles. In 1823 he petitioned Congress to send an exploring expedition to test his theory and got
twenty-five affirmative votes. With James McBride as collaborator
he published in 1826 *Symmes Theory of Concentric Spheres.*

Symmes believed the earth is composed of five hollow, concentric spheres, with spaces between each, and habitable upon both
convex and concave surfaces. At the North Pole, he supposed an
opening four thousand miles in diameter; at the South, six thousand. The sea extends through the openings, and seals, whales,
and fish pass through. Around each opening is a hoop of ice,
but within the hoop the climate is mild and even hot. Ocean
currents flow into the openings; volcanoes fringe the openings in
some places; sunlight is refracted into the hollow earth because
of the inclination of the poles.

The first appearance of this theory in scientific fiction is
in *Symzonia* (1820), by Captain Adam Seaborn (*pseud.?* perhaps
Symmes himself). Captain Seaborn narrates that in the year
1817, moved by the reasoning of Symmes, he projected a voyage
of discovery to enlarge scientific knowledge. He outfits a steamship and selects a crew for "sealing" in the South Seas. Reaching
the "icy hoop" at latitude 83°, they find an island alongside
which currents lead through the hoop. On the island they find
the bones of a great animal that Seaborn supposes came from
the internal world. After some mutinous mumbling by the crew,
Captain Seaborn sails on, drawn southward by a strong current;
the sextant shows a very queer latitude, near the equator. The

A Monument to Captain Symmes and His Theory, in Hamilton, Ohio.
(The photograph was obtained through the courtesy of
Professor Robert F. Almy.)

The inscriptions on the monument (with some letters chipped off, as
indicated by parentheses) read as follows:

West Side—   *East Side—*

(that appearing in the photograph)
John Cleves Symmes
join)ed the Army of the U. S.
   as an Ensign,
in) the year 1802. He afterw(ard
ro)se to the rank of Captain
an)d performed daring feats
of) Bravery in the Battles o(f
Lundy's Lane and Sortie from
   Fort Erie

Ca)pt. John Cleves Symmes·
   was a Philosopher,
an)d the originator of
"Sym)mes Theory of Concentric
Sph)eres and Polar voids."
He) contended that the Earth
wa)s hollow and habitable within.

crew members suppose they have passed the Pole and gone north on the other side, but Seaborn knows that they have gone over the rim of the world. They come to land on which they discover part of the prow of a ship, sewed together with white wire like platinum. Further on, a continent unrolls to the view; Captain Seaborn names it Symzonia. They reach a city, and Seaborn goes ashore. The people are friendly, exceedingly white people; their buildings and clothing are snow-white; they speak a musical language unintelligible to Seaborn. Interpreters teach Seaborn, and in turn, he teaches them; they learn quickly.

The people of this internal world have not one sun and one moon, but two, each dim, refracted through the open poles. They have developed a utopian civilization that includes all the arts and inventions of the external world and many more besides. The people are a kindly, calm, intellectual race. The ruler is the Best Man, elected by a legislature of Worthies, who in turn are elected for their virtues as the Good, the Wise, and the Useful. The internal world has an abundance of pearls, gold, and precious metals, which citizens use as baubles. Cupidity is unknown; there is no poverty; the goods of the world are shared in a system resembling socialism. Labor is state-regulated; money is a kind of ration-cards. Formerly, selfish men had lived in the land, but they had been driven out to inhabit the islands at the entrance to the internal world. Among inventions, the Symzonians have cigar-shaped dirigible balloons; to drive out the selfish during their civil war, they used flame-throwers capable of projecting burning gases for half a mile from tubes mounted on airships; they drive ships by shooting compressed air from under-water tubes "by the agency of a curious engine."

Because the utopian people of Symzonia fear to be contaminated, they direct Seaborn and his crew to depart. Stopping on his way out at the island, where he had left a sealing party, Seaborn picks up an enormous load of sealskins, and proceeds eventually to New York.

There is ample evidence that Symmes's theory interested Edgar Allan Poe; he refers to it in "Hans Pfaal" at the point where Hans observes the polar region from his balloon and sees evidence that the Pole is a great hollow.

Poe's story "MS. Found in a Bottle" (1833) is clearly an experimental fragment from a design to tell of an adventure in the hollow earth. After a collision, the narrator is hurled aboard a strange old vessel on which are men who seem to be the living-dead. It is drawn by irresistible currents toward the South Pole. The story ends abruptly with the description of the ship's behavior in a whirlpool and then its "going down." In the light of

Poe's interest in Symmes's theory, it is clear that the ship, which cannot sink, for it is porous and lighter than water, is going down into the interior of the earth. Poe's intention can only be surmised; perhaps at one time he planned to describe the interior of the earth as a spirit-world.

Poe's unfinished *Narrative of Arthur Gordon Pym* is likewise a fragment, describing a voyage destined for adventure in Symmes's hollow earth. The voyage is made up of mutiny, shipwreck, famine, cannibalism, and other horrors, but it draws the narrator, Pym, steadily toward the entrance to the internal world. The story ends—or breaks off—just before the descent, but many parallels with *Symzonia* show that Poe intended to follow the route of that book into the earth. *Arthur Gordon Pym* continually speaks of scientific discoveries that will amaze the world, but does not reach them. One long episode describes the search for islands formerly reported in the fifty-second latitude, but Captain Guy is unable to find them in the location given. Poe is evidently following a suggestion in *Symzonia* that the curvature at the rim distorts latitude, with the intention of finding the islands later in the same (apparent) lattitude. *Pym* describes the discovery on an island of the carcass of a strange animal, just as *Symzonia* had done; Pym's party discovers the prow of a canoe, as Seaborn had done. As Seaborn had left a party to take seals, Poe's Captain Guy prepares to leave a party to collect *bêche de mere*. The black islanders discovered, in Poe's story, at the entrance to a white sea apparently represent the exiles from Symzonia, described by Captain Seaborn as blackened by the sun. The islanders' fear of all things white, especially their terror when an explosion on board the *Jane Guy* spurts flame, apparently reflects their fear of the flame-throwing weapons of the internal world. Captain Seaborn interrupts his narrative for several pages to describe a colony of penguins; Poe interrupts his narrative for the same purpose. The warmth of the regions of the south and the strong southward-flowing current into which Pym and Peters are drawn indicate the influence of Symmes's theory.

But the tale breaks off. Poe describes a white mist and a great white figure that arise before Pym and Peters as they are drawn southward—and that is all, except Poe's note that Arthur Gordon Pym had suddenly died in Richmond. One can only surmise why Poe broke off his tale before he reached the main adventure. Perhaps he had become confused; *Symzonia* described a utopian land inside the earth; "MS Found in a Bottle" suggests that Poe meant to describe a spirit-world there; the "Arabic" symbols of Poe's book suggest that he may have planned at one time to describe the Lost Tribes of Israel in the inner world. The great

white figure that arises in Pym's path seems made up partly of
Magellanic clouds described in Symmes's theory as reflections
of New Zealand seen "across the rim" and partly of vague sym-
bolism. The detailed realism of *Arthur Gordon Pym* indicates
that it would have been a production far superior to *Symzonia.*

Apparently Jules Verne did not know of Symmes's theory, for
his continuation of *Arthur Gordon Pym, The Sphinx of Ice,* does
not suppose that *Pym* was moving toward the interior of the
earth. Verne's own *Journey to the Center of the Earth* (1864)
was inspired by more recent and more credible science, especially theories of geology about the formation of the earth and
the theory of evolution. Professor Von Hardwigg, a scientist,
learns from an ancient manuscript that it is possible to descend
into the earth through the extinct volcano Sneffels in Iceland.
The professor and a nephew descend the crater by means of a
rope, and then proceed along a volcanic tunnel, their way lighted
by an electric flashlight ("Ruhmkorff coil"). They see the geological history of the earth written in the rocks: "the sediment
from the waters which once covered the whole earth, formed
during the second period of its existence, these schists and these
calcareous rocks." They read, in layers of rock, the story of the
evolution of plants and animals. More than a hundred miles
beneath the surface, they find themselves beside an interior sea
above which curves a granite roof several miles high; even
clouds float in the firmament. Perhaps, the professor conjectures,
this great "vacuum" was caused by the sudden cooling of the
earth. Mushrooms forty feet high, mosses a hundred feet high,
giant ferns and grasses, and tremendous trees grow in the heavy,
tepid atmosphere. All this is the flora of the "second period"
of the world. The travellers sail the underground sea on a raft,
catch a fish of the Devonian period without organs of sight,
witness a battle between an ichthyosaurus and a plesiosaurus,
and discover a volcanic island with boiling springs. They find
the skeleton of a man of the "Japhetic family." A forest exhibits
the vegetation of the tertiary period. The explorers narrowly
escape a herd of mastodons guarded by a man twelve feet high
—obviously descended without change from some early epoch of
the earth's history. In flight, they use dynamite to blow a rock
from a tunnel, but start an earthquake and volcanic action that
bears them upward on their raft till they emerge with a stream
of lava on a mountainside in Italy. Except for its ending, this
tale presents a fairly credible scientific discovery. Teaching geology
and biology in the midst of an adventure, it is probably the first
piece of fiction to make prominent use of the theory of evolution.

3. To Other Planets

Professor George Tucker was Chairman of the Faculty of the University of Virginia when Edgar Allan Poe was a student there in 1826. Professor Tucker, writing as "Joseph Atterley," published in 1827 *A Voyage to the Moon*. Tucker followed the moon-voyages from the time of Godwin onward, adding to the established patterns several features of importance, among them the use of a counter-gravitational substance for interplanetary transportation, and the idea that a moon voyager must cross an airless void in bitter cold.

Ashore in Burma, the shipwrecked Atterley meets a Brahmin who has discovered a metal that tends to fly away from the earth. Coating a car with this substance, Atterley and the Brahmin fly to the moon. On the way, they look with interest upon the orb of earth and discuss various scientific theories about it, such as that the moon was whirled from the Pacific cavity when the earth was molten. They even discuss the possibility that the earth is hollow, but reject this theory. At the mid-point of their journey, their car undergoes a *bouleversement;* they weigh little; they throw off ballast before reaching the moon, and so land easily. They land in the country of Morosofia, where they find a tall, thin people of yellowish cast. The description of Morosofian society is satire. People on the moon are "doubles" of people on earth; "Glonglims," a race like Swift's scientists of Laputa, do such foolish things as eat the shells of nuts rather than the kernels (satirizing people who judge by superficial standards), and they make nails and hoard them. But among the inventions of the Glonglims intended to be absurd are steam-cookers, animal breeding to increase the size of animals, and internal combustion engines operated by explosions of powder. Visiting a second nation, Okalbia, Atterley finds a utopian race; Okalbians practise birth-control, have no capital punishment, and arbitrate disputes. After a time, Atterley and the Brahmin return to earth.

Poe's "The Unparalleled Adventure of One Hans Pfaal" (1835) is complex. It certainly owes a great deal to Tucker's *A Voyage to the Moon*. It narrates only the voyage to the moon, but Poe intended to continue the story in a second part describing life on the moon. The central portion of the story, that is, the description of Hans's voyage to the moon, is serious in tone, but an enveloping plot in facetious tone opens the story and closes it and seems to ridicule the whole idea. Apparently Poe was inspired to write about the moon by reading Tucker's book, but he did not want to use an anti-gravitational substance as a means of getting to the moon. From the description of the balloon in

Symzonia, he got the idea of sending his voyager to the moon
in a balloon. He worked seriously on this portion of his story,
consulting various sources of scientific information to make the
voyage credible; but when he read it to his friend J. P. Kennedy,
Kennedy ridiculed the idea. Poe then stopped work, before he
had written any description of life on the moon, and published
what he had written—the voyage only—as a separate story. To
forestall ridicule, he ridiculed it himself by surrounding it with
a facetious enveloping plot.

The facetious envelope we may dismiss here. But Hans's trip
to the moon is carefully worked out, even the radius of the moon
and that of the earth being taken into account in figuring the
distance. Poe has to suppose that some atmosphere exists between
the earth and the moon, since his method of travel is a balloon,
but he carefully prepares for an extremely thin atmosphere by
inventing a machine for condensing it. Hans's diary keeps a day-
by-day record of the appearance of the earth as he recedes from
it (including an inspection of the Pole to see whether Symmes's
theory is true), and of the moon as he approaches it. Following
Tucker, he describes gravitational effects between the earth and
the moon, including the *bouleversement.* There is a promise that
the "second part" of the story will yet be told. Considering the
solidity of his additions to the moon-voyages, one regrets that
Poe did not keep the promise.

Perhaps he did not do so because in the same year Richard
Adams Locke wrote his "moon hoax," a "news story" published
in the New York *Sun* as "Discoveries in the Moon Lately Made
at the Cape of Good Hope, by Sir John Herschel" (1835). It
created a sensation and very greatly stimulated the circulation
of the *Sun.* The story, presented with disarming scientific cau-
tion, purports to be based on information transmitted by Herschel
to the Royal Society. It describes years of work to perfect a
telescope with a magnifying power of 40,000, capable of repre-
senting objects on the moon eighteen inches in diameter. Through
it a reddish flora is first perceived, " 'precisely similar,' says Dr.
Grant, 'to the *Papaver Rhoeas* or rose-poppy of our sublunary
cornfields.' " Among lunar mountains, great claret-colored gems
are seen; then bison-like animals, adjusted to the conditions of
the moon with flaps over the eyes to protect them, the scientists
suppose, against extremes of light and darkness. Curious menlike creatures, with bat-like wings, are described; temple-like struc-
tures are seen. But finally, when the sun's rays struck the great
lens, it acted as burning-glass, and the observatory was burned.
The lay-reader of 1835 knew little of optics; what he knew of
the moon was not outraged by Locke's description.

Not to be caught napping, Poe pointed out several wrong details in Locke's story; his criticism of it was acid. Perhaps Poe had wished to work out something equally credible (possibly of a similar kind) for his "second part" of "Hans Pfaal."

A Fantastical Excursion into the Planets (anonymous, 1839) is less scientific, even though its Preface says that the author hopes "to excite in some young people, a desire for more real and proper instruction in astronomy." Imagination, as a guide, takes the narrator on a tour of Mercury, Venus, the moon, Mars, Pallas, Ceres, Juno, Vesta, Jupiter, Saturn and Uranus. Grotesque landscapes are in some accord with scientific beliefs—such as the mountains on the moon and the barrenness of Mars. But all the planets are inhabited by fanciful types of men drawn from mythology! On Venus sylph-like beauties sing rapturous love-songs; on the moon the doubles of men on earth get up a petition against the sending of lost articles there; on barren Mars furnaces blaze with ore from the mines, being made into weapons, and Martians parade in steel-clad phalanxes; Saturn is gloomy with cypress and Lethean streams.

Jules Verne might have written a first-rate voyage to the moon if he had not idolized his "master" Poe, misunderstood "Hans Pfaal," and written two exciting romances following it up in the spirit of its facetious enveloping plot rather than of its central story. *From the Earth to the Moon* (1865) and *Round the Moon* (1870) are not without science and invention. In fact, Verne invents a new means of travelling to the moon and works it out in detail; and he loads his books with scientific theories, facts and figures. But the mood is rollicking; some of the adventures are absurdities. The two features are simply sandwiched together, a slice of science and a slice of fun, in random widths. Following Poe, Verne does not describe adventures of his traveller on the moon.

For his envelope, Poe drew a puffing rabble in caricature of the Dutch; Verne drew the Baltimore Gun Club of hustling Yankees in caricature of the Americans. The Gun Club decides to shoot a projectile to the moon. An inquiry to the Cambridge Observatory yields reams of facts about the moon's distance from the earth and its apogee and perigee, with complicated calculations. The story digresses to describe the formation of the moon, indeed, of the solar system, but returns, amid Yankee antics, to serious discussion of the projectile to be shot to the moon from a cannon to weigh 68,040 tons by 400,000 pounds of fulminating cotton. In America it is easy to collect $5,446,675. for the project. When Michel Ardan of France applies to go up in the projectile, Congress makes him an honorary citizen. Finally

Ardan, President Barbicane of the Gun Club, and scientist Captain Nicholl are shot in a great cylindrical bullet from a giant gun in Stone Hill, Florida—a gun sunk nine hundred feet into the ground. (There is no Stone Hill, Florida; a hole nine hundred feet deep anywhere in Florida would fill with water. Verne was mocking the "practical" Yankees.) Though a hydraulic cushion deadens the shock of the start, everyone is knocked temporarily unconscious; protected glasses allow the travellers to observe from the projectile; air is supplied by a reaction of chlorate of potash. The trip is described in detail: temperatures are examined; a planetoid is barely missed; the travellers make detailed calculations, discuss astronomical problems, and get drunk on too much oxygen when a jet is left open. Their weight decreases; Nicholl drops a glass of water that remains suspended in the air; the projectile undergoes a *bouleversement*.

They prepare rockets to shoot against the moon to deaden their fall, but the planetoid has swung them out of their course, and they swing around the moon in an ellipse. Through their telescopes they examine the moon at an apparent distance of 1,500 yards. On the earth-side of the moon they find what scientists on earth have seen; on the "dark side" they see active volcanoes and water, and guess that life may exist in caverns. Finally the projectile completes its circuit of the moon, undergoes a *bouleversement*, and heads for earth. Sailors on the *Susquehanna* see a great, white-hot meteor fall sizzling into the sea, and a fleet that arrives to dredge for it finds the projectile afloat, flying a flag. Barbicane's notes are ready for a waiting world.

These two books present comic adventure; yet in them Verne worked out conditions to be met with on a trip to the moon from a wide reading of encyclopedic data concerned with science.

Edward Everett Hale's 'The Brick Moon" (1870-71) is less scientific, though likewise facetious. It tells the story of the inadvertent colonization of a home-made moon. To make it easy to measure longitude, a group of young men decide to send an additional moon into the sky to revolve as the earth revolves. They build a brick moon two hundred feet in diameter above two gigantic fly wheels turning in opposite outward directions, nearly touching. When the moon is rolled upon them, it will be hurled so far it will not fall back, but will remain suspended above one spot on earth. The hollow moon is braced by being filled with apartments whose walls are groined arches; workmen live in the apartments during construction. It breaks loose ahead of time, strikes the flywheels, and is cast into space—with thirty-seven people. It goes up nine thousand miles, beyond the earth's atmosphere, but takes its own atmosphere with it, including clouds for rainfall. Communication is established: the "moon" people can see big sheets of black cloth made into letters; they stand on the horizon of their world and (being very light) jump up and down in the Morse code. Provisions are sent up by means of the fly-wheels. The story suggests that people may be happy in a small world.

The wonderful journeys of 1817-1870 thus explored the possibilities of scientific fiction.

D. *Utopias and Satires*

The first half of the nineteenth century was rich in utopian experiments, especially in America, but most of them were in flight from the early stages of the industrial revolution. It had brought only smoke, slums, and riots in the mining towns. Few foresaw that machines might bring cleanliness, shining towers, and the good life. Utopian philosophers, such as Carlyle, Emerson, Thoreau, and Ruskin, thundered against machinery and called for a return to the middle ages, the farm, or the simple life. Utopian experiments were usually anti-scientific.

But here and there a maverick looked beyond the immediate railroad tracks toward a utopia that, like Mercier's, was set in the future. Mrs. Mary Griffith of Charlies Hope, New Jersey, published "Three Hundred Years Hence" in 1836. In this story, anticipating the heroes of Bellamy and Wells, Edgar Hastings goes to sleep; an explosion and an avalanche seal him hermetically in his chamber. Three hundred years later laborers excavating for a new street uncover him and wake him up. He meets a descendant of the same name and is piloted through the new civilization of Pennsylvania, New Jersey, and New York. Great social changes have taken place: women are emancipated, Princeton College teaches vocational and technical subjects, Negro slaves have been freed, tobacco and liquor have been prohibited, and war has been outlawed. This good world has been made possible through the development of machinery. A new power (not described) has superseded steam to drive locomotives and ships; "curious vehicles that moved by some internal machinery" are in common use. Other advanced machinery includes navigable balloons, the "self-moving plow," power-driven lawn mowers, haybalers, planters, cultivators, reapers and threshers, and delivery trucks. Machines "fill up gullies, dig out the roots of trees, plough down hills, turn water courses—in short they have entirely superseded the use of cattle of any kind." Houses are built of treated, fire-proof wood. Streets are immaculate pavements, washed and cooled by jets of water; the horse-and-buggy age has passed.

Great water-cooled, clean markets provide the goods of the world, including out-of-season vegetables. As no radical changes in government are described, except adoption of the single-tax on incomes and nationalization of railroads, all the social advances are due to mechanical invention. The utopia is "instrumental," that is, the utopian society is brought about through the development of science and the use of tools and machines.

Edgar Allan Poe was likewise a maverick, at least in his attitude toward the back-to-nature movement in New England. He frequently designed more than he executed, publishing fragments not fully worked out. His "Mellonta Tauta" (1849) seems to be such a fragment. It is partly satire, partly historical romance of the future, and partly an array of advanced machines for an instrumental utopia.

In a letter written from day to day, like a diary, Pundita of the year 2848 describes an excursion over the ocean in the dirigible balloon *Skylark*. Pundita frets because it moves only a hundred miles an hour; balloons with four hundred passengers speed past at a hundred and fifty. The ocean swarms with "magnetic propellers"; floating telegraph wires span the Atlantic; the railroads of "Kanadaw" run trains at three hundred miles an hour on rails fifty feet apart, while passengers "flirt, feast, and dance in the magnificent saloons." Pundita has watched with interest the erection "of a new impost on a couple of lintels in the new temple at Daphnis in the moon." The rivers around New York have been widened; the old city has been razed (partly by Earthquake) and is being made into a pleasure island for the emperor—for "Amricca," finally tired of mob-rule, has become a monarchy. The story ends abruptly.

Doubtless many such fragmentary prophecies of a world made new through the use of machines could be found. One thinks, for instance, of Tennyson's "Locksley Hall" (1842) with its vision of "argosies of magic sails," instruments in bringing about a "Parliament of man, the Federation of the world."

By 1871 science had begun to fulfill some of its promises; the earlier agonies of industrialization were passing; the burst of inventions, such as those of Edison in the last quarter of the nineteenth century, showed the Machine Age on the horizon; and the theory of evolution suggested not only an ancient past, but a limitless future, in which there might be racial self-direction.

It is natural, then, that many pieces of scientific fiction after 1870 employ the theory of evolution and the machines of science to present the Islands of the Blest.

CHAPTER FOUR

To the Islands of the Blest

Scientific Fiction, 1871-1894

BY 1871 IT WAS CLEAR that a Machine Age lay just ahead and that the future would, on this account, be different in many ways from the present. Naturally, the effort to prepare for this future took frequently the form of utopian or satiric fiction. Though machinery had brought wealth to a few, it had brought misery to many, but utopian writers believed that if the state should control industry, the increasing use of machinery could bring prosperity to everyone. The satirists doubted this result. Utopias and satires after 1870, describing more and more machines, sought in general an understanding of how machines would change the conditions of human life and how society could best meet the changed conditions.

By this time, the theory of evolution was public property. One interpretation of it supported a belief in progress, but another, a belief that civilization is artificial and liable to collapse. Belief in progress supposed that utopia might be realized, especially with the aid of machinery to relieve man of drudgery; belief that civilization is artificial supposed that the increased use of machinery would relieve man of the struggle for survival, sap his strength, and make him at last the slave of his machines. The fear was expressed that men, so recently savages, would use the forces of the new science to destroy themselves. Bulwer-Lytton's *The Coming Race* and Samuel Butler's *Erewhon*, making prompt use of the theory of evolution, stated the main ideas found in the utopias and satires of the period 1871-1894.

During the same period a great deal of scientific fiction narrated adventures of the kinds previously described. But the classifications of Chapters Two and Three must be altered somewhat. Since some of the marvellous inventions of this period are discoveries in physiology, mineralogy, and the like, the classification of "The Wonderful Discovery" is more suitable to include them than "The Wonderful Machine." And though the writers of scientific fiction continue to write tales of terror, the "Gothic" trappings are displaced (in such pieces as I have included) by a more highly rationalized supernaturalism. This change is reflected in the use of "The Occult and the Supernatural" to replace "The 'Gothic' Romance." It is necessary to add a new classification, "The Historic Romance," to designate both the tale of the future that is not primarily utopistic and the tale that, based upon the theory of evolution, turned to prehistoric times.

A. *Utopias and Satires*

Bulwer-Lytton's *The Coming Race* (1871) is based upon two hypotheses. The first, from the theory of evolution, is that man in the future will develop into an intellectual, self-controlled race surpassing our own in the same ways that we surpass savages. The second is that by gaining control over such forces as electricity and hypnotism man will establish a civilization in which there will be no toil, struggle, or poverty. In his earlier fiction, Bulwer-Lytton had speculated about occult forces and had attacked laboratory science. In *The Coming Race,* however, he supposes natural science may include psychic phenomena, not to be thought of as occult; he sees that this science may bring about a utopian condition, and his only doubt is whether this utopian condition may be desirable. The book is a utopia that includes some satire.

An American is led by an engineer to explore a deep crevice in a mine. The engineer is killed as they descend from the crevice onto a plain in the bowels of the earth, and the American is left alone. Under the "cavernous roof" above him flies "what appeared to be a small boat, impelled by sails shaped like wings." About him grows vegetation strangely like, and yet unlike, that above ground. Approaching a magnificent building, he sees what looks like a human being of great height and majesty of bearing. This man has wings folded over his breast and carries in his right hand a bright metal staff. His face is like that of no known race, "so regular in its calm, intellectual, mysterious beauty . . . with large black eyes, deep and brilliant, and brows arched as a semi-circle." The American is made welcome and after a time learns more of the Ana, as the people of the world inside the earth are called. They are a race stronger and grander than men, descended from men above ground who fled down caverns during prehistoric floods. Among the civilized portion of them, the Vril-ya, care and sorrow, passion and sin, do not exist. For a long time the Ana struggled as desperately as men above ground did, and then they discovered vril, an all-penetrating "electricity" that "comprehends in its manifold branches other forces of nature . . . such as magnetism, galvanism, etc." With the aid of this force the Vril-ya, little by little, made conquest of nature. Vril is available to the body through a wand which collects it from the air. Vril moves the automatons who serve the Vril-ya; it operates their machines, tended by happy children; it supports the Vril-ya as they fly on their mechanical wings with the grace of birds; it enables them to control the weather and to transmit thought from mind to mind—to learn the traveller's language, for instance, while he lies in a vril-imposed trance. It is the force that has made a perfected civilization possible. First it eliminated war, for with weapons of vril, war means annihilation. It eliminated poverty, crime, misery, and government, except a benevolent patriarchal rule.

By contrast with the societies of the earth's surface, the land of the Vril-ya seems utopian. When the American describes democracy, his host pities him and enjoins him to secrecy. And yet, the American finds himself restless among the Vril-ya; their perfectly rational society seems dull, without spurs. The feelings are never released. The sciences are highly developed, but the arts are held in some contempt. Bulwer-Lytton, foreseeing for the "coming race" both mastery of the forces of nature and the evolution of man into a more intellectual race, describes a static perfection, and he is dissatisfied because it seems dull. He fails to realize one implication of the theory of evolution, that life is dynamic, so that whatever stage of perfection man may reach is only a stage. Later utopias such as Well's *A Modern Utopia* do realize this implication.

Samuel Butler's *Erewhon* (1872) questions many of the assumptions of *The Coming Race*. The narrator, on an exploring trip to the interior of New Zealand, comes upon a civilization that had been farther advanced in the use of machinery than that of Europe, but that had discarded machinery, with the result that the men of Erewhon are "of the most magnificent presence, being no less strong and handsome than the women were beautiful." The narrator is treated kindly by two hosts in turn and falls in love with a daughter of each host. He is brought before the king, learns the language, investigates the customs, and escapes in a balloon with the daughter of his last host.

Butler's attack upon machinery uses ideas from the theory of evolution. When the people of Erewhon had developed machinery to a high degree, a philosopher arose who said that by a process of evolution machinery would develop consciousness, would enslave man, and finally would supersede him. Consciousness, the philosopher argued, may be of many kinds; who can say that a rose, for instance, exerts no conscious will as it creates a perfume man cannot manufacture? Perhaps the cells of the body have individual consciousness; perhaps a city, of wood and stone, with people moving through it like blood corpuscles, has consciousness. As there may be in the apparently unconscious cells of a potato such cunning and design as best fit it to thrive, there may be in a piece of machinery the cunning best suited to its purpose. This cunning may develop; already machines reproduce themselves and use man in the process exactly as red clover uses the humble bee. Already man is becoming enslaved; if machines should disappear, "so that the race of man should be left as it were naked upon a desert island, we should become extinct in six weeks." Reasoning in this way, the Erewhonians had destroyed machinery. As they used their bodies, they became a handsome and vigorous people.

Where Bulwer-Lytton predicts that the use of vril and the machinery it operates will enable man to develop himself fully, Butler fears that the increasing use of machinery may "so equalize man's powers, and so lessen the severity of any competition" as to cause survival of the unfit and "a degeneracy of the human race" till man's body weakens and becomes "purely rudimentary." These two attitudes toward the advancing Machine Age, shaped by two interpretations of the theory of evolution, underlie most of the utopistic writing of the period 1871-1894.

Jules Verne's nearest approach to a picture of Utopia is *The Five Hundred Millions of the Begum* (1879). Less philosophical than Bulwer-Lytton or Butler, Verne none the less states in two practical illustrations the problem of whether the development of machinery will be good or bad for mankind. His answer is that machinery may make life horrible if it is selfishly used, but may make it sweet, clean, and happy if it is used with that intention. The contrast includes other features. On the one hand, the spirit of Germany, regimentation, dictatorship, and science used for destruction are symbolized in Stahlstadt; on the other, the spirit of France, individualism, democracy, and science used for human welfare are symbolized in Frankville.

As usual, Verne tells a good story. Dr. Sarrasin of Douai

inherits, through a distant relationship, 527,000,000 francs from an Indian rajah: Professor Schultz trumps up a similar relationship and cheats Dr. Sarrasin of half the amount. Sarrasin establishes the city of Frankville in the wilds of Oregon to make use of all the latest conveniences of science; it is Sarrasin's experiment in Utopia. Thirty miles away, Professor Schultz etablishes Stahlstadt, resembling a combination of fortress, industrial section of Pittsburgh, and concentration camp. His aim is to manufacture munitions, to destroy Frankville, and finally to help Germany enslave the world. Stahlstadt employs thirty thousand German workmen subject to strict military discipline. But Max Bruckmann, in love with Sarrasin's daughter, manages to enter Stahlstadt as expert draftsman—and spy—and finally to get into the walled citadel of Schultz himself. Schultz exhibits his cannon able to shoot a projectile thirty miles, his new gun-cotton, his gas-shells containing carbonic acid to freeze whatever the gas touches, and his shells that fire in series like "Molotov breadbaskets." Max escapes to Frankville and warns the inhabitants, but they are powerless against Schultz. They wait in terror, but the Blitzkrieg does not come. Investigating, they find that one of Schultz's shells had blown up and killed him. Stahlstadt disintegrates, leaving Frankville to work out its utopian destiny. Perhaps to afford Verne a happy ending, Schultz was killed, but his death was an accident. The warning is clear that the terrible weapons of science could have wrecked Frankville.

Frankville itself is a model city planned to use all that science affords as people of democratic good-will use it. Its houses are one-family houses, each in its garden, each with its terraced roof. Benevolent capitalism flourishes; progressive education, especially in science, outdoor exercises, and labor-saving devices make life sweet, clean, and happy. There is nothing revolutionary. This Frankville, says Verne, is a sample of what science may make of our cities now; but watch out, he says, that science does not make cities like Stahlstadt.

W. H. Hudson, in *A Crystal Age* (1887), would follow the Erewhonians and abolish machines, to establish a matriarchal Golden Age. Smith, on a "botanizing expedition," is stunned by a landslide. He wakes in some vague future time to find a stately people dressed like ancient Greeks cultivating the soil. Though they speak English, they have never heard of England, Victoria, Napoleon, or even Shakespeare. Smith becomes one of a family living in an ancient and lovely mansion and working in the fields. He learns that many thousands of years ago a great catastrophe befell the human race; the few who survived chose to forget the old civilization and to build a better one. Machinery has been willingly forgotten, along with all systems, religions, -ologies, and -isms. But plants, animals, and men have developed wonderfully; intelligent horses come at whistle to stand in the plow-shafts.

At the head of each family is a Mother especially chosen to found a family; few are chosen, for few meet the high standards needed to improve the race. As a result of this directed evolution, the race has so improved that everyone lives in health and vigor to a great age; the Father (inferior to the Mother), for instance, is 196 years old. Machinery has no place in this sunlit society; it is a pleasure to earn daily bread in the sweat of the body.

Edward Bellamy in *Looking Backward* (1888) sought to face the Machine Age, instead of to dream it out of existence. The story follows the pattern of Mercier's dream into the future, with a surprise ending; it is not a dream, but a reality. Julian West, suffering from insomnia, is hypnotized in a soundproof vault in 1887; he wakes in 2000, under the care of his host, Dr. Leete. The new world is exhibited and explained to him. Naturally, he falls in love with Dr. Leete's daughter. He likes the new society, prepares to lecture on the nineteenth century, dreams that he is again awake in 1887, and awakens finally in 2000.

The book applies the theory of evolution to industrial organization, observes that with the increasing use of machinery corporations increase in size, and states that the inevitable result of this process—"industrial evolution which could not have terminated otherwise"—is state socialism. This socialism is a good result; the book is doctrinaire. At the same time, the intelligent use of machines to lighten labor and to provide everybody with plenty, instead of enslaving men to machinery or weakening their bodies through removing the struggle for survival, allows "natural selection to have a free rein"; marriages for love, instead of money, "preserve and transmit the better types of the race."

Capitalism had been "incompetent to the demands of an age of steam and telegraphs and the gigantic scale of its enterprises." The socialistic organization of society for the abundant, equable distribution of labor and goods came about when society was able to "recognize and co-operate with" industrial evolution. Machines, having given birth to the new society, continue to provide it with comforts and pleasures. Pneumatic tubes deliver goods over Boston in a few minutes; people have leisure to enjoy music, drama, and sermons sent out to everybody's home from central telephone stations; electrical devices perform all household labors. Labor-saving machines make it possible for everyone to retire at forty-five. Denying the implications of

Erewhon, Bellamy says that science, if socially controlled, will provide every citizen the opportunity to develop the best that is in him.

Looking Backward aroused intense excitement and controversy; "answers" to it sprang up like mushrooms. A typical answer was Richard C. Michaelis's *Looking Further Forward* (1890). It denies that the drift of industrial evolution is toward socialism, and attacks socialism by using the theory of evolution to support the statement that "Inequality is the law of nature and the attempt to establish equality is therefore unnatural and absurd."

William Morris would have socialism in his utopia, but no machines. In *News from Nowhere* (1890) the new day dawned when a revolutionary crowd destroyed machinery. The society he presents results from a combination of socialism, handicrafts, and enthusiasm for fourteenth-century art. The happiness and cheerful labor of the citizens of London in 2003 have had biological effects; men live longer and grow old later.

Theodore Hertzka's *Freeland* (in English, 1891) is more practicable. It describes an experimental socialistic state founded in central Africa; it has such success that the governments of the world determine to follow the example of the Freelanders. The utopian society of Freeland makes use of not only the machinery known at the time it was written, but also "automobiles" and gondolas driven by steam-wound spiral springs.

William Dean Howells's *A Traveler from Altruria* (1894) may properly bring to a close this survey of utopian concern with adjustment to the Machine Age, for it presents both satire and a utopian point of view. The method of the satire is to present American institutions, customs, and points of view as they seem to a visitor from Altruria, whose aloof, naively logical, and yet penetrating comments illuminate the unreason in ways and ideas long taken for granted. Finally, in a lecture to an American audience, the Traveler describes Altruria, a socialistic state that resembles a combinaton of Bellamy's mechanistic utopia and Morris's artistic one. The change that made Altruria a utopia was an "Evolution." At first, in Altruria, machinery had developed as in America; it seemed a monster that "devoured women and children, and wasted men." Perhaps this earlier "discipline" of competition was necessary in the "Evolution." Finally a socialist state was formed, by ballot and without bloodshed, and machinery was controlled for the social welfare. Now electricity performs all services in Altruria, driving trains at a hundred and fifty miles an hour and performing all labor except the handicraft work that Altrurians find pleasure in doing as art. Given the concentrated forces of the community to direct it, science is able to perform great public works, such as that of changing the climate of Altruria, formerly chilly, by cutting off a peninsula to alter an equatorial current. Altruria is a somewhere, an Island of the Blest, that America or any country may become.

In this book, as in nearly all utopistic writing between 1871 and 1894, fundamental influences upon the shape of the state have been the approach of the Machine Age and views of progress derived from the theory of evolution. Romances concerned with invention and discovery are, of course, concerned also with their social effects. The problems stated in the utopias and satires are, from 1871 onward, seldom absent, in more or less degree, from scientific fiction of any kind, except that concerned with the supernatural. Historic romances of the future, especially, include utopian and satiric material.

B. *The Wonderful Discovery*

The approach of the Machine Age naturally stimulated stories of invention and discovery. Jules Verne had found his pace and his audience. Lovers of the scientific tale waited breathless for Verne's next, and he, no less breathless, described invention after invention during this period.

Verne's three-part novel, *The Mysterious Island* (1870-75), is *Robinson Crusoe* up to date with every invention of nineteenth-century science, plus mystery and utopia. In 1865, five Union prisoners escape from Richmond in a balloon; winds drive them over the Pacific, and as the gas leaks out, the men drop near a desert island. Starting with nothing except engineer Cyrus Harding's knowledge of science, they develop the resources of the island and derive the conveniences of modern invention. Harding makes steel from coal and ores found in the island, and nitroglycerine from carbonate of potash, vegetable cinders, and saltpeter. They drain a lake to make their home in a granite cavern, build an elevator operated by a water-wheel, and set up telegraphic communication between their farm and their citadel.

But sometimes they are stumped, and then they receive mysterious aid. In need of quinine, they find a bottle of it on a table; they find tools on the sea-shore; and finally they receive a message over their telegraph to visit a cavern inside a volcano. The mystery is solved, for in the cavern they find Captain Nemo of the submarine *Nautilus,* dying. Their island is also his headquarters. He reveals the secret concerning himself that had been left a mystery in *Twenty Thousand Leagues Under the Sea*: he is an Indian Prince whom the English had despoiled. The castaways, rescued just before the volcano breaks into eruption, have been so happy on their island that they go to Iowa, then a frontier, to re-establish there the pastoral, but mechanized Utopia they had left behind.

Few imaginary discoveries are presented, but half the interest of the tale lies in Harding's ingenious mechanisms as he begins with desert island and ends with telegraphy.

Verne described the use of electric lights during the period when gas-lights were common. But in *Dr. Ox's Experiment* (1874) he began with an advanced type of illuminating gas and ended with a farcical story of the effects of pure oxygen upon the human system. Dr. Ox, having invented an inexpensive method for decomposing water into hydrogen and oxygen, is interested in discovering the physiological effects of oxygen in large quantities. As an excuse for laying gas pipes through the town, he proposes to light slowpaced Quiquendone with oxyhydric gas. When pipes are laid, he pumps oxygen into the town, with amazing effects; the pace of life quickens in plants, dogs, cats, horses, and men. Artichokes grow the size of melons, gourds the size of the belfry bell. The people get excited, riot, trump up a crusade against a neighboring town, march on that town, and then, out of reach of the oxygen, slow down and wonder what the excitement is about. Fortunately, an explosion wrecks the gas works.

Verne returned to his favorite, electric lighting by incandescent lamps, in *The Underground City* (1877), on the verge of its invention by Edison in 1879. A coal-lode is discovered in a mammoth cave in Scotland. Through the use of electric lighting it is possible to establish a mining town within the cavern, bright as day. The story, of course, includes adventure and a mystery, besides discussion of all that science knows about coal, its formation, and the world-supply of it.

Edward Bellamy of *Looking Backward* achieved that utopian best-seller only after other experiments in scientific fiction. Bellamy's *Dr. Heidenhoff's Process* (1880) is not a utopia, though in the dream-device of the book and in the discussion of the social uses of Dr. Heidenhoff's process the budding utopian may be detected. The process is a method of using galvanic batteries to induce controlled amnesia to eliminate unpleasant memories. Madeline Brand, who loves Henry Burr but is oppressed by morbid memories of another suitor who had seduced her, takes the treatment and emerges unable to remember even why she took it. The process may have important social consequences: criminals, even murderers, may be made into innocent men; society may establish hospitals for criminals, instead of prisons. Bellamy carried the idea over into *Looking Backward;* in 2000 "atavism" is treated in hospitals. But Dr. Heidenhoff's process is all a dream; in *Looking Backward,* the dream device is considered, but rejected, as Julian West re-awakens into 2000.

Verne's *The Steam House* (1880) presents the invention of what amounts to an elaborate auto-trailer drawn by a fast-stepping mechanical elephant, steam-driven. In this vehicle, fitted with electrical comforts, a group of Englishmen explore India beyond the railroads, hunt big game, visit cities, ford rivers—the elephant floats, his feet fitted with paddle wheels—and have hairbreadth escapes from treacherous natives.

In *The Star of the South* (1884) Verne toys with the idea of the artificial manufacture of diamonds and describes the attempt in great detail, but reveals at last that the apparent success is due to a zealous servant's placing a diamond in the crucible where his master hoped to find one. The novel, however, gives Verne an opportunity to describe diamonds and their structure, diamond mines, and from there all central Africa, as the diamond is stolen and has to be traced into the interior, with the usual fights with natives, treachery, and hairbreadth escapes.

Frank Stockton's "A Tale of Negative Gravity" (*c.* 1884) describes the invention of a machine that repulses gravitation. It can be carried in a knapsack and its "power" may be regulated; with it the narrator has a good deal of fun, as in climbing mountains and jumping fences. He speculates upon industrial uses for his invention, but as people think he is insane, he releases his machine and lets it fly away.

A more serious discussion of flight is offered in Tom Greer's (*pseud.*) *A Modern Daedalus* (1885), which describes a method of flying, its use to bomb England and force the English to grant freedom to Ireland, and then the new day of scientific progress that follows. John O'Halloran invents a mechanism for flying, a pair of wings strapped to the shoulders and steered by movements of the body, but otherwise secret. He plans uses for his machine that will bring about utopia, but his father and his brothers are then engaged in a rebellion against England. John flies to London and lights upon the dome of St. Paul's; a mob gathers, but he hides his wings before he is captured. The Home Secretary tries to get the use of the wings to suppress the Irish, but John escapes, incensed against the English, goes to Ireland, and there trains a company of fliers. Using bombs, they make short work of an English garrison and warships, helpless under attack from the air. When the English have granted Ireland independence, the wings are used for scientific exploration.

Robur the Conqueror (1886) is Jules Verne's contribution to stories of flying in a heavier-than-air machine. Though an exciting tale, as usual, it is likewise an expression of Verne's serious faith in the airplane and of his fear that it might be used for destructive purposes. Robur is a symbol: "Robur is the science of the future. Perhaps the science of tomorrow! Certainly the science that will come!" The future of aviation "belongs to the aeronef [airplane] and not the aerostat [balloon]." And when the science of the future produces the airplane, it "will greatly change the social and political conditions of the world." There are yet unbelievers, people who ridicule the idea of airplane flight; in the story Uncle Prudent and Phil Evans represent the blind who refuse to see, till at the end it is they who are left in ridicule. But significantly Robur will not yet make public the secret of his airplane, for "Nations are not yet fit for union." The secret will be revealed, Robur tells the people of the United States, "the day you are educated enough to profit by it and wise enough not to abuse it."

The Weldon Institute of Philadelphia is about to launch the greatest balloon ever constructed, a dirigible, driven by propellers fed by electric batteries. A stranger, Robur, appears, says that the balloon is outmoded, and explains the principle of heavier-than-air flight; he has to use pistols to keep from being mobbed. President Prudent and Secretary Evans, to cool off, stroll to the outskirts of the city; they are seized in the dark, and soon find themselves four thousand feet high in Robur's flying machine. The story halts for a long history of experimentation in heavier-than-air flight and a full exposition of the principles involved. The successful principle, Verne says, will be "Aeroplanes, which are merely inclined planes like kites, but towed or driven by screws." Robur's machine, the *Albatross,* employing this principle, is 112 feet long, in the shape of a ship's deck; seventy-four vertical screws give it lifting power; once in the air, it is sustained and carried forward by horizontal screws driven by electricity generated in batteries of secret composition. The airplane is made of tough, light plastics: paper mixed with dextrin and starch and compressed till hard as metal, a glass-like substance, and gelatinized fiber.

Besides the prisoners, the *Albatross* carries eight men in comfortable cabins, equipped with electric lights, instruments (such as compasses, thermometers, barometers) for use in flying, a small library, a portable printing press, a cannon with powder, dynamite, an electric stove, and plenty of food. At 120 miles an hour, the *Albatross* goes around the world, whale-shooting in the Pacific and cannibal-shooting in Africa. It is caught in a waterspout, crosses the South Pole, and is partly wrecked on a barren island. Finally Prudent and Evans learn its destination, Robur's stronghold on X island, where Robur intends to found a colony, to develop his science, and finally to conquer the world. (Robur is a symbol for science of the future.) Prudent and Evans, not yet ready for the future, destroy the *Albatross* with dynamite, but Robur escapes and later appears dramatically in Philadelphia in a new airplane, to laugh at his detractors and yet to promise the airplane to the world when the world is ready.

But Jules Verne did not hold to serious themes. His farcical tale, *The Purchase of the North Pole* (1889), is the story of a great invention that does not work because of a miscalculation. The North Polar Practical Association buys the Arctic regions for $2.00 per square mile. Behind the scheme are Barbicane & Co., who had made the trip around the moon; they have found coal at the Pole, and they intend to straighten the earth's axis, warm the polar region, and get the coal. They are going to load a tremendous cannon, a four-hundred-million-pounder sunk into a mountain in Africa, with Captain Nicholl's new explosive, melimelonite, and shoot it; the "kick" will straighten the axis. The world is in a frenzy, but when the cannon shoots, nothing happens. It develops that Maston's calculations, which had governed the size of the cannon, had been interrupted by a telephone call from a designing widow, and Maston had forgotten three cyphers. "To modify the conditions of the Earth's movement," Verne concludes, "is beyond the powers of man."

Probably deriving from both *Frankenstein,* whose theme it employs, and *Erewhon,* whose reasoning it employs, "Moxon's Master" (1893), by Ambrose Bierce, describes an automaton chess-player that becomes angry at a checkmate and destroys its creator. Moxon, the inventor, keeps his chess-player hidden, but argues with a friend that it is possible to create an intelligent machine. Following *Erewhon,* Moxon analyzes consciousness and reaches the conclusion that a machine thinks about the work it is doing. Experiments have shown him that plants think. He declares that even minerals think: the atoms of a mineral, moving freely in solution, arrange themselves into mathematically perfect shapes; frozen moisture aggregates in the symmetrical forms of snowflakes. The visitor to whom Moxon is talking leaves the house, but acting on a curious presentiment, returns, to find Moxon playing chess with the automaton. When Moxon moves to checkmate, the whirring of wheels is audible, "an effect such as might be expected if a pawl should be jostled from the teeth of a ratchet-wheel," and the machine reaches forward and strangles Moxon in its iron hands.

A wonderful discovery in mineralogy is described in Chamberlain's *6,000 Tons of Gold* (1894), and the book works out the social effects of this discovery. In South America (where a volcanic disturbance had split a mountain in two), Robert Brent receives six thousand tons of gold from an Indian tribe whose chief sees disaster in its possession. Buying a large steamship, Brent brings the gold to America and stores it in a private vault. He tries to administer his wealth for the good of society, giving millions to charity, science and education—especially $2,500,000. to Yale University for research in heavier-than-air flight. The new wealth stimulates invention. Brent is able to build a new kind of engine into his yacht *Mystery;* using liquefied carbonic acid gas under pressure, the *Mystery* crosses the Atlantic in four days. But he upsets world-finance. Prices rise, and efforts to feed the poor send prices higher. Finally, after an international conference, the bulk of the gold is loaded on a warship and dumped into mid-Atlantic. In this book, the discovery of gold has the effects predicted for the airplane: though capable of benefiting mankind, it almost wrecks the economic structure and almost plunges the world into war.

The effect of a tremendous charge of electricity upon the body is the basis of Conan Doyle's farcical story, "The Los Amigos Fiasco" (1894). The thriving town of Los Amigos has new electric generators propelled by waterfalls to generate six times the current of New York. A bandit is to be electrocuted; but the charge is too much for killing—it vitalizes. He cannot be killed: hanged, he comes down joking; shot, he remains spry with six holes in his body. The bandit has simply been drenched with life-force, here identified as electricity.

In 1894 H. G. Wells began the publication of scientific stories. The stories published in this year, however, are not as bold in describing imaginary discoveries as the ones to come later. Two of them, "The Stolen Bacillus" and "The Lord of the Dynamos," do not describe imaginary discoveries, but make use of actual science for purposes of fiction. "The Stolen Bacillus" tells of a bacteriologist who boasts to a disguised anarchist about a virulent culture in a test-tube. The anarchist steals the test-tube to poison the water-supply, but cornered, drinks the culture—which is really only bacteria that cause blue mold on monkeys. "The Lord of the Dynamos" tells the story of Azuma-zi, from beyond the Straits Settlements, who is employed to attend dynamos. He worships them as gods and to them sacrifices the engineer Holroyd by thrusting him against the switch.

In another story, Wells's "The Diamond Maker" (1894), the narrator meets a man who says he has learned to make diamonds and offers a huge diamond for a hundred pounds. The narrator

is skeptical, but intends to investigate; before he can do so, the
diamond-maker is accused of being an anarchist, scared away
by the police, and never seen again.

C. *The Wonderful Journey*

1. On the Earth

By 1871, few areas on the surface of the earth remained unexplored. But Jules Verne found the known world and actual machines just as amazing as imaginary ones. His *Around the World
in Eighty Days* (1872), for instance, exhibits the marvel that
the world can now be circled in eighty days.

Verne's *The Floating Island* (1876), a story of adventure
among the history and geography of the Pacific Islands, contains
a museum of imaginary inventions, most of them familiar in the
twentieth century. Indeed, the adventure is laid in the twentieth
century, in some unstated year.

Four musicians, finding themselves stranded in California,
accept the offer of a stranger to convey them to a large city,
cross a ferry operated by electricity, travel in an electric automobile, and are led to a hotel splendid with electric light. The
next day they discover that they are on a floating pleasure-
island owned by ten thousand American millionaires. It is an
oval, four miles long and three miles wide, built of land based
upon 270,000 caissons, and propelled by electric motors developing ten million horsepower. Electricity generated from petroleum
runs elevators, tram cars along metal streets, drays, moving pavements, telegraphs, telephones, stoves, incandescent lamps, "aluminum moons" (street lamps), and the fishing smacks that lie in the
"harbors." Electro-culture stimulates vegetables and flowers, regularly watered from "underground" conduits. The musicians have
been kidnapped because the millionaires, weary of phonographs
and "theatrophones," were pleased with their playing, heard from
Boston by cable-telephone.

After Verne provides his musicians with an inventory of these
wonders, he turns to geography and adventure: they tour the
Pacific amid lectures on the formation of islands, their geography,
and their inhabitants; they are attacked by Malays—and on to a
happy ending in New Zealand.

James DeMille's *A Strange Manuscript Found in a Copper
Cylinder* (1888) explores the unknown world of the South Pole.
The book was inspired partly by Poe's *Narrative of Arthur
Gordon Pym,* for the first stages of the journey offer details like
those in Poe's story, and the later discovery of a race speaking
a language resembling Arabic suggests the Arabic carvings in

Poe's story. DeMille apparently knew that Poe intended Pym to go inside the earth, but he rejected this destination as too fantastic. DeMille's traveller, passing through a cavern, fears that he may be going inside the earth and mentally reviews theories like those of Symmes.

The story has an enveloping framework: the central narrative is a manuscript found in a copper cylinder at sea and read aloud. Chapters of discussion of it include a good deal of scientific speculation. The central narrative tells the story of Henry More, shipwrecked in 1843 in a southern latitude. More and Agnew, a companion, left adrift in a small boat, are caught in a mysterious southward current. They come upon an island of black savages, apparently friendly but treacherous. More alone escapes from the savages and is again drawn southward toward vast mountains. When the stream draws his boat into a tunnel under a mountain, More speculates that he may be going into the hollow earth; but instead, he emerges on a placid sea surrounded by green land; populous cities, terraced slopes, and pyramids line the shore. He attributes the warmth of the air in this polar region to the flattening of the earth, so that internal heat of the earth warms the air.

Men who look like Arabs appear in a galley rowed by a hundred oarsmen; with feeble eyes, they blink in the sunlight. Heaping gifts on More, they lead him through a dark cavern to their underground habitation. There, taught by the girl Almah, More learns the language, which resembles Arabic. The civilization resembles the Egyptian, but inverts normal attitudes: these people see better during the long polar night than in the sunlight; they seek death as the highest blessing; they seek poverty, bestowing their goods on whoever will take them; though gentle, they practise cannibalism in a great sacrificial feast at the beginning of the dark season—butchering hundreds of eager victims; they consider hopeless love a blessing.

Yet no satiric purpose is clear in the book. It is a yarn of strange adventure constructed upon various scientific theories, especially the theory of evolution. As the manuscript is read aloud, the men reading it pause to discuss the phenomena described. Dr. Congreve, a physician, and Oxenden, an ethnologist, find that the story agrees with their knowledge. A sea-serpent that More describes is identified as of a species formerly in northern waters; Oxenden believes the people described are descendants of the Troglodytes, who were Arabian in race and once lived in contact with Egypt. Supposing them a Semitic people, the customs described, says Oxenden, could be accounted for by a natural evolution.

2. Into the Earth

Though DeMille rejected the theory of the hollow earth, others
did not.   William Bradshaw's *The Goddess of Atvatabar* (1892)
is an exotic development of the idea. A bizarre, often grotesque,
fairy tale of science, the book describes the discovery of a world
within the shell of the earth, lighted by its own central sun.
Rich young Lexington White and his coterie of scientists set
out to explore the North Polar sea. But they sail through the
open Pole, down a vortex to the inner world, and reach the
continent of Atvatabar, lying opposite the Atlantic ocean.

They encounter men who fly with wings operated by motors
that collect power from the air; these men conduct them to the
court of Atvatabar. The people of Atvatabar are far advanced
beyond those of the outer world in mechanical inventions. For
instance, they use power collected from the air; they have mechanical ostriches for cavalry; they make rain by shooting cold
gas into the air; they have seaboots, marine railroads, magnicity,
and airplanes as well as individual wings. In addition, they control soul-forces that can restore life to a dead body. Lyone, the
goddess, is killed by electricity, but is reincarnated by the force-
of-yearning of ten thousand twin-souls (lovers hopelessly separated) ; the ten thousand twin-souls grasp wands, each connected
by a wire to a great helix of terrelium; by yearning, they charge
an immense spiritual battery, and its vitality renews life in
Lyone. Proof of the scientific theory that animals evolved from
plants is found in the Garden of Tanje; there are, for instance,
such plant-animals as the Lillipoutum, a bird with roots on feet
and tail. This bird when hungry thrusts its roots into ooze on
river banks and feeds as a plant feeds. Gravity is very curious;
men weigh little in Atvatabar, and one can fly to a height where
he weighs nothing at all. This whimsy is hardly science, but it
shows what science can suggest in the mood of *The Arabian
Nights*.

William N. Harben, in *The Land of the Changing Sun* (1894),
is more practical in his description of an underground world,
for his wonders are simply advanced mechanical inventions. The
inside of the earth is not a Symmesian hollow-world, but a cavern
100 miles in diameter. Harry Johnston and Charles Thorndyke
are lost in a balloon near the North Pole. Landed near a lake
on an island, they are surprised to see a submarine emerge. They
are invited inside, in English, and taken down many thousands
of feet, to emerge in the cavern. A city lies before them; the
place is full of gold; the people have airplanes; they regulate
their temperature; their sun is a ball of light that rises in the

east, changes colors with the hours, and sinks in the west. They are taken before a king, the feudal civilization is explained to them, and they are shown the whole realm in a mirror based on telescopes, magnifying glasses, and reflectors.

The princess, with whom Thorndyke falls in love, explains to him that the country was first entered through a cavern two hundred years ago; its gold attracted men who decided to found a kingdom and to keep their secret—though they send men to the outer world to learn of inventions. Earlier they had used lamps, but finally they used electricity to construct a sun that runs on a track; its engineers change the color of the lenses with the hours. Meanwhile, Johnston discovers that the cavern roof has begun to leak; the ocean will soon fill the cavern. Naturally, the king orders all his people to the upper earth, where the princess and Thorndyke will be married.

3. To Other Planets

Apparently Jules Verne wanted to write a story of interplanetary flight, but could not bring himself to work it out fully and present it seriously. In *From the Earth to the Moon* and *Round the Moon*, he took his cues from Poe, but in *Hector Servadac* (1877), he struck out boldly on a course of his own, wavered, included facetious material, bolstered the adventure with scientific statistics and discussions, but finally has Hector himself doubt whether the adventure took place.

The story tells of a flight through space on a fragment of earth attached to a comet. Hector Servadac and his servant, Ben Zoof, knocked unconscious by something, wake to find themselves on an island. Exploring, they find fragmentary areas of the earth—such as a portion of the Rock of Gibraltar inhabited by two Englishmen playing chess, unaware that they are on a comet. From over the surface of their small "world" they collect various people, including an astronomer who explains what has happened, calculates every stage of their journey, shows them the planets in review, and predicts their return to earth. As they swing into the cold of outer space, they retire into volcanic caverns. When the comet gets almost to earth on its return, they take off in a balloon and land just where they had been picked up. The comet explodes.

Perhaps Verne's purpose was to weave into a readable yarn what he knew of planets, comets, and interplanetary space.

Serious throughout and more substantial than anything that preceded it, Percy Greg's *Across the Zodiac* (1880), in two crowded volumes, brings together much of the best in interplanetary voyages up to this time. Science in the book is carefully worked out. There are improbabilities, such as that evolution on Mars has proceeded as it has on earth, but otherwise Greg discusses with careful logic and point-by-point explanation the processes of a flight to Mars, describes in detail the civilization he finds there, including "Martial" inventions as solid as those of Verne at his best, and narrates an adventure that moves with the pace of a realistic novel.

A part of the careful construction is Greg's probability devices. The eccentric Colonel A—— takes a friend to his rooms and shows him a metallic case containing a long manuscript in cipher written on a metalloid alloy of aluminum and an unknown substance. Then the Colonel relates in detail how he acquired the manuscript: he saw what he believed to be a meteor smash into bits on a Pacific island and, investigating the crater, found fragments of human flesh and the manuscript.

This manuscript, when deciphered, tells the story of the discovery of apergy, an electric force operating counter to gravity. In a car propelled by apergy, the narrator sets out for Mars. The car is made of metal; its walls are insulated with cement; it receives light through small, round windows. The narration is detailed and explicit; problems are worked out, dimensions and quantities given, scientific theories discussed. Electricity generates the apergy and also decomposes carbonic acid to provide oxygen. Astronomical observations and mathematical calculations give reality to the narrator's flight. Gravitational effects are discussed: upsetting a coffee cup, he catches the coffee on its slow descent. As the car moves toward Mars at 40,000 miles an hour, the narrator observes the topography of that planet, its orange landscape, its gray seas. Reasoning in detail about forms of life, he prepares the reader for the possibility that men may inhabit Mars.

After testing the air of Mars, the narrator opens his car and steps onto that planet. Martial society he finds to be an advanced form of life on earth—a "coming race." Martials, who dress in Graecesque costumes, have dirigible balloons and automobiles driven by electricity along paved roads; they have trained animals for domestic services. Among their machines are a machine that writes from dictation (as the language is phonetic), guns to shoot poison gas in glass globes, electric tractors for plowing, cement-like plastics for building, numerous kinds of electric devices (such as lights, stoves, and long-distance telephones and chirographs), highly developed sewage-disposal systems that convert waste into fertilizer, three-dimensional talking-moving pictures, and photo-electric mechanisms for reproducing music.

The narrator is entertained by a host, who tells him of the customs and history of Mars. Mars, older than the earth, has reached a more mature stage; atheism is universal, except for a secret order, the Star, whose belief is in a God like the Christian God; the language is a logical one—its grammar is given; numeration is duodecimal; writing is a phonetic shorthand, like that of the dictation machine. The state is a monarchy, founded 13,218 years ago, when communism had failed; polygamy is practised; children are cared for by the state—and in general Martial civilization is advanced and scientific, but not utopian. The narrator is sent for by the Prince, who gives him half a dozen wives —in addition to his host's daughter, whom he has married. One of his wives contracts a Turkish disease, unknown on Mars, apparently from rose-seeds the narrator had brought with him. Since she has no resistance to this disease, she dies. Finally the narrator escapes the enmity of a member of the court-party by fleeing in his space-ship.

Without the exuberance of Verne's work, *Across the Zodiac* is the most fruitful single romance of interplanetary travel written before Wells.

By comparison, John Jacob Astor's *A Journey in Other Worlds* (1894) is a patchwork. Evidently Astor had read *Across the Zodiac*, for he uses apergy, and evidently something much earlier, for he describes Saturn as a world of spirits.

The book is divided into three parts, Book I, a semi-utopian description of the earth in 2000; Book II, a description of a journey to Jupiter and an exploration of it; and Book III, a description of a journey to Saturn. The story has a strong religious bias, the author evidently striving to reconcile religion and science by having the spirits of Saturn rationalize miracles.

Ayrault visits the planets because he is bored by the monotonous life in the super-Machine Age of the year 2000. Wind, tides, waterfalls, and the heat of the sun focused in lenses supply abundant energy. Electricity is broadcast into the air to drive vehicles at forty miles an hour; trains are moved at high speeds by attractive and repulsive magnets placed every fifty miles; "marine spiders" on bell-shaped feet swing across the ocean like pacing horses; aluminum airplanes are driven by electric motors; rain-making by the use of explosives regulates the weather; nature's food supplies have been replaced by synthetic foods; destructive weapons have made war impossible—to mention only a few of the commonplaces of 2000. Engineers are now working to equalize the climate by straightening the earth's axis; they are alternately draining and filling the Arctic ocean to vary the weight at the Pole as the earth swings to and from the sun.

Ayrault and his party find Jupiter going through a Devonian period, with mastodons, dinosaurs, and pterodactyls. From Jupiter, they go to Saturn, where they have many strange experiences among the spirits; for instance, a spirit breathing Biblical prophecies allows one of the travellers to see his own funeral. They learn such things as that Elijah knew the use of apergy, and his chariot was lifted by that force. The planetoid Cassandra, they learn from a spirit, is inhabited by unrepentant spirits. "Cosmos," a star at the center of the universe, is to become Heaven.

4. Into Other Dimensions

The science of the late nineteenth century foretold. not only a Machine Age, but the advance of mathematics toward relativity. Before 1895 conceptions of space in more than three dimensions and of space-time were common only among mathematicians.

A. Square (*pseud.* for E. A. Abbott), in *Flatland* (1885), seeks to present such conceptions in a series of analogies that the layman may grasp. *Flatland* is the autobiographical record of "A. Square," living in two-dimensional space, as he becomes aware of the mad possibility that space may be three-dimensional. The reasoning that leads him to comprehend three-dimensional space is the reasoning that would lead a person in three-dimensional space to comprehend space or space-time in four dimensions.

A. Square is an inhabitant of Flatland, two-dimensional space. He cannot imagine any other kind of space; his fellows look to him like lines, though they are really Triangles, Squares, Pentagons, and so on. In Flatland there is no up-and-down, an inconceivable idea; gravitation pulls toward the south. Social life is quite complex in this flat world; its limitations satirize those of the three-dimensional world. For instance, Flatlanders praise "men" for the regularity of their conformations.

Square has a dream in which he is transported to Lineland, where the stupids comprehend only one dimension. When he speaks to the king of Lineland, that monarch can see no source for a voice that seems to come from his own intestines; Square finds it difficult to explain two dimensions to the king, who cannot imagine moving his whole body in the direction of what he considers his insides. Then a Sphere visits Flatland from Spaceland: Square sees a circle growing first larger and then smaller and then vanishing. To Square the growth of the circle (seen as a curving line) is growth in *time*, but the circle speaks and says that it is really a Sphere that has moved across Flatland in *space*. The Sphere miraculously lifts Square into Spaceland so that he looks down upon Flatland, upon the insides of closed houses and even the insides of his neighbors. But when Square returns to Flatland and tries to describe to Flatlanders motion that is upward—yet not northward—he is declared mad and put into prison.

D. *The Occult and the Supernatural*

Speculaion regarding a fourth dimension leads, on the one hand, to such fiction as Wells's *The Time Machine,* but on the other, to "supernatural" visitations from non-Euclidean space.

The old theme of dual personality is given a laboratory setting in Stevenson's *Dr. Jekyll and Mr. Hyde* (1886) ; a drug-compound enables Dr. Jekyll to bisect his personality. Mr. Utterson, a close friend of the brilliant young physician, Dr. Jekyll, becomes aware that a revolting person, Mr. Hyde, has a strange hold on Dr. Jekyll. Hyde murders a man and disappears; Dr. Jekyll returns for a while to his former geniality, and then suddenly locks himself into his laboratory. Mr. Utterson breaks into the laboratory too late to save Hyde from suicide. He discovers a manuscript identifying Jekyll and Hyde as the same person and describing the process by which Dr. Jekyll bisected his personality.

The process purports to be one in advanced physiological chemistry. By means of his drug, Dr. Jekyll had enabled his baser nature to become embodied in the shape called Mr. Hyde; physical features melt and alter. Another dose reverses the process. At base, this is alchemy and allegory, but Stevenson calls it chemistry.

The theme of suspended animation is developed in William Clark Russell's *The Frozen Pirate* (1887). A man shipwrecked in the Antarctic comes upon a pirate ship wedged in the ice and filled with frozen pirates. One of the pirates, laid near the fire, shows signs of life; massaged and warmed gradually, he comes to life, though he had been frozen half a century. The next day, however, the total weight of his years descends upon him, and he dies. The explanation that freezing had suspended animation is as rational as that in Bellamy's *Looking Backward* or Wells's *When the Sleeper Wakes.*

A visitor from some realm of non-Euclidean space-time is described in Guy de Maupassant's "The Horla" (1887). The narrator gradually becomes aware of a strange hypnotic influence upon himself, and at the same time an invisible something drinks his glass of milk and visibly plucks a rosebud from its stem. He reads of similar presences in Brazil; perhaps this creature is something that developed in Brazil; perhaps it is a member of an invading party from another planet, creatures of a different order from man; perhaps it is superior in the evolutionary scale and is destined to supersede man. The narrator shuts the creature into a room and burns down the house—but the creature is not burned. The narrator is still pursued.

Ambrose Bierce's "The Damned Thing" (1893) presents another visitor from a dimension beyond the third. In fighting with Hugh Morgan the invisible creature that killed him comes between him and the newspaper man who tells the story. Though invisible, the creature was opaque enough to blot out parts of Morgan's body during the fight. A puzzled coroner's jury brings in a verdict of death at the "hands" of a mountain lion, but in Morgan's diary the newspaper man finds conjectures about the nature of the thing that haunted and killed him. As there are sounds beyond the range of the ear, there are colors beyond the range of the eye, and the "Damned Thing," Morgan conjectures, is a solid body—it bends down grasses as it walks—of such a color.

Perhaps a human being may stumble into the dimension from which the "Damned Thing" came. In "Charles Ashmore's Trail" (1893) Bierce tells the story of a man who goes through the snow to get a pail of water, but does not return. His footprints end abruptly half-way to the spring. Standing at the point where he vanished, his mother can hear him calling in faint tones, audible from no other point. Bierce appends to the story a discussion of non-Euclidean geometry pointing out the possibility that there may be "holes" in space, "pockets" caused by warping, which not even the ether pervades.

In general, the most important junction between stories of the occult and the supernatural and scientific fiction during this period lies in the story of some creature from a dimension beyond the third.

E. *The Historic Romance*

Sir Walter Scott and his numerous followers had made the historic romance popular. Two forces operated during the period 1871-1894 to bring certain types of the historic romance into the stream of scientific fiction. The utopian fiction stimulated by the presentiment of the Machine Age often included some synopsis of history in the future, and a natural development was the historic romance of the future. The theory of evolution suggested a new period of man's experience for romantic treatment, so that the historic romance of the prehistoric past appeared. Fears that civilization may collapse and man may return to barbarism suggested a romance of the future in which the setting is like that of the barbaric past—that is, the historic romance of the future-past.

1. In the Future

In the winter of 1870-71 a newly united and powerful Germany defeated France. French courage was no match for the new-fashioned methods of the Germans, based upon preparation, analysis, and the use of scientific weapons.

Sir George Tomkyns Chesney's "The Battle of Dorking" (1871) is a tale of the German conquest of England in 1875. It was written, avowedly, to stir England to prepare to face Germany. "There, across the narrow straits, was the writing on the wall, but we would not choose to read it." In this story, Germany suddenly annexes Holland and Denmark in 1875; England declares war on Germany; Germany seizes all shipping from the Baltic to Ostend and methodically prepares to invade England. The British navy attacks courageously, but it is powerless against the torpedoes of the Germans. The British are not prepared; at a feint of invasion on the east coast, troops rush there, while the Germans land in the south. British volunteers are shifted here and there in great confusion, without discipline or provisions. At Dorking, the lines face one another, but the Germans break through a flank, and London falls. It is all over. Canada and the West Indies join America; Australia, India, and Ireland become independent; Gibraltar and Malta are taken by Germany. England becomes a tribute-paying vassal. The science in the book is that of German organization and weapons.

The Kings' Men (1884), by Robert Grant and others, is less hard-headed and more romantic in its science. It tells the story of political intrigues in the twentieth century after George V abdicated the English throne and fled to America. The doddering old king proves unworthy of the sacrifices his adherents make to overturn the republic. Like other scientific fiction, the book is sprinkled with imaginary mechanical devices, such as guns that shoot electrically charged bullets and newspapers that issue from "tickers."

Inspired by socialistic ideas and by *Looking Backward*, Ignatius Donnelly, writing under the pen-name of Edmund Boisgilbert, published *Caesar's Column* (1890). The socialism is more Marxian, more conscious of class warfare, than in *Looking Backward*, where the people of the twentieth century meet "industrial evolution" with reasonableness, vote for socialism, and establish Utopia. In *Caesar's Column* the "haves" do not agree so readily with the 'have-nots." The increased use of machinery widens and deepens the gulf between the classes. The capitalist class controls the army and the weapons of science, especially swift dirigible airships and a secret poison gas. This class pushes the working

class deeper and deeper into squalor, till finally an underground
society of anarchists manages to gain control of the airships and
the army. In the orgy of destruction that follows, civilization
collapses. A small band of idealists flees to Africa to set up
a utopian state there and to preserve the seeds of civilization,
including machines, for the future.

The book is structurally a mixture of socialistic doctrines,
anarchistic intrigues, speeches, quotations of magazine articles,
star-crossed love-affairs, and revolution. Its setting is 1988. The
narrator, Gabriel Weltstein, has lived in Africa, and he arrives
in New York by airship, full of wonder at its radiance. This city
of ten million, sprawling all the way to Philadelphia, is heated
by water drawn from the earth's core and lighted by the earth's
magnetism; electric trains run on several street levels; airships
that make London in thirty-six hours are moored to "islands"
above the city. Gabriel eats at an automat that serves a dinner
selected by the pressure of the proper buttons; he selects news
from various parts of the world, presses buttons, and reads from
a ground-glass plate.

But in spite of these conveniences, human nature has not
softened. In the rich he sees "unbelief, cunning, observation,
heartlessness . . . a forcible and capable race; but that was all."
In the slums, where he is taken by an anarchist, he sees an "endless
succession of the stooped, silent toilers . . . shameless looks
. . . degradation . . . garrets, sheds—dark, foul, gloomy, over-
crowded." Naturally he joins the revolutionaries and takes part
in the reign of terror that breaks loose when General Quincy of
the air force joins them. Wall Street is blown up; the carnage
piles the dead in thousands, and the fanatic-leader Caesar Lomel-
ini pours concrete over them and engraves on it "the Death and
Burial of MODERN CIVILIZATION." Gabriel piles machines
into an airship and in it flies with kindred souls to Africa, to set
up there a socialistic state and wait for the opportunity to re-
civilize the world under socialism.

In *Caesar's Column* machinery widens the gulf between the
classes; it causes the collapse and implements it with horrible
weapons. But this is the result because machinery has been
wrongly used. Machinery itself is a good thing; it is a means
to Utopia. The little band fleeing from the carnage takes along
machines of every kind to be the instruments of the new age.

The tale of imaginary wars, combined with ideas of the coming Machine Age and with revolutionary and utopian materials,
yields finally such romances as George Griffith's *The Angel of
the Revolution* (1893) and its sequel *Olga Romanoff* (1894).

The Angel of the Revolution opens with the invention of the

airplane in the year 1903. Richard Arnold of London is enabled
to invent the airplane through the development of the internal
combustion engine and the combination of principles employed
in Jules Verne's aeronef and Hiram Maxim's aeroplane. He
realizes at once that possession of the airplane means power,
and he meditates whether to give his invention to the world.
The Tsar, for instance, might use it as a means of aggression.
He becomes acquainted with a man named Colston, a revolutionary anarchist, and is gradually led to join the Terrorists,
whose aim is to destroy tyranny and establish world-justice.
Meanwhile, the Tsar has developed dirigible balloons, and France
and Russia have planned secretly, the Terrorists learn, to invade
Germany, Austria, and England. The Terrorists manufacture
airplanes in preparation for the coming conflict; they manufacture also aerial torpedoes and test them out by blowing up the
fortress of Kronstadt. After rescuing some of their number en
route to Siberian prison camps, Arnold and other Terrorists fly
to an otherwise inaccessible valley in Africa, where they establish an arsenal. They build in Aëria, their African stronghold,
twelve airplanes with a cruising range of twenty thousand miles.

War breaks out between the Anglo-Teutonic Alliance and the
Franco-Slavonian League, involving all of Europe and most of
Asia. The Franco-Slavonians, with fifty dirigible balloons to
dump explosives, fire-shells, and poison gas on the enemy, overrun Europe, and finally England stands alone. A successful block-
ade of England brings on famine. Meanwhile organization of
trade unions is going on in America under the leadership of
the Terrorists, and in a long-planned uprising, the government
of the United States falls. Lord Tremayne (an English peer
among the Terrorists) then declares an Anglo-Saxon Federation
and offers immediate aid to England. The English king, fearing
the Terrorists more than the Tsar, refuses.

Aided by his balloons and by new, swift submarines, the Tsar
lands an army in England. Under terrific bombing from the air,
the English do not yield. "But this was not a war of men. It was
a war of machines, and those who wielded the most effective
machinery won battle after battle as a matter of course." Finally
the English, still defiant, are surrounded in London, and London
is methodically bombed to pieces. Offered another chance to
join the Anglo-Saxon Federation, the English king does so. The
American fleet is driven by new petroleum-burning engines and
is equipped with new-type underwater torpedo tubes; over it
flies the fleet of Aërian planes. Of course the Tsar's balloons
are no match for the planes; from the Tsar's army itself fifth-
column Terrorists organize into companies. The turning of the

tide becomes a rout; the Tsar is sent to Siberia; and the Anglo-Saxon Federation proclaims a World-State. Tyrants are banished, national frontiers are set up according to racial groupings, and armies, private profits, and private ownership of land and basic industries are abolished. From their stronghold in Aëria, the Terrorists impose peace, socialism, and benevolent over-rule, and guard their airplanes to see that the world obeys.

The sequel, *Olga Romanoff*, skips a century and opens with the surrender of the throne of the world by the Aërians in St. Paul's cathedral in the year 2030. They choose, however, to retain their utopian state in Aëria, the secret of the airplane, and the secret of vril—a powerful new electric weapon that was curiously anticipated by Bulwer-Lytton in the nineteenth century. They believe the world is ready to rule itself in peace. Socialism has worked well for a century; generations have grown up without any experience of war. Many inventions have made life good; for instance, monorail trains span the English Channel at two hundred miles an hour; ships of forty thousand tons speed over the oceans at fifty miles an hour; and power is cheaply derived from atomized carbon and petroleum. But Olga Romanoff, descendant of the last Tsar, plans to re-establish the Russian throne. She manages to capture Alan Arnoldson, the son of the president of Aëria, and to drug him with a poison that breaks down his will. He reveals to Olga the secrets of flying and of submarine construction, and in a cavern in Mount Terror, near the South Pole, Olga constructs a fleet of submarines and airplanes. With this fleet and the aid of the Sultan of Turkey, she then tries to secure world-dominion. As the battle rages with colossal destruction under the sea and in the air, news comes to Aërian astronomers from their colleagues on Mars—for communication has been established with Mars—that a comet of incandescent flame is on its way to the earth. The Aërians, abandoning the war, dig a cavern of refuge for themselves under a granite mountain. The passing comet burns the surface of the earth to cinders, killing all life. The Aërians finally emerge, with their seeds and machines, to begin a utopian repopulation of the globe.

The historic romance of the future, by 1894, had drawn from several of the streams of scientific fiction material for a spellbinding tale.

2. In the Past or the Future-Past

The theory of evolution provided Richard Jefferies with material for his *After London; or, Wild England* (1885), a story of the future-past. The romance is laid in the far-distant future, when civilization has collapsed into barbarism and is slowly emerging from it. The first part of the book discusses the downfall of the social system. The writer does not know what happened; he is trying to piece together a picture of the past as a scientist might attempt to describe the stone age on the basis of geological evidences. He is certain that there were great wars and conflagrations, and afterwards the country was overrun by animals. The records were destroyed, and with them knowledge of the arts and of science. Part of the change was geologic; perhaps the passing of a comet caused convulsions of nature. There are legends of lands that no longer exist; there is a lake in the heart of England under which ancient London partly lies. The few men left alive after the change were ignorant of the uses of such things as the "wires which were not tubular, but solid" over which the ancients communicated with each other.

The adventurous younger son of a chieftain rows across the lake in central England to visit the stagnant fen of what had been London. There he find skeletons, crumbling walls smeared with phosphorescence, and odors that turn even his barbarian's stomach. Finally he becomes chief of a shepherd tribe and sets out to build a city-fortress for his domain.

Another journey into the future when civilization has fallen is J. A. Mitchell's *The Last American* (1889), a satire that pretends to be a fragment from the journal of a Persian who discovers America in the year 2951. The Persians, surprised to come upon land, pick their way about "Nhu-Yok" and try to reconstruct from the ruins some idea of the ancient American civilization. The Persians find very amusing the "sharp, restless, quick-witted, greedy race" of "Mehrikans," perished from the earth because of a climatic change.

Austin Bierbower's *From Monkey to Man* (1894) is a story of the past, designed to illustrate the theory of evolution and to "solve" the problem of the "missing link." The story describes the activities of the two main species of apes on the "great divide," that is, at the time they ceased being apes and became men. The two species, the "Lali" and the "Ammi," are at war; one of them wins and is to evolve into men; the other is exterminated, leaving skeletons that confuse the anthropologists because they do not fit into the evolutionary scheme. During the course of their "war"—or complicated squabbling—the apes make many discoveries: how to make fire and to cook, for instance, and how to ride logs across streams. Finally the great cold comes, and the Lali remain in the cold till they become extinct, while the Ammi flee to the south and there develop into the first men.

* * * * *

The development of science in the last quarter of the nine-teenth century, especially the promise of a Machine Age—with consequent problems of social adjustment—and the theory of evolution, greatly stimulated scientific fiction. Needless to say, this development stimulated thought in every field and is re-flected in fiction outside our sphere. For instance, Thomas Hardy's story of frustrated love, *Two on a Tower,* was, he says, "the outcome of a wish to set the emotional history of two infinitesimal lives against the stupendous background of the stellar universe." And there is also the important genealogical novel, taking its rise in this period.

In the next period, 1895-1914, we have the work of H. G. Wells, who takes scientific fiction Across the Bridge of Time to the end of the world.

CHAPTER FIVE

Across the Bridge of Time

Scientific Fiction, 1895-1914

IN THE FICTION OF 1871-1894 described in the previous chapter, two influences stand out. The first influence is the effort to foresee the Machine Age and prepare for it, especially in the light of ideas of progress fostered by the theory of evolution. The natural result of this effort is the prominence of utopistic ideas not only in utopias, but also in stories of wonderful discoveries and in historic romances.

The second influence is Jules Verne.

During the next period, 1895-1914, utopias continue to be written, of course, but in general historic romances, especially those in the future, are the most important pieces of scientific fiction. Two reasons explain this fact. First, a utopia tends to be static. Once a socialistic utopia has been written and an anti-socialistic utopia has been written, a utopia employing wonderful machines, and a utopia employing no machines—what else is there to say about utopia? One way to say something more is to put the utopian state into action, to show it in the process of changing, say, in the midst of revolution. Then the result is the historic romance of the future. Second, utopias and satires had either hoped or feared some social development. But as the theory of evolution came to be more thoroughly understood, thoughtful men felt not so much hope or fear as resignation. It revealed how small men are in the scheme of life and how short their life-span is, compared with geologic time. Besides hope or fear, now a third attitude seemed possible, to suppose that life might go on for a geologic time, and before the end develop and collapse again and again, in any variety of ways. Thinking of this kind led to the historic romance of the far-distant future.

In the period 1895-1914, H. G. Wells replaces Jules Verne as the most important author of scientific romances. The differences between Verne and Wells are important. Verne was so lively that everybody read his stories, but he wrote as if for boys in their teens. Wells wrote as if for grown-ups thoughtful about the meanings of scientific progress.

Their training was different. Verne brought to scientific fiction skill in constructing farcical plots; Wells brought not only a university education in science, under Huxley, but the experience of lecturer in biology and author of a textbook in it. Verne's science was primarily shrewd guesses about inventions and encyclopedic facts looked up for the occasion; Wells's science was a competent grasp of scientific laws. Because he had this grasp, Wells brought to scientific fiction boldness of imagination, based on the geologist's sense of time and the astronomer's sense of space.

Verne's facetiousness and bubbling optimism, as well as his failure to treat fully the social meaning of machinery, contrast with Wells's tougher attitudes. Verne imagined a submarine, put some stock characters on it, and took a trip around the world. Wells, in general, tried to explain how people would behave in, for instance, the London of *When the Sleeper Wakes*. He finds the behavior altered by the altered conditions of life.

Wells was always interested in the social consequences of advancing science, and this interest not only gave his scientific fiction thoughtful substance, but led him into his later fields of utopian and sociological writing.

Wells brought also to scientific fiction the creation of characters. Whether or not one believes in his Cavorite or his Martian tripods, his people are credible, real people.

Of course other strains of scientific fiction, and other writers than Wells, made contributions during the period 1895-1914. Utopias and satires continue to appear. Variety in "The Wonderful Discovery" has necessitated the broader classification, "The Wonderful Adventure," broken into three subdivisions, "The Wonderful Machine," "The Wonderful Discovery," and "The Wonderful Event." Stories of wonderful journeys and of the occult and the supernatural continue. "The Story of Crime and Detection" is added to include a number of pieces in this field.

1. In the Future

A. *The Historic Romance*

H. G. Wells's *The Time Machine* (1895) resembles a utopia in some of its material, for it presents a developed society. But it does not present a desirable society, and if it is considered satire, it attacks a drift of human affairs that little can be done to alter. Previous historic romances sprang from social theory and an attitude toward the Machine Age; *The Time Machine* includes thought on these subjects, but it springs primarily from thought about the theory of evolution viewed as a development that may be upward for a geologically brief time, and then downward. But implicit in the picture is the process of historical development that brought it about. This process of development links the story to present human interests.

The Time Traveller invents a machine for travelling through time, which is considered a fourth dimension. In this machine he travels first to the year 802,701, when mankind has reached a second-childhood, and then on for thirty millions years till man no longer is to be found, and the earth itself hangs ready to plunge into the sun. The Time Traveller hoped to discover a "coming race" of men far ahead of us in their uses of machinery. Instead he finds a race of children on the surface of the earth, the Eloi, descendants of the masters of the world whose vigor declined when the necessity for effort vanished; and in caverns under the surface, a race of bleached nocturnal Morlocks, descendants of the laboring classes. From long-established habit, the Morlocks run the machinery needed for the comfort of the Eloi, but they live upon the flesh of the Eloi whom they serve.

The Time Traveller finds evidences of the summer of man's achievement, vast museums of machinery, now crumbled into rust. The struggle to achieve evidently had resulted in victory, but victory, in lassitude and decay. It is a ruthless process that nothing can halt, for the earth itself is subject to discreation. Toward the last, the sun hangs motionless in the sky; a stagnant ocean exhibits no flow of the tides; the thin air hurts the lungs; and great crustaceans exhibit the only signs of life. The Time Traveller comes back to his own time, to tell his story.

The Time Machine draws upon the sciences of biology, geology, and astronomy; from them it brings a cosmic perspective to scientific fiction; and it deals with areas of the imagination that properly belong to no other kind of fiction.

Wells's next romances of the future, "A Story of the Days to

Come" and *When the Sleeper Wakes,* are closer to the present. They describe the London of two hundred years in the future. Though they make use of the utopian pattern of a society that has highly developed machinery and though they contain a good deal of satire, they are primarily historic romances of life in a Machine Age. Instead of working out a society such as he would like to see, as Bellamy does, Wells works out the course of history in the future to show the drift of present tendencies. The stories describe a civilization founded upon mechanical progress, but no fundamental change in human nature has taken place. In social organization the dictatorship of an oligarchy of wealth has replaced the timid capitalism of our times. The gulf between the classes has widened; machinery has eliminated hunger and insecurity, but has made more and more men into machine-minders; the rich live an artificial life in effortless comfort. The arts, intellectual life, and religion have all become a ballyhoo that nobody takes seriously.

The London of the future, as presented in "A Story of the Days to Come" (1897), is a city of wonderful machines. Something like radio brays out such news as details about the accidents to the flying machines that ply around the world; food is grown on the land, but it is made synthetic before it reaches the hotel table—for there is no private dining; railways have been replaced by all manner of automobiles travelling between the five cities of England on many-laned highways built of a plastic Eadhamite; electric heating and artificial ventilation in the roofed-over city of London keep the climate constant; the use of wood has disappeared; travelling platforms eliminate walking. Machinery has destroyed family life; everyone eats in hotel-automats, splendid for the rich, refectories for the labor-minions. Progress has affected mental activity; one now remembers or forgets through hypnotism; education is by telephone; Elizabeth Mwres (Morris) has had "Lectures—not a solitary lecturer of ability in the world but she has had a telephone direct, dancing, deportment, conversation, philosophy, art criticism." Advertisements urge that Bruggles be dialed, for he "Teaches you Morals up to your Scalp! The very image of Socrates, except the back of his head, which is like Shakespeare. He has six toes, dresses in red, and never cleans his teeth." When the pace of life wears out at last, there are the Pleasure Cities and euthanasia.

Against this background, Wells tells a story of frustrated love. Elizabeth Mwres feels old-fashioned love for a poor young man, Denton. She is hypnotized to forget him, but Denton has her re-hypnotized to remember, and they romantically flee the city to live in an abandoned Victorian house. But use and wont have softened them; they cannot endure the old-fashioned hardships, such as fresh vegetables and the presence of dogs; as Denton says, "The World is too civilized. Ours is the age of cities. More of this will kill us." They go back to the city and, to make a living, surrender to the Labour Company. No man may starve, but once in the blue canvas of the Labour Company, always in blue canvas! Machine-minding drills the spirit out of them. Finally, Elizabeth's father dies, leaving some money, and they return to the life they can endure. It is an artificial, machine-tended life, but the only one possible for their generation.

Wells's *When the Sleeper Wakes* (1899) presents a larger, more detailed picture of the same London, this time in a story of attempted revolution. Graham of the nineteenth century is unable to sleep for many day on end. Suddenly dropping into a coma that lasts two hundred years, he wakes in a London of thirty-three million inhabitants. He finds it very strange. Aeropiles flit through the air; radio and television (perhaps using wires) have been developed; books have disappeared, and their place is taken by machines that render like-life dramas, some of them shocking. Graham finds that money was willed to him and was guarded by trustees; he slept, more was added and invested so well that Graham now owns half the world. His trustees, ruling the world, regiment the laboring classes into the Labour Company. But underground discontent breaks into rebellion when it is learned that the Sleeper has awakened. Men look to him for freedom. He is kidnapped by a revolutionary and taken to a meeting, but as fighting breaks out, he becomes lost. He wanders about the city. Finally the rulers send for the African police, who are coming in air-transports, and Graham makes a quixotic attack upon them, single-handed in an aeropile. He is killed, but perhaps the revolution will go on.

In this book, Wells's interest is largely sociological, that is, in the effects of the Machine Age upon human life. The city has engulfed mankind; the old individualism is impossible. Man has traded freedom for security. The king cuts antics in a music hall; the efficient dictatorship of Graham's trustees rules. Home life has gone; children are brought up in the crèche; hypnotism educates them and incidentally removes all the long, long thoughts of youth; morality has yielded to unscrupulous pleasure-seeking; culture is entirely "canned"; religion is a racket: "Brisk Blessings for Busy Business Men." Wealth is the only power.

Wells does not make it clear whether the rebellion succeeds, for the story ends as Graham dies; but if it does succeed, what hope is there for this society? It cannot destroy the machines that made it what it is, for that would be suicide. It can either remain regimented, or fight its way to confusion, without the barbarian's strength to endure the collapse.

The story of the future in Professor Simon Newcomb's *His Wisdom The Defender* (1900) is less concerned with the whole Machine Age than with the possible use of the airplane to bring an end to war. In 1941, according to *His Wisdom*, Professor Campbell of Harvard discovers an anti-gravitational substance called etherine. He also works out subsidiary inventions, a process for cheaply extracting aluminum from its ores and a "thermic" engine that operates automobiles and motorcycles on very little fuel. Then he sets about bringing universal, lasting peace to the world. After training a battalion of college football players to operate bullet-proof mechanical men—or tanks—submarines that use "thermic" power, and airplanes sustained by etherine, he issues an order to the nations of the world to disarm, and when they refuse, his submarines torpedo the navies of the world, his airplanes hover over every city, and his armored men stride among the armies and wrest guns from the soldiers' hands. An era of unprecedented progress dawns under the dictatorship of "His Wisdom the Defender," formerly professor of physics. The book presents a scientist's view not only of what machines might be invented, but of how they might be used to abolish war.

Another variety of historic romance is illustrated in Matthew Phipps Shiel's *The Lord of the Sea* (1901), an exotic tale of the future. The Jew Hogarth meditates man's unjust ownership of land and consequent taxation of the Jews. When a meteor with a heart of diamond falls upon the earth and Hogarth gets the diamond, he uses his wealth to build islands of steel, and then places these islands across the ocean lanes to levy a tax upon all sea-borne commerce until governments shall cease to tax land. Navies are powerless against him. Governments yield, but his islands are sunk by treachery. Then he is exiled with the Jews to Palestine and there becomes Shophet or Judge. Much in the book is simply weird or fantastic, but in plot the book is an historic romance that makes some use of science.

Shiel's *The Purple Cloud* (1901) makes even more fantastic use of scientific materials. Adam Jeffson sets out with an expedition to discover the North Pole, treacherously leaves his companions asleep and pushes on to discover it alone, finds at the Pole a lake wheeling about a pillar of ice engraved with a magic name, and returns to find his companions dead. An odor of almond blossoms fills the air. Jeffson returns to England and finds everyone dead; he wanders alone over the desolate earth for twenty years, burning the cities of the world. Old newspapers explain what happened: as he approached the Pole, a volcanic eruption filled the air with a cyanide gas that covered the world, except the Pole, and killed every living creature. Finally, when Jefferson burns Constantinople, he finds one woman alive, the daughter of the Sultan, and marries her, to become the father of a new race.

The science in Shiel's books is incidental to bizarre story and mood-picture of madness and desolation. The pillar of ice graven with a magic name, rather than the scientific explanation of the poison gas, sets the tone.

A very different kind of historic romance is Erskine Childers's *The Riddle of the Sands* (1903, republished in 1940 because of its apparent significance in the war). It purports to uncover a plot for the German invasion of England, and especially to give in detail the method that Germany would use in the invasion. Carruthers, the narrator, is invited to go with Davies on a yachting trip through the estuaries on the German coast. Davies suspects that the Germans are building fortifications there and planning ways in which German small-boats may harass naval strength like that of England. But the plans that they finally uncover, through a long period of investigation, are more sinister. The German design is to invade England by means of sea-going lighters, loaded with soldiers in the shallow estuaries (rather than at invasion ports), out of reach of any navy, and then towed in swarms across the channel, to land on shallow beaches, such as the flats on the Essex coast and on the Wash.

Rudyard Kipling's "With the Night Mail" (1905) purports to be an article published in a magazine of the year 2000 describing a balloon-trip across the Atlantic in a mail-ship. But in the description of the landing-towers, the swift flight itself, the hovering lights of other ships, the gleaming machines (Magniac's rudder, Fleury's vacuum-creating ray to assist the turbines, and the radio-like methods of communication), and the "Mark Boats" that patrol the Atlantic, one gets an oblique view of a whole social order. Aviation has so changed the world that governments have disappeared; world-control is in the hands of the Aerial Board of Control (the A. B. C.). This Board allows any individual or any nation to do anything—even wage war—so long as the person or nation does not interfere with the traffic *"and all it implies."* But as any anti-social action would in some way interfere with the traffic, the A. B. C. is simply world-dictator. The last government to capitulate to it was that of Crete, which finally became weary of its side-splitting comedy of parliaments, debates, popular movements, and tourists gaping at these relics, and asked the A. B. C. to take control.

Kipling's "As Easy at A. B. C." (1912) presents a sequel to

"With the Night Mail," though its setting is sixty-five years later, in 2065. It describes an attempt of the District of Illinois to break away from the Aerial Board of Control. Illinois is a backward place, largely farmland, devoted to singing Mac-Donough's Song against the People and to unveiling the statue of the Negro in Flames. The birth-rate has fallen; people are thinly spread over the earth, glad of the privacy in their separate houses. Privacy is good, but communications must be kept open, even in Illinois. When the A. B. C. liner lands, electric currents impede its men till someone on the ship sorts the currents and blows the fuse. In Chicago, the City Hall is being melted down into roadway plastic, and the people are defiantly gathered in the square singing MacDonough's Forbidden Song:

> Once there was The People—Terror gave it birth;
> Once there was The People, and it made a hell of earth!
>   (Then the stamp and pause):
> Earth arose and crushed it. Listen, oh ye slain!
> Once there was The People—it shall never be again!

But, government or no government—it does not matter to the A. B. C.—communications must be kept open. So the ship of the A. B. C. turns on a searing light that is torture to the nerves; then it turns on sound that "touched the raw fibre of the brain. Men hear such sounds in delirium." After the light and the sound, the crowds are grovelling. The A. B. C. takes control and re-opens communications. The glimpse into the future is brief and oblique, for Kipling sustains his point of view of the future itself. It is a strange world; even human nature has been remade by the airplane and all it implies—the A. B. C.

H. G. Wells continued to see woeful consequences in the multi-plying inventions of the Machine Age. The airplane had been invented by 1908, but no effective use had been made of it in warfare. Wells believed that it would be used in warfare with destructive results. *The War in the Air* (1908) places the blame for the World War of the 191-'s and for the social collapse that followed it upon the ever-widening gulf between man's social intelligence and his ability to manipulate such machinery as airplanes. The trouble lay, says Wells, in a cultural lag. "The development of Science had altered the scale of human affairs" and a "great civilization . . . was manifestly possible to mankind." Monorail trains span the English channel, and swift, two-wheeled automobiles are everywhere. But the world of the "hero," Bert Smallways, "the sort of pert, limited soul that the old civilization of the early twentieth century produced by the million," had "no sense of the State, no habitual loyalty, no devotion, no code of honour, no code even of courage." This is the situation in the democracies. But in the aggressor nations, especially in Germany, a more romantic, harder, and more ruthless leadership determines to use the machines of science for world-conquest.

War is precipitated by the development of the airplane and the dirigible balloon. Bert by accident gets Butteridge's plans for an airplane, and is cast adrift in Butteridge's balloon; he is brought down over a German army camp just as the dirigibles of Prince Karl Albert with their fleet of *Drachenflieger* (subsidiary airplanes) set out for New York and world-conquest. Taken along, Bert sees the naval battle in which the German airplanes destroy the American navy. Hereafter the "megatheria" of warfare, the great battleships, are obsolete, for "cheap things of gas and basketwork made an end of them altogether, smiting out of the sky." Bert sees the bombing of New York. Unable to surrender because its citizens are unruly and unable to be garrisoned from the air, New York is simply blown to ruins. Then other aggressor nations enter the field with new, secretly built types of airplanes. The Orientals attack the Germans over New York. Fighting breaks out all over the world, but the airplanes make it indecisive. Airplanes can destroy; they cannot garrison and hold. The economic system collapses, and as the years pass, the warfare becomes guerrilla over the world, the Purple Death follows, and nations break up into autonomous communities like those of the middle ages. But urban populations reduced abruptly to a peasant economy have none of the simple peasant arts. Within thirty years even the uses of machines are forgotten. This catastrophe is the logical outcome of the application of science to warfare.

In the effort to see in Wells's romance some forecast of the situation in the world of the 1940's one places beside *The War in the Air* Ferdinand Heinrich Grautoff's *Banzai!* (1908). It is less sweeping in its generalizations, less filled with destructive machines, but more thorough in its analysis of a method of warfare that has come into use. It describes the Japanese seizure of western America by fifth-column and Trojan-horse methods. Japanese propaganda has been busy in the Philippines, but there is no news of war there until an American warship is suddenly blown up. Meanwhile, in the United States, "bandits" seize railway trains and communication lines, and before anyone is aware of an organized Japanese threat, California, Washington state, and Oregon are cut off from the rest of the United States. Newspapers of the day before relied upon telegrams from Los Angeles to say that American naval war games are planned in the San Francisco harbor, and when there are explosions, citizens suppose them some scheme of Admiral Perry's and are amazed to find instead the Japanese fleet in the harbor. Japanese soldiers patrol the streets; the soldiers spring overnight from San Francisco itself, into which they have filtered for months, without uniforms. (The uniforms and arms came in packing cases.) It is the same in Seattle, Los Angeles, and elsewhere. The American soldiers are asleep when their sentinels are silently bound and gagged and the Japanese seize the barracks. Meanwhile American ships, loaded (by Japanese stevedores) with such goods as "optical instruments," blow up in mid-ocean; under the noses of American harbor defenses everywhere battleships of a new type appear, too squat in the water for aim at close range; balloons and airplanes cruise constantly over inland America, so that no surprise is possible. The war costs the Japanese nothing, for they levy upon the conquered territories for all supplies. They finally offer peace. They will allow the western states to return to the United States if they will also remain Japanese possessions, to be ruled half by Americans and half by Japanese, with unrestricted Japanese immigration. Finally a great battle is fought in the Rocky Mountains, and the Japanese are driven out.

Banzai! describes warfare by propaganda, "tourist" infiltration, seizure of nerve-centers, banditry, and surprise. Written by a German, it anticipates methods used in the 1940's.

These historic romances before 1914 look to the future, conceive it in terms of a Machine Age, and forecast many possibilities, from the long-range possibility of *The Time Machine* to the short-range possibility of Japanese attack upon America.

2.   In the Past or the Future-Past

The romance of the past generally follows the model of Bierbower's *From Monkey to Man* in telling a story of man at some critical point in his evolution. The romance of the future-past generally follows the model of Jefferies's *After London* in describing man after his relapse into barbarism. It includes some discussion of the reasons for the relapse and may serve the purpose of warning that civilization may decay if it makes too extensive use of machinery and so becomes too artificial.

Stanley Waterloo's *The Story of Ab* (1897), a romance of the past, was written to show that the supposed gap between paleolithic and neolithic cultures is not a gap, but an accelerated development due to adaptation and discovery. Waterloo tells a tale of Ab, a cave man who is born in the paleolithic, but lives into the neolithic time. Quite by accident, when a bent twig tied with a thong catches a piece of wood, Ab discovers the use of the bow. Because he kills his friend in a fight for the girl Lightfoot, Ab flees from the river basin that is now the English channel and comes to a strange country where burning natural gas issues from the rocks and lives there, secure from the beasts. Others join him, and to replace the caves of the old country, they erect huts. And this is the story, says the author, of the emergence of man into neolithic culture.

H. G. Wells's "A Story of the Stone Age" (1897) has the same setting in the Paris-London basin, and somewhat the same purpose. Ugh-lomi and his woman, Eudena, are forced to struggle against the conventions of their society, personified in Uya the Cunning Man of the tribe, and in this way the story is a companion-piece to Wells's "A Story of the Days to Come." Ugh-lomi and Eudena flee and when alone discover by accident how to push a stick through a hole in flint to make an axe; they come upon horses, and Ugi-lomi jumps upon one of them from a tree, has to hold on as it gallops away, and so learns to ride. But in the end they go back to the tribe, as the would-be unconventional lovers do in "A Story of the Days to Come."

Jack London's *Before Adam* (1906) develops the same theme as that of *The Story of Ab,* that men of the paleolithic and of the neolithic age overlapped. To this theme, London adds another, that of racial memory. The narrator says that what he reveals is what he has dreamed in very vivid dreams; when he studies evolution, he understands the significance of his dreams. The events really occurred to him and are embedded in his mind, to be remembered when he is asleep—as people who dream of falling are remembering some period of arboreal life. His dream, pieced together, tells of his childhood and youth as Big-Tooth in the mid-pleistocene period, a member of a paleolithic tribe. He dreams in detail of his dwelling in a cave, tormenting Saber Tooth the tiger, fighting with Red-Eye the bully, chasing the female Swift One, and with Lop-Ear learning to ride logs across streams. He dreams also of the Fire People, evidently a neolithic tribe, and their attack with bows and arrows, driving Big-Tooth and Swift One to a cave farther south, where they rear their family. The idea is implicit in the story that civilization is largely artificial and that in the core of his mind man preserves the old fears and old passions of the stone age.

London's *The Scarlet Plague* (1912) is the story of the future-past after an artificial civilization has crumbled and man is again primitive. Near the end of the twenty-first century old Granser is the only man alive who remembers the year of the plague.

He tells the story of it to the boys Boo-Hoo and Edwin. When the plague comes in the year 2013, Granser is Professor James Howard Smith of the University of California. Life seems a good thing, with all its foods, comforts, and machines; it seems secure; monorail trains and airplanes tie all the world together; disease is nearly exterminated. Then shortly after Morgan the Fifth is appointed by the Board of Magnates to be President of the United States, comes the plague, a scarlet rash that kills within the hour, and with it riots in the cities, fires, and flight. Finally Granser seems to be entirely alone in the world; he wanders for a long time, but comes upon the Santa Rosa tribe of seventeen people, besides two adult idiots. Sixty years have passed, and men are savages again; Boo-Hoo and Edwin snicker, amused at Granser's incoherent babbling. To himself Granser wonders and mumbles Jack London's theme. Gunpowder will come again, and through fire and blood and oppression, a new civilization will arise. It may take fifty thousand years to build, but it will pass, as all things pass—again and again.

A romance that brings the present into contact with the prehistoric past is Conan Doyle's *The Lost World* (1912). Professor George Edward Challenger, eccentric and bellicose scientist, leads an exploring party three thousand miles up the Amazon and into the mountains. There a line of cliffs surrounds a tableland as large as an English county. On it life has survived without evolutionary change since the Jurassic period. When the explorers climb onto the plateau, they find themselves among iguanodons, pterodactyls, and stegosauruses. They find also a tribe of ape-like men. Returning to England, Professor Challenger proves his discovery by the exhibition of a flying reptile.

In these ways the theory of evolution stimulated scientific fiction, providing material for romance in the geologic past and, as in *The Time Machine*, in the geologic future.

B. *Utopias and Satires*

In utopias and satires of the previous period, the theory of evolution is less important than the effort to foresee the Machine Age and prepare for it. But in many utopias and satires of the period 1895-1914 the situation is reversed; the effort to foresee the Machine Age and prepare for it is less important than the effort to foresee the future in terms of the theory of evolution.

Grant Allen's *The British Barbarians* (1895) brings to modern England a research-investigator from the twenty-fifth century. This man comes to Victorian England to investigate its "taboos," as a modern ethnologist might visit the Fiji Islands. Everywhere he finds taboos. Without luggage, for instance, he cannot get a respectable lodging, even though he pays in advance. Is "respectable" a widespread taboo? He borrows luggage on Sunday morning and wonders whether the taboo that he may not carry it through the streets is "a local cult, or is it general in England?" These taboos resemble those he had read about in his studies: the High Priest of the Zapotecs, for instance, is obliged to get drunk on a certain morning. In Uganda whoever appears before the king must appear stark naked; in England whoever appears before the queen must wear a tailor's sword. He finds taboos about property, costumes, the sexes, ancestors, labor with the hands, social classes, patriotism—all unfathomable to his view-from-the-enlightened-future.

The explanation he finds in evolution. Our race is descended from a monkey-like animal, Andropithecus of the Upper Uganda Eocene, an irrational creature. But here and there he finds a rational person, one of them a married woman whose husband is cruel to her. When the traveller is kind to her, and in fact violates a taboo, the husband shoots him, and he fades into the twenty-fifth century. The theory of evolution is in this way used to establish a point of view for satiric attack upon contemporary England.

In "The Child of the Phalanstery" (1899) Grant Allen describes eugenic practices in a society of the future, perhaps the twenty-fifth century of *The British Barbarians*. Clarence and Olive are allowed to marry only after the phalanstery approves their union for the good of the race, and the marriage rites are concerned with their duty to the state. When a malformed child is born to Olive, the rulers decree that the child must be chloroformed. On the day of execution—"Darwin, December 20"—the child is chloroformed in the name of the Cosmos and of universal Humanity.

The theory of evolution furnishes the foundation for H. G. Wells's *A Modern Utopia* (1905). Wells makes this clear at once: "The Utopia of a modern dreamer must needs differ in one fundamental aspect from the Nowheres and Utopias men planned before Darwin quickened the thought of the world. Those were all perfect and static States, a balance of happiness won forever against the forces of unrest and disorder that inhere in things. . . But the Modern Utopia must not be static but kinetic, must shape not as a permanent state but as a hopeful stage leading to a long ascent of stages." Wells's Utopia is a land symbolically described as a Somewhere beyond Sirius, but understood to be a Sometime. In it racial birth-direction is fundamental. The State itself demands personal efficiency, solvency, physical health—certainly freedom from disease—of all who marry and pays for and secures healthy births. Because the State recognizes the Will to Live and the perpetuity of aggressions in all life there is state-ownership of land, resources, and public utilities, but otherwise nothing to hinder individual development. Scientific research, however, is conducted on a world-wide basis: research paid for by state grants is conducted as if by the army corps, with telegraphic reports of experiments sent out like results of sporting events. Rulers are a "Samurai," men and women self-chosen among those who can stand the regimen, hardened by exercise, discipline, self-sacrifice, and periods of solitary meditation in the wilderness.

This Utopia, of course, makes full use of advanced inventions: plastics, electric air-conditioning, roofed-over cities, moving platforms in the streets, airplanes, and trains as comfortable as hotels. But it differs from earlier utopias in its emphasis upon the improvement of the race through the control of evolutionary development.

Earlier historic romances, for instance Griffith's *Olga Romanoff*, had described a catastrophe that overtakes the earth and the flight of a utopian-minded remnant into some cavern, there to preserve the seeds of civilization and later to bring utopia to pass. In *Underground Man* (in English, 1905) Gabriel Tardé describes a catastrophe that drives man underground forever, and there the utopian-minded survivors construct a Utopia. The first part of the book is historic romance of events in the twentieth century as recorded in the year 596 of the Era of Salvation by a historian among the underground men; the second part describes the disaster of the cooling of the sun after the winter of 2489; and the third part describes the plan to excavate the earth and the establishment of Utopia near its central fires.

With bold irony, Tardé outlines the struggle to achieve a mechanically utopian condition on the surface of the earth before the 2480's. "In this prehistoric era, formerly called the Christian" terrific wars had been fought between trains of armor-clad carriages; squadrons of submarines blew one another up with electrical discharges; and battles were fought between iron-clad balloons and parachutes carrying grape-shot. When peace is finally established, discovery of the last species of bacteria helps to eliminate disease and improve the race. Because of Graeco-Russian dominance, Greek becomes the universal language, with the consequent return to Homer and Sophocles as the primitive literatures become unintelligible, "even to the barbarous names of Shakespeare, Goethe, and Hugo."

Then the sun turns red; the seas become ice; the air begins to fall in flakes of nitrogen and oxygen. The remnant of mankind that gathers about a giant stove in Arabia is, of course, made up of only the most fit, such as artists' models inured against the cold. When Miltiades exhibits proofs that heat and electric power may be got from the interior of the earth, men begin to burrow.

Into their colossel crypts men bring the choicest treasures of libraries, museums, and art galleries. Constant temperature, light, and power are available, supplied by "thermic cataracts by the side of which all the cataracts of Abyssinia and Niagara were only toys." Men construct a genial, artistic Utopia, using electric power and machines, among them monocycles and electric trains, but chiefly developing man's talent for art, for instance, in bas reliefs in stone dwellings along the roadway tunnels. Birth control limits the population to the fit: no woman will consider marriage to a man who has not contributed some distinguished work of art to the world. In this Utopia may be traced influences from Morris, as also from Wells and from the theory of evolution.

Robert Hugh Benson's pair of utopistic books, *Lord of the World* and *The Dawn of All*, vary the usual pattern in an attack on the Machine Age, socialism, and "humanitarianism," and present a plea for Catholicism.

Lord of the World (1908) describes the victory, in the world of 2000, of the religion of Humanitarianism (humanity-worship) and the conquest of Europe by its prophet, Felsenburgh, just before the second coming of Christ and the end of the world. Perhaps Humanitarianism and Felsenburgh are symbols of the Antichrist. The world of 2000 has seen the triumph of the Machine Age, largely as Bellamy and Wells had described this triumph. Air-conditioned cities are partly underground; swift motor cars speed along many-laned highways; "volors" (airships) fill the air; news is flashed upon great electric placards; and euthanasia is administered regularly in appointed hospitals. The world has become socialized. National languages linger, but everyone speaks also Esperanto. Three great empires remain, the Eastern, the European, and the American, with their three religions, the Eastern mysticisms and, in struggle for the West, Catholicism and Humanitarianism.

Socialistic-positivistic Humanitarianism (having swallowed up Protestantism) seems about to win the world-struggle. Catholics plan to blow up Westminster Abbey, and in revenge Rome is razed by a hundred volors. Felsenburgh, a sort of Christ-of-the-Humanitarians, is swept amid popular enthusiasm into the Presidency of Europe. As persecution of the Catholics continues, Percy Franklin, the last Pope, assembles his cardinals in Palestine, and prays. When he does so, points of light descend upon him from

Heaven, and the Lord of the World comes, and evidently the
end of the world: "Then this world passed, and the glory of it."

Lord of the World is a utopistic satire describing, Benson says,
"the kind of developments a hundred years hence which, I thought,
might reasonably be expected if the present lines of what is
called 'modern thought' were only prolonged far enough."

The Dawn of All (1911), however, is a utopia that attempts
"to follow up the other lines instead," and to sketch the world
as it may be if lines of "ancient thought" should be prolonged.
That is, the book presents a Catholic Utopia. The usual sleeper
wakes to find himself a Monsignor, secretary to the English
cardinal, in the year 1973—suffering from amnesia. The world
of *The Dawn of All* has made the same kind of mechanical
progress as in Benson's earlier book; but in addition, forces
transcending science, studied by scientists and reconciled with
science, perform miracles. All the world has become Catholic
except a few small groups, among them the German socialists
of Berlin; but when the Pope arrives, the Germans are converted,
and all the world is subject to the Catholic Church. The social
organization is that of the church hierarchy and the medieval
guild; the Church controls education, science, and art. Debates
no longer concern questions of whether God exists, but whether
there is a distinction between the miracles of the Church and
the miracles wrought by psychology.

In Wells's *The World Set Free* (1914) the destructive use of
atomic bombs in warfare brings about a world-chaos that, in
turn, brings about the rational settlement of world-affairs. The
result is Utopia, especially as intra-atomic power now supports
the arts of peace. Holsten invents a method of using the internal
energy of atoms in 1933; he releases his material only slowly,
for fear of its misuse, but by 1953 the Holsten-Roberts engine
begins to replace other forms of power. Highways throng with
machines that cost a penny to run thirty-seven miles; Redmayne's
helicopter, allowing for straight up-and-down hovering, revolu-
tionizes aviation. But these inventions bring on social ills: coal
mines close; oil is worthless; the stock market is in a panic. As
the unemployed march, Germany attacks England and France
with atomic bombs. These bombs are continuing explosives, furious radiations of energy that dim to half in seventeen days and
then dim to half again, but leave Paris, for instance, simply a
crater.

As the world flares to war with atomic bombs, it becomes
apparent that war must be stopped without question of victor
or vanquished, or mankind will perish altogether. Leblanc of
France calls a world-conference of kings, presidents, ministers,

journalists, and scientists to meet on an Alpine mountainside. Rulers abdicate, and the Council gathers all the Carolinum (atomic bombs) in the world, outwits a treacherous King of the Balkans in his scheme for world-conquest, and sets itself up as the World State. Everyone on the world is given a vote; uninhabited wildernesses are systematically opened up; populations are spread through the country (for the cities are still exploding craters); and the English language, shorn of grammatical vagaries, is adopted as a world-language. Science flowers as a world-wide co-operative enterprise fully supported by the State. Science, it is seen, is the awakening mind of the race.

Utopia as described in these books of 1895-1914, is nearly always a condition of the future, usually a dynamic condition, employing machinery, but emphasizing the continued development of man.

C. *The Wonderful Adventure*

1. The Wonderful Machine

In all these books the most frequent machine of the future is the airplane.

H. G. Wells's "The Argonauts of the Air" (1897) describes the flying of the first airplane and the disaster of this flight. This invention, guided through years of experiment by a photographic study of the flight of birds and Lilienthal's methods and slowly developed toward the most "far-reaching alteration in the ways of humanity . . . effected since history began," is popularly called "Monson's Folly" until Monson, goaded by ridicule, recklessly flies it before the steering-gear is perfected and pays for his success with his life. But Monson's tragic success will guide the next of that gallant band who, says Wells, will sooner or later master the air.

Edward Bellamy was doubtless inspired by the invention of the phonograph to write "With the Eyes Shut" (1898). Taking a journey by train, the narrator is surprised to see the newsbutcher enter with phonographic books and magazines; fitted with earphones, the instruments allow him to "read" and at the same time enjoy the scenery. Stations are announced by phonographic annunciators; in his hotel, the phonographic records recite the news and clocks announce the hours in words; he finds phonographic books equipped with a panorama that unrolls views of the story as the "book" recites and so sees the play *Othello* as he sits in his hotel room. Bellamy is famous for his social doctrines in *Looking Backward;* he was also interested in machines themselves.

H. G. Wells's "The Crystal Egg" (1897) tells a story of an interplanetary television apparatus, invented not on earth, but on Mars. A sending-and-receiving apparatus in the form of a crystal ball is, however, found on earth. The story of the crystal itself is subordinate to that of life on Mars as an antique-dealer named Cave views it through the strange "egg." Wells at this time was no doubt working on *The War of the Worlds*, published the next year, and the red vegetation, the twin moons, the shining canals, and the strange tentacled creatures of the Martian landscape provide partial views of the world from which the invaders come later. But now the crystal has been lost, for when Cave dies, his wife sells it without knowing its value.

Before 1900 scientific fiction, made popular by the romances of Jules Verne, branched out into juvenile literature. On the juvenile, or dime-novel level, tales of wonderful machines appeared by the hundreds, usually in a series. A typical series is the "Frank Reade" stories. Noname (*pseud.* for Lu Senarens) published weekly adventures of a boy-hero in his 'teens, the son of a "famous inventor." He is in love; he has a rival whom he always outdistances; he invents wonderful machines, outdoing his father; he foils the villain who is always trying to steal the secret of his invention. Broad Irish or good-natured darkey "comic relief" is invariably present. Details of the machine are always vague, but it is usually something made familiar by Verne or other writers of scientific fiction.

A typical production is Noname's "Young Frank Reade and His Electric Air Ship or A 10,000 Mile Search for a Missing Man" (1899). Frank tells his father that his airship is built of aluminum and a thin alloy of steel; it is fitted with electric engines, raised by "steel rotoscopes with a revolution of mighty swiftness" and propelled by "aluminum blades with steel bearings." The pilot sits in a luxurious pilot-house and operates the ship from an electric key-board. The action is partly the minstrel-comedy of Scipio, a "black coon," and Larry, a "belligerent Oirish lad," and partly the foiling of the villain, Luke Snyder, "Member North American Scientific Society, LL. D., F. R. S.," who tries first to spy on the airship and then to blow it up. "You young whipper-snapper!" he says when foiled. "You dare insult Luke Snyder? You shall pay for this," for Luke Snyder "neither forgets nor forgives!"

The "Frank Reade Library" was issued weekly from 1892 through 1899 and occasionally later. It described such inventions as a steam-horse, a steam-man, a steam-tallyho, a steam team, an electric air canoe, an electric submarine, an electric robot, and an electric armored car. The inventions were always used for

"Price 5 Cents" — but now a Collector's Item

good purposes, such as using the electric tricycle to break up the African slave trade. There were other similar series, among them the Tom Edison, Jr., series, Happy Days series, Pluck and Luck series, and Boys' Star Library. These pieces then retailed for five or ten cents. Following up these series, such books as Victor Appleton's Tom Swift juveniles have continued the stories of marvelous inventions by a boy-inventor. Beginning in 1910 with *Tom Swift and His Airship,* the titles include *Tom Swift and His Electric Rifle* (1911), *Tom Swift Among the Diamond Makers* (1911), *Tom Swift and His Air Glider* (1912), and *Tom Swift and His Photo-Telephone* (1914).

Love in this fiction is always pure; social attitudes are conservative. Whatever their value as literature, these juveniles doubtless diverted many a weekly allowance from soda-pop to the newsstands. The health of America, in body and mind, was not threatened by this variety of juvenile fiction.

Wells anticipated the army tank in "The Land Ironclads" (1903). In the light of Wells's explicit description of tanks, their principle of operation, and their effect upon infantry, it is difficult to understand why the British waited until 1916 to employ the first tank in warfare. Wells's story scores the conservatism of the War Office, and this conservatism, as well as the invention itself, may be considered an anticipation.

Trench warfare has reached a stalemate. Then one morning, from the enemy trenches, appear great iron-clad cruisers, "Something between a big blockhouse and a giant's dishcover," firing from portholes in their sides. The tanks advance across trenches, crawling on thick, stumpy feet, "reminding one of . . . the legs of caterpillars." The feet are hung on the rims of wheels: eight pairs of big pedrail wheels, each about ten feet in diameter, each a driving wheel and set upon long axles free to swivel around a common axis. Soldiers inside the tanks operate automatic rifles sighted by means of a camera-obscura and surveyors' cross-wires. The defending army is completely routed; the old general fumes in contempt of "ironmongery." Wells makes clear that victory in the future belongs to men who use the machines of science.

Jules Verne had described airplanes, submarines, and automobiles; by 1905 all these wonders had been invented. Not to be outdone, Verne combined them all into one machine. *The Master of the World* (1905) brings Robur the Conquerer back into fiction, not this time as the hero, the symbol for advancing science, but as the villain-inventor, a symbol for science gone mad with destructive power. The story is told as a detective story from the point of view of the police official Strock, who is detailed to investigate smoke and flame at intervals appearing above the peak of Great Eyrie mountain near Morganton, North Carolina. Strock finds the peak a sheer precipice that he cannot scale. Then mysteries appear: at an automobile race in Wisconsin a strange vehicle appears, streaks down the track ahead of everything else, and vanishes; along the New England coast a vessel is seen moving at a great speed; a submarine emerges from Lake Kirdall in Kansas. The governments of the world advertise for this machine, but a letter received in Washington from "The Master of the World" says that these offers are despised, for the Master can take anything he wants. After a series of maneuvers, Strock sneaks upon the submarine as it lies in Black Rock Creek in Lake Erie, but is taken captive. He finds it an electrically driven combination of ship, submarine, airplane, and automobile. It is made of aluminum and has folding wings and retractile wheels. When government vessels chase it to the brink of Niagara, it takes to the air. Robur flies it to the hideout-workshop inside the circular precipice of Great Eyrie. It becomes evident to Strock that Robur is a madman who intends to terrorize the world. But instead he dares to fly into an electric storm, is struck by lightning, and falls into the sea. Though the idea is not worked out, the romance suggests very strongly Verne's fear that the machines of science might become weapons of terror in the hands of madmen.

2. The Wonderful Discovery

Side by side with the romance of invention flourished the romance of scientific discovery. Where Verne's typical contribution to scientific fiction was largely made up of imaginary machines, Wells's typical contribution was generally concerned with discoveries in the natural sciences. *The Time Machine,* setting the pace for Wells, is, for instance, concerned with the theory of evolution.

Wells's "Æpyornis Island" (1895) is likewise concerned with evolution. On a tiny island near Madagascar, Butcher finds some great eggs buried in a mud that smells like creosote. Deserted by his servants Butcher is forced to eat two of the eggs, an egg lasting him more than a week. He finds the second egg, warmed by the sun, in the process of hatching out a "chick," and the third finally hatches out a great bird. During an enforced stay of several years on the island, Butcher rears the strange creature. One day, angered by a shortage of food, it attacks him. He kills it and ultimately gives its bones to a museum, which mounts and labels them the largest ever found of the extinct *Æpyornis vastus.*

An even stranger discovery is described in Wells's "In the

Abyss" (1896). By means of a bathysphere constructed to withstand tremendous pressure, Elstead visits the bottom of the sea
and finds there intelligent bipedal vertebrates with something
like a civilization; the creatures apparently regard Elstead as a
god and offer him organized worship. Elstead descends five miles
to the ocean floor, where the pressure is a ton and a half to
the square inch, but "it's jolly thick steel," with enormously
thick glass in the circular windows. Elstead is carefully let down
by a clock-work mechanism that, in turn, is to raise him. He
fails to come up at the appointed time; but later he does come
up unconscious, with a force that sends his sphere rocketing
into the air. He tells of finding on the sea-bottom creatures half-
reptilian, half-human in appearance; the creatures breathe through
gills, support globular bodies on frog-like legs, and carry weapons
of bone in their frog-like hands. They make noises to one another,
capture the sphere, and drag it to a roofless "city" like a ruined
abbey, built of "water-logged wood, and twisted wire rope and
iron spars, and copper, and the bones and skulls of dead men."
One that seems to be dressed in a robe of scales leads the creatures
in something like a chant as they prostrate themselves before the
sphere. Finally the sphere breaks through its holding ropes and
rises to the surface. Scientific men, hearing the story, suppose
these creatures may be, like us, descendants of the great Therio-
morpha of the New Red Sandstone age.

Using the theme of *Frankenstein,* the principles of evolution,
imaginary discoveries in plastic surgery, and suggestions from
Swift, Wells produced in 1896 one of his most powerful and
terrible books, *The Island of Dr. Moreau.* The narrator, Prendick,
is shipwrecked, but is picked up by a dirty little steamship loaded
with animals. The animals are unloaded on an island, and Prendick is forced to get off, too. The men on the island besides
white-haired Dr. Moreau and his assistant, Montgomery, seem
queer, bestial people: a servant has pointed ears, covered with
fur; a man drops on all fours to lap water from a stream. In
Moreau's locked laboratory some bloody surgical operation is
going on; screams and moans issue from it. Prendick believes
Moreau is vivisecting human beings, and he flees. He comes upon
the huts of the Beast Folk, dim, dirty, and grotesque. There he
is welcomed and led to the   Sayer of the Law who chants, as
all chant, an insane litany: "Not to go on all-Fours; *that* is the
Law. Are we not Men? . . . Not to claw bark of Trees; *that* is
the Law. Are we not Men? . . . *His* is the House of Pain. . . .
His is the Hand that heals." Moreau and Montgomery arrive,
and when Prendick flees, shout to him to return, that there is
no vivisection of men.

Returning, Prendick learns the truth. Moreau, fleeing from prejudice against vivisection, came to this island to pursue his researches. He has advanced step by step toward the manufacture of human beings from animals by plastic surgery, blood trans-fusion, bone alteration, skin grafting, and alteration of chemical rhythms, larynx, fixed ideas—hypnotically supplanted by other fixed ideas—and even the emotional structure of the brain. "I am a religious man, Prendick, as every sane man must be," says Moreau; he has sought the laws of this world's Maker all his life, and in this search has found it necessary to be "as remorse-less as Nature." Little by little, his products have been more and more like men, less like swine, dogs, or apes. But none has satisfied him; they have dribbled into the huts, to chant the law and try to keep themselves erect, while Moreau has gone on and on to fresh creation.

But the "men" begin to revert, old instinct to stir in their flesh as soon as Moreau's hand is lifted from them. One day a rabbit is found bitten through and through. Sure the Leopard Man is guilty, Moreau goes to the huts to punish him, but the Leopard Man, cornered, kills Moreau. Montgomery gets drunk and gives drink to the Beast Men, and he is killed. The Beast People gradually go more and more on all-fours, lap up water, etc.; the Monkey Man jabbers Big Thinks, strings of words without meaning. After months among them, Prendick escapes on a raft to England. There he sees the beast in the faces of men everywhere; reason, like the Law, struggles feebly against instinct. In church, for instance, the preacher jabbers Big Thinks, and Prendick walks in fear among his fellow men. Swift's con-clusions about human nature in "The Voyage to the Houyhnhnms" are here re-enforced by the theory of evolution.

Frank Stockton's *The Great Stone of Sardis* (1897) presents the geological discovery that the core of the earth, beginning fourteen miles below the surface, is solid diamond. By 1947 great mechanical progress has taken place: electrically propelled ships, made in two parts connected by a ball-and-socket joint, eliminate rolling at sea; moving platforms eliminate walking in the cities; electric monorails span the continent; flying ma-chines and submarines are in common use, the submarines em-ploying a device for extracting air from the water as fish do. In this setting, the inventor Roland Clewe of Sardis, New Jersey, invents a submarine that goes to the North Pole; he next invents an X-ray mechanism that sends its rays to any desired depth in any substance and exposes the surface at the end of the rays. It will be useful in surgery and in mining. With this "artesian ray" he looks into the earth, and at fourteen miles sees a clear transparency. He invents also a projectile that automatically bores through solid matter. The projectile falls from its holder and starts downward; at fourteen miles down, it stops. Clewe goes down the shaft to investigate and comes to solid diamond. After breaking off a few pieces, he fills up the hole. This discovery leads him to new knowledge about the formation of the earth: it was originally a comet of diamond but when it approached the sun, the sun's rays heated it as a burning glass is heated, and the surface burned to ashes that form the present surface-layer of the earth. Caught by the sun, it became a planet.

Wells's next romance of discovery, *The Invisible Man* (1897), presents a more thoughtful fantasy. In fairy stories, invisibility is a boon; an invisible man has tremendous advantage. But in a world of natural law, says Wells, an invisible man would be at a disadvantage. He must either go naked and catch cold, or cover his face when he clothes his body; dogs smell him and bark; drivers of vehicles do not slow down as he crosses the street.

The Invisible Man tells the story of Griffin, who discovers a laboratory method for making himself invisible, believes that he has enormous power, institutes a reign of terror, and is finally beaten to death by a mob. Griffin, swathed in bandages about his head, comes to a village inn; mysterious things happen, such as doors opening and closing and furniture jostling about through no visible agency. But Griffin needs a partner. He seeks the help of a physician, Dr. Kemp, to whom he tells the story of his years of experimentation to find some formula in molecular physics to make flesh invisible as sea larvae are invisible. He discovered the formula and, in the midst of pain, rendered himself invisible. Then he discovered that he is forever cut off from normal human activities. But with Dr. Kemp for partner, he says, he can rule the world. Kemp betrays him, and there is a complex and grotesque fight as Griffin battles the police and citizenry of a whole town but is finally cornered, caught, and beaten to death.

Griffin became invisible through a physiological change, but in Wells's "The New Accelerator" (1903) the narrator and Professor Gibberne become invisible by increasing their speed of motion to a point beyond visibility. Professor Gibberne discovers a drug to speed up all bodily processes at the same rate. When he and the narrator take a dose of the stimulant, they seem to themselves to move at the normal rate, but everything else seems to halt. The world is silent, except for slow pattering noises, sounds analyzed into their component vibrations. A glass dropped hangs almost motionless, slowly drifting down. They go onto the leas where a motionless band is playing and hear a "sound like the slow, muffled ticking of some monstrous clock." The narrator finds that the friction of walking sets his trousers afire. When the drug wears off, after what seems half an hour, they discover that only two or three seconds have passed. Perhaps this drug, the new accelerator, is "the beginning of our escape from that Time Garment of which Carlyle speaks."

A relativity of size is the subject of Wells's *The Food of the Gods* (1904), and its theme the escape from the trivial and the traditional. The story opens as a tale of marvelous discovery, but it closes as an allegory of the conflict between the large ideas of the new world of science and the limited ideas of the old world of tradition.

Professor Redwood, a physiologist, explores the laws of growth and discovers that men and plants grow by spurts; Mr. Bensington, a chemist, discovers a substance always present during growth. The two scientists put their conclusions together and suppose that they may make growth continuous. They experiment with a new Food on chickens. The chickens grow outrageously, but the Food gets spilled over and wasps get it; rats get it; it gets into grass. The chickens, as big as horses, escape into the village of Hickleybrow and create a panic. An engineer, Cossar, leads an expedition to exterminate the giant rats. Meanwhile, Mrs. Skinner, formerly in charge of the chicken farm, begins to feed the Food to her grandson, Caddles; Cossar, a man of vision, insists that it be fed to children and feeds his three sons; Redwood feeds his son; a man named Winkles gets the Food for a Princess on the continent. It causes havoc everywhere that it leaks out: giant cockroaches, eels that kill sheep, huge flies and spiders. "It seemed even to wise men that the Food was giving the world nothing but a crop of unmanageable discontented irrelevancies." Caddles, meanwhile, becomes a giant boy and is set to work in a stone quarry single-handed; Cossar's sons grow up aware of some destiny that the world has for them.

But the world resists all bigness. It becomes a political issue. The Cossar boys want to tear up the winding, narrow roads and build fine, straight roads; they would tear down the slums and erect clean houses. But real-estate agents stop them. Caterham, running for Prime Minister, wins on the promise to oppose the Big. Caddles, puzzled by his strangeness and isolation, wanders up to London and is shot down by cannon. And at last all the giants—Redwood, the Princess, the Cossars, and others from out-of-the-way places—gather in a fort. The little people swarm at them, but the giants reply by shooting explosive bombs of the Food. It will give every living thing that feeds on it a new growth. The book ends as the giants challenge the world: "For greatness is abroad, not only in the Food, but in the purpose of all things!" They insist (and this is Wells's message) upon the right of change and growth; they insist that, in the end, however opposed, the earth belongs to the great and wise. Their weapon is the spread of the Food, the product of science.

Conan Doyle's "The Horror of the Heights" (1913) is typical of many less serious stories of wonderful discoveries. It uses arguments from evolution to support the idea that gaseous creatures live in the upper air. Seven miles above the earth in an airplane, his motor sputtering in the thin air, Joyce-Armstrong sees a bell-shaped creature of enormous size, pinkish with green tentacles, but transparent as a jellyfish. Then he sees air-snakes of smoke color. Gliding down rapidly, he is attacked by a monster of glue-like consistency, but a bullet through what looks like a gas bag deflates the creature, and it releases its hold. Joyce-Armstrong comes down, but goes up again. Portions of his plane and a notebook are found. The last entry records that he is forty-three thousand feet high, with three of the creatures beneath him. "God help me, it is a dreadful death to die!"

These stories are, in general, the result of speculations in evolution and physiology.

3. The Wonderful Event

Stories of wonderful events form a considerable body of scientific fiction within the period 1895-1914.

H. G. Wells told many stories of man's conflict with imaginary creatures. "The Flowering of the Strange Orchid" (1895) describes what a wonderful plant does when brought back to England. Wedderburn purchases an orchid of an unidentified species— one found crushed under the body of the collector Batten. When Wedderburn plants the orchid in his greenhouse, it blossoms, gives off a stupefying odor, and finally grasps Wedderburn with blood-sucking tentacles. When his housekeeper comes to look for him, she finds him nearly dead. Wells's "In the Avu Observatory" (1895) also tells of a strange, destructive monster in Borneo. Something prehistoric that has survived in the wilderness flies like a bat into the Avu Observatory and wrecks it. Also hitherto unknown to science are the *Haploteuthis ferox* of Wells's "The Sea Raiders" (1897). From somewhere in the depths of the sea the creatures appear in swarms along the Devonshire coast, prowl, prey on bathers, and then suddenly vanish into the abysses of the sea.

Wells's next story of a wonderful event, "The Star" (1897),

describes a disaster of astronomical proportions. A wandering star invades the solar system. It strikes Neptune and wraps it in a mantle of flame, and the two globes fall toward the earth as one mass of incandescence. But it is deflected by Jupiter and does not strike the earth on its way to the sun. Yet over Japan and Java and eastern Asia, hot gases and ash stream from the volcanoes; the earth reels with earthquakes; the snows of Thibet melt and pour across Hindostan; cities are shaken from their bases; "the thunder and lightning wove a garment round the world." For months the disturbances continue, slowly abating. When the sun appears once again, it is larger and hotter, and Iceland and Baffin's Bay are pleasant lands of green vegetation. Martian astronomers, viewing the effects on earth, are surprised at the little damage done; the white discolorations around the poles are shrunken, and that is nearly all. "Which only shows how small the vastest of human catastrophes may seem, at a distance of a few million miles."

In *The War of the Worlds* (1898), these Martians, "minds that are to our minds as ours are to the beasts that perish, intellects vast and cool and unsympathetic," invade the earth, green with the vegetation and gray with the water that are sparse on Mars.

Astronomers on earth observe a curious spurt of flame on Mars, but suppose some volcanic action there. Then the first cylinder buries itself in English sand; crowds gather to see the "meteor." They send for soldiers when the top unscrews and a grayish bulk heaves itself from the cylinder. The Martian is a fungoid-looking globe with dangling tentacles, a V-shaped mouth, no brow, no chin, and immense eyes. When men advance to communicate, something like a sword of flame leaps to them; at the touch of this flame, iron and glass melt, water explodes into steam. More soldiers arrive, but the Martians stay in their pit, working on something; perhaps they cannot get out of the pit. Then suddenly a Martian strides out, and another and another, each one on a tripod of steel, higher than houses, stepping over the pine trees. Soldiers fire their cannon, but the Martian heat-ray explodes their battery.

Night after night new cylinders fall. As the Martians come towards London, the population stampedes out of the city in terror. Besides the heat-ray, the Martians have a black smoke that writhes over the ground and poisons; it destroys Richmond, Kingston, and Wimbledon. A Martian reaching the coast is attacked by a battleship till a heat-ray is "driven through the iron of the ship's side like a white-hot iron rod through paper," but sheer momentum carries the ship into the wading Martian to cut him down. The narrator sees a Martian capture some men and fling them into a basket. Hiding in a house with a curate, the narrator observes the Martians close up, at their camp. He sees the intricate, swift, and perfect handling machines and the pulpy, bodiless brain-masses that make up the Martians. Martians do not eat or digest or even have a stomach; they simply inject the blood of other living creatures—men—into their veins. They do not sleep; they are without sex, but give birth by budding. They appear to communicate without sound, by some kind of telepathy.

Going toward London, the narrator comes upon an artilleryman who has a plan for moving men underground, living there, studying the Martian machines and mastering them, and finally emerging to fight the Martians. The narrator wanders on. Then there is a strange silence, broken by a distant wailing ululation. The Martians are dying in their machines. It is learned that bacteria kill them. Without bacteria on Mars, they had no resistance to disease, and in drinking the blood of men, they had drunk all man's diseases. Men coming back to London at last learn much from the Martians' machines, especially the secret of flying.

Of all Wells's scientific stories, perhaps *The War of the Worlds* is the purest, the least sociological, as a romance of science. Using the theory of evolution to account for the Martians' development, the story extends evolution logically. Studying the reaction of men to a cosmic catastrophe, Wells creates unforgettable characters, such as the clergyman who can think only of Sodom and Gomorrah and the wasted effort of the Sunday Schools. The Martians derive from the biological laboratory; their mechanical "limbs" from the caustic thought of Butler's Erewhonian philosopher; the bacterial dénouement apparently from Greg's *Across the Zodiac*. It is a tale of wonder and terror for modern times, more terrible than anything "Gothic."

Wells returned by 1903 to stories of the discovery of strange biological specimens. Perhaps the threat to man's dominion of the earth may come from insects, rather than from Mars. "The Valley of the Spiders" tells the story of the attack by huge spiders upon some men in a desert. The spiders have bodies half as large as a man's hand and webs that carry them through the air like sails.

This conception is developed in Wells's "The Empire of the Ants" (1905). Hearing rumors of a great pest of ants, the Brazilian government sends a gunboat into the territories of the upper Amazon. The men on the gunboat find organized, poison-carrying ants; the ants have seized a steamship, which wallows derelict with a few bloated bodies upon the decks; and a Portuguese sent aboard to investigate is bitten and dies. The captain of the gunboat comes to a deserted village; everyone is dead or has fled before the ants. The captain is helpless except to fire his cannon at some houses. These ants are credited with a knowledge of fire and metals and engineering; they tunnel under a river wider than the Thames. Holroyd muses upon what may happen if presently they store knowledge, use weapons, form empires, and sustain a war against man.

D. *The Wonderful Journey*

1. On the Earth

Romances of wonderful journeys on the surface of the earth abound in the period 1895-1914, especially in juvenile literature. These romances frequently have some relationship to science.

Jules Verne's *The Sphinx of Ice* (1897) is a sequel to Poe's *Narrative of Arthur Gordon Pym;* Verne, however, does not suppose that Poe's story is directed toward an adventure inside the earth, but continues the story with the discovery of the South Pole and then of Pym's body held by magnetism to the magnetic pole of the Antarctic. The tale is one of Verne's poorest. Verne not only misunderstands the destination of Poe's *Narrative,* but alters and explains away a number of the facts Pym's journal had recorded, to force liaison with his own tale.

Other tales describe the discovery of strange peoples. Edward Bellamy's "To Whom This May Come" (1898) describes the narrator's shipwreck among an island people who, through a process of evolution, have acquired the power of telepathy and who, therefore, have lost the power of speech. The people are described as descendants of soothsayers driven from Persia some centuries before. Their seemingly occult powers are due simply to "slight acceleration . . . . of the course of universal human evolution," which is destined in time to lead to "direct mental vision on the part of all races."

H. G. Wells describes a race that has lost the power of sight and has evolved in its place an extraordinary keenness in all the other senses. In "The Country of the Blind" (1904) the mountaineer Nunez ventures beyond "Parascotopetl, the Matterhorn of the Andes" and there tumbles over a precipice into an isolated valley. Into this valley, many generations ago, people slightly touched by Spanish civilization strayed and, because of a disease that affected their eyes, lost the power of sight. But they have developed a pastoral life dependent upon keen hearing and smelling. Nunez, far from realizing the proverb that "in the country of the blind the one-eyed man is king," finds himself, for the weakness of his other senses, held to be feeble-minded.

Desiring to marry a daughter of the blind people, Nunez is ordered to have his eyes put out to restore him to sanity. He flees in terror, but is killed trying to scale the precipice. Perhaps Wells is remaking the point made in *The Invisible Man,* that the person with unusual powers is at a disadvantage in society. The proverb that he would be king belongs to fairy story; that he would be considered an idiot is the reality suggested by science.

2.   Into the Earth

Journeys inside the earth during this period yield stranger romances.

One of them is John Uri Lloyd's *Etidorhpa* (1895). Combining material from mystic sources with unusual explanations for natural phenomena, the book offers an explanation for the origin of the earth, describes it as hollow, and narrates an adventure inside it.

The book is presented by Lloyd, as written by Llewellyn Drury, who tells of his experiences in receiving the central manuscript from I-Am-the-Man. Meditating alone, Drury is conscious of a presence in his room; he looks up to find a gray-bearded stranger there. This stranger, who possesses the ability to dematerialize and to pass through a solid wall, declares he is no phantom, and then reads his manuscript.

I-Am-the-Man, interested in occult studies, is taken by a guide to the entrance of a cavern in Kentucky and there is turned over to a strange creature, his host, a being in stature like a man, but with blue skin and a face without eyes or sockets. Following his host, I-Am-the-Man plunges into the cavern. His host senses the way through darkness and water as they go down into the earth, finally to emerge onto dry land; their way is illuminated by a diffused light filtered through the earth. They pass a forest of colossal fungi, sweet in odor and taste, and then cross salt beds. I-Am-the-Man finds that gravitational attraction has almost disappeared, and he is able to float down declivities and across abysses. They come to a placid lake, like a sheet of glass. To cross it, the host produces a metal boat that travels nine hundred miles an hour by means of an ethereal current or magnetic force. Travelling for five hours at this speed, they are protected from any rush of wind by a shield of force that surrounds the boat.

The host explains the interior structure of the earth. The earth-forming principle is a sphere of energy that, spinning through space, collects matter as a bubble might collect dust; this matter, forming the earth-crust, is nowhere more than eight hundred miles thick; it is firm and solid on both convex and concave surfaces and its gravitational pull is the same on both surfaces, but in deep caverns gravitational pull diminishes. At one place, near the Pole, there is an opening into the interior—the verge of the earth-sphere. To this point I-Am-the-Man is led. He is told that he must prepare to lose his material aspect; matter is but a manifestation of energy or spirit, and he is to enter the inner world of spirit. Following his host, he plunges into the abyss and there floats, drifting until he wills to go to the opposite shore of the earth's inner crust. In this phase, he converses with his host by telepathy. On the inner crust, I-Am-the-Man is turned over to another host who is to lead him to Etidorhpa—and the story closes.

Physical phenomena, natural laws, and science are not discarded in favor of supernatural explanations, for it is explained that the strange phenomena are natural. The author pleads that the domain of the natural sciences be extended to include esoteric phenomena, especially conceptions set forth in the book.

An older tradition in scientific fiction is continued in Charles Willing Beale's *The Secret of the Earth* (1899). It is built upon Symmes's theory of the hollow earth. Furthermore, making use of material from Poe's *Narrative of Arthur Gordon Pym*, it correctly supposes that Poe's *Narrative* is an unfinished story of a trip inside the earth. The method of travel, however, has been modernized; it is by airplane.

The Attlebridge brothers, Guthrie and Torrence, have invented an airplane. At first they are unable to get capital to develop their invention, but suddenly Torrence meets a mysterious sailor and from this time on has plenty of money. Finally the airplane, partly supported by an anti-gravitational principle, is ready to fly. As they depart in it for the North Pole, Torrence unfolds to Guthrie the secret he has had from the sailor; the sailor had visited the inner world, but had not found anyone to believe him. Because Torrence believed and promised to make the trip and demonstrate the fact to science, the sailor gave him pearls and gold brought from the inner world. Proceeding northward, the airplane crosses an ice barrier and then comes to a warm region. Past lofty mountains, they proceed to the inner world. They discuss Symmes's theory at length. They pass roofless houses—for there is no rain or change of climate in the interior —and finally bejeweled men in a gorgeous ship. They come to a city of white and gold. Torrence believes that the interior of the earth was man's first home, and from that fact stem the legends of Eden and a Golden Age. After crossing an equatorial desert, they come finally to the temperate zone again and then pass out into the darkness of the South Polar outer world. Unfortunately an accident wrecks the airship.

Exploration in the twentieth century has, of course, shown that this haunting, recurrent Symmes's theory is contrary to fact; the world inside the earth must remain forever in the realm of romance. But up to the very date of Commander Peary's discovery of the North Pole in April, 1909, Symmes's theory continued to attract adherents. For instance, Willis George Emerson's *The Smoky God,* describing a voyage to the inner world through the open North Pole and out through the South, was published in 1908.

The explorer, Olaf Jansen, finds, like the Attlebridge brothers, that the interior of the world is the Garden of Eden. Olaf and his father, fishing north of Spitzbergen, are overtaken by a storm that drives them northward. They soon see a strange, dull-red sun on the "northern" horizon, but this sun they later learn is in the center of the earth. It is the "seat of electricity," called by the inhabitants of the inner world "The Smoky God" and believed to be the "throne of 'The Most High.'" They come to a land, the capital of which is called Eden, inhabited by giants twelve feet high, clothed in Graecesque tunics and shoes with golden buckles. The people of this land have developed the uses of electricity; it "surcharges" the atmosphere and "vitalizes" plants and animals alike. Electricity operates "flying cars" and aids in "communion with one another between the most distant parts of their country on air currents." Plants and fruits are gorgeous: grapes the size of oranges, apples as large as a man's head. The language resembles Sanskrit. Olaf concludes that the inner world is the cradle of the human race and that its discovery must alter all "physical, paleontological, archaeological, philological, and mythological theories of antiquity." Footnote references to scientific writings that accord with the discoveries of the story take up, on some pages, more space than the text; Olaf's maps and manuscript are to be presented to the Smithsonian Institution.

The next year Commander Peary reached the Pole without finding the polar opening.

3. To Other Planets

Narratives of voyages to other planets are numerous in the period 1895-1914.

H. G. Wells chose to call his story of interplanetary travel *The First Men in the Moon* (1901). It is indeed the first to be scientifically consistent, except in the invention of an anti-gravitational substance. Wells argues even this point. As Bedford's manuscript says: "I would like to see the man who could invent a story that would hold together like this one."

The narrator, Bedford, strikes up an acquaintance with the scientist, Cavor, who is trying to manufacture a substance opaque to gravitation. Gravitation, he says, is a form of radiant energy, like heat or light. Glass is transparent to light, nearly opaque to heat; a solution of iodine in carbon bisulphide is transparent to heat, but opaque to light. Metals are opaque to electrical energy: sheets of metal cut off wireless rays. But no known substance is opaque to gravitation. "Cavor did not see why such a substance should not exist, and certainly I could not tell him." Then one day Cavor is successful: the chimneys of his laboratory jerk off and fly heavenward. Fortunately, the sheet of Cavorite flies up, too, or it "would have whipped the air off the world as one peels a banana."

Cavor builds a sphere of glass and metal and coats it with sections of Cavorite that can be electrically rolled up like roller blinds. In this sphere they depart for the moon, able to guide themselves by rolling up blinds to let any heavy body attract the sphere. Without weight in interplanetary space, they float to the center of the sphere. They approach the moon, a dead world of extinct volcanoes and lava wildernesses, alternately blazing and freezing in absolute zero. Using the pull of the sun as a brake, they come drifting down into a "snow" of frozen air. They witness the lunar sunrise, "a stupendous scimitar of white dawn with its edge hacked out by notches of darkness." But as the sun's heat touches the snow, it becomes a thin air; "sticks" burst rapidly into life and grow. Testing their way, Bedford and Cavor climb onto the moon.

Weighing only a sixth of their weight on earth, they run and jump, stumble and get lost. They hear rumbling sounds, the clank of machinery, and a great cylinder-head opens on the surface of the moon; up a tunnel come flabby, slow-moving beasts two hundred feet long, prodded by Selenites, insect-like men, erect, goggle-eyed, with tentacles and arms projecting from cylindrical body-cases. Hungry after flight, Cavor and Bedford eat a pulpy vegetable; it makes them drunk and sleepy. When they wake, they are shackled in a prison inside the moon. Bedford and Cavor, led captive, observe vast machines that manufacture the cold, bluish light that runs in conduits along the tunnels. Expected to walk a thin bridge across a bottomless chasm, Bedford strikes at his captor, and his fist goes clean through: "He smashed like some sort of sweetmeat with liquid in it." Bedford and Cavor escape and climb upward through tunnels to the surface. The lunar day is waning; they wander, separate, and look for the sphere. Cavor is re-captured, but Bedford finds the sphere just before the dark and cold descend, and in it he returns to earth. The sphere is left on a beach; there a small boy clambers into it, and it is gone like a rocket.

That is the end of the adventure; so far, it is pure scientific romance. But Wells had not described lunar life, and in this description there is opportunity for satire. When Bedford publishes his story, Mr. Julius Wendigee tells him of fragmentary wireless messages coming from Cavor on the moon. The moon, Cavor finds, is a sponge of rock, partly natural, partly artificial caverns; the "volcanoes" of the moon are excavated rock; in the center is an ocean; air is denser as it flows through the moon's interior. The inhabitants of the moon are developed from insects, differentiated and specialized into many kinds and sizes; specialization is artifically stimulated by education and surgery: one has a vast fore-limb; another is all legs; another is all lop-sided brain; another is a linguist, and another is a rememberer (historian). For instance, Phi-oo and Tsi-puff, linguist and re-memberer, easily learn Cavor's language. Others are artists, math-ematicians, or physicians. Each works at his own task and enjoys doing nothing else; when workers are not needed, they are drugged and laid aside. Cavor is taken for an audience with the Grand Lunar, a great bladder-brain pulsing with "undulating ghosts of convolutions writhing visibly within." The Grand Lunar questions Cavor about life on earth and is amazed at its aim-lessness, its wars, its use of the same sort of men for all kinds of work. The Grand Lunar supposes that men may wish to invade the moon—and the messages from Cavor cease.

This satire on human specialization is a product of the creative imagination that applies to bees and ants the principle of evolution that produced man.

The less scientific, more traditional voyage is continued in such books as George Griffith's *A Honeymoon in Space* (1901). A wealthy British peer, Lord Redgrave, supplies an inventor funds for developing the "R. Force," an anti-gravitational force that results from breaking gravitation up, as electricity is broken up, into positive and negative. A space ship, the *Astronef*, is constructed and Lord Redgrave takes his bride on a honeymoon through space in it. Before starting, however, he averts a world war by exhibiting this flying machine and demonstrating the helplessness of armies against it. Lord Redgrave and his bride visit the moon, Mars, Venus, Jupiter, Callisto, Ganymede, and Saturn. The romance sums up the wonders of interplanetary flights described in fiction from Cyrano de Bergerac to 1900, though, published in the same year as Wells's *The First Men in the Moon*, it shows no influence from Wells's harder-headed book.

But even *A Honeymoon in Space* is too austere, has too much science in it and not enough love-rivalry and personal adventure, for the pulp-paper magazine fans of the 1920's and 1930's. The formula for the pulp-paper story (reflected, for instance, in the "comic" sheets of newspapers) demands, *mutatis mutandis,* a gold-and-jeweled society in towered cities on a strange planet, a beautiful queen, a space-traveller in love with the queen, a jealous rival, an antagonistic high-priest, death-dealing rays for weapons in a fierce, chromatically repeated struggle, hairbreadth escapes, and finally the victory of the hero and sometimes his marriage to the queen. This formula-story draws incidentally from science, largely from some traditional features of scientific fiction, and largely from the romance-of-travel into strange civilizations as developed by H. Rider Haggard.

Garret Putman Serviss's *A Columbus of Space* (1909) follows this formula so colorfully that the romance ran through several editions as a book and was then serially republished in *Amazing Stories* in 1926. In this story, Edmund Stonewall discovers a repulsive force based on atomic disintegration, builds a car, and takes three friends with him to Venus. Landing on a part of the planet that is perpetually dark, they discover ape-like cave dwellers; one of the travellers is captured and is to be sacrificed, but the others save him by killing the high priest. After crossing an ice-barrier, they reach the warm regions of Venus and find there a highly developed race of Venusians—a beautiful people, superior to men, who communicate by telepathy. The lovely queen, Ala, saves them from a mob, and she and Edmund fall in love. Edmund has a rival, Ingra, who plots constantly to get rid of the men from earth. They explore Venus, visit a zone of great swamp, and barely escape a monster of prehistoric kind. Finally Edmund and Ala are happy on an idyllic part of the planet, but Ingra appears with a party to attack them. Ingra seizes the space ship and almost gets away with it, but airplanes catch him on the edge of a jungle. Back in the capital city, the high priest is opposed to Ala's marriage with Edmund, but Ala, as a queen, defies the priest. As Ala's party is about to be victorious, Ingra flies by in an airplane and starts a destructive fire in which all the travellers from earth perish except the narrator, who comes back to earth to tell the story.

The foregoing plot-outline is a skeleton. Dozens of incidents cannot be included, for the story is all action and color. The people of Venus are Graecesque idealizations of men and women; the capital city is a futuristic dream of New York, stage on stage; the matriarchy at war with the priesthood suggests popular ideas of Egypt or Phoenicia. What it amounts to is the use of "science" as a background for extravagant romance of the *Prisoner of Zenda* type. The "science" adds exotic color, opportunity for extravagance.

Yet another variety of interplanetary voyage describes visits to the planets as a means of teaching geology and astronomy—just as Waterloo's *Story of Ab* tells a story to illustrate a theory of evolution. Mark Wicks's *To Mars via the Moon* (1911) is stodgy as a romance, and certainly the home-folks discovered on Mars are not credible. But the bulk of the book is presentation of information about the solar system. As the author says, he intends to set forth "the most recent and reliable scientific information" so that "the book may be referred to with as much confidence as any ordinary textbook." The author lists the names of scientists whose works he has studied. But in the narrative portions of the book, describing a trip to the moon and to Mars in a car of "martalium," the conventional materials of previous scientific fiction are found.

4. Into Other Dimensions

The fourth dimension in stories of 1895-1914 is generally incidental to some other feature. For instance, Wells's *The Time Machine* makes use of the fourth dimension as time; stories of the supernatural treat the fourth dimension as a spirit world.

In the same year that Wells published *The Time Machine* carefully explaining that the fourth dimension is time, he also published "The Story of Davidson's Eyes" (1895), which assumes that the fourth dimension is spatial. Davidson, in his laboratory, has something happen to his eyes during a thunderstorm. Though he remains in London, he sees a southern ocean, an island, and a ship, rather than the city. For several weeks he lives in one world, but sees in another, until gradually his "unreal" vision fades away. He later discovers that what he saw happen during these weeks actually happened in the South Seas. Professor Wade, explaining that an electrical shock warped Davidson's eyes so that he saw in a fourth dimension, suggests that "two points might be a yard away on a sheet of paper, and yet be brought together by bending the paper round."

E. *The Occult and the Supernatural*

Wells's "The Plattner Story" (1896) describes a trip into a fourth dimension that is, this time, a world of spirits. The story assumes the co-existence in the same space of two worlds, the world of the living and the world of the dead. But a living person may somehow be "exploded" into the world of the dead and back again, with no change except that his anatomy is reversed. Gottfried Plattner, says the story, undoubtedly disappeared, and he undoubtedly had his internal structure transposed: once right-handed, he is now left-handed; his heart, once normal, is now on his right side. Mathematicians say that the only way to transpose the right and left sides of a solid body is to take it outside space as we know it into a fourth dimension.

Plattner, a schoolmaster, teaches elementary chemistry; when Whibble brings him some green powder found in a lime kiln, he experiments with it. It explodes, and Plattner is no longer there. He cannot be found anywhere until he smacks squarely into headmaster Lidgett one day, in his garden. Plattner's story is that he is stunned by the explosion, and then horrified when some of the boys walk through him. Then he finds himself in a dim green world of silence, with a village like a cemetery; its inhabitants are globular heads at the top of tadpole-like bodies. The heads watch him, as they watch all the living, dimly visible. They seem to be the dead, whose morbid interest is in the working out of trains of consequences they have laid. Plattner sees them gather eagerly around a dying man whose widow-to-be is tearing up his will. Plattner runs, falls upon the bottle of green powder, and is exploded into Lidgett's garden.

Well's "The Story of the Late Mr. Elvesham" (1896) is a Jekyll-and-Hyde story of a wonderful elixir. Elvesham, old, wealthy, and decrepit, discovers a chemical compound that makes it possible for men to exchange bodies. He inveigles a healthy young man, Eden, into partaking of liquor containing the compound. After a confusing experience of being in two places at once and of remembering clearly events that happened before he was born, Eden wakes to find himself irrecoverably in the feeble body of Elvesham.

George Du Maurier's *The Martian* (1896) is the story of an indwelling spirit from the planet Mars and its influence upon its host's life. Barty Josselin, believing that he is going blind, meditates suicide, but he goes to sleep and wakens to find a note in his own handwriting telling him not to commit suicide. The note is signed "Martia." Martia tells him, in trance, that "she" is a spirit inhabiting Josselin and evident to him at times when he feels a gravitational pull northward. When Josselin sleeps, Martia dictates to him (and he writes) novels that have "as wide and far-reaching an influence on modern thought as the *Origin of Species*." Martia says that "she" comes from Mars, and "she" reveals to him something of the advanced civilization of Mars.

H. G. Wells's "The Man Who Could Work Miracles" (1898) offers no explanation for the strange power given to Mr. Fotheringay to do anything by a simple exercise of the will. Fotheringay, who does not believe in miracles, is astonished during an argument to discover that things happen as he wills them. He wills minor miracles, such as to have an extra egg on his plate; then he goes to talk with Maydig, the curate, who is convinced by exhibition. As the evening is getting late and Maydig and Fotheringay are a little excited, Maydig suggests that Fotheringay imitate Joshua and command the earth to stand still. Fotheringay does so, but "he had made no stipulation concerning the trifling movables upon its surface," and there is an immediate hurricane, "everybody and everything had been jerked violently forward at about nine miles per second." As the surface of the earth is being destroyed, Fotheringay manages to will that he be let down softly and given time to think; then he wills that everything be as it was before and also that he lose the power to work miracles. These desires also come to pass. As in *The Invisible Man* and "The Country of the Blind," miracle-working is criticized in the light of scientific law; it would not give a man power, but disaster.

Jules Verne's *The Castle of the Carpathians* (1900) is pseudo-supernatural; mysteries and spectres are finally revealed to be the work of modern mechanical devices. The scene is "Gothic," an isolated village in the Carpathians near the deserted castle of the once-powerful family of Gortz. The villagers believe the castle haunted, but two intrepid travellers, Count Franz Télek and his man Rotzko, investigate and discover that Rodolphe de Gortz and a scientist, Orfanik, living there in seclusion, are using mechanical devices to terrorize the countryside. The chapel bell rings, intense flames spring up with spectral appearance, sirens sound, monsters appear in the clouds (projected there by huge reflectors), iron plates about the moat shock the unwary—for they are connected with electrical batteries. The tale sounds like "Gothic" supernaturalism till the villain Science is unmasked at the end.

H. G. Wells's "A Dream of Armageddon" (1901) is the story of a dream, or a series of consecutive dreams, of the kind of future Wells described in *When the Sleeper Wakes*. When he is dreaming, the narrator lives in a future world of airplanes and Pleasure Cities. He dreams finally of a war that destroys civilization and in which he is killed; after that, he has nightmares. The story implies that the dreamer lives in two periods, one of them the future furled backward (as in a fourth dimension) to overlap the present.

Rudyard Kipling tells a story, in "Wireless" (1902), of temporary metempsychosis made credible by analogy with the phenomena of wireless telegraphy. An imaginative, consumptive druggist, Shaynor, in love with a girl named Fanny Brand, is seized by the urge to write poetry. He has never read the poems of John Keats. But after many rewritings and erasures, he emerges from strenuous throes of composition with "The Eve of St. Agnes." In the next room a young man has been engaged in equally strenuous efforts to operate a wireless instrument. The implication is that the soul of Keats is in wireless communication with Shaynor. The wireless-operator's efforts to explain wireless, especially his talk of parallel wires and magnetic fields, also explain the metempsychosis.

The foregoing stories indicate how science contributed to occult and supernatural literature during the period 1895-1914.

F. *Crime and Detection*

During the latter part of the nineteenth century, Sir Arthur Conan Doyle gave great impetus to the detective story. Sherlock Holmes and the hundreds of detectives made in his image solve crime-puzzles by using a "scientific" rationale that includes wide knowledge of chemistry, physics, and medicine, as well as unerringly logical deductions.

Arthur B. Reeve's detective, Craig Kennedy, employing a technique like that of Sherlock Holmes, adds to it a wider use of science and the use of imaginary mechanisms. Reeve's creation, in the period 1910-1914, met with popular acclaim, and Reeve proceeded to capitalize upon this popularity by writing a large number of stories of crimes detected by the microscope, the dictaphone, chemical analysis, and similar means.

As most of the stories about Craig Kennedy fall into a single pattern, to examine the pattern will indicate the use of science. In "The Poisoned Pen" (1911) Kennedy solves a murder mystery by demonstrating that letters sent to the actress who has been poisoned were written on both sides of a sheet of paper. On one side was a note, ostensibly from a physician, instructing the actress to take a certain "headache" powder and then to drop the note into a jar of ammonia. In ammonia the writing on one side of the paper vanished, and writing appeared on the other side that threw agents of the law completely off the trail. Kennedy's method is to collect the evidence quietly, mystifying Jameson (his "Watson") and the reader, and then to call together all the principals in a laboratory and demonstrate his conclusion.

Richard Austin Freeman's Dr. Thorndyke works in the same tradition. His "Watson" is a Dr. Jervis. Dr. Thorndyke's science is not always so flashy, so seemingly imaginary, as Kennedy's; his method is the same. Dr. Thorndyke is a physician whose specialty is criminal medicine, and whose deft laboratory assistant, Polton, can do anything from prepare eggs on toast without the use of fire to create a reproduction of handwriting so clever that no expert, except Dr. Thorndyke, can detect the forgery. In *The Mystery of 31, New Inn* (1913), Dr. Thorndyke suspects that a piece of sugar is poisoned. He examines it with a chemist's knowledge: for foreign crystals on the surface, for alkaloid content, for arsenic content, and so on.

In the stories of Reeve and Freeman, the science pretends to be laboratory science. But an imaginary discovery in science is sometimes found as the basis for a story of crime and detection. Jack Harrower's "The Brain Blight" (1913), for instance, is a complex story of crime based upon the discovery of a drug that causes deterioration of the brain, and of an antidote for the drug. Dr. Keenton, travelling in South America, gets some of the brain-blight from Valdoza, who discovered how to make it from a rare plant. After finding an antidote for the blight, Dr. Keenton manages to poison millionaires with it and then to charge each one $10,000. for a cure.

In these ways, stories of crime and detection have made use of the materials of science.

*   *   *   *   *

Largely through the work of Jules Verne and H. G. Wells, scientific fiction by 1914 had exploited imaginary inventions and discoveries and had made imaginary applications of the laws of science for the purposes of romance. It had appeared on every level of literary achievement, from the dime novel to the stimulating and artistic stories of Wells and Kipling. It had been used for the serious examination of human destinies in utopias and satires and in historic romances of the future.

CHAPTER SIX

Beyond the Mountains
of the Moon

Scientific Fiction, 1915

H. G. WELLS remarks in his Preface to *Seven Famous Novels* that he is through writing scientific fiction, for "The world in the presence of cataclysmal realities has no need for fresh cataclysmal fantasies. That game is over." But it is not over. Mr. Wells, busy "trying to make a working analysis of our deepening social perplexities," has almost quit the game, but others have continued it. In fact, more of this fiction has been produced since 1914 than ever before. Much of it has been a serious effort to make our cataclysmal realities graphic, to explore the relation of man to himself, his society and his ethics as they are affected by science, and to illustrate the utopian opportunities and the frightful dangers in recent scientific discovery. Perhaps the need is greater than ever that fresh cataclysmal fantasies may shape apprehension in an increasing number of minds and lead to the determination that the possible worst may not come to pass.

Three phenomena characterize the scientific fiction of 1915 to 1946. One is the development of the cosmic romance; the second is a tendency to employ scientific fiction to explore psychological, moral, ethical, and even metaphysical problems; and the third is the rise of magazines devoted entirely to scientific fiction.

Where Wells devoted only one romance, *The Time Machine,* to man's final destiny before the end of life in the universe, the fiction of the past few years has made this destiny a frequent theme. It is the theme of Olaf Stapledon's *Last and First Men,* for instance, a cosmic romance whose hero is Mankind and whose villain a nearly eternal Fate. The background is not the earth alone, but the solar system. In a later book, *Star Maker,* even this background is widened; the director (if not the villain) is the Star Maker; and the background is at least one universe. A characteristic difference between scientific fiction before 1914 and after that date is this widening of the romance to cosmic proportions.

At the same time, Stapledon has led the way in the use of scientific fiction to explore man's adjustments to new ethical values. Indeed, to see human nature from the point of view of an advanced mind is the effort of his *Odd John;* and his *Sirius* is a similar effort to see human nature in some detail from a viewpoint entirely outside humanity.

The rise of magazines devoted to scientific fiction is an evolution. The dime-novel literature of the 1890's included the Frank Reade stories imitative of Jules Verne's. During the 1890's occasional pieces of scientific fiction appeared in such magazines as *All-Story.* The popularity of these "different" stories, as they were called, led to publication of more and more of them and finally to the founding of *Amazing Stories* in 1926, the first of the "scientifiction" magazines. *Amazing Stories* at first republished stories by Poe, Verne, and Wells, and then later published new pieces as a staff of writers was built up. At the same time, *Weird Tales,* occasionally publishing scientific fiction before this time, published more and more of it. With the success of *Amazing Stories,* other magazines with such titles as *Wonder Stories, Marvel Tales, Astounding Stories, Astounding Science-Fiction,* and (in England) *Scoops,* came into existence. Sometimes a new magazine has appeared for only an issue or two and disappeared. But several are thriving today.

There are even fan magazines, that is, magazines about "scientifiction" magazines, their stories, and their writers, such as *The Fantasy Fan* and *Fantasy Commentator.* The latter has been for some time publishing thoughtful articles about phases of scientific fiction and portions of an enormous bibliography of scientific and fantastic fiction. Clubs, with buttons, slogans, and grips, have flourished. Moving pictures have filmed many pieces of scientific fiction; magazines with the standing of *Scribner's* have published it; newspapers have published it; it has appeared for some years in "comic" sections of newspapers—daily comic strips, Sunday color-features, and "comic books"; Tarzan, Superman, and Buck Rogers are known to every schoolboy; the Big Little books of the dime-store counters include scientific fiction;

On the Newsstands of the 1930's

department-store book-counters display it. Scientific fiction on this level is a social phenomenon of the 1930's and 1940's.

Since the unique feature of this fiction is its concern with the imaginary, and hence the "amazing" or "astounding," it has described greater and greater marvels, and at the same time kept popular interest avid by portraying heroes in constant danger from interplanetary pirates, villains, etc. Stories of atomic bombs and the use of atomic power have long been conventional in this fiction; as Mr. A. Langley Searles, editor of *Fantasy Commentator,* remarks, atomic power in fiction had become by 1936 "so trite that a successful magazine story could never be based on such a theme—it had completely lost its novel touch." The cosmic romance is a standard feature, a convention. Any story may be set on Jupiter (or perhaps on Antares or even in a new universe), ten thousand to ten million years from now, and up.* Wide popular reading of this fiction, much of it well written, prepares the way for the more serious efforts, such as that of Stapledon, to explore man's destiny with serious purpose.

The present chapter attempts to cut a cross-section through various types, kinds and qualities of scientific fiction published in recent years. It describes books by Wells, such widely popular books as Huxley's *Brave New World* and Hilton's *Lost Horizon,* and some representative stories from the magazines.

The leading exhibits are classified as "The Cosmic Romance." This classification swallows up what has been included in two former classes: "The Historic Romance" and "The Wonderful Journey." The Cosmic Romance is subdivided into three parts, "In Space," "In Time," and "In Space-Time." The other classifications continue as in previous chapters.

---

* In this treatment of the entire career of scientific fiction, most pieces so unknown to the general public that stories must be summarized, I find it impossible to do justice to thousands of the stories appearing in the magazines. I can only present a few samples that seem to me representative. No doubt stories I have not read may be more representative or better in quality than those I select. For adequate commentary on the stories in the magazines I refer readers to the fan magazines. Perhaps a recent collection may be recommended, **The Best of Science Fiction,** edited by Groff Conklin and published by Crown Publishers, New York, 1946.

A. *The Cosmic Romance*

1. In Space

The Cosmic Romance set in Space includes wonderful journeys to other planets than the earth, or to such worlds as the world within the atom. Frequently however, the emphasis is not upon description of the alien world, as usually in the Wonderful Journey, but upon romantic adventures in this world.

Platonism and science seem, at first glance, strange companions, but the frontier regions of physics have looked for some years like mysticism. At any rate, C. S. Lewis's *Out of the Silent Planet* (1938) employs physics to support Platonism.

The philologist Ransom, a Cambridge don on a walking tour, is unable to find accommodation at an inn; he stops at an isolated house where a "professor" lives. There an old school-fellow, Devine, and a physicist, Weston, after some whispering, receive him. He is drugged, and when he awakes, he is on a space-ship 85,000 miles from the earth. The ship is going to Mars. It is a globe, built in cabins around a smaller globe, which serves as flooring, for in space "downward" is toward the center of the globe. Ransom does not understand what operates the ship, some exploitation of "the less observed properties of solar radiation." Through space, the travellers receive not only blinding light, but vitalizing impulses from rays that never penetrate the atmosphere; "he felt his body and mind daily rubbed and scoured and filled with new vitality." As the space-ship enters the atmosphere of Mars, all sense of direction disappears in confusion, and the lights of the universe seem turned down. Ransom suddenly thinks, with a vision that never afterwards deserts him, that the "earths" are holes in the living heaven, "rejected wastes of heavy matter and murky air, formed . . . by subtraction from the surrounding brightness."

At first Mars is so strange that no ideas of it are clear in Ransom's mind: "you cannot see things till you know roughly what they are." Colors are chiefly purple; vegetables on thin stalks rise twice as high as English elms; the place looks like a submarine forest; stalky, large-chested distortions of earthly bipeds appear. Ransom flees into the strange forest. After a night of solitude by a lake, he sees emerge from it a creature six or seven feet high, "something like a penguin, something like an otter, something like a seal." The creature is friendly; from a pouch it offers Ransom an invigorating drink; it speaks in what Ransom, as philologist, recognizes as language. Ransom goes to live with a tribe of these creatures in a canyon. He had often thought of going to another planet, but it is very strange being on Malacandra (Mars): "waking, sleeping, eating, swimming, and even, as the days passed, talking." He tells these hnau (rational creatures) that he came from the sky, but they are not foolish; they know he came from an earth. He learns that there are three genera of hnau on Malacandra: the Hrossa, among

whom he lives, devoted to a pastoral life and the development of
song and poetry; the Seroni, who live on the hills, astronomers
and scientists; and the Pfifltriggi, miners and artists of the plains.
The ruler of the planet is Oyarsa, an eternal, invisible spirit
whose dwelling is space; the eldila, invisible messengers of Oyarsa,
communicate with the hnau and speak the will of Oyarsa. In
turn, Oyarsa is a lesser spirit than Maleldil, whose servant he is.

Then Oyarsa sends an eldil for Ransom: a thin voice speaks
from the air. Guided, Ransom sets off across the mountain tops
to the island-city of Oyarsa. As he journeys, he learns of the
eldila, creatures whose bodies are movements swift as light:
"To us the *eldil* is a thin, half-real body that can go through
walls and rocks: to himself he goes through them because he
is solid and firm and they are like cloud." Oyarsa rules Malacandra; no one thinks of breaking His laws. For every earth
there is an Oyarsa. When Ransom is called before Oyarsa—whom
he cannot see—he is questioned. Once the earth (Thulcandra)
was one of the community of planets, but then, long before man
appeared, the Oyarsa of Thulcandra became bent; there was a
great war, and finally the Bent One was bound to Thulcandra
at the will of Maleldil. Since then the earth has been a silent
planet, except that perhaps, Oyarsa thinks, Maleldil may have
"taken strange counsel and dared terrible things, wrestling with
the Bent One in Thulcandra."

Weston and Devine do not believe in Oyarsa, but suppose
trickery. They say that they came to Malacandra to prepare it
for an invasion by men; they look upon the Malacandrans as
inferior creatures: "Our right to supersede you is the right of the
higher over the lower." But Oyarsa wonders whether Maleldil
wants any race of hnau to live forever; it seems to him a
teaching of the Bent One who breaks all other laws in the name
of the lesser law of self-preservation.

At any rate, Oyarsa commands Weston, Devine, and Ransom
to go back to earth; He says that any space-ship coming again
to Malacandra will be disintegrated. As Ransom leaves the
space-ship on earth, there is a flash of light, and the space-ship
vanishes.

A post-script relates the thought of the book to the Platonism
of the twelfth century, when Bernardus Silvestris used the word
Oyarses to mean the tutelary spirit of a planet. In this book, the
world of the invisible is not a supernatural world, but the world
suggested by intra-atomic physics interpreted through Platonism;
as in Platonism, material actuality is only a gross manifestation
of reality.

Akkad Pseudoman (*pseud.* for E. F. Northrup) presents in

Zero to Eighty (1937) much less of a romance, but much more of a practical scientist's investigation of the possibilities of interplanetary flight. In fact, the romance is only a vehicle to carry the discussion of conditions under which interplanetary flight may be possible. It owes little to the tradition of scientific fiction, but is based upon experimentation. A "Technical Section" of forty pages presents the mathematical calculations, drawings, photographs, and descriptions of apparatus on which the author bases his story. The Preface says: "In short, one purpose of this book is *to prove* the possibility (sufficient funds being available) of doing all that is herein described." The science is "believed to be entirely consistent with current proved facts. . . . Back of the technical portion of the book is a not inconsiderable expenditure of money, devoted to experimentation and collection of data by laboratory tests."

Perhaps to keep the reader's interest alive, the book contains a love-story, an attack by bandits, and a shipwreck. But the central feature of the book is detailed description of the efforts of Akkad Pseudoman to construct a missile for going to the moon. Experiments begin in 1945, at which time rocket-driven airships are in practical use. The principle employed is a combination of electric gun (employing high-frequency magnets) to give a missile an initial velocity, and rockets to propel the missile in space. Small missiles containing animals are shot for various distances; problems of air-supply in space and of steering are investigated. Chemicals supply air; rockets in the tail of the missile steer it. Velocities are figured; the velocity at the mouth of the gun must be seven miles per second; heat from air-friction may be neutralized by alcohol cooled with dry-ice and allowed to evaporate. Finally, on June 28, 1961, Akkad and his friend Jean are shot from an electric gun two hundred kilometers long built across Mount Popocatepetl; rockets pick up the velocity after they leave the earth's atmosphere. They go to the moon. They observe the moon as they circle it, and without landing, they return to earth.

Zero to Eighty is scientific fiction employed by a scientist to set forth possibilities that lack of funds prevents him from working out. The author is not without standing in scientific circles.

Two books by Edwin Balmer and Philip Wylie, *When Worlds Collide* and *After Worlds Collide,* pick up the more traditional material of scientific fiction and expand it to the proportions of cosmic romance.

In this pair of romances, two bodies from outer space invade the solar system; astronomers calculate that one of the bodies will strike the earth and engulf it, but the other will pass by it. To avoid destruction, groups of scientific men build rockets and, just before the collision, convey invading parties to the approaching world that will not strike the earth. The earth is destroyed and hurled into space by one of the invading bodies; groups of men land on the other, find the cities of a long-extinct civilization upon it, and adjust themselves to a new world, as the planet takes up an elliptical orbit about the sun.

When Worlds Collide (1932) opens with the discovery, by the astronomer Bronson, of a dead sun, Bronson Alpha, and its planet, Bronson Beta, on their way to the solar system. Scientists form the League of the Last Days to work for some method of transferring selected men to Bronson Beta, which will not collide with the earth. Unable to save all mankind, the scientists, led by the world's greatest physicist, Cole Hendron, select five hundred of the best brains and fittest bodies: scientists, physicians, linguists, and capable, beautiful women. Then they prepare to use the newly discovered power of atomic disintegration to convey a space-ship across space. They have two years, for on the first approach the alien sun will not strike the earth; it will circle the sun, and destroy the earth on the return. As the worlds pass near the earth disasters occur: "The great plateau of inner Thibet dropped like an express elevator nine hundred feet. South America was riven into two islands. . . . North America reeled and shuddered, split, snapped, boomed and leaped. The Rocky Mountains lost their immobolity and danced like waves of water." Cities, of course, go to pieces; New York sinks under the sea. Yet thousands of men remain, now desperate; space ships building in various parts of the world are focal points of fierce wars. Hendron's party is assaulted, but saved as disintegrating atoms are turned upon the attackers. Finally, as the Bronson bodies again approach the earth, this time to collide, Hendron's two space-ships are ready; rockets that split beryllium atoms are in place; and the remnant of mankind departs. Travelling toward Bronson Beta, they see Bronson Alpha strike the earth. "The very earth bulged. Its shape altered before their eyes. It became plastic. It was drawn out egg-shaped. . . . A great section of the Earth itself lifted up and peeled away, leaping toward Bronson Alpha with an inconceivable force." Veered by the collision, earth and Bronson Alpha, one flaming mass, drive out of their orbit into space. But guided, slowed down, and manipulated by their rockets, Hendron's space-ships land upon Bronson Beta. The travellers find breathable air and drinkable water.

After Worlds Collide (1934) describes the exploration of

Bronson Beta and adjustment to the new planet. Men find that days are fifty hours long; two hundred and five days make up a year; summers will be brief and hot, winters long and cold, near Mars. They find glass-roofed dead cities, metal roads, flying machines of a strange type, an inter-city electrical plant operated from a central station, and even stores of strange meats and vegetables canned in transparent metal. But other rocket ships reach this world, too, one from England and one from Asia. The Asiatics are communists who wish to have the whole planet for themselves. They seize the power plant and threaten to cut off the heat from all cities except their own when the planet is in the cold region near Mars. But their leader is finally assassinated, and the central-heating plant falls into the right hands.

In outline, these books are typical of many stories of the destruction of the earth and the escape of a utopian remnant of mankind to a new world. Of course the books contain a love story; personal jealousies, rivalries, and adventures furnish the narrative body with details.

A serial in *Amazing Stories,* A. Hyatt Verrill's "Beyond the Pole" (1926), describes a civilization on a warm Antarctic continent. It is a civilization of intelligent crustaceans that have, for the time, enslaved even more intelligent ants. The ants revolt, seize the power plants, and at the end of the story seem about to conquer the crustaceans.

The story is found in a cylinder attached to the leg of an albatross. It opens with a narrative of shipwreck; alone, the narrator climbs mountains beyond the South Pole; the land he finds warm, apparently from the warmth of a volcanic earth. He sleeps; when he awakes, an erect creature like a lobster eight feet high is standing by him. This creature flashes thought to him in a way that he later learns to be like that of radio: thought is sent out by the lobster's antennae. The narrator is taken in an airplane operated by an invisible force, not machinery, to the cemented-stone city of the crustaceans. There he finds a civilization based upon the use of metallic sulphur, which, like rubber, can be made a plastic of many forms and uses, and which, subjected to some disintegrating process, gives off light, heat, and power, especially from a great power house. Giant ants that once struggled with the crustaceans for dominance are kept captive. The lobsters are a product of evolution, now controlled; they hatch from eggs tended in a central depository; the young are trained for specialized tasks. For instance, without books, historians carry all records in their minds. Since everyone is conditioned to his special task and has no desires beyond it, there is no government. All the goods of the state are shared equally. The many uses of metallic sulphur have superseded all other machinery: boats, automobiles, and even wheels have long been discarded.

Meanwhile, the imprisoned ants escape, flee to an isolated section, prepare for military assault, and advance. The narrator does not see the outcome of the battle that breaks out, as he flees to an island, but he believes the ants will conquer the now peace-loving crustaceans.

This story is made up of various traditional materials, such as the warm polar regions, discovery of the narrator by a host who treats him kindly and takes care of him, the civilization of specialized insects as in Wells's *First Men in the Moon,* the destruction of all machinery except one wonderful kind of machine, and the socialistic organization.

Equally derived from many sources is Edgar Rice Burroughs's Tarzan of the Apes. As romances, moving pictures, newspaper strips, and "comic" books, the Tarzan yarns have been worldwide best-sellers for twenty years, perhaps because Tarzan is every teen-age boy's day-dream of himself. In original conception, Tarzan, son of Lord and Lady Greystoke, brought up by apes in an African jungle to be as strong as they are and as agile in the tree tops, and yet to master them because he has the mind of a naturally-educated man, is a variant upon the romance of pre-history. But in the constant stream of Tarzaniana that have poured from Burrough's pen, Tarzan has adventured in nearly every locale of scientific fiction.

Tarzan at the Earth's Core (1929) illustrates Burroughs's use of traditional material. The adventure takes place in Pellucidar, which, "as every schoolboy knows, is a world within a world, lying, as it does, upon the inner surface of the hollow sphere, which is the Earth." This conception of Pellucidar is based upon "a book written about 1830" and "another work of more recent time," that is, possibly upon Seaborn's *Symzonia* and Emerson's *The Smoky God.* In a previous romance (for *Tarzan at the Earth's Core* is plucked from an endless stream), David Innes had bored a mechanical prospector through the earth's surface, to emerge in Pellucidar. After various adventures, he had been captured by the Korsars. Radio messages had reached Jason Gridley in Tarzana, California, and Jason, before setting out to rescue David, sought the aid of Tarzan in the African jungles. In a zeppelin manufactured from a metal "as light as cork and stronger than steel," discovered by Tarzan in the Wiramwazi Mountains of Africa, the explorers set out for the inner world via the open North Pole. The typical phenomena described by earlier writers—the hoop of ice, the erratic behavior of the compass, the warmth of the polar regions—are observed on the journey.

Tarzan's adventure begins, however, when the airship has come to rest in a prehistoric jungle in Pellucidar. Tarzan swings off into the jungle, like the fearless lone-hunter that he is; when he fails to return, others go to look for him—Jason Gridley in an airplane that is soon felled by a flying reptile. The romance thus keeps three or four adventures going all at once, in alternating chapters. Each chapter is brought to a close with Tarzan or Jason in deadly peril; two or three chapters later, the peril is averted by daring and physical prowess.

The fact that the adventure is laid inside the earth has little significance. The apes of the internal world, who rescue Tarzan from a prehistoric tiger, speak "the primitive root language of created things," and therefore, the same language as the apes of Tarzan's jungle. Even the Snake Men, evolved from snakes into egg-laying, non-mammalian "men" with three-toed hands, reptilian skins, and two short horns, speak this language. Tarzan's own adventures include capture by a bird-reptile, a pteranodon, and escape; capture by the wild men of Clovi, and escape with Jana the Red Flower of Zoram; capture by the Snake Men, and discovery of his lost Waziri warriors who overcome the Snake Men; capture by the Korsars and release when the airship comes upon the ship of the Korsars. Jason Gridley's adventures are equally thrilling. Naturally, the airship, hovering over the city of the Korsars, forces the Korsars to release David Innes, and naturally Jana the Red Flower of Zoram is to come to the upper world with her lover Jason.

The book, like all the Tarzan books, is all excitement, hairbreadth escapes, scraps of evolutionary theory, slices of scrambled geology and paleontology, and fragments taken from the traditions of scientific fiction.

Another story making use of the traditional material is Ray Cummings's *The Girl in the Golden Atom* (1919). The central idea is that of O'Brien's "The Diamond Lens," plus some romantic adventures from Alice's Wonderland and Gulliver's Lilliput. In an opening like that of *The Time Machine*, a Chemist discusses with a group the relativity of space, which, says the Chemist, is both infinitely large and infinitely small: every atom is a solar system, and our solar system is but an atom of some larger universe. He then describes the production of a microscopic lens powerful enough to look into the atoms of a wedding ring. In an atom, he sees a girl and falls in love with her. With the aid of a drug that causes the cells of the body to reduce their bulk without changing their shape, he goes into the atom in the ring. There a war breaks out, and the Chemist, like Gulliver in Blefuscu, helps the friendly king defeat his enemy by taking a drug that makes him grow to giant size: he stamps down the forest in which enemy soldiers are hiding. Then he returns to his own world, but promises to return to the world of the atom and to the girl Lydia. He has been gone from earth only two days, for time is relative, too. This story is romance and fairy-tale, but its patter of scientific explanation makes it popularly acceptable in the twentieth century.

E. E. Smith and Lee H. Garby's "The Skylark of Space" (1928) was, when published, the pride and joy of *Amazing Stories* fans. This complicated serial is chiefly a story of intrigue, rivalry, and struggle that are only incidentally set in a background of astronomy, life on alien planets, and marvellous inventions.

Richard Seaton discovers X, a catalytic that releases the intra-atomic energy of copper; Reynolds Crane, a millionaire, helps him to build a space-flier. The Steel Trust, meanwhile, steals some of X and constructs a space-flier like Seaton's *Skylark*. Perkins, a super-criminal detective employed by Steel, abducts Margaret Spencer and Dorothy Vaneman, the former in posses-sion of damaging knowledge and the latter Seaton's sweetheart, and takes them into space. There the Steel Trust's space-flier is in danger of being drawn into a dead sun, but the *Skylark* locates the ship and draws it out; Perkins is killed. The *Skylark* goes on to many adventures, especially on Osnome, a planet inhabited by intelligent beings. Nalboon, Emperor of Mardon-dale, entertains the *Skylark* crew, but plots to secure the *Skylark* for war against an enemy nation, Kondal. The travellers escape to Kondal, and there Crane and Margaret and Seaton and Dorothy are married. Mardondale attacks Nalboon with an air-armada employing waves of unbearable light, sound, and heat; the *Skylark*, covered with impenetrable substances, destroys the armada in a fierce battle. The travellers receive court-honors and then depart for earth.

The story exhibits wonders in abundance. The force liberated by X supplies an irrestible pull toward its focus, apparently in infinity, and an irresistible repulsion; speeds of flight, then, are superior to the speed of light. A subsidiary invention is the object-compass, which remains focused on any object: it is used in tracing both a detective in Washington and a space-ship across interstellar space. The trial-flight of the *Skylark* is a one-hour jaunt around the moon. In space, the *Skylark* lands on very queer worlds; one world is full of platinum and prehistoric monsters and animated trees that fight animals with branches like spears. Another world is inhabited by people who are pure mind, but are able to materialize themselves and appear in any shape; for instance, one appears in the space-car, the double of Seaton, speaking English and aware of everything in Seaton's mind. These creatures say that men are very low in the scale, such as their world exhibited ten million years ago. The planet on which their final adventure takes place is inhabited by men of high intelligence and an advanced civilization, adorned in metallic collars, abundance of diamonds and rubies and other emblems of barbaric splendor—but no clothing. They have an electrical apparatus that, clamped on the head, immediately changes the convolutions of the brain to teach language; the religion is a mixture of science and theology: a belief in a First Cause whose supreme law is Darwinism.

Perhaps the notable quality of this story (as typical of many stories on the "amazing" level) is exaggeration. Space measured in light-years is crossed like crossing the street; the strange planets, ablaze with diamonds and gold, are inhabited by creatures who do not have man's limitations. And yet feeble man is hero and wins the great fight for Kondal.

But even exaggeration pales beside the grotesqueness of Otis A. Kline's *The Planet of Peril* (1929). In this story, a Dr. Morgan has conducted psychic research that enables him to exchange the personalities of inhabitants of various planets. Morgan transfers Robert Grandon to the body of Prince Thaddor of Venus; Thaddor is then in prison for aspiring to the hand of Princess Vernia. He (Thaddor-Grandon) escapes into a fern-forest with Vorn Vangel, Morgan's ally on Venus. Thaddor is surrounded by Uxpo warriors, the Fighting Traveks, but, defeating their captain in a duel with the scarbo (scimitar), he becomes their leader. Princess Vernia attacks Thaddor and the Uxpo warriors with ten thousand airmen in gyroscope cars. (There are counterplots at the capital during her absence.) Thaddor's men, fighting with torks (machine guns firing poison-gas bullets), are overwhelmed; Thaddor escapes, but saves the princess from an amphibian reptile. Thaddor and the princess are cast away at sea in the country of flying grampites, or vampires, who capture the princess and take her to their aerie in a volcano; Thaddor ventures through a lake of sulphur to rescue her, but in escaping in an airplane whose controls are strange, he lands in the Valley of the Sabits, six-legged burrowing creatures with armored skin.—The story goes on in this fashion through dozens of perils and miraculous escapes, till finally the princess is restored, and Thaddor (Grandon) is made emperor of Venus.

The story is filled with quasi-scientific material; unearthly beasts, space-ships, airplanes operated by psychic power, one-wheeled automobiles, underground men from whom evolution has removed eyes, and the like. In this fairy-story as grotesque as Irish legend, the "science" is mere excuse for wonders that are beyond explanation.

2. In Time

Herbert Best's *The Twenty-Fifth Hour* (1940) was published during the first year of World War II. Describing the breakdown of civilization over the world and the near-extinction of mankind, it foretells a course that the war could have taken. Troops of the United Nations reached Berlin before the Germans perfected their final rocket-bombs and the atomic bomb; otherwise perhaps either world-wide submission to the Nazis or disaster like that described in the novel would have been inevitable.

In the story, two scientific methods of destruction bring about the great collapse. First, defensive methods fail before the ever-increasing power of bombs to destroy the brain-centers of the modern state, the cities, and hence means of factory-production and distribution. Governments, social organizations, economic systems, and industry fall to pieces. Armies are left stranded, without food and supplies, communication with any central authority, or assurance that any homeland survives. These "torn remnants of armies, navies, air forces and even city mobs" become ruthless roving bands. "Westward, as far as the Atlantic, raged raping, looting, anarchy." Across the Atlantic, as the war spreads to America and becomes a national death-struggle, a second method of destruction wipes out populations: disease germs specially bred for virulence are loosed to kill all human life in the cities.

The story is told in terms of the experiences of Captain Hugh Fitzharding of England and Ann Shillito of Chicago. Soon after everything falls to pieces, Captain Fitzharding fights his way northward across Europe with his dwindling company of soldiers; they seize a chateau, kill the men, draw lots for the women, and fortify themselves to resist invaders.

As America is experiencing a severe economic upheaval just before entering the war, Geoff Shillito, condemned to die of tuberculosis, sails his small yacht to the Caribbean, and his sister Ann goes with him. They live idyllically for a while at St. John's island and then take up trading from island to island to increase their slender stores. While they are at sea, the bacteria come; they discover ports of the dead and return to St. John's. The dead lie everywhere; ships at sea wallow helplessly, without crews. For eight years, they live alone, cultivating a garden, raiding dead towns for canned goods. Geoff goes at last to Baltimore, but returns with news that he found no one alive. They sail for Europe.

Meanwhile, Captain Fitzharding's men have melted away; he has become, like men everywhere, a lone prowler, wandering from country to unknown country. Most men have died, too weakened by civilization to adapt themselves to barbarism. Life is "simple, bare-footed, skin-robed, fireless. Cannibalism was now the accepted mode of life." On the coast of Spain, Fitzharding sees Geoff Shillito come ashore for water and kills him. He boards the skiff, and with Ann sails on. They are repulsed at Gibraltar; black warriors with spears keep them off the coast of Africa.

Finally, however, they arrive at the Nile and attract an oar-driven navy of Egyptians; even though they plainly belong to the race of "animal men" of Europe, the Egyptians desire to copy the lines of their boat and learn to maneuver it, and so give them a home. In Egypt alone, a Mohammedan people is beginning civilization all over again.

In general outline, the book is a grim and serious analysis of what might have happened, and of what may happen if totally destructive warfare breaks again upon the world.

An older story, dealing with another grave, though more distant, danger of the Machine Age is Edward M. Forster's "The Machine Stops" (1928), a psychological and philosophical study of humanity in an age when the Machine has conquered. The Machine is self-operative, self-repairing; men, living each alone in a cell in the bowels of the earth, are served all the objects of desire at the touch of buttons; direct communication or direct experience of any kind is loathsome. Men communicate by radio-television; when they go from place to place (though all places are alike) they go in closed cabins of airplanes.

The life of Vashti, a woman of this distant future, consists of eating, sleeping, and listening to lectures and giving lectures, through the Machine. From her son (removed from her in childhood) she receives a call to visit him; he has a new, heretical idea. When she goes, reluctantly, he tells her a revolting story of his visit to the surface of the earth, where he had almost perished in the foulness of untreated fresh air. Was he reverting to some savage type, this son to whom she had taught the use of his stops and buttons? But he insists that there may be life outside the Machine, that "it has robbed us of the sense of space

and the sense of touch . . . paralyzed our bodies and our wills.
. . . We exist only as the blood corpuscles that course through
its arteries."

This story attacks trends in our own Machine Age, "those
funny old days, when men went for change of air instead of
changing the air in their rooms." Man had grown strong in
battle with "Night and day, wind and storm, tide and earthquake," but the Machine that gave man victory in this battle
also softened his muscles, made first-hand ideas horrible to him:
"Let your ideas be second-hand, and if possible tenth-hand, for
then they will be far removed from that disturbing element—
direct observation." Finally even God is only the Machine, whose
prophets describe the peace that passeth understanding, "to repeat certain numerals out of the Book of the Machine," and the
"ecstasy of touching a button, however unimportant, or of ring-
ing an electric bell, however superfluously."

Finally the Machine begins to break down: it fails to render
music perfectly, fails to supply drugs or euthanasia. Then it
stops. Men crowd from their tunnels in terror, touching one
another for the first time in ages; they fight in the darkness and
die like flies. Men, their bodies white pap, their minds the last
sloshy stirrings of a spirit that had reached toward the stars—
and achieved the Machine—perish. But a few remain, a few
savages on the surface who had refused to embrace civilization.

Sidney Fowler Wright's *The World Below* (1929) is likewise
a thoughtful romance of the future. But where Wells's time-
traveller had found civilization to go forward to the conquest of
nature, and then to decay in a long second-childhood of the
race, the time-traveller of *The World Below* finds that when
civilization rises to its height, catastrophic forces sweep it out
of existence, old forms of life disappear and new forms take their
places, in a never-ending cycle.

Danby is put into a room; the professor will send him through
time. After sleep, Danby wakes 300,000 years from now on a
smooth stone in the slow dawn of a sun larger and nearer to
earth; days are four times as long. The stone is beside a cliff
along which runs a path of polished stone. He watches a furred
creature, strangely human-looking, come running down the path;
the creature slips, and cabbage-trees reach out and grab the creature and drag it toward them. Danby manages to get the creature
away from the cabbage-trees, but the creature is dying. Danby
speaks, and the creature is shocked at the barbarous sound; it
converses without words. Danby observes the creature to have
arms and legs, but also tentacles below the knees; the eyes have
a human quality; the ears are protected by a flap; the mouth is

lipless, a slit; gills lie underneath cheek-pads; the tail is bifurcated, with paws at its ends. From the creature, Danby learns that it is an Amphibian, allied with the Dwellers and with them at war with the Killers. The Dwellers are giant men who live within the earth; the Killers are beasts who rule the surface of the earth, as Amphibians rule the sea. The creature entrusts Danby with a message and sends him on to meet other Amphibians. Crossing a chasm over an invisible bridge, Danby is attacked by frog-like animals; in a tunnel he is plucked by blood-sucking pink roots; he is captured by a Dweller, who puts him into a basket, but he escapes. He comes at last to the Amphibians, who are marching, singing a wordless song.

From them, Danby learns much. The Dwellers are the masters of the earth, the men. Advanced in science, they are now seeking to overcome the recurrent danger to all civilizations: "countless civilizations . . . had successively destroyed themselves by the misuse of their own discoveries," with a regularity that suggested a fundamental law. The Dwellers know of ancient men, "existing for a short period, too transient and too barbarous for the Dwellers to be likely to consider them worthy of any study. . . . They killed each other in many violent ways, and rewarded those who devised fresh methods for their own destruction. The stench of their diseases rose in the sky till the other planets protested." The Amphibians are going to rescue their leader from the Killers; Danby is sustained in the rapid pace by the nervous energy he receives from holding an Amphibian hand.

After a battle of wills—psychic forces that impede the body— the Amphibians drive the Killers from their arsenal and rescue their leader. Some of the Dwellers arrive, and they take Danby to their world underground. They go through tunnels in whose transparent walls samples of past civilizations are kept caged, alive. In a great room, the Dwellers talk with an animal stored with information, a book; when the animal dies, Danby learns, its brain is preserved as a record that may be read. The Dwellers ask Danby for information about the False-Skin Age—for the Dwellers wear no clothes. Danby is cleansed of diseases under a ray-machine and is put into a cage.

Danby does not understand all he sees any more than, says the author, a native of the English island of 500 B. C. could understand modern London. The world into which he goes is much farther removed from us in time than we are from 500 B. C. The logical assumption, says the book, is not that men simply increase, grow more and more, but that one particular species vanishes, and another vanishes, again and again, and life fulfils itself in ways that look upon our ways as barbarous.

The book is thoughtful romance built upon a theory of evolution in cycles.

Stanton Coblentz's "After 12,000 Years" (1929) is one of scores of stories of the future found in *Amazing Stories*. While the narrator is the subject of an experiment in suspended animation, the doctor is killed; the narrator wakes up in the year 12,201. Strange men appear, earless and toothless, and take him in a flying machine to a roofed-over city of mountainous towers. Streets are filled with a din of vehicles. The sleeper is thrown into a cell; he is fed capsules of food; doctors examine him in amazement, noting fingernails and hairs on his arms—traces of atavism. He is slowly taught the language, a corrupted English; he learns the social organization. There are four classes, the ruling Political-Financial class of wolf-faced people; the Intellectual, or large-headed; the Laboring, or small-headed; and the Military, stony-faced with small heads. These species are not allowed to intermarry, for the social ideal is that of the ant-hill, the specialization of each type for its duties. The sleeper is finally assigned to tend cages of insects. For many ages bacteria and insects have been used in warfare, as in the Bubonic War of the eighty-ninth century and the War of Malarial Germs, spread by mosquitoes, in the one hundred and fifteenth century. There are now three great nations, Panamica (Americas), A-uria (Eurasia), and Afalia (Africa). The A-urians, vengeful because Panamican engineers have altered the Gulf Stream, begin hostilities.

The sleeper, given lessons in patriotism by a phonograph, is sent to scatter termites by airplane over the enemy's country. He witnesses a battle in which warrior ants are used. Then fleas bring the Scarlet Death—and civilization crumbles. The sleeper comes back to Panamica to find the girl Luella and with her flees to Borneo, a "backward" place not engaged in the war.

Ray Cummings's *The Man Who Mastered Time* (1924) is an even more fantastic thriller of future wars. Loto Rogers, born in the atom of *The Girl in the Golden Atom* and its sequels, is a chemist experimenting on the time-factor in proton motion. He suddenly sees a man imprisoning a girl in a glass house. The scene is, of course, in the future. To rescue the girl, Loto invents a time-airplane. He travels past the rise of a mechanical civilization, an ice age, an invasion of earth from other planets, and finally to the year 28,300. He finds the girl Azeela, but is taken prisoner when the captor turns an electric paralyzer upon him. Loto's friends follow him in another time-airplane. A war is raging between the barbarians of the Noth and Arans of the Orleen country. The Arans are a luxury-loving class, served by the Bas. A third class is made up of scientists; Azeela's father is one of them. Toroh of the Noths time-travels through various civilizations to find strange weapons of attack, such as a whirling knife magnetized to find its prey and a magnetic machine that pulls down airplanes. When the Noths win, the scientists blow up both Arans and Noths and free the Bas. Then Azeela comes with Loto to the present world. On the level of the popular thriller, the story presents a basic pattern for the adventure in time.

Trips to the past are less frequent in scientific fiction from 1915 to the present. Sometimes romances tell the story told in H. G. Wells's "The Grisly Folk" (1921), describing the clash between the Neanderthal grisly men and the true men, penetrating Europe from the southward. Wells describes the Chellean giants of about 350,000 years ago, and then the ape-like Neanderthal sub-men who follow them, and then tells the story of Wauch and Click, true men of a tribe who trek northward into England and battle the Neanderthal sub-men.

John Taine's *Before the Dawn* (1934) provides a trip through time to that past when great reptiles were masters of the earth. "John Taine" is the pen-name of Eric Temple Bell, Professor of Mathematics at the California Institute of Technology, past-President of the Mathematical Association of America, and member of the National Academy of Science. His story concerns the evolutionary past revealed by biology, but it makes use of theories in mathematics and physics to bring this past into the present as if on a motion-picture screen.

The story is presented by the scientist Langtry, inventor of the "electronic analyser" that explores atoms and causes the light absorbed into them to re-portray the scenes upon which it fell eons ago. The device is cleverly and thoroughly rationalized: it "does for light what a phonograph does for sound . . . unweaves from the slightly modified atoms all the history of the light which, ages ago, robbed them of a few electrons." But it is clearly only a device to enable the author to paint a graphic moving-picture of the past.

The analyser is first used experimentally to date an archaeological specimen by measuring the light liberated from its atoms. Then engineers of the American Television Corporation study the chance flashes of scenes, scrambled pictures that materialize in the air, and learn how to project natural dramas into a great theatre.

As atoms of various specimens, including meteorites and fossils, are analyzed, vivid scenes from the prehistoric world appear. Great races of reptiles grow to maturity in a desert, struggle for survival, and perish before a plague of green flies. A great cold descends upon the earth; volcanoes burst out of the sea; animals flee from the Arctic southward over a narrow land-bridge, etc. The scientists follow the adventures of one group of great reptiles over several years and even feel a kind of pity as two of them, "Jezebel" and "Belshazzar," live out their lives of violence and futility, discover the principle of the lever to survive a little longer, and finally die. One hardly credits the fantastic invention that serves as means for this display, but the romance is a fine example of what science can do in providing colorful drama laid in the distant past.

3.   In Space-Time

The successor to H. G. Wells in the disciplined use of science for romance is Dr. Olaf Stapledon, lecturer in Liverpool University, England, on literature, industrial history, psychology, and philosophy, and author of various books on philosophical and ethical topics. Stapledon's romances deal not only with evolution, but with the new space-time revealed in twentieth-century mathematics and astronomy. His scientific imaginations are carefully worked out, but it is clear that he is not interested in them alone. He is concerned with the philosophic meaning that is expressed in them.

In *Last and First Men* (1930), Stapledon undertakes "to invent a story which may seem a possible, or at least not wholly impossible, account of the future of man." He believes that "controlled imagination in this sphere can be a very valuable exercise for minds bewildered about the present and its potentialities," for to romance of the future, with the imagination thus controlled, "is to attempt to see the human race in its cosmic setting, and to mould our hearts to entertain new values."

Last and First Men is the story of the human race from the present to the extinction of the eighteenth and last species of men on the planet Neptune, some 2,000,000,000 years in the future. The story is told by a member of the eighteenth species of men speaking through the mind of the author. This Eighteenth Man may be considered a symbol of the end as it influences, or ought to influence, the means. That is, the book offers symbolically an attempt to foresee the final goals toward which human life is moving. During this "brief music that is man," in the concert of the cosmos, the incessant downpour of generations exhibits many features that men today cannot understand even when the exterior is seen, any more than a cat in London can comprehend finance and literature. Stapledon's many variations of human life in this future explore the possibilities that lie in time and in the principle of evolution.

In the century after the World War of 1914-1918, there is a brief, tragic conflict between France and England; neither side wants war, but basic conflicts of temperament bring it about. The war is halted by an appeal to idealism: "The spirit of France and the spirit of England differ . . . but only as the eye differs from the hand. Without you, we should be barbarians. And without us, even the bright spirit of France would be but half expressed." But the collapse of a plane that carries bombs renews the war, till England and France are exhausted and in eclipse. Germany leads Europe until a Russo-German struggle brings collapse, and then the formation of a European confederacy. Then America is ascendant; through press, radio, moving picture, and televisor, it drenches the planet with the crassest pleasures of New York and the religious fervors of the Middle West. For a brief interval, a Chinese physicist presents a method for disintegrating the atom. It blasts a fleet of American planes coming to invade Europe, and then the Chinese, seeing the dangers in this invention, destroys his secret and kills himself. America continues to attack: poison gas floods Europe and leaves it a wasteland. Asia unites under China, and two rival cultures rule the world: American wealth, power, and activity, and Chinese pessimism, nostalgia, and passivity. When the dichotomy leads to war, Americans attack with bacteria that disintegrate the nervous system. The result, in the year 2400, is the formation of a World State with an American president and a Chinese vice-president.

Till the year 4000, the world is Americanized under a World Financial Directorate: Finance, Flying, Engineering, Surface Locomotion, Chemical Industry, and Professional Athletics. Science and religion are united in the worship of Divine Energy. The continents are artificialized; industry and agriculture interpenetrate; slender cruciform pylons three miles in height and half a mile in breadth are scattered over the earth uniformly; the Sahara is a lake-district of sun-proud resorts; the arctic regions are warmed by directed ocean currents. Man's normal life-span is two centuries; his amusements are, for instance, the dance of the airplanes.

Then earth's coal and oil, lavishly spent, are suddenly exhausted. Bacterial war breaks out, and with it the spread of the American madness. The dark age that follows lasts for a hundred thousand years. But civilization rises again, this time in Patagonia; windpower and water-power develop, and science re-discovers how to break up the atom for power. At the height of the new age, war

breaks out; in Patagonia mischief-makers begin the disintegration
of a mountain, and atomic contagion spreads. Mountains dance,
tidal waves mangle the coasts, the earth heaves and burns; and
when the steam subsides, twenty-eight men and seven women are
left alive in a region near the North Pole.

They settle in Siberia, except one man, two women, and two
monkeys, who settle in Labrador. Ten million years after the
Patagonian disaster, two varieties of the Second Men inhabit
the earth; of them the intelligent variety is gigantic in size,
hair-covered, long-lived (dying at two hundred or more). Their
mentality is esthetic and scientific: "Little children delighted
to hear how the poor things called Illusions were banished from
the Country of the Real, how one-dimensional Mr. Line woke up
in a two-dimensional world, and how a brave young tune slew
cacophonous beasts." As the generations of long-lived, eager
Second Men advance, their science attacks the twin problems of
Ideal Man and how to remake human nature. They approach
Utopia, till the Martian invaders come.

The Martians come as a cloud. On Mars, with its sparse
atmosphere, life developed from sub-vital dust as disparate floating
molecular organizations that finally became united by a neural
"radio." As man is made of specialized cells united by nerve-fluid,
Martians are made of cell-entities united by sensitivity to ethereal
vibration. The typical Martian organization is a cloudlet; systems
of cloudlets may unite into a larger Martian, and on up to the
group-mind of the planet. Martians come to earth as ultra-
microscopic units travelling on gravitational fields, and then collect
into cloud. They perceive no radiations from men and suppose
them unconscious machines controlled by the incoherent, but
doubtless sentient, radio stations. Men fight Martians with artificial
lightning for three hundred thousand years; but Martian units,
breathed into the body, create insanity, and before the Martians
depart men become like children for a dark age of thirty million
years.

Then the Third Men appear in the wilderness: brown-skinned,
golden-haired, cat-faced, with "six antennae of living steel" for
fingers and with hearing so developed that they may run through
a wood blindfolded. Civilizations rise utilizing wind, water, tidal
power, and the earth's internal heat. Biological control enables
them to breed specialized types for specialized work. They develop manipulative skills, especially in biology, manipulating even
the foetus and the germ-plasm to direct evolution. Finally they
create the Fourth Men, the Great Brains. The first of the Fourth
Men is a Great Brain in a ferro-concrete turret forty feet across.
Hundreds of servants bring him information and specimens: he

creates a detailed history of the world; he is a university of all languages, for instance, and even an artificially created language. Then when ten thousand of the Fourth Men are created, they annihilate the Third Men and use automatons. The Great Brains finally conduct research to determine the perfect man and create the Fifth Men—men to live for three thousand years each by a system of self-repair of all tissues. The brain capacity is twice that of the Second Men; they communicate by telepathy; the sixth finger is tipped into two minute fingers and a thumb. "The vast economic routine of the world-community is carried on by the mere touching of appropriate buttons." Yet, the arctic regions are left wild; dangerous animals, formerly annihilated, are reconstructed; and for vacation a Fifth Man spends a decade amid the dangers of the Arctic wild. For scores of millions of years, the Fifth Man develops "art, science, and philosophy, without ever repeating itself or falling into ennui," for "the higher a mind's development, the more it discovers in the universe to occupy it." They explore space in cars of artificial atoms, and time, the past eons of the earth. But the moon approaches the earth and will fall upon it. The Fifth Men destroy the semi-intelligent life of Venus and go to Venus, where the destruction of Venerian life, though a necessity, leaves the Fifth Men with a sense of guilt.

"Man's sojourn on Venus lasted somewhat longer than his whole career on the earth." Under the attack of bacteria on Venus, the Fifth Men sink into a dark age. The Sixth Men appear, after some millions of years; they are seal-like amphibians. The Seventh Men, developed from the Fifth along with the Sixth, are pygmies organized for flight through the air, with streamlined bodies covered with wool and fingers elongated to hold a flying membrane stretched from foot to finger-tip. The Seventh Men endure for a hundred million years, but so greatly enjoy the thrills of flight that they leave their industrial machines to cripples. After a war, the Seventh Men in despair commit suicide, flying into a volcano; from the cripples develop the Eighth Men. They go underground, utilize the planet's internal heat, and construct an engineer's paradise. But at the height of their development, they discover a luminous nebula on its way to the sun; it will make life on Venus unbearable. With atomic power to make Neptune habitable, they journey to Neptune.

The sun absorbs the nebula and doubles in size; Neptune becomes torrid except at the poles. During the long sojourn on Neptune, ten species of men develop one after another. The Sixteenth Men gain control of the movement of the planet and swing it into a temperate region. At last, the Eighteenth Men appear, with occipital eyes in addition to an astronomical eye on the crown of the head. They live in towers of translucent materials, high above the surface of Neptune; ordinary flight is by means of radiation belts; liners fly at great speeds; vessels a mile or more in length go regularly to other planets. Instead of books, minute tapes inserted into a pocket instrument set up "telepathic" vibrations. Men live for a quarter of a million terrestrial years, spending an adolescence of a thousand years in the Land of the Young, going through all the experiences of the race. The original two sexes have developed into many subsexes, and people live in sexual groups easily brought into telepathic unity to think as a single mind, each to share all the memory, temperament, and past experience of every other. At intervals, the Last Men think as a racial unit. Men even throw themselves backward in time to experience the life of the past and to influence that life—as the "real author" of this book does.

But the problem of mind in the cosmos has not yet been solved. Decay of the sun indicates that life in the solar system must end. It is impossible to propel Neptune to another solar system, but myriads of minute bodies of life, with definite evolutionary bias to develop toward men, are being propelled on electromagnetic wave-systems throughout the universe, perhaps to take root. "It is very good to have been man."

Stapledon's next book, *Last Men in London* (1932), a corollary to *Last and First Men,* presents the ferment of ideas in the modern mind as it is influenced by the astronomical view of man's destiny; that is, it presents the World War of 1914-1918 and its aftermath as seen through the eyes of a Neptunian Last Man, who, in turn, looks through and influences the mind of a citizen of the present, Paul. The Last Man in this book is a symbol for the objective intelligence of science, especially in the field of ethics. Its theme, says the author's Preface, is "man's struggle in this awkward age to master himself and to come to terms with the universe."

The story opens on Neptune. The Last Man enjoys a long holiday with a woman named Panther, flying and swimming; they dine on foods prepared by photo-synthesis and brought from the colonies on Uranus and on delicacies from their own orchards. They watch a five-mile-long food-ship from Uranus come to dock; and then they prepare for the experience of the Race Mind. For an interval, every person on Neptune is linked in direct telepathic communication, as the cells of a body may be linked in a single action. The Last Man tells something of himself and of Neptunian society. He describes his thousands of years of primitive experience as a youth, his scientific preparation for his life-work—the exploration of the past—and his manifold sexual, religious, and racial experiences. He describes work on Neptune: manufacture is routine performed by machinery, overseen by scientists. Men work creatively in science, in the arts, or in history. To enter the past, the Neptunian goes to an underground room in the Arctic and, after adjusting mind and temperament to an era of the past, enters a trance.

He awakes in an English child named Paul and in him grows up, chiefly observing, but now and then tentatively making suggestions to Paul. As Paul grows to manhood, the World War breaks out, a clash of nationalities as absurb to the Neptunian as for "a man to favor his left eye against his right." Many Neptunians, studying the past, influence men during the war: a statesman suddenly sees himself and his world and plans and ideas as through the mind of another person, perhaps on the other side of the conflict. These visions hinder single-minded destruction, but tend to enlarge the human at the expense of the animal. Paul is torn in an agony of conflicts, but finally gets into the war in the ambulance service.

After the war, there seems for a time hope that men will reconstruct their world intelligently, but the corrosive effect of frustration and guilt undermine any constructive program. Men become "less trustworthy, less firm . . . less rigorous in abstract thought . . . more avid of pleasures, more prone to heartlessness." Realization of the deterioration stimulates it. A friend of Paul's, also stirred by Neptunian thought, wonders whether man can make a new world with the existing human species, or whether it must be destroyed and another made. The Neptunian, aware that the dark age is coming and of the eons of rise and fall of species, returns to Neptune.

A third book, Stapledon's *Star Maker* (1937), is a sequel to *Last and First Men.* Its theme, however, is not merely the story of Man, but the story of Life and Mind in the Cosmos through all times, that is, within the circle of eternity. It seeks to suggest all possibilities in the infinite and eternal and finally to see these possibilities as they may appear to the Star Maker. Beginning in the here and now, it sweeps in a spiral through space, and then in another spiral through time, to reach finally the four-dimensional sphere of infinity-eternity. It seeks to offer an explanation for the mystery of life and space-time as the explanation may be surmised from biology, astronomy, and mathematics.

A narrator, in England, walks into an open field and looks upward at the stars and muses on them. As he muses, his imagination spirals out through the solar system, across inter-stellar space and through myriads of systems till finally it finds an Other World, the most similar in all the universe to this earth.

The Other World is a satiric picture of this one, strange enough to seem unreal, but like enough that absurdities there caricature absurdities here. The satire presents an aloof picture of how man's absurdities may look if seen through alien eyes. In the Other World, men are somewhat like men here, but they have spout-like mouths, equine nostrils, and strange senses, such as taste-buds on the feet and hands for sensing the flavors of metals, woods, and earths. In this world, not pigmentation, but racial odors determine antagonisms and persecutions, unless wealth may purchase for a sweet-smelling person in a salty nation an "honorary salting." A radio that directly stimulates brain-centers sends out not sound alone, but touch, taste, odor, sight, and sound; a man may retire to bed, with a radio-cap on his head, and live a richly stimulated life without ever moving; the Broadcasting Authority supplies doctors and nurses to attend to his bodily functions; pressure on a button provides electric massage to replace exercise. These features of the Other World satirize our prejudices and our reliance upon second-hand experience.

With him, to enlarge his perceptions, the narrator takes Bvalltu, his host in the Other World, to visit yet other worlds. As they travel from planet to planet, they inhabit the minds of hosts, who in turn join them, till finally the composite mind of the narrator is something like a cross-section of the Cosmic Mind. They visit many strange worlds, many manifestations of life evolving in alien ways. One world exhibits men with only one leg, one arm, and one nostril, but three eyes on the top of the head. One world exhibits "men" developed from a marine animal like a star-fish, the head developed from the feeler claw, the legs and arms from the four other claws; the mouth is in the middle; the nostril is used for speaking; the head bears five eyes. Another race reproduces by budding; parents conceive by breathing the pollen of the community, given off as a subtle perfume during periods of group emotion. Among the more highly developed races is a symbiotic race of paired ichthyoids and arachnoids—fish and shelled-spiders—a "spider" no bigger than a chimpanzee inhabiting a hollow behind the fish's ear. Exchange of endocrine products takes place. The fish are introvert, the spiders extravert, but the partners (except for brief periods for sexual matings) together develop the arts and sciences, electric power, and philosophy. Another world exhibits composite beings, avian creatures like sparrows that act with a flock-mind in a telepathy of "radio" waves that amounts to a single center of consciousness. There are plant-men, sleeping, rooted vegetables or trees by day, but active animals by night, roaming sometimes far from the detached roots.

In all the worlds visited, life struggles upward toward realization of some utopian dream, falls back, and struggles upward again. In many worlds, an adjusted socialism (perhaps democratic or dictatorial in political form), eugenic reproduction, biochemical control of life-processes, the use of sub-atomic power, and telepathy bring their inhabitants close to utopia.

Some worlds discover how to alter the orbit of a planet at will by firing sub-atomic rockets; for interstellar travel, sometimes taking thousands of years, a planet forms an artificial sun and takes it across the void. Some worlds, setting out to colonize "empty" space, end by attacking other worlds. Fleets maneuver among the stars to annihilate planetary systems. Highly developed worlds resist the robber-worlds with telepathic pressure, psychological penetration amounting to interplanetary fifth-column activity. At the end of the wars, the symbiotics (arachnoids and ichthyoids) are spread from world to world; crowded, they create their own worlds, hollow globes of concentric spheres enclosing air around the ocean at the center of the globe.

Following this utopian condition inhabitants of a world, meshed together in direct neural connection to form a world-mind, by telepathy interlock a galaxy into a single consciousness. Each conscious individual enjoys the sensory impressions of all the races in a system of worlds.

The multi-minded narrator then spirals through time to a period when stars surrounded by their rings of planets, natural and artificial, begin to explode. Search for an explanation leads to the discovery that stars have conscious life. The outer layers of a mature star are tissues of incandescent gases that live by intercepting the flood of energy from the star's heart. The outer layer is the "brain," receiving the faint stimuli of the star's cosmic environment. Impeded in their cosmic dance by the artificially created planets, the stars take the only revenge they know: they explode. Galactic-minds are finally able to enter into telepathic communication with the stars and to feel the "gentle titillations, strokings, pluckings, and scintillations that came to it from its galactic environment." The motor activity of a star, which seems to astronomers mechanical because they do not understand the psychological nature of the star, is its normal physical movement in relation to other stars. After telepathic communication is established, the stars are willing to be surrounded by their "vermin."

Speeding onward through time, the narrator sees the universe run down; stars, planets, or their inhabitants can do nothing to restrain the constant flow from high to low potential. Ranging backward and forward, the narrator observes the history of galaxies, from first awareness as nebulae, lentoid bodies compact with tingling currents, on to the end, when stars, inhabited by intelligent swarms of minute worms, glow only at their centers, and finally die.

In a supreme act of vision, the narrator views the birth of the cosmos. The Star Maker, brooding on a past not pleasing, is goaded by discontent into fresh experiment. The Spirit objectifies for Itself an atom of Its infinite potentiality:

"Then the Star Maker said, 'Let there be light.' And there was light.

"From all the coincident and punctual centers of power, light leapt and blazed. The cosmos exploded, actualizing its potentiality of space and time. The centers of power, like fragments of a bursting bomb, were hurled apart. But each one retained in itself, as a memory and a longing, the single spirit of the whole."

The Star Maker is "an effulgent star . . . the centre of a four-dimensional sphere whose curved surface was the three-dimensional cosmos." The Star Maker is in essence Creator, aloof, divine, and passionately intent upon His work of art. The narrator sees many universes, the Star Maker's experiments: at first, non-spatial, though physical; a musical universe, with creatures in a dimension of musical pitch; universes in humanly inconceivable dimensions; in some universes (as in ours) space expands; in others, it contracts. Our universe lies between the immature and the mature creations. In the mature creations, for instance, a creature sometimes has an active life in every temporal dimension; or again, for instance, a creature faced with several possible courses of action, takes them all, thereby creating many distinct temporal dimensions and distinct histories of the cosmos.

The Star Maker's ethic is the ethic of the artist: pain and destruction are necessary parts of the eternal harmony. He is ruthless, for "virtue in the creator is not the same as virtue in the creature. For the creator, if he should love his creature, would be loving only a part of himself; but the creature, praising the creator, praises an infinity beyond himself." From this vision the narrator awakes on a hill in England.

What can be said of Stapledon's imaginations? They are by no means idle ones. They are philosophical developments of ideas implied in biology, astronomy, and mathematics. The realities cannot be specifically as Stapledon has imagined them, for our knowledge of space and time is limited to a small area. But in the same way that analysis is superior to guesswork, Stapledon's fantasies are superior to simpler, more egocentric forms of prophecy.

Other writers of romances in space-time present either fragments of conceptions like those of Stapledon or purely fanciful stories. A fragment is Donald Wandrei's "The Red Brain" (1927), in *Weird Tales*. It is the end of the universe, and the dust of disintegration has blotted out all life except on Antares, whose inhabitants are sexless brains, liquid and formless; they live, protected from the dust, underneath a crystal dome. The great brains gather to think as one brain about how they might check the dust; such schemes as vacua-developers rooted on Betelgeuse have failed. Among them is a Red Brain, different from the others and felt to be a genius. It elongates itself, becomes tense with thought, and announces that it has a plan. As the other brains tune in to think its thoughts, it sends out thoughts of hate that kill them all. "The hope of the universe had lain with the Red Brain. And the Red Brain was mad."

Taylor L. Hansen's "The Prince of Liars" (1930), from *Amazing Stories,* is built upon the relativity of time. A stranger appears in the modern world who says that he is Gnostes, a Greek of the time of Pythagoras; he was captured by men of Allos and taken to that planet. He returns to earth at brief intervals to gather information for Allos, but ages of earth-time pass between his visits; within his normal life-time, he returns in the Middle Ages and again in the twentieth century. Men of Allos, he says, are developed from a creature like the fly, but they are large, plumed, and intelligent. Living far from their sun, men of Allos manufacture their own light and heat; they live in glass-roofed cities of metal towers; they converse by means of telepathy. Having mastered gravitational forces, they go from place to place in the universe to gather scientific information. In comparison with their slow-paced world (though there life seems normal), the earth speeds through time like a top.

Visions of the Star Maker are found even in short stories. Clifford Simak's "The Creator" (1935), in *Marvel Tales,* presents a grotesque fantasy of creation. The narrator and Scott Marston travel in a time machine to an unknown destination; they arrive in the laboratory of the Creator. The Creator is a pyramid of light; before Him is a bowl of pulsing matter. This, says the Creator to the earth men and to the other grotesque creatures from the universe, is the universe from which they have all come. The Creator says that He intends to destroy the universe, but He is thwarted by a sphere-headed, thin-limbed "walking stick man" from some alien planet, who turns upon the Creator a purple ray that transfixes Him. Then the creatures from the universe (including animal-like creatures and tentacled heads) decide to return to their worlds. The narrator and Marston get back only so far as the last days of the earth and find it inhabited by degenerated men, living in caves: "Earth's proud cities have fallen into mounds of dust," and the planet is swinging near the dying sun.

The idea of space-time is a relationship demonstrable only in mathematics. To use abstract formulas as plot-material for romances necessarily yields fantasy. This fantasy may be disciplined to produce such work as that of Stapledon, or it may be developed in an idle way.

B. *Utopias and Satires*

The Machine is in human life to stay. Recent utopias, therefore, picture a world of machines well used to relieve men of drudgery; satires picture man's slavery to the Machine in a Machine Age.

In general, utopias of the previous period, 1895-1914, stressed the evolution of man; human nature must be evolved into utopian human nature. Whether this change can be effected is an important question in utopian writing since 1915. A few utopias, especially H. G. Wells's *Men Like Gods,* express the faith that the social and psychological sciences may show the way toward self-directed evolution into Utopia. Satires that picture a world of the future lack this faith.

Wells's *Men Like Gods* (1923) makes use of space-time as a device for getting typical citizens of this world, and especially the author's eyepiece, Mr. Barnstaple, into the utopian world. Mr. Barnstaple is riding down the road in his automobile, bound for a vacation; with a snap, he is on a finer road through a sweeter countryside, in Utopia. As he learns later, two utopian scientists, experimenting to rotate a portion of their world into the F dimension, rotate it into our world, lying next theirs as two sheets of paper lie side by side. And yet it is clear that this Utopia is a symbol for our world after three thousand years.

Two other automobiles ride into Utopia, one containing a Conservative leader, the Secretary of State for War, a fine lady, a chauffeur, and a priest, and the other containing a playboy lord, a moving picture actress, and a chauffeur. Barnstaple, eyepiece for Wells, learns the principles of Utopia; the others react to it according to their natures and standards. Communication is at once established, for telepathy is common in Utopia—though some "words" are lost to some of the visitors, who have no information in their minds for comprehending what they "hear." They learn that there is no government in Utopia; anarchism is practical because everyone is interested in work; no one is antisocial.

The historical progress toward Utopia begins at a period like that of our nineteenth century, in "outbreaks of the scientific intelligence" manifested especially in the development of mechanical power; the first response of the general population is proliferation, following Malthusian principles to fill the earth to the limit of subsistence with two thousand million inhabitants. "Upon this festering, excessive mass of population disasters descended at last like wasps upon a heap of rotting fruit." Science is misused, commercialized, made a hunt for profitable patents in an Age of Confusion. Toward the climax of this age, as the earth seems slipping into a new dark age, the social and psychological sciences begin to develop. The result is control of population, not merely limitation, but discrimination among births to eliminate the dull, the idle, the defective, and the malignant, with the result that "The vast majority of Utopians are active, sanguine, inventive, receptive, and good-tempered." The population of the world is reduced to two hundred and fifty million men of almost a new kind: "beyond man toward a nobler humanity. They were becoming different in kind." There is no want and no inactivity; the old bases for competition are gone; the new bases are service and distinction.

The secret is chiefly that man has learned to control evolution. Evolution, as far as nature is concerned, is purposeless. Nature takes no heed of any standard of excellence. "She will lift us up to power and intelligence, or debase us to the mean feebleness of the rabbit" indiscriminately. But through control of evolution, man attains Utopia.

Men bring evils into this Utopia. They bring diseases, to which the Utopians have lost resistance. Men are isolated on a crag, where they foolishly, except Barnstaple, plan to seize control of the unarmed utopian world. The Utopians simply revolve the whole crag into a new dimension and then return it; the earthlings are, of course, completely cowed. Mr. Barnstaple, taking no part in the "rebellion," instead continues to view the utopian world, especially its scientific achievements. "In Utopia to make a novel discovery was to light an intellectual conflagration." Science, art, engineering, and history are the concern of all the people. Where science on earth has progressed for only two hundred years, with only a few hundred researchers in each generation, in Utopia: "We have gone on for three thousand years now, and a hundred million good brains have been put like grapes into the wine-press of science." To help in a new experiment in dimensions, Barnstaple is voluntarily revolved back into his world, to return from his vacation a healthier man.

The development of science to create utopia is the core of

Otfrid Von Hanstein's serial, "Utopia Island" (1931), in *Wonder Stories*. The narrative describes how the discovery of an Incan treasure enabled the German scientist Alesius to establish an experimental university on an island in the Pacific and then to kidnap willing scientists to conduct research. There is an intrigue for the treasure, but the conspirators are outwitted.

On the island is the city of Santa Scientia, founded to be the University of the World, to show how science may bring about utopia. To populate the island with others than scientists, Olympic games are held there with a hundred thousand selected guests besides the athletes. A beginning-utopian population is secured, along with recognition of the island as an independent nation by the League of Nations, pledged to protect it from all invasions. In Santa Scientia buildings are of steel and glass, with parks on their roofs; transportation is by cars in tubes propelled by compressed air and magnetism; the sumptuous hotels are nearly automatic in operation; pressure on buttons, for instance, brings in dinner. To typewrite, one dictates into a selenium cell, and a perfect typescript results; to read, one puts a scroll into a machine that reads aloud. Medicine extends the normal life-span to a hundred and thirty. The guarantee of the League of Nations enables the island to drop all secrecy and to become a research-laboratory, an experimental-station in utopia, for the world. This story is in the tradition of Verne, rather than Wells, but it indicates how ideas of the development of science to bring about a utopian world find expression in popular form.

James Hilton's *Lost Horizon* (1933) was one of the most popular utopias of the 1930's, as best-seller and as moving picture. Yet its appeal has been neither to the "intellectuals" who read Wells, nor to the "masses" who, perhaps, read *Wonder Stories,* but to the conservative middle classes—restless with frustration. The narrative is adventurous and sentimental; the utopia is singularly old-fashioned, a utopia found in an isolated place in Tibet, rather than either a utopia in the future or one to be brought about through scientific development.

Conway is kidnapped by airplane (along with others) and brought to Shangri-La, on the Tibetan plateau. In an isolated valley there a civilization, whose basic principle is moderation, is happy under the moderate control of a lamasery; the rule is a kind of gentleman's code, custom rather than law. The society is pastoral and idyllic, though secret emissaries go constantly to the outer world to learn of progress in science and invention. Such secrets have been mastered as the secret of longevity: the High Lama is nearly two hundred years old. Now about to die, the High Lama selects Conway as his successor and tells him of his duty to preserve in Shangri-La "our books and our music and our meditations, conserving the frail elegancies of a dying age," for a dark age, heralded by wars, is soon to descend upon the world. Under the rain of bombs, there will be not even flickering centers of culture; "there will be neither escape nor sanctuary, save such as are too secret to be found or too humble to be noticed." Shangri-La, both secret and humble, may preserve its records and its culture for "a new world stirring in the ruins." Science plays little part in this utopian retreat, except that all its benefits are treasured there, employed in moderation. The wide appeal of this sentimental romance of utopian escape is manifest in the late President Roosevelt's humorous use of "Shangri-La" to describe the base from which Doolittle's fliers attacked Tokyo, and later the location of the "Manhattan Project"; everybody understood immediately what he meant.

Chalmers Kearney's *Erone* (1943), published during the war, is likewise a sentimental piece of writing, but it has a more earnest core of social analysis and of practical suggestion for bringing about Utopia. The utopian plan, which is presented in the general story-pattern found in many older pieces, is based upon two theses: (1) that we have the economic, industrial, and scientific means to create a world of abundance for all, and lack only the will to discard the profit-motive that generates excess and want side by side; and (2) that spiritual rebirth leading to the application of Christian principles is necessary to bring about human happiness.

John Earthly, an engineer, "had a dream—a vision, if you like" that the scientists of Erone (Uranus) transported him to that planet and back again by means of a new invention, "the inter-planetary dissolution transmission and deposition of a living man." During his stay on Erone, Earthly is entertained by a host, Nitram Yeldir, professor in the University of Astroradio Scientific Research, and his daughter, Doreece. Of course, Earthly falls in love with Doreece, and marriage is prevented only because it is necessary for Earthly to return to earth at the outbreak of the war. Yeldir and Doreece exhibit their nearly perfect society, conduct Earthly through their cities and their mechanical wonders, and explain to him the economic and spiritual principles that underlie this happy state..

The Eronians make use of the advanced inventions of scientific fiction: three-dimensional television in color; tea-tables that roll in at the touch of a button; devices for focusing the heat of the sun; electrical processes for regulating plant-growth, and the like. The underground monorail system, on which Doreece serves as an engineer, is given detailed attention; the author is advocating a similar system for use on earth. The cities of Erone are metropolitan areas of flowered parkland around self-sufficient tower-communities—"the best of the New York skyscrapers . . . with ample space between each." In the center rises a gigantic domed tower, the combination Civic Center and Cathedral.

The economic system is a modified socialism. Everything, except such personal property as a separate home, furniture, and bicycles, belongs to the state; all men are expected to "do anything that might be necessary in the service of the state." Vast public works are in constant construction. The most honored people of Erone, Yeldir explains, are "a new aristocracy—the people who did things—engineers, scientists, architects." In return the state provides abundantly for everyone. Each year the National Bank gives each citizen a credit for about $5,000, an adult's share of the year's national dividend—"the sum total of all the national earning power." It is not necessary to use any part of this credit for ordinary needs: transportation and all public services, even food in restaurants, are free. All emergency needs are antici-pated: for example, if a couple about to marry desire to have their own home in the country, the state issues a credit sufficient to build the home and deducts the amount—without interest of any kind—from their credits over a period of fifty years. Earthly visits a captain of industry who presides over happy workers operating labor-saving devices in a vast factory; he visits the beautifully planned mill-community. Though this mill-manager is paid (or credited) for his work in additional shares of the national dividend, he is not allowed to accumulate money; any excess at the end of a year is canceled.

The Eronians are deeply religious. Earthly comes upon the President of the Council at worship in the Cathedral at the heart of the Civic Center. Moved by a deeply religious spirit, the Eronians worked out Utopia by applying Christian doctrine to all aspects of life: "We applied the laws of the Most High and formed humanity into one great family with equal rights and an equal share of the world's wealth . . . achieved true economics—the world-wide economy of Love."

Though this utopian romance goes no more profoundly than a Sunday-morning sermon into the means for bringing about the necessary spiritual rebirth, it reflects a thought with which more analytical writers are struggling today, that some revolution is needed in man's spirit, as well as in the fields of economics and application of scientific invention.

Robert Herrick's *Sometime* (1933) is a combination of utopia and satire. It begins as utopia, established chiefly as a point of view for satiric comment upon the modern world. The utopia is the world of a thousand years in the future, but its particular locality is a sunny lakeside city in the fertile Sahara. The old Xian (Christian) civilization was about to collapse anyway, especially through a series of wars in the twentieth century, but a new ice age that thrust glaciers down through Europe and North America and destroyed all society there brought about the great adjustment. The adjustment is eugenic control of population, the abolition of private property, the establishment of a world-state with few laws—an anarchy that depends upon good will—and education to change human nature. The motto of the new world is " 'Human nature as it may become' and 'Life as it may be,' with enormous variety, perpetual change, for thousands upon thousands of years yet to come." The Machine helped wreck the old society, but "The disease was deeper." The new society uses machines finer and more automatic than the old. The disease lay in the "animal kind of evolution with its wastes, cruelty and futility" as opposed to "ordered evolution." In the new world, the young march out to work, singing; they have remade the African desert into a garden. They have dropped prejudice and pruriency: all ages, sexes, and races bathe together naked; "the preposterous cult of virginity no longer had any repute in the modern world." Now humanity is no longer "teased and tortured by sex obsessions and repressions"; men may concentrate upon essential concerns. But parenthood is of intense concern to the state; people mate as they please, but only those approved by the most rigorous tests, physical and intellectual, may wear the gold-braided chiton of parenthood.

Cities are planned mazes of ivy-clad dwellings set in gardens. Automatic machines are everywhere: great air-liners bring the China mail; to operate a pleasure boat, one steps in and sets a dial. To read a book from the public library, one plugs in a switch, and it is read to him from a reel, or it may be thrown from microfilm upon a wall. Nearly everything is made of bright plastics. Life is long, but lethal temples offer refuge for those who wish to leave the world pleasantly.

Against this background, the present world-confusion is thrown. Professor Felix, historian and archaeologist, takes an exploring party to the ruins of New York, Washington, and Chicago. He comments upon the wastes of the robust individualism, the high-pressure industrialism, the complex legal system, and the vanished professions of soldiers, policemen, priests, lawyers, and private physicians, and the folly of the old architecture and the old monetary systems.

The hope for utopia, in *Sometime* and *Men Like Gods*, lies in directed evolution, especially the control of human nature.

But perhaps men will master the techniques for controlling human nature and then will use these techniques to create merely animal happiness, that is, contentment and stability. That is the conclusion of Aldous Huxley's *Brave New World* (1932). In this book, scientific technique enables men to hypnotize human nature and condition it to any mould desired, and the desired mould is a world whose motto is Community, Identity, Stability.

This satire pictures the world of A. F. (After Ford) 632. It opens in the Central London Hatchery and Conditioning Center, where human ova, fertilized in test-tubes, are treated to produce five grades of human beings: Alphas (highest in intelligence), Betas, Gammas, Deltas, and semi-moron Epsilons. The Bokanovsky process for breaking up an embryo into as many as seventeen thousand identical twins, socially predestined human beings, makes it possible for the first time in history to "really know where you are." After decanting (being born from bottles), babies are predestined and conditioned: Epsilon embryos, for instance, destined for labor in the tropics, are put in hot tunnels alternated with cold; hard rays add discomfort to coldness; they are bred to thrive on heat, to dislike cold. Babies destined to be workers are given books and flowers, and then frightened and electrically shocked: "What man has joined, nature is powerless to put asunder." Hypnopaedia, through speakers under the children's pillows, makes Gammas, for instance, glad they are Gammas; they do not have to work as hard as Betas, and they are not stupid like Deltas.

They have no inhibitions; largely sterile, or taught "Malthusian drill" in contraception, children are encouraged in erotic play; men and women love as casually as they attend the movies; only viviparous birth is obscene.

The new world-order came into being after the Nine Years' War that began in A. F. 141 and was fought to economic and social collapse with airplanes and disease germs. There was a choice then between World Control and stability, or barbarism. The Controllers were successful when they turned to ectogenesis, neo-Pavlovian conditioning, hypnopaedia, and a campaign against the past. In the new world, life is full of pleasure; even the old men copulate, harmlessly; there is no leisure from pleasure, and if time yawns, there is soma, a drug with all the virtues of Christianity and alcohol and none of their disadvantages: "half a gramme for a half-holiday, a gramme for a week-end, two grammes for a trip to the gorgeous East," without pains to return for "scampering from feely to feely, from girl to pneumatic girl, from Electro-magnetic golf course to" other mechanical pleasures. Machines are everywhere: individual helicopters, rocket planes for crossing the Atlantic, the feelies (talking moving pictures in three-dimensional technicolor, with electrical apparatus for "feeling," and accompanied by symphonies in odor), monorail trains, state euthanasia, and crematoriums that recover the minerals from the body. A hotel room is laid out with: "Liquid air, television, vibro-vacuum massage, radio, boiling caffeine solution, hot contraceptives, and eight different kinds of scent," and a notice announces Escalator-Squash-Racquet courts and an Obstacle and Electro-Magnetic golf course.

Bernard Marx, who had somehow got too much alcohol in his blood-surrogate when he was an embryo, is discontented. He goes to a religious service, in Solidarity: the loving-cup of strawberry-ice-cream-soma is passed around, and the liturgical refrain is sung:

> "Orgy-porgy, Ford and fun,
>   Kiss the girls and make them One.
> Boys at one with girls at peace;
>   Orgy-porgy gives release."

But it does not give release to Marx's discontent. He goes with beautiful Lenina to America and shocks that exemplary female because he wants to talk a little before going to bed. In America, they visit a reservation for savages and there meet Mr. Savage, brought up on Shakespeare. Mr. Savage is brought back to London. His sense of humanity is outraged; he is furious at a feely; Lenina comes into his room and strips, and he rages; he tries to incite factory-Deltas to revolt, but police quell the disturbance by unrolling Anti-Riot Speech Number Two (Medium Strength). Mr. Savage is taken to a Controller, who explains to him why the world has had to choose stability. Not all men can be Alphas; it has been tried on an experimental island, with throat-cutting results. Factories must be run, and "An Alpha-decanted, Alpha-conditioned man would go mad if he had to do Epsilon Semi-Moron work—go mad, or start smashing things up." Science is not at a standstill, but it is controlled; inventions are filed in the patent-office and held there, for every "discovery in pure science is potentially subversive." The Controller says, "I'm interested in truth. I like science. But truth's a menace, science is a public danger. As dangerous as it's been beneficent. It has given us the stablest equilibrium in history." But it could also bring on something worse than the Nine Years' War. Mr. Savage ends by killing himself.

Brave New World thus accepts the postulate of *Men Like Gods* that human nature may be changed, but raises the problem of the direction that change must take; in a Machine Age, can it be changed to yield an Alpha-plus democracy (or even anarchy of men-of-good-will), or would the self-determination of Alpha-plus minds end in aggressions to be stopped only by a change toward Community, Identity, Stability?

Another answer to this question than the suppression of science and the proliferation of sub-normal human types is offered in *Useless Hands* (1926), by Claude Farrère (*pseud*. for Charles Bargone). This satire says that, with the multiplication of automatic machines, hands to run them become unnecessary. Owners may solve the problem of the unemployed by destroying the unemployed.

In 199— James F. MacHead Vohr, "wheat king" and head of the American Siturgic Monopoly, is dictator of the Western Hemisphere, dependent upon him for all its bread. From a magnificent palace he directs the activities of 360,000 workers in the "Blocks," a city of steel skyscrapers divided into neat, tiled, electrically served apartments, all alike. The workers are well fed and well clothed, but the monotony of their work de-humanizes them: "Easy work it was, all mechanical . . . Open or shut a regulator; lift a water-gate or lower it; start a grinder running; slow it up, accelerate it, stop it; regulate the rotation of a screw, modify the circulation of a multiplier; . . ."

All life is conditioned by machinery: "Machines of child-training, of education, of teaching; birth-machines, nursing machines, training machines, directing, correcting and perfecting machines, an arsenal of adapting machines: machines of apprenticeship; machines of feeding; wheat machines, meat machines, preserve machines; dressers, builders, fitters; machines of euphony and euphory; perfume machines, harmony machines . . . euthanasian machines, last of all!" In this world, a workman of broad intelligence retrogresses; an artisan becomes a day laborer; a day laborer, an animal.

The workers rebel against the monotony of their life and begin wrecking machines. Vohr reasons that the fittest should survive, and the Machine is fittest. Therefore Vohr turns upon the workers a ray that disintegrates them; from his tower a scientist dissolves 360,000 men.

The message of these satires is that the stumbling block between us and Utopia is human nature and the frames of thought and feeling most comfortable to the ego. The development of science has provided the materials for a utopian world, but men in control of these materials, for one thing, view concentrated wealth with pride. Huxley's *Brave New World* of aggressive Alphas and factory-Deltas is hard to wave aside. On the other hand, as we enter the Atomic Age, rebuild Europe, and scatter our cluttered cities, we have an opportunity to replace outworn frames. The effort to speed this result is the most important aim of serious scientific fiction.

C. *The Wonderful Adventure*

1. The Wonderful Invention

Every kind of scientific fiction since 1915 is filled with wonderful machines and inventions. But some stories are primarily concerned with a wonderful invention and its use.

Bernhard Kellermann's *The Tunnel* (1915) describes the building of a railroad tunnel under the Atlantic ocean from New York to Biscaya, Spain, a co-operative enterprise of the governments of Europe and the United States. A successful tunnel, of course, has been driven from the continent to England. But engineer Mac Allan's dream of a tunnel through the bed rock of the Atlantic is not easily realized. Finally, when a financial giant, Lloyd, contributes his millions, boring starts from Spain and from New York; thousands of men are employed in the grinding toil and heat; a fire breaks out; volcanic explosions occur; mobs stone and kill Allan's wife. But after twenty-four years, the first train, stream-lined to go 295 kilometres a hour, makes the trip in twenty-four hours.

The idea in this novel is developed in Gawain Edward's *The Earth Tube* (1929). Romance, adventure, and world-struggle are added to give the story action. Unaccountable earthquakes disturb South America; scientists conclude that a tunnel is being constructed from Asia to South America through the center of the earth. They suppose some sinister purpose, but they cannot get government officials to credit their theories. Finally the eastern end of the tunnel is found near Buenos Ayres. Asiatics have used an indestructible metal to construct the tunnel; through it they have used gravity to transport men and machines for the conquest of the Americas. The chief machines are tanks of the impenetrable metal undulal; their drive to conquer the Western Hemisphere cannot be stopped by ordinary means. As a last resort, King Henderson secretly enters the Asiatic stronghold; he is captured and condemned to death, but he escapes, with the secret that liquid air can destroy undulal—and the story ends with the defeat of the Asiatics.

These two stories indicate two stages in the development of scientific fiction: first, the conception of a marvellous invention, and then the narration of a series of world-shaking events (and private heroisms) that grow out of the invention. The trend, it is to be observed, is toward the historic romance.

Sir Arthur Conan Doyle's "The Disintegration Machine" (1929) describes a fantastic invention that is, likewise, prominent in such fiction as, for instance, *Useless Hands*. Doyle's belligerent scientist, Professor Challenger, is invited to witness the invention of Theodore Nemor, a machine for dispersing the molecules of any substance placed between its poles, and then, miraculously enough, reassembling them when the current is reversed. Challenger is sceptical until Nemor disintegrates (and re-integrates) Challenger's friend Malone. Then Nemor makes the mistake of boasting that his machine can disintegrate battleships coming between poles placed on separate ships; officials, unquestionably Russian, were seen idling in the lobby. Challenger pretends scepticism and has Nemor get into the machine to be himself disintegrated. When Nemor has disappeared, Challenger destroys the machine and thus saves the British Empire.

An even more wonderful invention is described in Edmond Hamilton's "The Metal Giants" (1926), from *Weird Tales*. The scientist Detmold learns how to construct a brain of metal and to give it consciousness by passing T-waves through it. After still further experimentation, Detmold gives it not only arms, animated by magnets from the thought-currents of the brain, but also self-sufficient power of thought; the brain can think because of internal atomic changes rather than any waves passed into it from outside. Finally it surpasses all expectations, thinking with acuteness to solve scientific problems. Detmold goes away for a brief while, and then the brain undertakes its own development; it constructs metal giants three hundred feet high, without brains but animated from the metal brain by remote control; these giants attack and destroy a town and are setting out for conquest of the world when Detmold returns, grasps the situation, constructs a great metal wheel, and rides down the tiny brain in the center before the encircling metal giants can stop him. The giants, of course, collapse when their central brain is smashed, but in falling they crush Detmold.

The idea of the "Metal Giants" is expanded and complicated in Eando Binder's "Adam Link's Vengeance" (1941). Adam Link, the first metal man constructed by Jack Link, is lonesome; he seeks to commit suicide by disconnecting the wires that keep him conscious and by having clockwork then drip acid onto his iridium-sponge brain. A sinister scientist, Hillory, frustrates this plan, re-connects Adam's neural system, and (remembering Frankenstein's monster) suggests that Adam needs a mate. With Hillory's help, Adam creates a metal woman, Eve, and has Kay

Link, Jack's sister, educate her by a system of electrical thought-transference. Eve's mind, therefore, becomes a feminine mind. She and Adam love one another. Then Hillory shows his hand; by a trick, he gets Adam and Eve to adjust metal helmets over their heads, and when they have done so, their motor-impulses are remote-controlled by Hillory's mind from a metal helmet he wears. Hillory will use them to gain power. He sends Eve out to rob and murder. Adam writhes in agony of conscience, but when Kay comes to see him, he has to tell her nothing is wrong because Hillory controls his organs of speech. Kay senses, however, that something is wrong and privately disconnects the metal helmet. Adam attacks Hillory; Eve, directed by Hillory, attacks Adam. Adam is hurled over a cliff, but he repairs his broken body and attacks again, this time to kill Hillory and, unavoidably, Eve. Now that Eve is dead, Adam again meditates suicide.

Invention of a marvelous kind of television forms the basis for an exciting narrative of love, danger, and struggle for control of the world, in George McLociard's "Television Hill" (1931), from *Amazing Stories*. Tom McManus, newspaper reporter, is invited by Cyrus King and Bob Wentworth, scientist-inventors, to observe the uses of a new kind of television. Power rays are projected any desired distance from sending towers; at the end of their path, the rays pick up images and return them along the sending rays to the receiving apparatus at the station; the images are then transmitted to an instantaneously sensitive screen. The result is that from Television Hill any event in the world, on its surface or under it, may be witnessed.

McManus films news-reels of events in all parts of the world, as they happen; telegraph service informs him, for instance, of a disaster in South America; television "picks up" the disaster as it is occurring; McManus photographs the result and has local news-reels available within a few moments. This monopoly is profitable. Meanwhile, McManus falls in love with Diane, King's daughter just returned from five years in Europe. Then suddenly a block of the South American coast is cut off; directing mechanisms will not focus on it; the scientists discover sabotage in their apparatus. It is finally discovered that a group of schemers, belonging to a secret organization seven million strong, also has this kind of television. These schemers plan to use it to conquer the world. They offer to include McManus, King and Wentworth in their organization, and when the inventors refuse, an artificial cyclone is sent to destroy Television Hill; rays stop the Cyclone, but bolts of lightning and mysterious fires finally destroy Television Hill. McManus flees with Diane—whom he discovers to be not Diane, but her double and a member of the conspirators, now in love and therefore repentant of her share in the destruction. The sinister scientists of the conspirators are left in control of great powers not yet used.

This thriller is filled with detailed description of the principles of operation employed in various machines; the principles sound reasonable, but they depend upon chemical action that is not explained, such as that of the liquid that reacts to television rays like photographic film, but almost instantaneously changes back to the unexposed state, and hence presents a series of pictures in motion. Other items in the story typical of scientific fiction are the scoffing at the scoffers (for anything is possible to science), the belief that this invention will alter the course of human history, the fondness for gigantic, polished machines, and the employment of a love-and-spy plot.

The invention in Gardner Hunting's *The Vicarion* (1926) is even more marvellous. Radley Brainard perfects the vicarion; it reproduces scenes from any point in the past, present or future, as a moving-picture machine reproduces pictures, but in three dimensions, with color, sound, scent, and even heat. The invention is based upon the impression events make upon the ether, and then upon a method for tuning to the right etheric vibration and condensing the ether-held impression of the event; this condensed impression, held in a bomb, can be released within a stated space, where the events themselves seem to take place. Events are not confused (though there must be thousands in any given portion of ether), for every event has its own wavelength. A single event may be recorded and reproduced over and over.

When the vicarion is made public, it creates first a sensation, and then chaos; naturally it wrecks the motion-picture business; governments try to prohibit it, for it reveals scandalous events in the private lives of judges and senators. Theatres for the vicarion spread. It records battles of the past, the Paris mob of 1792, the Battle of the Marne, the Confederates' yell at Antietam, the interior of a Russian prison. The world becomes demoralized, unable to concentrate on the present because of its fascination with the past. Secrets are revealed. "A notorious dive at a nearby beach suddenly closed its doors, after one scene from its parlors was shown in the prosecuting attorney's office." Buyers see into sellers' accounts; heirs look at wills that lie secretly hidden in strong boxes. Finally, so great is the chaos, a mob storms Brainard's house; he makes a speech to the mob, but the mob breaks in anyway. The flesh-and-blood Brainard is himself in the mob, and the appearance that the mob attacks is the image of himself as Brainard rehearsed it weeks ago. But the vicarion has to go; the raw realities of life are more than the nerves of mankind can stand.

In these ways, the machines foreseen by Jules Verne and largely realized in the twentieth century have been replaced by increasingly fantastic ones, especially in the fiction of the magazines.

2. The Wonderful Discovery

Physiological discoveries form the basis for numerous stories since 1915.

John Taine's *The Iron Star* (1930) describes the discovery of a ray that causes the human body to degenerate in the direction of the apes. This ray is an emanation from an iron-like substance found in a meteor that fell in central Africa. To destroy this baleful substance, scientists use X-rays that initiate atomic disintegration.

A strangely brutish man named Swain, formerly a missionary to Africa, visits Dr. Colton in Chicago for a diagnosis. Colton can find nothing wrong known to medical science, but he notes the thickening of certain bones, the growth of hair on Swain's body where hair does not normally grow. Leaving Colton's office, Swain rushes with animal-like eagerness to his rooms, throws open a suitcase empty except for an iron-like tack, takes a deep breath and is satisfied. Reappearing on the streets, he swings through trees in a park, steals bananas from a fruit stand and eats them whole, etc.

To solve the mystery that he knows is somehow connected with Swain's African life, Colton and the physicists Big Tom and Little Tom Blake go to Africa, taking X-ray apparatus; Swain goes as a "guide." Through a complex series of adventures that lead into central Africa, the party following Swain (who has committed a robbery and fled) comes to caves in which Swain and his native carriers have disappeared. Ape-like creatures led by a giant leader block their path, then fight among themselves until all are killed except the "Captain." The caverns are found to contain strange drawings of meteorites, and an extremely heavy metal that gives off emanations that cause a kind of drunkenness. Swain is killed in an overflow of water from a lake.

The "Captain" brings his wounded arm to be treated by Dr. Colton, who discovers that the "ape" is a degenerated man; henceforth the Captain, though brutish and inarticulate, serves as their guide and protector. The scientists proceed through the jungle, past a glade where a carved iron face stares at the sky, and finally, through many dangers, to a shrine of the heavy metal, out-cropping from the ground. The Captain indicates that the metal must be destroyed.

The scientists reason out the mystery: the metal, which they name "asterium," must be part of an exceedingly dense star that fell as a meteor long ago; pieces of its ore protrude over a large area; causing drunkenness, it was worshipped as a god by the natives, but it causes degeneration. The rays destroy mineral matter in human tissues, especially in the glands, altering the chemical composition of their excretions. The Captain was formerly a white man, who retains enough reason to know that the substance must be destroyed. They reason that a substance so dense and radioactive may be easily disintegrated and so, in spite of drunkenness near the ore, play X-rays upon it. "The X-ray waves were short enough to start the atoms of that dense element and their hard little cores jumping about . . . some of the nuclei got a real sweep to their oscillations, and burst clean out of their shells—the rings of electrons spinning about them like stars round a sun."

Lightning springs from the mass; all flee in time to escape a tremendous explosion; storms rage and the earth shakes as atoms explode throughout the widespread ore. Days later, when the train of fire reaches a mountain containing the ores, an explosion kills the Captain. After they are back in Chicago, a manuscript left by Swain reveals further details. The Captain had been a man named MacKay who had associated with Swain; Swain had wished to cure himself of his terrible addiction, but had so far deteriorated that he could not take the final step of revealing the full secret to Dr. Colton.

This well-rationalized romance is typical of the best scientific fiction written for no other purpose than to entertain. The scientific discoveries form a core for the story of African adventure.

On the other hand, the physiological discovery in Aldous Huxley's *After Many a Summer Dies the Swan* (1939) is incidental, though it is used to form an ironic climax. Most of this realistic and bitter novel is divided between satiric attack upon the American millionaire art-collector and gross Philistine, Mr. Stoyte, and philosophic discussion by the mystic, Mr. Propter. But an interwoven thread of the story concerns the effort of Dr. Sigmund Obispo, Stoyte's private physician, to discover the secret of longevity—an effort liberally supported by the aging Stoyte, who is terrified at the idea of dying. Obispo's researches center on the intestinal flora of the carp, a fish that lives for centuries. Jeremy Pordage, employed to read and catalog the Hauberk Papers for Stoyte, comes upon a diary written by the Fifth Earl of Gonister, who sought longevity by chopping up and eating the intestines of freshly killed carp, lived an active life for past a hundred years, committed an obscene sexual crime at that age, gave out that he was dead, substituted a body, and then retired into a great cellar.

After various events, this thread of the story comes to a climax when Obispo and Stoyte invade the underground rooms of the Hauberk family and find there the Fifth Earl alive, just over two hundred and one years old. But unfortunately he has degenerated into an ape-like creature grown over with red hairs, unable even to talk—a "foetal ape." This, reasons Obispo, is "one of the mechanisms of evolution . . . The older an anthropoid, the stupider." Horrified at the grotesque "success" of their journey, Stoyte none the less wants to know how long it might take for the degeneration to set in.

For the story "In the Abyss," H. G. Wells had rationalized from the theory of evolution to describe the discovery of verte-brated bipeds at the bottom of the ocean. Sir Arthur Conan Doyle's *The Maracot Deep* (1929) makes more use of materials from mythology. Explorers discover not only the Lost Atlantis, but men living there, on the bottom of the ocean, in a roofed-over city. Enormous pressures are explained away, rather than ex-plained, and even the devil makes an appearance.

Dr. Maracot, an eccentric scientist, organizes an expedition to explore the floor of the ocean on a plateau around a deep called Maracot Deep, because formerly discovered by Maracot. The scientists in the expedition, besides Maracot, are the engineer Bill Scanlan and the zoologist Cyrus Headley, the narrator of the major portion of the story. Exploration is to be in a steel sphere thick enough to withstand great pressures. When the ship *Stratford* reaches the proper point, the sphere is let down to the shelf of the plateau, 1800 feet; there a giant lobster-like animal attacks the sphere and nips the connecting cables. The sphere rolls off the plateau into the Deep and settles 30,000 feet down. The ocean floor is illuminated by phosphorescent light created from the decay of the droppings of sea animals; the explorers see the roofs and towers of buildings, covered with curiously Phoenician inscriptions; pressures seem not to be great in spite of the depth. Then suddenly a man in a transparent envelope appears beside the compartment, which is opened to allow him to enter. He furnishes the scientists with glass-like air-filled coverings for their bodies and leads them into an enclosed city, which they later discover to have a population of several thousand.

The city is lighted by fluorescent electric light. The explorers are given comfortable beds to sleep on, and then coffee, hot milk, rolls, fish, and honey. After they have rested, the explorers are

led into a room where, by concentrating their thoughts, they
reflect what they wish to convey in an image on a screen. The
Atlantans (for such are these people) have gone far beyond
other men in science; they have mastered etheric vibration, and
thought expressed on the screen is an application of etheric
vibration—a mechanical telepathy. Headley at sight falls unaccountably in love with Mona, daughter of one of their hosts, and
she with him. From day to day, they learn more of Atlantis:
air is manufactured in a pump that circulates it through the
city; food is made of chemicals poured into machines and treated
with heat, pressure, and electricity, so that "flour, tea, coffee, or
wine was collected as the product."

The explorers are shown the history of Atlantis; a prophet,
Wanda, who was also a scientist, foresaw in a trance the coming
of the deluge and the sinking of Atlantis. Therefore, in spite of
jeers, he constructed a water-tight roof over a portion of the
city, prepared the machinery for pumping air, and stored away
supplies. Chosen people are saved in the city when the waters
rise amidst the bursting of volcanoes. This occurred eight
thousand years ago. Science, following the leads established by
Wanda, has advanced to use intra-atomic power. The Atlantans,
however, do not have radio, and they are interested when Scanlan
manufactures a radio that picks up programs from London. The
explorers venture outside the city in their glass-like protectors,
and explore the ruins of a temple to the Lord of the Dark Face,
Baal-Seepa. In the midst of the temple, they come upon this devil,
clothed in black tights. For the desecration of his temple, he
threatens to destroy Atlantis, and a few days later materializes in
the assembly hall. Nothing is effective against him until Dr.
Maracot springs upon the dais and commands him to cower, and
the devil vanishes in a pool of putrescence. Dr. Maracot reveals
that the spirit of Wanda came to him in a trance and gave him
power over the devil. It is also revealed that Headley and Mona,
unaccountably love-stricken, are re-incarnations of people who
lived in old Atlantis and were there lovers.

Meanwhile, the London radio furnishes information that a ship
is looking for traces of the explorers; the explorers and Mona
have themselves fitted with glass bells in which they rise to the
surface and are rescued.

T. S. Stribling's "The Green Splotches" (1920), from *Adventure* magazine, describes a discovery in a South American valley
in which the natives say the devil himself resides. The DeLong
Geographical Expedition finds, at the entrance to the valley, clean-
picked skeletons of animals and a man, arranged in a row to
illustrate evolution. A guide fires a gun and runs; at the point

where he disappears, the men find green splotches that analysis shows to be chlorophyll. Standifer meets a strangely intelligent Indian who gives him gold; the next morning Standifer's hair is white and there is a running sore on his leg; apparently the gold carried in his pocket is radium-irradiated. Then an "Indian" appears with a lump of pure radium; he has the ability to read anyone's mind and to speak English. He comes, he says, from a land called One; in his land his name is 1753-12,657,109-654-3, but he may be called Mr. Three. His nation lives in the radium age, he says, after having passed through a steel age, an aluminum age, and a uranium age; the men of One use molecular energy. The stranger looks with amusement on a game of chess; he has never seen the game before, but he defeats the expert Demetriovich in ten moves. He then describes "Cube," the chess-game of One, played in the mind (without a tangible board) with 256 pieces moving in three dimensions. It becomes apparent that Mr. Three is inhabiting the strangely changed skin of the guide that disappeared; he is handcuffed and shackled, but a few minutes later handcuffs and the guide's skin are found in the tent, and the copper-colored Mr. Three sits smiling on a boulder nearby. Electric shocks paralyze a man who seeks to shoot Mr. Three. Mr. Three answers questions: he is one of a group of scientists from One who have come to earth to collect specimens, and he wants the man Pablo as a specimen. Mr. Three uses electric shocks to drive the whole group to an "aluminum zeppelin" in the valley, Pablo is taken on board, and the "zeppelin" rises at such speed that it turns all the colors of the spectrum in succession, as they watch it disappear. The explorers conclude that the craft is from the Planet Jupiter; the strange powers may be due to the fact that Jovian blood, shown in green splotches, is chlorophyll, capable of converting solar radiation directly into energy. Dr. DeLong is awarded the Nobel Prize for his discovery.

These two romances, *The Maracot Deep* and "The Green Splotches," are typical of the more fantastic among the discoveries described in scientific fiction since 1915. Many other stories of discovery concern efforts of a mad inventor to rule the world.

Murray Leinster's stories, "The Storm that Had to Be Stopped" (1930) and "The Man Who Put Out the Sun" (1930), from *Argosy*, describe the efforts of Preston to make himself world-dictator. Preston discovers a way to cut off heat-rays from the sun; the atmosphere over an area affected by his rays absorbs all the sun's heat; the earth below freezes, the warmed atmosphere rises, and a terrific storm results. Operating from a broadcasting station on an island, Preston demands that the world capitulate; the storm increases in violence; soon Arctic cold will sweep down upon Europe and America. But finally the use of tanks and bombs enables the scientist Schaaf and police-inspector Hines to destroy Preston's apparatus, though Preston escapes.

In the sequel, Preston operates from another island to cut off all light from the sun. He sends Hertzian waves into the Heaviside layer to give it an electric field opaque to light. He again sends out demands that he be made Emperor of the Earth, but again Schaaf and Hines reach his stronghold and, in spite of Preston's attack with freezing rays, overpower him. The army and navy then bombard the island, destroy it, and restore light to the world. But the secrets Preston discovered are, finally, of benefit to the world; power to replace coal and petroleum may now be drawn directly from the sun.

3.   The Wonderful Event

Wonderful events are often, of course, dependent upon wonderful inventions and discoveries, and no clear line of division can be drawn between them. Stories that are chiefly interested in what happens because of the invention or discovery may be classified as stories of wonderful events.

The wonderful discovery in Philip Wylie's *The Gladiator* (1930) is like that of Wells's *Food of the Gods,* except that it yields gigantic strength of nerve and sinew, rather than size; but the theme is that of *The Invisible Man,* that a person with extraordinary powers is a solitary and outcast man, doomed to failure in all the plans suggested by his advantage.

Abednego Danner, professor of biology in Colorado, discovers a method for impregnating the embryo of animals with chemical substances that give nerves and tissues the hardness and strength of steel. He experiments with tadpoles that break open their tank and with a cat that becomes as strong as a lion. Then, as his wife is with child, he gives her an opiate and injects chemicals into her body to strengthen the child. When the boy, Hugo, is born, he shows symptoms of great strength, but as he hurts those he plays with, he is taught to suppress his strength as an evil thing and to play alone. In college, he enables a weak football team to play an unbeatable game, until in a moment of forgetting to hold himself in, he kills an opponent. He works for a while as a strong man in a circus. He tries love, but frightens the girl Charlotte, who loves him but finds him abnormal and leaves him. When the war breaks out in 1914, he enlists in the foreign legion; bullets and bayonets barely scratch his skin; he wipes out whole batteries single-handed. Just as he is about to put into execution a plan to capture the German high command and the Kaiser, the armistice is signed. He works on a farm; he is caught up by radicals agitating for the freedom of prisoners but he is disillusioned to find that the radicals really do not want the prisoners freed—as Hugo could free them. He drifts into South America, where the archaeologist Hardin, learning Hugo's secret, dreams of creating a race like Hugo, to clean up the miserable world and start afresh with a utopian people.

Underlying this romance of adventure is a psychological study of the strong man in a world of weaklings and especially of Hugo's sense of frustration and his failure to find adjustment anywhere. When the boy Hugo is attacked by a farmer's boy, he fights reluctantly, but finally enraged, hurls the boy over the spectators' heads, with the result that the town turns against him: ministers pray over him, doctors examine him and prescribe medicines to weaken him, and he is scolded and nagged by everyone, for instance, the blacksmith, whom Hugo could easily tie into a knot. Everywhere around him lie great deeds to be done, but people do not want great deeds done; humanity prefers "protecting its diseases, its pettiness, its miserable convictions and conventions, with the essence of itself—life. Life not misty and fecund for the future, but life clawing at the dollar in the hour, the security of platitudes . . . the needs of skin, belly, and womb."

Hearing his story with sympathy and imagination, the scientist Hardin dreams of a race of Titans: "You are the beginning of the new. We begin with a thousand of you. . . . You produce your own arts and industries and ideas. . . . Then—slowly— . . . Conquer and stamp out all these things to which you and I and all men of intelligence object." Going alone to a mountain peak to think over this dream, Hugo is struck by lightning and killed.

To some extent, *The Gladiator* illustrates the statement in the introduction to this chapter, that a new phenomenon in serious scientific fiction since 1914 is the exploration of psychological, moral, and ethical problems. Hugo Danner's injection stimulated bone and flesh. Other romances present the superman of stimulated mind. If we cannot easily find an injection that will stimulate the mind and heart to higher functioning, at least we can imagine the birth of a genius and study his reactions to our common life, his struggles to throw off its clogs, and his glorious, inevitable failure that leaves a little sediment of new wine in the common cup.

Before he abandoned the "game" of "cataclysmal fantasies," H. G. Wells had suggested this thesis in *The Food of the Gods*. He repeated it in *Star-Begotten* (1937). Mr. Joseph Davis finds both himself and his wife disturbed by strangely lucid question-ings of established ideas. The fancy strikes him that perhaps cosmic rays are affecting himself and his wife; perhaps, he reasons, supermen of Mars are bombarding the earth with rays that will cause evolutionary mutations into a finer type. Exceptional figures have appeared in history, "Confucius, Buddha; men with strange memories, men with uncanny mathematical gifts, men with unaccountable intuitions. Mostly they have been persons in advance of their times, as we say, and out of step with their times." Perhaps Martians, bombarding earthly men with rays that affect the tissues of the mind and heart, are bringing into existence a clearer-headed, simpler, and intellectually more powerful kind of man. The world is heading for world-wide war, "floating on a raft of rotting ideas . . . an accumulation of once-sustaining institutions, customs, moral codes, loyalties, sapping one another . . . a vast accumulation of drift-wood—floating debris." Perhaps the world after the smash-up will be a saner world, when star-begotten human beings take control: "What *would* a world of human beings that had, as Davis put it, *gone sane* be like?"

Olaf Stapledon's *Odd John* (1936) is a romance concerned with this new man—or superman. Stapledon's cosmic romances presented the story of mankind, and then of the universe, chiefly to "mould our hearts to entertain new values"—new social and ethical values suggested by the longest possible range of view, the greatest possible emergence from the shell of self, here, and now. *Odd John* tells the story of a boy who is born with a mind that immediately apprehends these values, judges human ideas and behavior in their scale, seeks to collect the few like-minded of the world around him to establish Utopia, and is crushed by the weight of a hostile mankind.

The book is a detailed psychological study, a biography of John Wainwright, born after a foetal period of eleven months to the brilliant physician Thomas Wainwright, and Pax, his wife, of deep, still feeling. John develops slowly, but learns with rapidity and insight when his mind ripens so that he can apprehend a subject at all. He immediately perceives the inadequacies in ordinary conclusions. For instance, given an abacus a short while after he learns to talk, he rapidly learns to count, ponders, and then comments that the numbering system is not a good one because it counts in tens, rather than in twelves. Shortly afterward, he amazes mathematicians from the University by discussing with them relativity and curved space as if he "has *seen* it all already for himself."

As John grows up, he comes to feel it his mission to "advance the spirit" on this planet, either "by taking charge of the com-

mon species and teaching it to bring out the best in itself, or
. . . by founding a finer human type of my own." To get money
for his project, the boy invents labor-saving devices, markets
them, and, learning finance, uses the money to accumulate more.
He studies his own emotions, then world-institutions, movements,
and ideas, learning rapidly, reaching new conclusions. For example, cutting through the accretions of myth and ritual, he
analyzes the Church as an institution in feeble touch with a
great truth—truth perceived darkly through a glass twisted by emotional and intellectual egoisms and the inability of the human
mind to visualize the Spirit. "How splendid it might be," he
comments, "if only they could keep from wanting their God to
be human." He perceives that science has brought man to the
place where he somehow must be more intelligent than he ordinarily is, for "Mechanical power, you see, is indeed vitally
necessary to the full development of the human spirit, but to
the sub-human spirit [ordinary man] it is lethal."

Foreseeing a disastrous world war, John turns his back upon
the "bloody awful species" of ordinary-man and sets out to
preserve the best achievements of the spirit in some utopian
retreat, whence he and a few like-minded others may rebuild
after the debacle. To harden himself and come to grips with
his own spirit, he goes alone and naked into the winter wilderness of Scotland; there he not only struggles with nature's ele-
mental furies, but so concentrates upon the development of
mental power that he is able to establish telepathic communication with others of his kind scattered through the world. After
the ordeal, he seeks them out, guided by pictures in their minds
that flash into his own. In a small boat driven by atomic power,
accompanied only by the narrator (his ordinary-human biographer), John visits France, Egypt, India, China, etc., and picks
up strange young supernormals. In Egypt, John communes with
Adlan, who had lived for 384 years but has been dead for
thirty-five; Adlan had learned to explore the past and the future,
and in an exploration of the future meets John's mind. Adlan
teaches John how to explore the future telepathically. A blind
Tibetan monk, Langatse, refuses to join the group because he
wishes to continue to praise the Spirit in religious meditation,
but he agrees to guide the colony by telepathy.

The supernormals are highly differentiated individuals; for
instance, Jelli of Hungary, a girl with a head that looks like
a croquet mallet, has the power to distinguish colors and forms
imperceptible to normal eyes; and Sigrid of Sweden has the
power to comb out tangled minds, somewhat as a psychoanalyst
might do clumsily through consultation.

They go to an island in the South Seas and establish homes, a meeting house for telepathic conferences and for worship, and laboratories. Deriving power from atomic disintegration of radioactive elements, their experiments are of many kinds; for instance, they manipulate the embryo to stabilize a superior human type. After a brief period of happiness, they see into the future and realize that the nations of the world will not let them live. Discovery comes, and the navies pounce upon them. Though they have atomic power that would enable them to destroy their enemies, they know they would have to fight the entire world to preserve their integrity, and "When we had finished the great slaughter, should we be any longer fit mentally for our real work, for the founding of a finer species, and for worship? No!" So John sends his biographer away, and as a shipload of armed men approach the island on December 15, 1933, something happens: the whole island sinks into the sea.

No summary can do justice to *Odd John*: it is a detailed psychological study of the supernormal mind in a world of normal hates, prejudices, selfish moralities, and stupid maladjustments. Stapledon's subtitle reads, "A Story Between Jest and Earnest." The story, let us say, is a jest; but the attempt is earnest enough to grapple with the problem of human inadequacy and to show that the wisest and most spiritually intuitive in human thought is everywhere impeded by the worst and finally overwhelmed.

Stapledon's *Sirius* (1944) is another effort to see human nature from the point of view of an objective intelligence. Where Voltaire, in "Micromegas," had brought an inhabitant of the stars to earth to view man objectively and make a few observations, Stapledon undertakes to look at man critically, keenly, and in detail from underneath. The exceptional and non-human mind is placed in the brain of a dog. The dog Sirius retains his canine senses, both those superior to man's (particularly his olfactory powers) and those inferior (particularly his dim, color-blind eyesight). Though loving human beings with dog-like affection, and occasionally hating with wolfish rage, Sirius is sufficiently outside humanity to observe man objectively.

The story of Sirius is narrated as a biography by Robert, who is in love with Plaxy Trelone, the dog's closest human affinity. Thomas Trelone, a scientist at Cambridge University experiments with the introduction of a hormone into the blood stream of a mother to increase the bulk of the cerebral cortices and refine the nerve-fibres in the unborn young. His experiments produce big-headed mice, guinea pigs, and rabbits, all quick at finding their way through mazes, but all sickly; later experiments produce superior sheep-dogs that prove very helpful to Welsh farmers. Then Sirius is born, apparently the most helpless of a litter; Sirius develops slowly, at the same rate as a human being. Trelone brings up Sirius along with his little girl, Plaxy; Sirius's intelligence seems at least equal to Plaxy's. As Plaxy learns to talk, so does Sirius, though his desperately practised speech is limited by inadequate vocal organs: "no outsider would suspect his strange noises of being any human language at all."

The most desperate conflict in Sirius, studied with careful pity in the record of his growth, is that "between what he later called his 'wolf-nature' and his compassionate civilized mentality." As he grows up, his love-life is that of a dog; he is carried away by the odors of bitches, but after the heat, he finds the bitches stupid; the puppies that he fathers are not supernormal, and he has no interest in them. Impeded by weak eyesight and the lack of hands, Sirius learns to read and write. He has difficulty distinguishing C, G, D, and O, and the like, but he perseveres; he writes with a special glove for his paw, equipped with a penholder. Both his awareness of the human ranges that lie beyond him and his proximity to the canine make Sirius all the more eager to grow in mind and spirit; he studies poetry and music, learning to sing in a voice extremely sensitive to tune; he reads history, science, and the Bible, "though vast tracts of literature meant nothing to him, save as verbal music, because his subconscious naure had not the necessary human texture to respond to them emotionally, nor had he the necessary associations in his experience."

Trelone talks frequently with Sirius, seeking to meet his mentality on a common ground; Sirius understands, though sometimes Trelone's grave reasoning seems a little less than the ultimate wisdom. Sirius's extra-human sense of smell and the queer way he sees shapes give him unusual powers; for instance, no matter what people may pretend, certain overtones of odor define their emotional states, even meanings deeper than they can express. Since most people suppose him "only an animal," they indulge in unprintable vulgarities and obscenities in his presence. "What roused his contempt was their proneness to insincerity," for he has no inhibitions about mere obscenities.

Sirius, directed by Trelone, serves an apprenticeship as a sheepdog for a Welsh farmer, concealing for the time his most remarkable powers. Then he is taken to Cambridge to study and be studied. He observes intellectuals and feels contempt for their limitations, such as their neglect of powers he would have given a paw to possess. For instance, they undervalue their hands:

"Many of them, in fact all but the surgeons, sculptors, painters, and research workers, were wretchedly clumsy with their hands, and by no means ashamed of it." Artisans, he finds, are even considered vulgar because they work with their hands, "the most glorious human organ, the very instrument of creation." Providing material for research papers in psychology, Sirius writes a pair of them himself: "The Lamp-Post" and "Beyond the Lamp-Post." His sense of smell tells him that even the big-shot scientists, presumably dedicated to the search for truth alone, are often little men inside, "itching for personal success, for the limelight, or (worse) scheming to push someone else out of the limelight, or make someone in it look foolish or ugly." He finds them obtuse about everything that is not human, incapable of realizing imaginatively any other kind of spirit.

Sirius discovers religion. Its forms make no sense to him, but the odors of a Cathedral service are a seductive reek. "Washed in the Blood of the Lamb" softly sung resolves for the time his "haunting conflict between pity and blood-lust. . . . His guilt [he had killed a ram and a pony] was washed away." Life in the laboratory becomes stultifying to Sirius, even though he is allowed to roam through Cambridge and is supplied a series of sleek bitches.

Sirius goes to London and observes the life of the dock yards and the curious class-conscious disunity among mankind; men mistreat not only dogs, but one another. He goes to work for a cruel man who resents his intelligence and finally attempts to shoot him; in a rage, Sirius kills the man. Sirius is shielded by Trelone. Then the war breaks out, and during a bombing raid, Trelone is killed by falling masonry. Terrified, Sirius wanders back to Plaxy and lives alone with her. Rumors that Plaxy is living in sin with a man-dog cause outbreaks of violence. When Plaxy is conscripted for war service, Sirius becomes a hunted creature, an outlaw. Maddened to frenzy by hardship, loneliness, and a series of indignities, Sirius kills a man and eats part of him. There is no place in man's world for him: "I could only be at home in a sort of Alice-in-Wonderland world." Sirius is discovered and killed, suffering, as Plaxy meditates, "something that is common to all awakening spirits on earth, and in the farthest galaxies."

Now that description of ever-larger machines and ever-widening cosmic horizons is becoming trite in scientific fiction, these books by Stapledon show that the whole field of psychological, social, ethical, and philosophical interests may be thoughtfully treated and made graphic in romances.

An adventure on an island where evolution has created extraordinary forms of life is narrated in S. Fowler Wright's *The Island of Captain Sparrow* (1928). Charlton Foyle, after interfering between a captain and a mutinous crew, is put adrift in the North Pacific. He comes to an island of towering granite and enters its bowl-like interior through a tunnel. There he discovers the descendants of the pirate band of Captain Sparrow on one end of the island, a forest between, and a priest-like race of white men isolated from Europe for ages, on the other. In the forest live men with horns, hairy bodies, and hooves. Though the degenerate pirates hunt and eat these "animals," they have also interbred with them, so that some of the pirates have hooves or horns. For centuries the original inhabitants on the other end of the island kept their number to eighty by sacrifice of the oldest or weakest member whenever a healthy child was born. This custom strengthened the race, in spite of inbreeding, but the pirates brought diseases, and the race is flickering out. Only a priest, his wife, and a child are left, and they are dying. Domesticated birds the size of ostriches, but older in the evolutionary scale, perform agricultural work for the priest. After a number of adventures, including a love affair with a wild girl who has escaped the pirates, Foyle finds himself at last alone on the island with the girl and the child of the isolated race; the pirates have fled; the priest and his wife are dead. Because the island is something like a paradise, they remain on it.

The "science" in the book uses the terms of biology, though the results sound more like mythology.

George Allan England's *The Golden Blight* (1916), though perhaps equally fantastic, is a blast against war, particularly capitalism as a source of war. A scientist who is also a radical, John Storm, discovers a Zeta-ray that alters the molecular structure of gold to crumble it into ash; the ray may be manipulated to be effective over any area. In agony because of the war and other injustices wrought by capitalists, Storm calls upon Murchison, the richest man in the world, to order that the world disarm. When he refuses, Storm destroys all gold in the Wall Street area. Panic follows, and assassins seek to kill Storm. But he escapes and then methodically destroys all the gold in Europe and America. Meanwhile, Braunschweig, a German financier, cannily supposes that, when the effects of the ray wear off, the gold-ash will revert to gold; he collects all the ash in the world. It does return to gold in the presence of Braunschweig and other capitalists, but in doing so generates heat so intense that they are all killed. By this time, the people of the world are so disillusioned that they set up an international socialism. The gold is left where Braunschweig had piled it.

The romance, though full of excitement, is also propaganda; it quotes arguments from economists, altruists, and socialists, using material from such writers as Bernard Shaw, Zola, and Ruskin, and such books as Kirkpatrick's *War, What For?* Storm's demands are single-minded and vehement: "Just this: International Disarmament, the Abolition of War, World-Peace. . . . War must cease. You understand me? *War must cease!*" War is "a big killing game for profits—the wholesale murder of the working-class in defense of the interests of the ruling class." When gold is destroyed, the first results are world-delirium: "hundreds of thousands clamoring, yelling, fighting, even bleeding in the frightful violence of that terrorized struggle for news." But the Socialists remain calm and take control. Storm modestly declines all credit for the utopian condition that follows: "Not I! Science has worked this miracle; and by her hand she shall yet bring mankind to perfect knowledge, perfect light!"

Karel Capek, whose drama *R. U. R.* added the word *robot* to the languages of the world, also wrote *The Absolute at Large* (1927), a loosely organized narrative, without a central character, of the destruction that overwhelms civilization when the unchecked spirit of the Absolute is released through the discreation of imprisoning matter. In 1943 an engineer, Marek, invents a Karburator to utilize atomic energy by burning up the atom. In early experiments, curious results are noted. Matter yields energy and disappears, but there is something left behind that fills men with religious fervor. Marek says it is God. "What is left behind is pure God. A chemical nullity which acts with monstrous energy. Being immaterial, it is not subject to the laws of matter."

The Karburator, of course, replaces machines operated by steam, electricity, or other sources of power. The result is very queer: people love their neighbors, but insist that their neighbors adopt their religion; banks give away money to the poor; people see visions; everyone becomes fanatically religious. Religious wars break out over the world and are fought to a frenzied finish. As the last battle is raging among thirteen armies of one individual each, the effects of the released Absolute wear off and order is gradually restored. Police hunt out dens where pre-war Karburators are kept and where dissolute people still congregate for religious orgies.

A similar picture of world-wide disaster is drawn in F. Wright Moxley's *Red Snow* (1930). On August 17, 1935, a purple cloud dims the brilliance of the sun; from it falls a flaky precipitate that drifts through all solid objects and sinks into human flesh; no human being escapes. It causes an itching sensation, but no other immediate inconvenience; then scientists discover that it has made everyone sterile. No children not already conceived will ever be born. Ten months after the "snow" falls, the last child is born. The romance traces the disintegration of society under the realization that the race of man is doomed. At first there is prosperity; people spend wildly because there is no need to save. Then religious crusades break into wars fought with airplanes, cannons, bombs, capsules of deadly gas, and disease bacteria. All labor quits work; all means of transportation break down; animals multiply over the earth. Steadily, ever accelerated by wars, world-population declines. At the end of the book, the last man alive, Preston, is taken into a chariot by a strange being that is not a man.

In *The Absolute at Large* and *Red Snow* at least half the world-wide misery is due to man's irrational behavior. In R. C. Sherriff's *The Hopkins Manuscript* (1939) men face a cosmic disaster, with orderly courage, but when the "disaster" turns out to be a blessing in disguise, human nature brings on a war that destroys Europe.

In large part, *The Hopkins Manuscript* is a psychological study of how a commonplace Englishman faces disaster. The "manuscript" is discovered 1000 years from now by the scientists of the Royal Society of Abyssinia; it is treasured as a historical document that throws some light upon the "dead civilizations of Western Europe." Written by Edgar Hopkins during his last days, it tells the story of his life during the year that preceded the fall of the moon into the Atlantic Ocean, during the lunar disaster, and during his brief stay in London while the disorganized nations of Europe were overrun by the armies of the East.

Edgar Hopkins, a retired schoolmaster, lives in the suburban village of Beadle, and his chief interests in life are his prize chickens, his garden, and his satisfactory housekeeper; his social life consists of membership in the amateur British Lunar Society. At a meeting in the summer of 1945, the President reveals that the moon is steadily falling and will strike the earth on the third of May, 1946. Members of the Society are asked to keep this matter secret till science and the governments of the earth can work out a way to meet the disaster. With difficulty Hopkins guards his tremendous secret till finally the governments have worked out a plan, and the ministers of the Church are chosen to announce the approach of the moon. Reactions in the village of Beadle are various, from the truculence of the doctor and the violence of the saloon-keeper to the quiet courage of the impecunious aristocrat, Colonel Parker.

As the moon grows visibly larger, an army engineer arrives

to direct the building of an underground shelter. There is a fine spirit in the English village; cricket matches are organized for moonlit nights. Then the hurricanes come.

On the fatal night, Hopkins decides not to enter the dugout, but, like Colonel Parker, to stay in his own home to face whatever death may come. He sees the sky become wild with a blood-streaked fury; through the dust-clouds, the heavens pant "like the shattered lung of a dying giant." There is a roar of waters; part of the house collapses. For a while, air is splashed from the earth. Hopkins falls to the floor, bleeding at the ears.

In the morning, the valley is flooded with mud; a steamship lies on its side in the garden; an earthquake has ripped open the dugout. Colonel Parker's house collapsed upon him, and only Parker's children, Robin and Pat, seem to be alive. Gradually, however, as they reconstruct their lives around an economy that includes no electric lights, they become aware of other people who survived in other places. They learn from an aviator sent out by the government that the moon fell into the Atlantic and (as a cavernous body) collapsed; it bridges Europe and America.

A ten-year plan of reconstruction gets started. Electric lights come back; towns are planned and built according to utopian visions. Hopkins is happier than ever before in his life. Then explorers discover gold, coal, and iron on the moon. England needs a corridor to the sea, below Spain, and the only corridor possible would cut the continent of Europe off from the moon. The nations snarl; fanatic leaders arise; ideas of a confederated Europe and a sharing of the new wealth are scorned by truculent dictators. A confused war breaks out, every nation fighting for itself. This war drains all resources, all the young men; reconstruction is stopped; the trains stop running. Hopkins hears that armies of Selim the Persian are overrunning Europe, and Europe, divided, cannot face Selim. Society falls to pieces in England; only a few roving bands, here and there, inhabit London. There are no young. Hopkins ends his manuscript, and Abyssinian scientists find it in the wilderness-ruins of ancient London a thousand years later.

The message of the book—for it seems more than mere entertainment—is that mankind can stand disaster, even almost annihilation, so long as men stand together, but animosities, nationalisms, and passions bring about disaster even greater than that of the fall of the moon.

These stories are typical of the wonderful events described in scientific fiction in recent years. Perhaps a climax of the wonderful is reached in such a story as John Russell Fearn's "The

Blue Infinity" (1935), from *Astounding Stories*. It narrates how science gains such control of the forces of nature that men are able not only to take the earth on a trip across the universe and through its shell into another one and back again, but also to repair an injury to the sun.

A wandering star rips open the corona of the sun with the disastrous effect that, through the gap, electrical forces play upon the earth, destroy Australia, and threaten to destroy the earth. But Eunice Banks, daughter of the astronomer Rodney Banks, has inherited secrets in the control of astronomical forces. She proposes to take the earth away from the dangerous sun and to transport it to Alpha Centauri to become a planet there. She has a machine to send out waves neutralizing the gravitation holding the earth to the sun; another machine can concentrate gravitational force to triple the attraction between the earth and Alpha Centauri; and another will allow the earth to travel at a speed superior to the speed of light by curving the ether from its path and forming an "ether tunnel." Light, it is explained, travels at only 186,000 miles per second because of its friction through the ether. Men dig themselves underground for the trip through space; lines of force are set up to hold the atmosphere in place; and the earth, piloted by Eunice Banks, sets out for Alpha Centauri.

But the machine for tripling the pull toward this star breaks under the strain, and the earth plunges blindly through space; it reaches the rim of the universe and breaks through it. It comes to rest in a new universe whose laws are different from those of the old; for instance, though earth retains its own gravitation, there is no gravitational pull between astronomical bodies; another kind of force, a ring of force, holds bodies in place. Because the heat of the new sun is almost unbearable, Miss Banks resourcefully repairs her machines and draws the earth back into its familiar universe. But in gigantic batteries she has stored up bands of force from the alien universe. She returns the earth to its old sun, hurls the alien bands of force against the sun to repair its rents, and settles the earth—now the only planet, as the sun has absorbed the others—in a comfortable orbit.

This is a fairy-tale of astronomy. To describe this kind of science, Olaf Stapledon's cosmic romances build up a civilization able to sustain it. One feels some inadequacy in Eunice Banks. None the less, such fragments from the cosmic romance are popular in recent scientific fiction.

D. *The Occult and the Supernatural*

The tale of terror thrives today with new rationalizations from science. The Elder Things of ancient myth are explained to be, perhaps, life-forms from an alien planet, and the "ectoplasm" of spirit mediums is likely to show up with a molecular formula.

Howard Phillips Lovecraft's "At the Mountains of Madness" (1936) combines material from the "dreaded *Necronomicon* of the mad Arab Abdul Alhazred," the closing chapters of Poe's *Arthur Gordon Pym* (along with a suggestion from "Ulalume"), and geology and the theory of evolution; the result is a tale of terror with every effect of the supernatural. The story is told to discourage any further scientific expeditions to the South Pole, by a scientist who took part in the ill-fated Miskatonic University Expedition.

In this expedition, two whaling-boat loads of scientists, graduate students, and their assistants go to the region of the South Pole. When they reach Ross Island, a student named Danforth identifies Mount Erebus as Poe's Mount Yaanek. But these literary identifications (even when birds like those of *Pym* are seen) do not interest the scientists. The party separates into two groups. The group headed by Lake, the biologist, ponders markings found in the slate that indicate Cambrian or pre-Cambrian life there, something more than five hundred million years old. Lake goes forward to a range of mountains higher than the Himalayas. Boring beneath the ice-crust, he breaks into a hollow space, a tunnel filled with well-preserved animals of a kind never seen before: eight feet long, and barrel-shaped with star-shaped heads. The hide is tough; the blood is greenish like the sap of vegetables. Lake dissects one of them; the dogs are furious. Then a windstorm cuts off communication between groups.

The main party looks for Lake. The dissected bodies of the strange creatures are found and carefully buried. Then Lake and the others are found dead; one man is missing; another man has been curiously dissected. The narrator and Danforth take airplanes to cross the lofty mountains. They come to a city of towered stone buildings stretching for a hundred miles in geometric patterns. Exploring in the city, they find carvings that enable them to read its incredibly ancient history. When earth was young and the South Pole was warm, the Elder Things—no doubt those spoken of in the Pnakotic Manuscripts and the *Necronomicon*—came to earth, filtered down from the stars. The city was built nearly a thousand million years ago. These Old Ones, shaped by an alien evolution and possessing powers

that man does not have, created the life of earth; they manufactured "multicellular protoplasmic masses capable of molding
their tissues into all sorts of temporary organs under hypnotic
influence" to serve them as slaves. (The amorphous masses must
be the Shoggoths of the *Necronomicon*.) The land-masses of the
South Pole broke up into continents; alien creatures from yet
other planets came to do battle for earth; the Old Ones fought
with atomic weapons and throve till the great cold came. Then
they retreated first into the sea, and then into a sea in the interior
of the earth.

Finding a tunnel, the explorers venture downward. They come
upon the body of the man missing from Lake's camp, frozen and
preserved; acrid odors rise. They come upon headless bodies of
the star-headed creatures, the bodies sucked dry of blood. Then
a mist rises and a formless thing advances, coming down the
tunnel like a piston in a cylinder. The narrator and Danforth
barely escape alive; their plane takes them over the mountains as
strange birds cry, as in *Arthur Gordon Pym*, "Tekeli-li!" Perhaps
the formless thing is simply Shoggoth, shapeless, living protoplasm,
from fragments of which all life on earth evolved through the
millenniums.

A similar quasi-scientific mythology underlies a great many
stories from Lovecraft's pen, especially *The Shadow Out of Time*
(1936).* This time, the discovery of the weirdly awful past
that is none the less rationally explained, and the bringing of
this past and the present into juxtaposition, are accomplished by
(1) The metempsychic transfer of the mind of the narrator into
the body of a member of an eldritch race that dominated the
earth before the forms that produced man appeared, and then
(2) the narrator's discovery of ruins from this ancient time
and his recognition of their familiar symbols.

The story is presented as a manuscript writen by Professor
Nathaniel Wingate Peaslee of Miskatonic University and presented to his son, a professor of psychology. Following experiences so strange his mind can hardly credit them, Peaslee

---

* Howard Phillips Lovecraft (1890-1937) was one of the most sensitive
and powerful writers of our generation in the field of the quasi-scientific
tale of terror. Both the stories described here were originally published
in *Astounding Stories*. Similar pieces appeared in *Amazing Stories* and
Weird Tales. Lovecraft built up a following of readers who regard him as
a twentieth-century Poe. His work seems worth wide literary recognition,
delayed perhaps because he published in magazines. Since his death, Ark-
ham House, Sauk City, Wisconsin, has collected his stories and published
them as *The Outsider and Others* and *Beyond the Wall of Sleep*. August
Derleth has a biography and critical commentary, *H. P. L.: A Memoir*,
published by Ben Abramson, New York.

must formulate them for his son, above all to warn mankind to abandon the explorations of the strange stones in Australia.

The background is known to the general public: in 1908, while lecturing to a class in political economy, Peaslee slumped into a stupor; he awakened a victim of amnesia, able to speak only a stilted English; his behavior estranged his wife; he insisted on pursuing researches into ancient, forbidden documents in out-of-the-way corners of the world; after some years, he awakened from the amnesia to complete the sentence he had been speaking to his class in political economy.

Peaslee's conscious mind remembers nothing of the lapse of years. But in repeated, consecutive, horrible dreams, his lost years come back to him. Dreaming, he is in the grip of a non-human entity, dwelling in a civilization of vast stone cities, one of a Great Race that lived "somewhat less than 150,000,000 years ago." This Great Race had come "from that obscure, transgalactic world known in the disturbing and debatable Eltdown Shards as Yith," to inhabit strange bodies and to conquer an elder, half-material, "horrible elder race of half polypous, utterly alien entities which had come through space from immeasurably distant universes," drive it underground, and seal it there. Members of the Great Race, including Peaslee, are "immense rugose cones ten feet high, with head and other organs attached to foot-thick distensible limbs spreading from the apexes. They spoke by the clicking or scraping of huge paws . . . and walked by the expansion and contraction of a viscous layer attached to their vast, ten-foot bases." They rove "all over the habitable world in titan airships or on the huge boat-like, atomic-engined vehicles which traversed the great roads" and delve curiously "into the libraries containing the records of the planet's past and future." They are masters of the secret of time-travel; with mechanical aids, "a mind would project itself forward in time, feeling its dim, extra-sensory way till it approached a desired period." Then it would seize a victim, as one had seized Peaslee. The victim would be compelled to inhabit the body of the creature, to submit to questions, and to write out a descriptive history of his own time; while the alien creature would inhabit his victim's body and explore the new world. The exploration completed, the process is reversed; all memory of the experience is blotted from the conscious mind of the victim.

In his dreams, Peaslee becomes acquainted with the other victims: a mind from Venus of the incalculable future; one from a moon of Jupiter six million years in the past; minds from the "winged, star-headed, half-vegetable race of paleogean Antarctica; . . . one from the wholly abominable Tcho-Tchos;

two from the Arachnid denizens of earth's last age," and so on. He learns from the Great Race that it will live its vast span, and then in the face of deadly peril, perhaps rebellion by the imprisoned horrors underground, the "cream of the Great Race" will skip over man's brief age and enter suitable bodies of "the mighty beetle civilization" that is to follow.

Supposing that all these dreams are sheer dreams, Peaslee writes an article describing his visions for the *Journal of the American Psychological Society*. Then a letter from Australia reports that stones with carvings such as he describes are to be found in a desert there. Miskatonic University organizes an expedition; miles of the stones are found, half uncovered by the shifting sands. The fragment of a memory draws Peaslee to a particular spot, where he finds an entry into a cavern—a gallery familiar to him in all its details. He proceeds across tumbled masonry, down tunnels, and into a room; he searches in a cabinet opened by a combination he "remembers"; he finds the astounding article he seeks. Then something damnable, something not material, that whistles like a sighing wind, seems coming through the darkness, up out of the dreaded doors that had been sealed. Peaslee flees, stumbles, crawls, and scrambles, till somehow he finds himself in the desert. He has dropped the priceless record he had sought and he dares not return for it; but he had seen it under his flashlight for a moment, the story of his own time, written in his own handwriting on sheets of perdurable metal.

These stories by Lovecraft meditate a combination of the measureless past of geology and astronomy, some grotesque suggestions from the theory of evolution, and ideas from various mythologies. They are splendid examples of scientific fiction turned to the uses of the tale of terror.

It is to be noted that these stories by Lovecraft, though written to inspire terror, do not deal with the supernatural, that is, spirits or spooks. But André Maurois's "The Weigher of Souls" (1931), though using materials of terror—dead bodies and spirits—seeks to make these materials seem the commonplaces of laboratory analysis. The narrator, a Frenchman, goes to London to visit Dr. James, whom he had known during the War; he goes with Dr. James on his rounds at St. Barnaby's hospital. At dinner, James brings the conversation to the subject of immortality. The narrator thinks life but a tissue of images and sensations: "Sensations cease with the sentient organs . . . bound up with the existence of a nervous system." But James believes cells would not organize into a living body if there were not a vital fluid; at death, perhaps this vital fluid simply leaves the body to return to some common stock. "Why shouldn't there be a principle of the conservation of life, analogous to that of the conservation of energy?" That night, the narrator goes with James to experiment on a body recently dead. It is weighed on a sensitive scale; weight diminishes steadily, as the body loses moisture; but a little more than an hour and a half after death, the body takes three sudden drops in weight. Nothing is seen to leave the body, but perhaps, says James, it has lost a form of energy; energy possesses mass, as any post-Einsteinian physicist knows.

Back in Paris, the narrator talks with the physicist Monestier, who suggests that an invisible energy—say, the "psychons" that are the electrons of the soul—may be made visible if irradiated with ultra-violet rays. The narrator goes again to James and observes him collect souls in bell jars; under ultra-violet light, a soul looks like a swirling of cigarette smoke. Souls of strangers, put into the same jar, glow dimly; souls of brothers burn with the luminosity of a full moon. Dr. James asks that his soul be put into the same jar as that of his dead wife, but when he dies some years later, a local doctor breaks the jar before the narrator can arrive. The story is both a tale of the supernatural, and yet simply the description of a laboratory experiment with "psychons."

Maurice Renard's *New Bodies for Old* (1923), dedicated to H. G. Wells, develops the ideas found in *The Island of Dr. Moreau* into a tale of Satanic surgery and even of soul-transference.

Nicolas Vermont goes to visit his kindly Uncle Lerne, whom he finds strangely changed, eccentric, and engaged in clandestine activities in a greenhouse. When Nicolas explores, he finds evidence of curious grafting: animals and plants are grafted together, so that trees have animation, rats have leaves growing from their tails, and dogs do not seem doglike. He comes upon the half-buried body of Klotz. When Nicolas falls in love with Emma, a woman whom his uncle also loves, the uncle imprisons Nicolas and operates on him, taking his brain and putting it into the body of a bull and putting the bull's brain into Nicolas's body. When Emma makes advances to the bull in Nicolas's body, Nicolas gores him and kicks out the brain. Uncle Lerne operates at once and restores Nicolas's brain to his own body; the bull's brain and body die. Meanwhile, Lerne is greatly interested in Nicolas's motor car; one day, in the automobile, he dies. After his death, Nicolas learns the truth, that Klotz had killed Uncle Lerne and put his own brain into the uncle's body. Now that the body is dead, Klotz's soul has somehow got into the motor car. The car behaves in strange ways; it is finally nailed into a box, where it "dies"—becomes a mass of putrescent decay.

Though the book is ghastly with horrors, there is a great deal of quasi-science in the explanations of events. When Nicolas is put into the bull's body, for instance, he finds that all his sensory perceptions change: blood looks green, for instance, and trees and grass red; odors and sounds are such as Nicolas has never experienced before. Yet it is not pure science that animates Lerne (Klotz); he desires at first simply to make himself wealthy by selling bodies to old, weak millionaires; and he desires later to find immortality, as he thinks he may by discovering how to make the soul enter into machinery. But apparently the animation of a piece of machinery, instead of rendering the soul immortal, renders the machinery mortal.

The story of *Frankenstein* is presented in modern guise and with chemical formulas in Clyde C. Campbell's "The Avatar" (1935), from *Astounding Stories*. Dr. Michael Earle, as the climax of a career of bio-chemical research, finds the secret of life to lie in regulated overcharges of electricity. Working from a model furnished by a sculptor, he creates a "perfect man," David. He wishes to create a race of perfect men, but he needs money; scientific organizations scoff at him. But handsome David becomes a moving-picture star and earns a great deal. Then David gets ambitions of his own; he joins a Terrorist organization and, through the force of his personality, wins such support that he becomes world-dictator. Dr. Earle then asks for means to create a race of men like David, but David wants only a mate, the perfect woman to match himself; he will have no others like himself to challenge his dictatorship. Dr. Earle, in remorse, slips into David's bedroom and slits his throat.

An interesting feature of the story is the elaborate discussion of the chemical formulas necessary to create protoplasm. The following is one sentence among dozens: "When diketopiperazine is hydrolyzed by acid, the dipeptide—glycylglcine is obtained." But this is simply the elixir-of-life theme given a "chemical" formula. The political discussion describing David's rise to power is likewise elaborate, but childish. The Terrorists, for instance, say: "I want to see the World State in power—so we can have exquisite cities of the most subtle color patterns and eugenics and handsome airships and no money."

The foregoing tales of terror illustrate various ways in which the theories and formulas of science may be used to give a new rationality to stories of the occult and the supernatural.

E. *Crime and Detection*

In the same way the "detective story" overlaps into scientific fiction. In recent years, stories of crime and detection have issued from the presses in a flood. Many of them, of course, contain material from scientific fiction; some contain a little science; some, as the following examples show, are simply scientific fiction given the plot-interest of detective fiction.

Alexander Laing's *The Cadaver of Gideon Wyck* (1934) purports to be the narrative of a medical student who examines the circumstances surrounding the murder of Dr. Gideon Wyck. For a number of months before and after Dr. Wyck is killed, various women give birth to symmeli in the hospital attached to the medical school. These symmeli, five in all, are progressively more and more like mermen or mermaids; they live only a short time after birth and are afterwards dissected. Dissection shows tissues like those of a creature midway between the lower forms and man; they are obviously "atavistic flesh from a human type modified by obscure and powerful forces."

It is revealed that the women giving birth to these creatures had all been seduced by Dr. Wyck; during their pregnancy, he had hypnotized them. It is surmised that Dr. Wyck, a specialist in embryonic medicine, experimented with them in an effort to induce and control mutations in the embryo. Dr. Wyck's laboratory was wrecked before his death, but evidence suggests that the women had had their lower extremities immersed in cold salt water while the torso had been bathed in heat and subjected to various chemical and electrical forces. Though the story is primarily concerned with crime and its detection, an elaborate interest in the story is the effort of Dr. Wyck to exert pre-natal influence.

Such a story is a detective story that also contains science. Other stories are pieces of scientific fiction that employ crime-and-detection as a plot device.

Erle Stanley Gardner's "A Year in a Day" (1930), from *Argosy,* makes use of the idea in Wells's "The New Accelerator" to tell a story of crime and detection. Various millionaires receive instructions to send money to a certain man, or death will result at a specified time. A millionaire surrounds himself with guards, but at the appointed time chokes and dies. By tracing the origin of the notes demanding money, a scientist, Swift, finds a doctor who manufactures capsules that speed up bodily processes as much as three thousand times. Under the influence of a capsule, a man is invisible. The doctor dies of heart disease when Swift attacks him, but Swift continues his search; he takes some of the capsules and finds himself invisible to normal sight, but able to see a number of thieves, likewise invisible to others, busy looting banks and jewelry stores. Taken to be one of the thieves, Swift penetrates to the den of the leader and overcomes him. The scientific explanations are the same as those in Wells's story; the plot of crime and detection is simply superimposed upon the earlier fiction.

A. L. Burkholder's "Dimensional Fate" (1934), from *Wonder Stories,* is the narrative of a man about to be executed for murder. The courts will not believe his story, and the mechanism has been destroyed, but the story explains, he says, the death of Joseph Burnett. Leopold Dochler and Burnett make a machine that translates them into a fourth dimension; they enter a curious, craggy world; a many-legged, man-headed monster attacks them; they flee back into the world, but the monster comes, too, on their machine. The monster picks up a pistol and shoots Burnett. Dochler manages to work the controls so as to send the monster back into the fourth-dimensional world; to insure that no other monster "comes through," he destroys the machine. But the police refuse to believe Dochler's story.

Anthony Skene's "The Man Who Stole Life" (1933), in *Detective Weekly* (English), tells how Blake, detective, and men of Scotland Yard discover and kill a Nabob. The Nabob is suspected to be responsible for a number of murders in which the victims apparently die of old age before they can tell their story completely. Blake follows a young woman to the Nabob's house and observes how the Nabob straps her into a chair and turns upon her powerful beams that seem to sap her life. Blake is himself captured and strapped into the chair, but his assistant arrives to save Blake. In the struggle, the Nabob is knocked against an electric switch and killed. Blake discovers that the man is the inventor of a machine that extracts life-force from his victims and then, in turn, delivers the life-force to the Nabob, who, records show, is 147 years old.

George O. Smith's "Identity" (1945) offers another example of the way the crime-story may furnish action for scientific fiction. This yarn from a recent issue of *Astounding Science-Fiction* is also, I think, a fair example of current run-of-the-mine scientific fiction from the magazines. In an offhand manner, it makes use of wonders of the world in the future, marvellous mechanisms of all kinds (rays capable of atomic disintegration, interplanetary space-ships, the matter-duplicator, etc.), telepathy, and psychic control of matter, without bothering to rationalize these features long familiar to readers of the magazines.

Since these wonders are casual commonplaces, the basis for

the story has to be a fight of some kind—in this story, a crime, a search, and a villain chasing a hero. As far as the action of the story is concerned, the plot might have been laid in the "wild West" or in gangland. For good measure, the threads of a love-story weave through the plot.

Cal Blair enters a building of the Solarian Medical Association and steals a kiss from Tinker Elliott, bent over a microscope. He discovers that his diabolical twin-brother, Benj, has been visiting Tinker and passing off as himself—a revolting idea in this world where the matter-duplicator can duplicate also people, and to be a duplicate or pose as one is cause for revulsion.

The ghost of Hellion Murdoch, long-dead interplanetary-pirate and scientist-genius, mails to Cal the key to his long-lost treasure; the key is a cryptogram involving the use of a "cavity resonator and antenna system." Cal supposes the treasure may not be anything, after all, for ancient coins or jewels may be easily duplicated and have little value. Gangsters attack Cal and force him into a space-craft; rival gangsters in another space-craft rescue him and take him before gang-leader Benj. (Among the oaths to spice this yarn is Cal's "I'll be psyched if I do.") Cal escapes by jumping from a window and meets Tinker in a bar; they refresh themselves with Callistan loganberry, roast knolla, and palan. They discuss the horrors of duplication and talk of the great wars fought by armies of nineteen million men duplicated from a thousand originals, then thirty-eight millions, and the final peace-time strain on the home-front when "several thousand men tried to live in one old familiar haunt."

Inspired by Tinker, who accompanies him, Cal sets out in a space-ship for Venus, to find Murdoch's hoard. Transferring to a 'plane at a station on Venus, Cal begins the search. In the Vilanortis Country, Benj waits in his flier to intercept Cal, whom he traces by radio beams. Near the hoard, the brothers crash, and then fight it out with needle-beams till a white-hot point quenches itself in Benj's throat. Tinker suffers a fractured vertebra in the crash. She sends Cal on to find the hoard, because she knows Murdoch was an illegal neuro-surgeon and supposes his treasure may be something to help her. Sure enough, the hoard is a report of research conducted on live primates and recorded so clearly in three-dimensional pictures that a child can follow directions and repair damaged nerves. Cal operates, and after a short while, Tinker is well.

Crime and detection, cops-and-robbers, gangland fights, and interplanetary piracy appear frequently in the scientific fiction in the magazines.

* * * * *

In the foregoing chapters, I have defined scientific fiction as the story of an imaginary invention or discovery in the natural sciences and consequent adventures. I have classified typical pieces according to the kinds of experiences narrated, and have offered brief summaries that I felt to be necessary in this pioneering presentation, because the pieces are not generally well known. The classification shows that pieces of scientific fiction are not isolated units. They form parallel parts of a body of literature that has developed with singular unity of substance and clarity of evolution. The central group of stories seems to be those that begin as marvellous inventions and trips to other worlds and then develop through historic romances into cosmic romances. Close to it, often overlapping, is the group containing utopias and satires. Subsidiary groups of fiction dealing with the occult and with crime and detection have developed as writers saw opportunities for deepening the tale of terror by using the materials of science or for combining the excitement of a chase and a story of invention.

Looking now at end-products, we may tentatively conclude that the cosmic romance has gone about as far as it can go until some radically new view of the cosmos may be manifest in science itself. The hey-day of the magazines was the 1930's. Though I have found it impossible to present the vast bulk of magazine stories in this work, and perhaps in choosing *representative* stories have made choices that "fans" will contest, I have just read through and laid aside the latest issue of two magazines. I seemed to be reading something I had read several times before. On the other hand, another myth-maker the size of Lovecraft may arise, and the new fields treated by Stapledon in *Odd John* and *Sirius* have been merely introduced, rather than exhausted. Finally, though our daily lives may follow their accustomed routines calmly, as in 1903-1910 most people were calm under the spread of man's new wings, the fact is that we are entering the Atomic Age. More books like *Twenty-Fifth Hour* may serve a useful purpose; and there is need for books of a kind I cannot define, because I have not seen them yet—books to present a graphic, convincing study of the paths that we may follow and to show the right one.

PART II

And Space Anatomized

CHAPTER SEVEN

Scaffolding

Structure, Narrative Method, and Characterization

BECAUSE SCIENTIFIC ROMANCES treat inventions and discoveries that are imaginary, they have the task not imposed upon other fiction of making the improbable seem true. They must describe machinery in some detail, in order to make it credible, and yet must keep a narrative going. Their subject-matter is intellectual, rather than emotional, and yet, to be popular, they must have emotional interest. Therefore, an analysis of scientific fiction may point out many special features. A surprising unity of method and substance is evident, though no formula fits every story.

A. *Structure*

1. Plot

Many scientific romances exhibit a story within a story. Paltock's *Peter Wilkins,* following a tradition of the imaginary voyage, presents an enveloping story to tell about Peter Wilkins, how he was found, and how he was got to tell his story. After this introduction in a commonplace background to vouch for his truth, Peter Wilkins tells his story of a wonderful journey. This method, usually presenting the wonderful journey or the wonderful discovery in a manuscript found by the author, who himself vouches for the manuscript, is very common in scientific fiction. It removes the central adventure from the reader by one degree (and sometimes more), but it tends to suggest realistic proofs that the manuscript is authentic. Greg's *Across the Zodiac* for instance, tells a story found in code in a wrecked cylinder; the wreckage of the cylinder, with its pieces of flesh and strange metal, vouches for the truth of this manuscript. DeMille's *Strange Manuscript Found in a Copper Cylinder* presents not only a manuscript found at sea, but a good deal of sceptical discussion, pro and con, regarding its authenticity; throughout the reading-aloud of the manuscript, scientists discuss it. Lloyd's *Etidorhpa* contains similar interludes to discuss the validity of the assertions made in the manuscript of I-Am-the-Man; scientific experiments are worked out to prove that the seemingly impossible is true. The author of Emerson's *The Smoky God* is only presenting, he says, the manuscript that Olaf Jansen gave him on his deathbed; manuscript and maps are being presented to the Smithsonian Institution. Sherriff's *The Hopkins Manuscript* purports to be a manuscript narrating Hopkins's personal experiences, dug from the ruins of London after 1000 years by scientists of the Royal Society of Abyssinia. The device of the long-lost manuscript is a favorite one in scientific fiction.

A variant of this device is that of a letter or series of letters or narratives to contain the central story. Doyle's *The Maracot Deep* is put together from several accounts, though chiefly three separately written narratives of Cyrus Headley. Often a story, told in general by the omniscient author, departs from a central narrative to describe a subsidiary adventure, which may be included as the diary of a person taking part in it; this method is used, for instance, in the diary of Eliot James in Balmer and Wylie's *After Worlds Collide*.

Because a piece of scientific fiction often presents (1) events in the world of everyday and (2) an adventure in an imaginary world, it has a tendency to break into two parts. When the author's main intention is to discuss (3) the social significance of an imaginary discovery, the fiction may break again between the adventure (2) and the discussion (3). The breaks, however, are not all in so neat a pattern. Jefferies's *After London* breaks into two parts, the first of which is a historical account of the relapse into barbarism in preparation for the adventure in Part II. John Jacob Astor's *A Journey in Other Worlds* presents three Books, first a sketch of the world of 2000 A. D., second a detailed trip to Jupiter, and third, other trips. Stockton evidently found the story of discovery in *The Great Stone of Sardis* too slight to stand alone, and therefore linked together two stories, one of the Great Stone and another of Arctic exploration, in alternating chapters. Wells's *The First Men in the Moon* shades gradually from the events in everyday surroundings into the trip to the moon, but after Bedford has been brought back to earth, the romance continues, to include Cavor's description of life on the moon along with social satire not present in the adventure proper. Wells's *The Food of the* Gods describes the discovery of the Food and its immediate consequences in Book I, tells the story of Caddles in Book II, and discusses the social significance of the discovery in Book III. The romance is continuous, but the emphasis is clearly shifted. Tardés *Underground Man* first offers a satiric description of the world of the future before the catastrophe, then a romance of the catastrophe, and finally a utopian picture of the adjustment after it.

The historic romance, especially, often more or less abandons central characters and tells the story of world-wide conflict or disaster in a panorama of scenes. Wells's "The Star" offers a panorama of world-disaster as an alien star passes the earth on its way to the sun; the star and its effects are viewed by policemen, seamen, milkmen, men in China, and so on, and the views are the scenes of the story. Wells's *The World Set Free* similarly shifts scenes from one place to another in a panorama of world disaster. Parabellum's *Banzai!* has no central character; scenes of the Japanese invasion are presented as views by this person or that one, somewhat alternated with chapters discussing the political or military situation as a whole. Huxley's *Brave New World* acquires a central character in Mr. Savage only in the second half of the book; the first half is made up of snapshots from a few lines to several pages in length.

When there is a continuous central story, it is often a slight one as a framework to carry other material. Nearly all of Verne's romances, though the plots may be complex, are padded with geographical and scientific information and then filled in still further with purely episodic adventures. *Twenty Thousand Leagues Under the Sea,* for instance, is made up chiefly of geographical information about the sea bottoms of the world. The story of Butler's *Erewhon* is very slight; social commentary and satire make up the bulk of the book. The story of Howells's *A Traveler from Altruria* is almost non-existent; the book is made up of conversations comparing the Altrurian point of view with that of America. Wicks's *To Mars Via the Moon* offers a story only as a framework for lectures on astronomy. Sometimes there may be a sufficient story that is, however, laid aside for long chapters of discussion. Boisgilbert's *Caesar's Column,* for instance, inserts speeches, articles from magazines, and long discussions; England's *The Golden Blight* similarly quotes at length from economists and writers on social subjects. Pseudoman's *Zero to Eighty* even presents the papers read before a scientific society.

Frequently the central story is one of world-struggle, and the "hero" is simply the author's eyepiece who becomes involved in that struggle. In Wells's *When the Sleeper Wakes,* for instance, Graham wakes up at the beginning of a revolution; he takes some part in it, but he is largely the observer of forces and events that sweep past him. Similarly, Bert Smallways, typical citizen, is drawn into the world-struggle of Wells's *The War in the Air;* he is a convenient medium for seeing some events close up: "To such a spectator as Bert it presented itself as a series of incidents, some immense, some trivial, but collectively incoherent." In chapters that drop Bert altogether, Wells offers discussion that draws the events into a coherent picture. In the fiction from *Amazing Stories* and similar magazines, the idea of the story is often a new invention, and "story interest" is superimposed upon it. This superimposed story is often one of mystery or of crime and detection. The narrative interest in Smith and Garby's "The Skylark of Space" is largely the struggle of the Steel Trust to gain control of the secret solution "X"; several cross-firing detective agencies are employed; here are murders, secret passages, wonderful codes, and all the paraphernalia of the detective story.

Another device that may include the foregoing features is that of presenting the story as the narrative of a historian in the distant future. In this narrative the world-history growing out of scientific discovery is usually central. Simak's "The Creator," for instance, is "written in the elder days as the Earth rides close to the rim of eternity." Stapledon's *Last and First Men* is "dictated" to a narrator of the present by one of the Eighteenth Men, who views the whole of man's life as a kind of symphony in which, for instance, "the careers of the First Men and of the Second Men are each a single movement" more fully developed than later movements because the readers of the book are "themselves tremors in the opening bars of the music" and "it is best that I should dwell chiefly on things near to them, even at the cost of ignoring much that is in fact greater." Stapledon's *Star Maker,* following somewhat the same pattern, offers the book as a frank imagination from a cosmic point of view that begins at a point in England and first spirals out through space, including wider and wider pictures, and then spirals through time, to view an ever-widening era of past and future. Suspense is replaced by increase in boldness of the imagination; climax is gained by increasing the range through space-time.

In other stories, devices for gaining suspense and for reaching a climax are more like those in other fiction. Verne's favorite method for gaining suspense, for instance, is to keep two or three or more adventures going at the same time, to drop one adventure at a point of danger to the hero, and then to pick up another adventure and lead it to a similar point of danger. This is the technique of Burrough's Tarzan books. In *Tarzan at the Earth's Core,* for instance, Tarzan is brought to a crisis of inescapable peril, and the chapter ends; the next chapter takes up Jason Gridley's experiences and carries Gridley to a similar point of danger; then Tarzan's adventures are resumed, and so on. Sometimes suspense is gained through presentation of an amazing fact, then explained through "cut-backs." Campbell's "The Avatar," for instance, opens with Dr. Earle's plea to physicians to help him in creating other artificial men than David. As physicians scoff, the story cuts back to explain the creation of David. In a piece of scientific fiction, the climax (which is often also the dénouement) is usually the collapse of the forces set in motion by the imaginary invention or discovery. In Wells's *The War of the Worlds,* for instance, the climax is the unexpected death of the invading Martians through the agency of disease-germs. This climax is usually prepared for, but the preparation is hidden for the sake of surprise; in *The War of the Worlds* the facts that Martians have eliminated disease-bacteria and that they drink human blood are made clear earlier in the story; presumably no reader guesses that man's diseases will kill the Martians.

2. Openings

A problem that every writer of scientific fiction must solve is that of how to introduce the imaginary invention. The writer must gain the reader's interest and convince him of the truth of the narrative, and yet prepare him for the unusual and for willing suspension of disbelief in it.

A favorite opening, imitated from imaginary voyage literature, is the opening in a commonplace setting of everyday events, often the life-story of the narrator. Madden's *The Reign of George VI* plans to tell of events in the twentieth century, but it opens with a discussion of major trends in the politics of the past seventeenth century and advances gradually to the twentieth century. Voyages of imaginary discovery may open with some statement of the reasons for undertaking the voyage followed by a discussion of commonplace preparations for it. Seaborn's *Symzonia,* for instance, opens with a statement of a project for discovering a passage to a new world; nothing else extraordinary is encountered for a good many pages. Tucker's *A Voyage to the Moon* offers typically a biographical sketch of the narrator followed by a story of shipwreck and the very gradual introduction of the idea of travelling to the moon. More recent fiction generally discards the shipwreck found in the imaginary voyage, but opens with narration of commonplace events. Wylie's *The Gladiator* draws an opening picture of a commonplace, henpecked professor and his wife living in the small college town of Indian Creek, Colorado; Professor Danner's experiments in biology are introduced gradually as experiments on animals, before he conceives the idea of giving his son nerves and muscles of steel. In Lewis's *Out of the Silent Planet,* Ransom, enjoying a walking tour between terms at Cambridge, stumbles into adventure only because he cannot find a rooming place at an inn.

The natural opening for the story within a story is a commonplace discovery, usually of a manuscript. Mary Shelley's *Frankenstein,* for instance, is introduced by Walton's letters to his sister; Walton is making expeditions to the Arctic on whaleboats for his health and to investigate signs of a temperate zone around the Pole. The discovery of the emaciated Frankenstein driving across the ice on a sled is not reached until the fourth letter; the central story is what Frankenstein tells. Frequently the discovery of the manuscript, or the central story in whatever form, is preceded by a prologue. In Verrill's "Beyond the Pole," for instance, Dr. Abbott Lyman presents the central manuscript after a prologue describing how, while doing ornithological research on Desolation Island, he found an albatross hampered by a cylinder attached to its leg.

Verne's favorite opening is the statement of a mystery of some kind. *Robur the Conqueror* opens with mysterious events taking place all over the world: trumpetings come from the air; flags appear on monuments. Verne's *Master of the World* opens with the assignment of a federal detective to investigate the strange fires seen above a mountain in North Carolina. Von Hanstein's "Utopia Island" opens with the mysterious disappearance of eminent scientists all over the world. Balmer and Wylie's *When Worlds Collide* opens with the mysterious mission on which David Ransdell is sent from Australia to New York; Ransdell learns the contents of the box he is carrying only after he completes his dangerous mission.

In recent scientific fiction a favorite opening has been the challenging statement of some scientific principle not generally understood. A group of scientists, including, however, some layman to whom the principle has to be explained, discuss this principle, and then the story following illustrates it. Cummings's *The Girl in the Golden Atom,* for instance, opens with a doctor's challenge of the statement that there is no such thing as the smallest particle of matter; his *The Man Who Mastered Time* (like Wells's *The Time Machine*) opens with a round-table discussion of the nature of time.

But much scientific fiction, especially in recent years, is bolder; it plunges at once into the imaginary situation. Griffith's *The Angel of the Revolution* opens with "Victory! It flies!" to describe the invention of the airplane. The future historian in Tardé's *Underground Man* loses no time: "It was toward the end of the twentieth century of the prehistoric era, formerly called the Christian, that took place . . . the unexpected catastrophe." Forster's "The Machine Stops" opens with "Imagine, if you can, a small room, hexagonal in shape, like the cell of a bee." After the room, the rest of the Machine Age is described, and the story is under way. Huxley's *Brave New World* opens on a lecture-tour of students through the Central London Hatchery. In the opening of Best's *The Twenty-Fifth Hour,* Captain Fitzharding's half-starved soldiers are wandering through a desolated Europe. What had happened, the story of the great collapse, is reserved for gradual revelation later in the story. Stapledon's opening for *Odd John* challenges the reader at once to consider the central, startling point of view of the satire: "When I told John that I intended to write his biography, he laughed. 'My dear *man!*' he said. 'But of course it was inevitable.' The word 'man' on John's lips was often equivalent to 'fool.'" Stories of the prehistoric past usually plunge into the midst of the narrative: Bierbower's *From Monkey to Man* opens with Sosee on a limb sucking a mango five hundred thousand years ago; Waterloo's *The Story of Ab* opens with baby Ab bawling for his mother on the approach of a hyena; London's *Before Adam* opens in the same way, with a child screaming at the approach of a wild boar. In similar ways, a large proportion of recent stories plunge at once, into the story.

3. Endings

Another problem that every writer of scientific fiction must solve is that of how to end his fiction, that is, to dispose of a machine that is not available to the public or to keep others from verifying the route to an imaginary world.

In the worlds of the future entered by a sleeper—and sometimes in a story concerned with an imaginary voyage to other planets or with an invention—the old-fashioned ending was the waking of the sleeper. In Mercier's *Memoirs of the Year Two Thousand Five Hundred,* for instance, the sleeper simply wakes at the end of the fiction. This tradition continued until Bellamy rejected it in *Looking Backward,* though it is sometimes found later, as in Benson's *The Dawn of All.* A similar dodging of responsibility for an imaginary discovery is the author's doubt, at the end of the book, whether the adventure took place. Verne's *Hector Servadac* returns to its starting point, and Hector doubts whether the adventure took place; perhaps he and Ben Zoof dreamed it. Howells's *A Traveler from Altruria* likewise ends with the departure of the Altrurian and then wide-spread doubt whether such a place as Altruria exists.

The favorite ending, however, is the loss or destruction of the marvellous secret, such as the destruction of the space-flier in Wells's *The First Men in the Moon* when a small boy tampers with the controls and flies off into space. (The *First Men in the Moon* has two endings, the end of the adventure proper and then the end of the postscript when the Grand Lunar prohibits further messages from Cavor to Bedford.) Similarly, the space-flier is destroyed at the end of Lewis's *Out of the Silent Planet.* The space-car of Greg's *Across the Zodiac* has been smashed to bits before the central manuscript is found. Verne's *Mysterious Island* comes to a close when a volcanic eruption destroys the island. Jekyll dies with his secret in Stevenson's *Dr. Jekyll and Mr. Hyde.* In Wells's *The Time Machine,* the Time Traveller takes a second trip into time and does not return. In Wells's *The Invisible Man,* the Invisible Man is beaten to death; the tramp Marvel secretes his formulas, but he can make nothing of them. The invasion of Wells's *The War of the Worlds* comes to a close when bacteria kill the Martians; Graham is smashed to earth, and apparently to death, to end Wells's *When the Sleeper Wakes.* The airplane of Beale's *The Secret of the Earth* is wrecked in the Antarctic. Lightning strikes Robur's machine in Verne's *The Master of the World.* At the end of Hilton's *Lost Horizon,* Conway has gone to look for the forgotten passage to Shangri-La and has not returned.

The ending that somehow destroys the evidence continues to be typical in scientific fiction up to the present. Detmold, of Hamilton's "The Metal Giants," has to destroy the metal brain he created. The scientists of Taine's *The Iron Star* use atomic disintegration to destroy the last particle of "asterium." Earthly, in Kearney's *Erone,* either was killed during the German blitz over London or went back to Erone. As the navies approach their island-retreat, the supernormals, in Stapledon's *Odd John,* destroy themselves by sinking the island into the sea; in *Sirius,* the dog becomes an outlaw and is shot. The narrator of Lovecraft's *The Shadow Out of Time* tells his story to prevent further investigation of the Australian ruins; if what he has seen is fact, there still lies "upon this world of men a mocking and incredible shadow out of time." But perhaps it was all a dream: "I did not bring back the metal case that would have been a proof, and so far those subterrane corridors have not been found."

But some writers more boldly assert that the imaginary invention is available; it has been given to the public, or it may be found in a particular museum. In Emerson's *The Smoky God,* for instance, the manuscript and maps of the route to the inner world are being given to the Smithsonian Institution. In Cummings's *The Girl in the Golden Atom,* the ring containing the atom in which the adventure took place lies in the Museum of the American Society for Biological Research. In Wells's *The War of the Worlds,* the handling machines of the Martians are said to have taught scientists a good deal; they are now being subjected to further study. The secret rays of Leinster's "The Man Who Put Out the Sun" will, within a few years, says the story, replace all coal and petroleum.

Historic romances of the future, of course, end with either the establishment of world peace, as in Griffith's *The Angel of the Revolution,* or the collapse of society, as in Wells's *The War in the Air* and Forster's "The Machine Stops."

Sometimes the ending is ironic. Butler's *Erewhon,* for instance, concludes with a plea for subscriptions to a stock company to civilize the Erewhonians: "Please subscribe quickly. Address to the Mansion-House, care of the Lord Mayor, whom I will instruct to receive names and subscriptions for me until I can organize a committee."

B. *Narrative Method*

In narrative method, the special features of scientific fiction are those growing out of subject-matter. Since an imaginary invention or discovery lies beyond common experience, the teller of the tale, the "point of view" of the narrator, is often a single "veracious" person. Every trick is used to make the imaginary adventure seem probable; where realistic fiction relies upon the principles of human behavior in normal situations to create belief, scientific fiction uses innumerable means to support the improbable. Love-romance and passion, important in most fiction, have no intrinsic place in scientific fiction, but are often included in a conventional pattern. Humor, too, whose source usually lies in character, plays a subsidiary rôle.

1. Points of View

Many scientific romances are narratives of a single adventurer's experiences written by himself. The method is inherited from the typical imaginary voyage; the strange adventure is one man's experiences, and he alone knows what happened. Many stories (especially the utopias and satires) contain "propaganda," and the single narrator may conveniently stop at any point to comment upon a situation or a custom and to express his own ideas about it; the author, through his character, can state the most revolutionary opinions without first-hand responsibility for them. Finally, when the veracity of the narrator is established in various ways, the first-hand narration is an excellent probability device.

Usually the first-hand narration is in the form of a manuscript; its discovery is described and its author's veracity established in an enveloping plot. Then the narrator tells his story. A typical manuscript is that in Kearney's *Erone.* Before his death, John Earthly simply gives his engineer-friend a manuscript describing his interplanetary adventure. This simple device is varied in several ways. One of the ways is illustrated in Verne's *Twenty Thousand Leagues Under the Sea;* an enveloping plot describes how M. Aronnax is captured and taken on board the submarine *Nautilus;* from then on, the story is M. Aronnax's tale of his experiences. The narrator in Bulwer-Lytton's *The Coming Race* starts his adventure in the company of an engineer, but the engineer is promptly killed, so that the narrator is left alone, the only person who can tell of his experiences. Lloyd's *Etidorpha* contains a single narrator's story within a single narrator's story. An enveloping commentary vouches for Drury; Drury describes in detail the way I-Am-the-Man came to him; and then the central story is the narrative I-Am-the-Man reads to Drury and leaves with him. Adam Jeffson, the "last man" in the world in Shiel's *The Purple Cloud,* writes his story as a diary for his own emotional relief; the diary is seen in a vision by the prescient Miss Wilson. Kipling's "With the Night Mail" purports to be a magazine article written in the distant future to describe the narrator's experiences in crossing the Atlantic.

Another frequent method in scientific fiction is that of telling the story from the point of view of a historian of the future. The historian sifts the data surrounding an event, a world-catastrophe; or the arrival at a utopian state of affairs, and then presents the history of what happened. For example, Jefferies's *After London* describes the historian's effort to sift, from positive records, from relics, and from "what the old men say," the truth about the collapse of civilization and the descent into barbarism. The historian of Newcomb's *His Wisdom* says that "We who live in this Golden Age never tire of comparing our happy lot with the backward condition of our forefathers"; he then offers the story of the change. Tardé's *Underground Man* purports to be the history of the three phases through which the world passed from its life on the surface of the earth in a Machine Age to its present utopian life underground; the historian, of course, lives in the underground Utopia. He presents records and quotes, for instance, extracts from the great speech of Miltiades as it has been preserved on phonograph records. In Stapledon's *Last and First Men* the historian of the future is one of the Eighteenth Men who informs and speaks through the mind of the author: "Before closing this preface I would remind the reader that throughout the following pages the speaker, the first person singular, is supposed to be, not the actual writer, but an individual living in the extremely distant future."

In Stapledon's later books, the story is told by a biographer-friend of the central character. Two complementary points of view are presented at the same time. The biographer presents the extraordinary, usually satiric, point of view of the central character and then comments upon it in his own character. In *Odd John,* John's own attitudes toward ordinary life "displayed the sympathetic though aloof interest of an anthropologist observing the customs of a primitive tribe." Then John's friend the biographer comments upon John's views as they seem to a normal human being. The same general method is employed in *Sirius,* though with interesting variations. First, the dog's own point of view is a curious one, difficult for Sirius to state in man's language, and difficult for a man-biographer to define. As Sirius tells Trelone, "In making me, you made something that sees man from clean outside man, and can tell him what he looks like." The camera-eye focused critically upon man is sharp, immediate, and familiar—obviously an advance in depth over extra-human viewpoints in other fiction. Second, the biographer, Robert, has a man's natural tendency to look down upon a dog. Furthermore, Robert is in love with Plaxy, and his desire to marry Plaxy is frustrated by Plaxy's feeling that her life is linked with Sirius and she must sacrifice everything to shelter and guard him. So Robert, though he understands the situation, has good reason to feel antagonism for Sirius.

Sometimes stories written by an omniscient author none the less choose this or that character and follow him through a series of adventures; then sometimes the author steps outside the

limited character's point of view and comments upon the larger
scene. This method is a favorite with Wells. In *The War of
the Worlds,* for instance, Wells describes the fall of the Martian
cylinders through a narrator writing in the first person and
describing both his experiences and observations and what he
hears of events elsewhere. Then as new cylinders fall in various
places, Wells shifts the point of view to that of the narrator's
brother to describe the panic in London, the proclamations in
the newspapers, and the flight. Then from time to time, Wells
abandons even the brother and writes, for instance, to describe
what a balloonist would have seen if he had been suspended above
this or that part of England. Portions drop even this limitation
and present Wells's comments from an entirely omniscient author's or historian's view. Wells's method in *The War in the
Air* is somewhat the same; he looks both through Bert Smallways
and then down upon Bert; often he abandons Bert altogether.

A good deal of what must be told in a piece of scientific fiction
is explanation of the phenomena observed. Writers handle the
problem of this exposition in a variety of ways. The single narrator may describe what he sees and then offer his conjectures;
he may explain in terms of what he learns later; and he may
save up a good deal of explanation for a chapter or so of
exposition. In Bulwer-Lytton's *The Coming Race,* for instance, the
narrator speaks of phenomena "at first too strange to my experience to be seized upon by my reason," but through repeated
trances and other methods he is furnished with information
that allows him to give "the following details respecting the
origin and history of this subterranean population." In *The
Time Machine* Wells explains the theory of time-travelling by
having his Time Traveller explain it in the opening pages of the
book to a variety of people, including laymen. As they are led
to understand it, of course the reader likewise is led to understand it; their questions and objections are, supposedly, those
of the typical reader. In Wells's *When the Sleeper Wakes,*
Graham is at first confused; he understands little of what he
sees in the world in which he awakes. Naturally, he asks questions and receives answers; as he learns, the reader learns.
In the midst of the struggle that breaks out, Graham is lost
on the public ways. He takes a seat beside an old man and,
through questions, gets the old man started on reminiscences.
These reminiscences give both Graham and the reader a coherent
picture of the history of London during Graham's sleep and of
the present state of affairs.

An interesting device is used in Renard's *New Bodies for
Old.* When Lerne (that is, Klotz in Lerne's body) has imprisoned

Nicolas's brain in the body of a bull, Lerne taunts Nicolas by whispering into his ear—now that he cannot reveal the secret— the full story of his experiments in grafting and brain surgery. Frequently the scientist takes with him on his adventure some ignorant but curious character; this person asks questions, and the scientist explains. Verne uses this device constantly. It is the excuse for all the elaborate astronomical lectures in Wicks's *To Mars Via the Moon.* Sometimes, as in McLociard's "Television Hill," the young man in love finds his sweetheart ignorant but curious, and he explains to her in detail; the girl's extreme curiosity is later explained by the fact that she is a spy for a rival group of scientists.

An interesting satiric device that is also useful for exposition of ideas is one used in satire from *Gulliver's Travels* to the present. To explain an abstract idea to a person either stupid or naively reasonable—and also to make the reader see this idea objectively—the narrator finds it necessary to phrase the idea in something like basic English. In a well-known passage in *Gulliver's Travels,* the Houyhnhnms cannot understand the word *lying,* as it stands for something outside their experience; it has to be translated as "saying the thing which is not," an obviously irrational thing to do. In Lewis's *Out of the Silent Planet,* Ransom has to translate Weston's creed of the survival of the strongest for the benefit of Oyarsa. When Weston says, "Our right to supersede you is the right of the higher over the lower," Ransom has to translate it as, "Among us, Oyarsa, there is a kind of *hnau* who will take other *hnaus'* food and— and things, when they are not looking. He says that he is not an ordinary one of that kind. He says that what he does now will make very different things happen to those of our people who are not yet born."

2.   Probability Devices

The greatest technical problem facing the writer of scientific fiction is that of securing belief. Scientific fiction, with its central adventure outside normal experience, cannot rely upon "universality." It has the difficult task of securing the reader's suspension of disbelief in something outside human experience, in order for the reader to enter imaginatively into the story.

The oldest and perhaps the soundest method for securing suspension of disbelief is that of embedding the strange event in realistic detail about normal, everyday events. This device, taken over from the imaginary voyage, is found, for instance, in Godwin's *The Man in the Moone.* The opening chapters introduce nothing extraordinary; one is inclined to believe from the beginning when a book offers, in the opening sentence, such "realistic" details as the following: "It is well enough and sufficiently knowne to all the countries of *Andaluzia,* that I *Domingo Gonsales,* was borne of Noble parentage, and that in the renowned City of *Sivill,* to wit in the yeare 1552. My Fathers name being *Therrando Gonsales,* (that was neere kinsman by the mothers side unto *Don Pedro Sanchez* that worthy Count of *Almenara,*). . . ." Holberg's *Journey to the World Under-Ground* offers similar particulars, including the names of the consuls and senators of Bergen in the Year of Our Lord 1665, when the journey is undertaken. Locke's "Discoveries in the Moon" is filled with particulars, including the citation of the issue of the Edinburgh *Journal of Science* that originally carried the story; few people, as widespread belief in the "moon hoax" indicates, were aware that the *Journal of Science* had ceased publication before this date. Among other details, Locke gives the most careful, dated description of the makings of the great telescope; the first cast, opened on January 3, 1833, was imperfect; a new cast was made on January 27 and opened early in February.

Verne, likewise, offers minute details. *Five Weeks in a Balloon,* for instance, figures every pound of hydrogen and every pound of air displaced by it, in the filling of the balloon, lists every article packed into the car, and states every detail of date, time (to the minute), and topography. Throughout all his stories, the same encyclopedic detail is found. In *Twenty Thousand Leagues Under the Sea* the *Nautilus* appears under the following circumstances: "The 13th of April, 1867, the sea being beautiful, the breeze favourable, the *Scotia,* of the Cunard Company's line, found herself in 15° 12′ long. and 45° 37′ lat. She was going at a speed of thirteen knots and a half." A variation of this device of giving place and date is to give blank places and dates, suggesting that actual places and dates would offer identification unpleasant to someone. Bulwer-Lytton's *The Coming Race* says that, "In the year 18—, happening to be in——" the beginning of the adventure took place. Wells did not offer the elaborate statistics that Verne offered, but he likewise sought verisimilitude in the use of realistic details. Prendick's escape from the *Lady Vain,* in *The Island of Dr. Moreau,* is, says Wells, widely known through newspaper accounts, but some of the accounts are wrong in detail, especially, he says, that quoted from the *Daily News* of March 17, 1887. Doyle's *The Lost World* offers a Foreword to withdraw the libel actions of Professor Challenger, widely expected by the public. Furthermore, this book includes photographs of the distinguished looking gentle-men-in-beards who took part in the expedition. The photographic plates are, notations say, "From a photograph by William Rans-ford, Hampstead."

A related method is that of naming prominent scientists (real or imaginary), speaking of certain imaginary details as well known, and offering footnotes that refer to these and similar items. Locke's "Discoveries in the Moon" is based upon information furnished by Dr. Andrew Grant, collaborator with the younger Dr. Herschel, who himself is transmitting his notes to the Royal Society; Herschel is preparing a book that will be issued shortly. Poe's "The Facts in the Case of M. Valdemar" likewise deals with a well-known case; in fact, says the story, the piece is written to counteract widespread misunderstanding and false rumors. In Verne's *From the Earth to the Moon,* the Gun Club sends to the Harvard Observatory for a report on the practi-cability of the plan to send a missile to the moon, and the full report from Harvard is printed. Scientific men "of such eminence as Adams and Jenkins, find nothing incredible in" the vertebrated creatures of Wells's "In the Abyss." Wells's "The New Ac-celerator" was first published in *The Strand Magazine* in 1901; in this magazine, says the story, the picture of well-known Professor Gibberne, dicoverer of the "new accelerator," appeared, "I think late in 1899," and Gibberne is described in terms of what the "reader may, perhaps, recall" from that picture. Mr. Bensington of Wells's *The Food of the Gods* is a Fellow of the Royal Society; Professor Redwood, of the same story, is Pro-fessor of Physiology in the Bond Street College of London Uni-versity. Emerson's *The Smoky God* has numerous footnotes to well-known author, title, volume and page of item after item substantiating portions of the story. Stribling's "The Green Splotches" is "Transcribed from the field notes of James B. Standifer, Secretary DeLong Geographical Expedition to the Rio Infiernillo, Peru, with introductory note by J. B. S.," and finally, "It may interest the reader to know that the Nobel Prize was awarded to Dr. Gilbert H. DeLong for the series of brilliant deductions set forth above.—T. S." The narrative of Verrill's "Beyond the Pole" describes an apparatus like a radio; a foot-note explains that the narrator, in the Antarctic for some time, could not have heard of this recent invention. The same story offers footnotes quoting from the New Bedford *Mercury* of August 14, 1917, to substantiate details of the narrative.

These tricks, though effective, are so old that they have a worn transparency. Perhaps a sounder method is, as Wells says, "to *domesticate* the improbable hypothesis." The writer must trick the reader "into an unwary concession to some plausible assumption and get on with his story while the illusion holds," and then, "As soon as the magic trick has been done the whole business of the fantasy writer is to keep everything else human and real." Perhaps Wells himself illustrates this device better than anyone else. Most of Wells's stories contain just one improbable item; all of the story that follows it has the consistency and logic of a universal principle. Invisibility has to be granted in *The Invisible Man;* if it is granted, what happens to Griffin thereafter is not fantastic (the fantastic advantages of invisibility are rejected), but somberly and unexpectedly realistic. Cavorite has to be granted in *The First Men in the Moon,* but the adventure following its discovery, though fantastic, asks for no further suspension of critical judgment; even the Selenites sound like probable inhabitants of the moon as scientists understand it. At the end of the story, Wells dares the reader to find a "man who could invent a story that would hold together like this one."

Attention to consistency, of course, involves preparation for following events. The reader is led gradually from the commonplace to the imaginary, but while still immersed in the commonplace, he notices, as if from the corner of his eye, little inexplicable facts. Then, when the imaginary fact is stated, its improbability is lessened because it explains the facts noted, perhaps, as strange, but accepted in their background of the commonplace. Wells is a past-master in the use of this device. The improbable fact in Wells's *When the Sleeper Wakes* is that Graham should sleep for two hundred years, but the opening chapters describe his nervous exhaustion, his inability to sleep for days and days, his taking of drugs, and finally the physical fatigue he has induced to make him sleep. The conditions under which he goes to sleep, sitting upright in a chair, are abnormal; the sleep is a "cataleptic rigour"; quite naturally, we suppose, he sleeps for an abnormal time.

Another probability device is the classic one elaborately worked out by Swift for *Gulliver's Travels.* The publisher, in "The Publisher to the Reader," vouches for the apparent truth of the whole and for Mr. Gulliver's reputation for veracity. Master Abeline, adding a chapter to Holberg's *Journey to the World Under-Ground,* says that the narrator, Klimius, dying in 1695, had lived "a sober and pure-minded man well thought of in his community." Greg's *Across the Zodiac* is, on the title page, presented by the publisher as "deciphered, translated, and edited" by Percy Greg, and an elaborate and detailed enveloping plot describes the circumstances under which Greg got hold of the central manuscript, in a strange cypher. Authors' prefaces and

introductions shamelessly assert, as the prologue of Lloyd's
Etidorpha does: "My purpose is to tell the truth." Prefaces like
that of Childers's *The Riddle of the Sands* point out that the
true names of persons taking part in the adventure must be
concealed in matters of such national importance. Authors, like
the narrator of Maurois's "The Weigher of Souls," "have hesi-
tated a long time before setting down this story," and this
narrator would not dare believe it at all if he were not "eye-
witness of the facts I am about to relate." The publishers precede
Laing's *The Cadaver of Gideon Wyck* with a statement "To the
Reader," saying that the story was received from a reputable
literary agent who is ignorant, as the publishers are, of the
author's identity; customary royalties are reserved for the author,
should he wish to present proofs of his authorship. Packages
of manuscript reached the agent postmarked from various cities.
The author's purpose is to tell the truth, in spite of danger to
himself.

The narrator's veracity is often stated in terms of his contempt for cheap fiction that tells improbable yarns. Swift's
Gulliver's Travels, for instance, expresses the hearty wish that
every traveller, before he is permitted to publish his voyages,
should be obliged to swear to their truth before the Lord High
Chancellor, for unscrupulous authors impose the grossest falsi-
ties on the unwary reader. In Smith and Garby's "The Skylark
of Space" chemists ridicule the liberation of atomic energy and
classify it with perpetual motion; the method of travelling through
space described in the story is not of that class.

Sometime the narrator's story is a death-bed statement, as
Emerson's *The Smoky God* is. Burkholder's "Dimensional Fate"
is the statement of a man wrongly accused of murder and now
awaiting execution. Sometimes the narrator, lost in some alien
world, entreats whoever finds the manuscript to notify his rela-
tives; in Verrill's "Beyond the Pole," for instance, the narrator
asks that the person finding the manuscript notify friends in
New Bedford, Massachusetts, U. S. A., or at least get the story
into a reliable newspaper. Sometimes the manuscript is written
as a warning to science. Peaslee, in Lovecraft's *The Shadow Out
of Time* must "formulate some definite statement—not only for
the sake of my own mental balance, but to warn" scientists to
leave the perilous stones in Australia forever unmolested.

Sometimes the author's preface is an "Appeal to the Public"
to give his story credence, because matter-of-fact people who
have heard the truth have laughed at it and called the author
crazy. Tucker's *A Voyage to the Moon* says that Atterley is
without honor among his friends, in spite of objects he has

brought from the moon, but he trusts the judgment of a wider public. Poe's *Narrative of Arthur Gordon Pym* has a preface stating that Pym feared to publish what necessarily sounds like an improbable fiction, until finally Mr. Poe of Richmond suggested that it be published under the garb of fiction, to be signed by Mr. Poe; but now that the story is out, the facts should carry conviction through their consistency. The narrator of O'Brien's "What Was It?" says that he is prepared to meet incredulity and scorn, but he has, after mature consideration, resolved to tell the truth as simply and straightforwardly as he can.

The narrator frequently brings back from his experience some token that can now be seen; it is often placed in a public museum. In Swift's *Gulliver's Travels* Gulliver brings back tiny cattle from Lilliput. In Tucker's *A Voyage to the Moon,* Atterley has presented a pair of anti-gravitational shoes to "Madam ——, of the New York Theatre," who is thus enabled to delight audiences with her agility. At the end of Verne's *Five Weeks in a Balloon* the official record of the flight is placed in the archives of the Geographical Society. A cast of the strange monster in O'Brien's "What Was It?" is being placed by Mr. Escott in a "well-known museum of this city." The æpyornis bones of Wells's "Æpyornis Island" have been sold to a dealer near the British Museum, and a lawsuit, "Butcher *vs.* Dawson," is being waged for Butcher's salary while he was marooned on the island. Wells's Time Traveller in *The Time Machine* pulls from his pocket two flowers such as the Medical Man present has never seen before. Gottfried Plattner, in Wells's "The Plattner Story," brought back from the fourth dimension a transposed body; Plattner has before-and-after photographs that clearly show the transposition.

Of course, if the story is true, the reader wonders why particular directions and formulas are not given. Authors dodge this question in various ways. Greg's *Across the Zodiac,* for instance, starts out to describe the method by which the Martialists (Martians) break up the atom; at the critical point, however, the editor inserts in brackets: "About half a score lines, or two pages of a ordinary octavo volume like this, are here illegible." The narrator of Greer's *A Modern Daedalus* withholds "any clue to the mechanical principles involved" because they "must for the present remain my own exclusive property." In Wells's *The Island of Dr. Moreau* the principles of Moreau's surgery are explained in general and the results are seen, but Prendick (the narrator) is never allowed to enter the laboratory when Moreau is at work.

Of course writers are aware that readers see through these tricks and that, after all, they suspend disbelief because they are willing to do so. For this reason, no doubt, writers sometimes frankly avow their romances to be fiction. Even this frankness is very old. Daniel's *A Voyage to the World of Cartesius* has a prefatory "General View" that praises Lucian of Samosata for "the most advantageous Method that possibly could be thought on. He proclaims forthwith to his Readers that whatever he shall say is false." Daniel then promptly acknowledges that, in spite of his devices to "preserve the strict Law of probability" in his narrative, his story is likewise false. Even the Time Traveller of Wells's *The Time Machine* finally casts doubt upon his carefully devised and consistent story; he challenges his hearers to treat his assertion of its truth as a mere stroke of art; then he says: "And, taking it as a story, what do you think of it?" The narrator of Wells's "The Plattner Story" says that: "Frankly, I believe there is something crooked about this business of Gottfried Plattner," but he is unable to put his finger on the crooked factor. The narrator of Verne's *The Master of the World* supposes people will not believe him, and says: "I can scarce believe it all myself." Stapledon, wishing to describe the whole universe through all eternity, gives up any device whatever; his narrator in *Star Maker* goes to walk under the stars, sits down on a knoll, and imagines an adventure through all space and time. John tells his biographer in *Odd John* that he may "perpetuate the biography—as fiction, of course, since no one would believe it." In such cases, as Kearney's *Erone* states, "The record is the thing; and its message is real."

3. Love Interests

The love story is not an organic part of scientific fiction; many pieces contain no love-interest at all. But one of the persistent traditions of the voyage to another world is that the traveller is there received by a host who has a lovely daughter, and the traveller falls in love with this daughter.

In the great bulk of older scientific fiction, the love-interest is very slight. In the work of Poe, Verne, and Wells there is no love interest worth mention. Most of the characters are either young men not emotionally entangled, such as Arthur Gordon Pym or Griffin in Wells's *The Invisible Man,* or married men who only now and then think of their wives in order to wonder, like the narrator in Wells's *The War of the Worlds,* what has happened to them, or scientists who seem to have no domestic connections, unless comic ones. Graham's interest in Helen

Wotton in Wells's *When the Sleeper Wakes* is a variant of the host's daughter tradition, but even this interest is casual. Bert Smallway's Edna, in Wells's *The War in the Air,* giggles through the opening chapters, but she is forgotten through the major portion of the book and serves finally only as something to draw Bert back to England. There is no woman at all in Wells's *The First Men in the Moon* or his *The Island of Dr. Moreau.*

But when Hollywood made a moving picture of *The Island of Dr. Moreau,* a beautiful girl in danger was introduced into the story to widen the public who would be interested in the picture. This necessity for widening the public probably accounts for the inclusion of a perfunctory love story in recent scientific fiction, especially in the magazines. The method is foreshadowed in such a book as Griffith's *A Honeymoon in Space;* the narrative concerns a trip to various planets, but a honeymoon is made the occasion for the trip, and the newlyweds indulge in appropriate love-passages throughout the book.

Frequently the love-interest takes the form of a triangle. The type is illustrated in Balmer and Wylie's *When Worlds Collide* and *After Worlds Collide.* Eve, the daughter of the scientist Hendron, is engaged to marry Tony at the opening of the adventure; then she is strongly attracted to David Ransdell, whose admirable qualities cause Tony both admiration and jealousy. Eve vacillates between the two men throughout the two novels, but in the end marries Tony. This love affair could be cut from the story without affecting any major action.

Sometimes the love-interest, though not organic in the adventure, furnishes motives for the action of the story. In Smith and Garby's "The Skylark of Space," for instance, the character Seaton is in love with Dorothy Vaneman, and Crane falls in love with Margaret Spencer. The Steel Trust has the girls abducted and taken to another planet in order to make Seaton and Crane surrender their secrets. This abduction furnishes the motive for Seaton and Crane to make their voyage through space. On a strange planet, in the country of Kondal, the heroes and their sweethearts are united in marriage.

Love is often the inspiration for the hero's heroic decisions. In Griffith's *The Angel of the Revolution,* the inventor Richard Arnold falls in love at sight with Natasha, daughter of Natas, Master of the Terrorists; she loves him, but cannot speak to him of love until their task of liberating mankind has been accomplished. After Arnold has, under Natasha's inspiration, defeated the armies of the world and established peace, they are married. In Doyle's *The Lost World* a somewhat comic love story fulfills the same purpose. The narrator, Malone, is in love with a petulant girl named Gladys. She insists that, to win her, he must perform some heroic action, and to do so he goes with Professor Challenger on the expedition to the Lost World. When the conquering hero returns to his Gladys, however, he finds her married to a diminutive clerk, but Malone, now more mature, is able to console himself with his share of diamonds from a crater in South America.

4.   Humor

The satires, of course, include irony as a basic humorous device. Poe is facetious in "Hans Pfaal" and elsewhere as a means, no doubt, of evading responsibility for his extravagant fiction. Verne follows Poe in surrounding some of his scientific stories, such as *From the Earth to the Moon,* with an envelope of caricature and horse-play. He imitates this facetiousness from Poe; it is largely absurd exaggeration. For instance, in *Doctor Ox,* Verne describes the effects of abundant oxygen upon vegetable life as follows: "Asparagus attained the height of several feet; the artichokes swelled to the size of melons, the melons to the size of pumpkins, the pumpkins to the size of barrels, the gourds to the size of the belfry bell, which measured, in truth, nine feet in diameter . . . . "

Wells's scientific romances contain humor of two kinds. The first is humor of character. Wells frequently draws a limited character into the midst of world-catastrophe in order to observe him with amusement. When the Martians come, in *The War of the Worlds,* the only thing the curate can think of for days is that God does not seem to appreciate all the work the curate has done in organizing Sunday Schools. The curate was walking with the Spirit in the cool of the evening—and then, Sodom and Gomorrah! He is as baffled as a rat in a maze. Though Bert Smallways, in *The War in the Air,* is the "hero" of the book, Wells describes him with a similar detached humor; when New York is destroyed, Bert gapes and says, "Gaw!" Dozens of Wells's characters are limited in the same way. A second kind of humor in Wells's romances is a grim irony, the irony of man's pomp in the face of nature's power, or the irony of man's wishful thinking in the face of facts. Prince Karl Albert, of *The War in the Air,* cuts a sorry figure on Goat Island; even Bert perceives how artificial his tinsel is, and shoots him. Griffin, in *The Invisible Man,* dreams of world-dominion, but the reader sees all along that invisibility is a terrible handicap.

A similar ironic humor-of-character is frequent in descriptions of how limited people react to cosmic disaster. In Sherriff's *The Hopkins Manuscript,* for instance, the news that the moon will strike the earth and, perhaps, destroy it, is announced from the pulpit in Beadle. Hopkins sat tense, waiting for some explosive reaction, but none came. The villagers were slow in grasping the facts, and there is considerable humor in the description of their reactions. After the services, a grandmother, for instance, is hazy about the sermon:

" 'He says the world's going to end, Grandma!'

" 'Eh?' said the old lady.

" 'He says,' bawled the girl, 'the world's going to end!'

"The old lady's eyes lit up with a gleam of memory.

" 'That's more like old Vicar Hutchings,' she cackled. 'Vicar Hutchings used to say that every Sunday.'

"I heard the girl still shouting as they turned the bend in the lane.

" 'He says, it's going to end on the 3rd of May!'

" 'That's what old Vicar Hutchings always said,' murmured the old lady. 'But Vicar Hutchings never gave no date.' "

Stapledon's fantasies are shot through with a subtle humor, often wittily phrased irony, but sometimes whimsy. This whimsy is most delightful, I think, in passages like the following from *Sirius.* In describing the youth of the young dog and his girl-companion, Plaxy, Stapledon says: "When Sirius acquired by observation of the family's super-sheep-dog, Gelert, the habit of lifting a leg at gate-posts to leave his visiting card, Plaxy found it hard to agree that this custom, though suitable for dogs, was not at all appropriate to little girls. She was deterred only by the difficulty of the operation. Similarly, though she was soon convinced that to go smelling at gate-posts was futile because her nose was not as clever as Sirius's, she did not see why the practice should outrage the family's notions of propriety."

On the whole, however, scientific fiction is not a humorous kind of literature.

C.   *Characters*

The interest of scientific fiction is chiefly in things, ideas, and discoveries, rather than in people. For this reason, perhaps, though a few characters found in this fiction are memorable, many are not even individuals, but types. Occasionally a character develops, grows more mature, as Bert Smallways does in Wells's *The War in the Air;* nearly always a character learns, especially if he adventures into a utopian society; but for the most part, characters in scientific fiction are static. Even when a character's

outlook broadens, his emotions undergo no development; his
personality does not mature. Julian West, in Bellamy's *Looking
Backward,* for instance, enters Utopia with an open mind; he is
surprised; he listens respectfully to his host; he falls in love
with his host's daughter; the reasonableness and happiness of the
new life are apparent to him; he dreams himself back in the
nineteenth century and is horrified; and he awakes again into
Utopia. But throughout it all, he is essentially static. He is a
typical adventurer into a strange world. We may compare him
with Gulliver in Swift's *Gulliver's Travels,* who, in spite of his
intellectual growth, never progresses emotionally beyond the
horse-sense taught him by the Houyhnhnms; or we may compare
him with Barnstaple in Wells's *Men Like Gods,* who returns
to London healthier than he was, and his wife thinks an inch
or two taller, but hardly a changed man in anything except
point of view. Such characters make up the rational pupils who,
as it were, attend school in Utopia.

A more complex hero is superman, either a natural genius
or a product of some scientific food of the gods. He is usually
a misfit at single-handed war with the world. In stories concerned chiefly with adventure, his personality is simple. He is
Captain Nemo of Verne's *Twenty Thousand Leagues Under the
Sea,* Natas of Griffith's *The Angel of the Revolution,* and
Preston of Leinster's "The Man Who Put Out the Sun." In
other stories, his character and his relations to the world of
normal men are the main interest. Hugo Danner in Wylie's *The
Gladiator* is a superman of nerve and brawn; all his adventures
spring from his strength; but his powers place him also mentally beyond the pale of the normal world and a little above its
limitations. Stapledon's *Odd John* is altogether a study of
superman whose superiority lies in intellectual grasp and spiritual insight. The book is written to exhibit the new light John
throws on the muddled affairs of mankind, man's insistence that
they remain muddled, and John's inevitable martyrdom.

Scientists in scientific fiction fall roughly into three classes:
the eccentric who resembles the absent-minded professor; the
ruthless scientist devoted to truth alone; and the utopian idealist.

Of the three, the eccentric is perhaps the most common. He
may be an emotionless machine like Phileas Fogg of Verne's
Around the World in Eighty Days. He may be a narrow and
opinionated specialist, like each of the group of scientists in
Bradshaw's *The Goddess of Atvatabar,* whose names suggest their
characteristics: Professor Rackiron, electrician and inventor; Professor Starbottle, astronomer; Professor Goldrock, naturalist; and
Dr. Merryferry, ship's physician. Or he may be more subtly

developed, like Cavor in Wells's *The First Men in the Moon*. Cavor is: ". . . a short, round-bodied, thin-legged little man, with a jerky quality in his motions; he had seen fit to clothe his extraordinary mind in a cricket cap, an overcoat, and cycling knickerbockers and stockings . . . he never cycled and he never played cricket. . . . He gesticulated with his hands and arms and jerked his head about and buzzed. He buzzed like something electric. You never heard such buzzing. And ever and again he cleared his throat with a most extraordinary noise."

Scientists Bensington and Redwood of Wells's *The Food of the Gods* are "quite undistinguished-looking men as indeed all true Scientists are." Bensington wears boots cut into slits because of his numerous corns; Redwood is so nondescript "that it is hard to find anything whatever to tell the reader" about him. Doyle's Professor Challenger of *The Lost World* and other stories is a giant with an enormous head, a face and a spade-shaped beard like an Assyrian bull, a chest like a barrel, huge hands covered with black hair, and a bellowing voice. Like Challenger, Higgins of Balmer and Wylie's *After Worlds Collide* is strongly opinionated and finds nothing right in any other scientist's theories.

The scientist whose sole passion is the ruthless pursuit of truth is a frequent character. Dr. Moreau of Wells's *The Island of Dr. Moreau* thinks nothing of pleasure or pain; he stabs a knife to the hilt in his leg to show his contempt for pain. He thinks only of finding out "the extreme limit of plasticity in a living shape." The right or wrong of his experimentation with living creatures does not trouble him: "The study of Nature makes a man at last as remorseless as Nature." This passion for truth, or it may be power, is found in others of Wells's characters. It spreads outward from the laboratory to include Machiavellian world-conquerors, such as Prince Karl Albert of *The War in the Air*. The scientist Weston of Lewis's *Out of the Silent Planet* scorns all moralities except those of science: "Yes—anything whatever . . . and all educated opinion—for I do not call classics and history and such trash education—is entirely on my side." John and his supernormal friends in Stapledon's *Odd John* are similarly ruthless where the slaughter concerns only a few individuals. After they rescue survivors from a wreck in the Indian Ocean, they learn that if they bring the men ashore they will have to give testimony in court. As appearance in court may endanger the secrecy of their project, they shoot the survivors. On the other hand, John and his friends turn the same ruthlessness upon themselves and commit suicide rather than indulge in wholesale slaughter when the world's navies descend upon their island. In Huxley's *After Many a Summer Dies the Swan,* Dr. Obispo is not only ruthless, but cynical and amoral with a refined sensuality; he torments the object of his lusts partly to study her reactions.

These ruthless characters and their codes spring from that interpretation of the theory of evolution that views life as a struggle for survival in a Nature red in tooth and claw and from the interpretation of science as knowledge beyond good and evil.

In spite of ruthlessness and an amoral code, the scientist whose sole passion is the pursuit of truth is often an idealist; when he ignores human feeling in the present, he does so because he thinks in geologic terms. Present pain may be a means toward a final truth that may bring about human happiness. The scientist Hardin of Wylie's *The Gladiator,* for example, dreams of creating a race of Titans like Hugo Danner. They are better fitted to survive, and to supersede, even if to supersede means to destroy and to stamp out the cherished objects of little men's labor and affections.

Characters of yet another type, a favorite with Wells, are those bystanders who are unwittingly swept into adventure. They do little, but they see and experience and, therefore, serve as the eyepiece of the author. Prendick, in Wells's *The Island of Dr. Moreau,* is such a character. The various characters of Wells's *The War of the Worlds* are simply intelligent and observant citizens whose chief activities in the fiction consist of running away, hiding, and observing. Bert Smallways, in Wells's *The War in the Air,* plays the rôle of stage-hand in a play that he does not even understand. These characters, as Wells depicts them, represent the typical man-on-the-street brought suddenly face-to-face with the cataclysmic effects of sciences they do not comprehend.

*   *   *   *   *

The values of scientific fiction have not, in general, depended upon craftsmanship. Writers close to the first rank, such as Poe, Verne, Wells, Kipling, and Stapledon, have contributed to it, and where a first-rate writer has written scientific fiction, the romance is of first-rate literary quality—a truism applicable as well to the love story or the realistic novel.

CHAPTER EIGHT

Substance

Conventions and Content-Patterns

Since scientific fiction tells the story of an imaginary invention or discovery and the adventures that follow, naturally it differs from other fiction chiefly in substance, that is, in what the story tells.

At first glance, Mary Shelley's *Frankenstein* and Wells's *The Time Machine* do not seem much alike. But resemblances between *Frankenstein* and Wells's *The Island of Dr. Moreau* are more apparent. And when these pieces of fiction are included with others, as it were superimposed upon one another, it is evident that the stories fall into patterns that exhibit variety in details, but similarity in outline.

The story of a piece of scientific fiction is ordinarily that of an adventure into a strange world or that of the invention of a wonderful machine; frequently the two are combined. In numerous adventures into a strange world, similar features of this world are observed; the same things happen. Likewise, in stories of imaginary invention, the same experiences recur again and again. The present chapter exhibits the patterns into which these recurrent adventures and experiences fall.

A. *Patterns in Adventures of Many Kinds*

1. The Inhabitants of a Strange World

In many journeys to a strange world, the traveller discovers men like those of the known world, but usually of a finer physical type. In Seaborn's *Symzonia,* for instance, the traveller to the world inside the earth is struck with "The exquisite beauty of the women, the graceful dignity of the men, the chaste decorum and sincere politeness of all." They are a reasonable people, self-controlled and intellectual, in short, the men and women of Utopia. In Butler's *Erewhon,* likewise, the traveller finds men "of the most magnificent presence, being no less strong and handsome than the women were beautiful." The people who live inside the earth in Harben's *Land of the Changing Sun* came originally from the surface, but they are none the less "the finest specimens of physical health that could be imagined . . . remarkably strong . . . with healthful color and . . . intellectual energy." Even on a planet outside the solar system, the travellers of Smith and Garby's "The Skylark of Space" find a "superbly molded race" like men of earth, even though their skins are a glistening green.

Travellers discover other types of true men. The Time Traveller of Wells's *The Time Machine* finds men of the eight hundredth millennium beautiful and graceful, but frail and childlike with a "Dresden china type of prettiness." Evolution has smoothed the features of mankind, but removed strength along with ruggedness. These are the Eloi. But, as the Time Traveller discovers, another branch of man has degenerated into the bleached, anthropoid, nocturnal Morlocks who live underground. Similarly in Coblentz's "After 12,000 Years," men evolve into various types, such as giants with small, stupid heads who do manual labor, and wolf-faced men who engage in politics. Stapledon, looking still farther ahead to see the rise and fall of eighteen distinct species of human beings, describes the magnificent Eighteenth Men of 2,000,000,000 years in the future. They have more fingers than men have, and one of them is split into three minute organs of manipulation; they have occipital eyes, as well as an astronomical eye on the crown of the head, and the two ancient sexes have branched into many sub-sexes. And yet they are men.

Stapledon describes no other true men in the universe because he believes that infinite variety is implied in the design of the Star Maker and, therefore, in the operation of evolution. The realization that inhabitants of other planets would hardly be man-like was stated in scientific fiction even before Darwin's statement of the theory of evolution. The anonymous *Fantastical Excursion into the Planets* supposed in 1839 that "certainly size, bulk, gravity, climate, difference of length of days and years" on various planets must indicate a "vast variety of nature." In the work of Wells the principles of evolution are worked out; intelligent creatures are evolved in natural ways from other genera than those producing man. For instance, Wells's "In the Abyss" describes an intelligent vertebrate living in the depths of the ocean and developed there to fit the conditions of that environment. It is a creature with a globular body "poised on a tripod of two frog-like legs and a long thick tail," with a hand like a frog's; its mouth is reptilian; in place of ears, it has gill covers; its eyes are large and protruding to see in the dim glow of phosphorescence. For his Selenites in *The First Men in the Moon*, Wells supposes the controlled evolution of insects in a cavernous moon. The first Selenites that Bedford sees are something like upright ants, with whip-like tentacles; because gravitational pull is slight, the Selenites' feet and legs are flimsy. Faces are insect-like, with bulging eyes at the side; necks are long and jointed. After Cavor has lived for some time in the moon, he describes a variety of types, artificially created: "They differed in shape, they differed in size! Some bulged and over-hung, some ran about among the feet of their fellows, some twined and interlaced like snakes. . . . The strange and most insect-like head . . . underwent astounding transformations; here it was broad and low, here high and narrow, here its vacuous brow was drawn out into horns and strange features, here it was whiskered and divided, and there with a grotesquely human profile. There were several brain-cases distended like bladders to a huge size. . . . There were amazing forms with heads reduced to microscopic proportions and blobby bodies." The Selenites, developing from something like ants, differentiate them-selves according to their tasks in society, binding themselves as Chinese women used to bind their feet, or stimulating this or that organ with special foods and drugs; the result is a wide variety of sub-species evolved from one insect prototype.

After Wells, of course, this suggestion of evolution from a non-anthropoid species produced a great variety of creatures. The creatures of Verrill's "Beyond the Pole" are likewise evolved from a non-anthropoid prototype; they are erect bipeds, but they have eyes on stalks, tentacles, scales instead of hair, and pincer-fingers of several sizes and kinds. Like the Selenites, Verrill's creatures hatch from eggs carefully tended and treated to dif-ferentiate the species into sub-species. Also like Wells's Selenites, they train one sub-species to be rememberers and historians and therefore have no need for written records. The narrator meditates that "beyond the shadow of a doubt, these creatures had been evolved from some lobster-like ancestor." Many varie-ties of creatures strangely evolved, from either anthropoid or non-anthropoid genera, are found in the fiction of the magazines.

Stapledon's romances explore nearly every imaginable route of evolutionary development. *Last and First Men* describes seventeen species of men evolved, under varying circumstances, from the present species—including the artificial species of Fourth Men and Fifth Men. The same book also describes alien evolutions; when men move to Venus, for instance, they find there intelligent creatures developed from something like the swordfish. Three manipulative organs, or "hands," lie sheathed in the "sword," but may be extended beyond it. The strangest creatures described in *The Last and First Men* are the invading Martians evolved from a sub-vital form in accordance with the conditions prevailing on Mars. The living unit is ultra-microscopic, "far smaller than the terrestrial bacteria, or even the terrestrial viruses." Borne on dust-particles in the dry air of Mars, they feed on minute wind-borne chemicals and absorb solar energy by photo-synthesis. The unit is without any more consciousness than an individual cell in the human body, but a neural system analagous to radio enables clouds of these units to maintain a vital organization dominated by a "group mind."

It would seem that the imagination can scarcely go farther than this and still maintain a basis in logical possibility. But Stapledon's *Star Maker,* exploring the whole universe, presents hundreds of other varieties more or less consistent with the principles of evolution. On one planet, for instance, the narrator finds that evolutionary processes have not duplicated organs; the resulting creature has one leg and a tail for locomotion, a single arm (prolonged into three forearms), one nostril, and one ear, but a three-pronged proboscis bearing three eyes. On another planet, intelligent life has developed from something like a starfish. Beginning with five prongs and a stomach, the creature specialized one prong for perceiving and developed a brain (and five eyes) in it; it specialized four prongs for locomotion, and finally developed "hands" on two of them; spines developed into organs of electric perception; the mouth remained in the center of the body. On another planet, a symbiotic race develops from fish-like arachnoids and spider-like crustaceans that ride on their backs. Up to puberty the young of both species are free-living individuals; but, as their symbiotic organization develops, each seeks out a partner of the opposite species. The union which follows is life-long, and is interrupted only by brief sexual matings. The arachnoids are extravert and scientific, their partners introvert and artistic; the union, more or less telepathic, results in a well-rounded symbiotic creature that develops one of the great civilizations of the universe.

The foregoing species of intelligent creatures seem grotesque, but they are explained by known laws and develop according to them. The merely grotesque—or purely fanciful—creatures of scientific fiction may, perhaps, be defined as those whose evolution remains unexplained. Many such grotesque life-forms appear in scientific fiction. Locke's "Discoveries in the Moon," for instance, describes creatures on the moon like intelligent orang outangs, but with the membranous wings of bats. Because no process of development is offered to account for this combination, it seems a fanciful juxtaposition less acceptable to logic than the creatures described by Stapledon that are, in fact, far stranger. Wells's Martians of *The War of the Worlds* are more acceptable, though the narrator can only surmise regarding their development. They are bodiless heads; they have no nostrils, a pair of eyes, a beak, and sixteen whip-like tentacles around a mouth that opens into the lungs. The heads contain heart and brains, but no digestive apparatus; they feed by injecting the blood of other creatures into their own veins. They are sexless, but reproduce by budding; they do not sleep. Machines take the place of limbs and muscles.

In more recent scientific fiction, many sorts of grotesque creatures can be found, usually made up—like the inhabitants of the moon that Locke describes—of combinations of life-forms on the earth. The Snake Men of Burrough's *Tarzan at the Earth's Core,* for instance, are like men; they even speak the common language of Pellucidar. But they have three-toed hands, reptilian skins, pointed ears, and two short horns. Smith and Garby's "The Skylark of Space" describes flying monsters with the fangs of tigers and the shapes of spiders; one monster is armor-plated: "It seems to combine all the characteristics of bird, beast, and fish, and even to have within itself all the possibilities of both bisexual and asexual reproduction." Kline's *The Planet of Peril* contains a menagerie of nightmares, among them scaly hyenas with three horns, and grampites, that is, bat-winged vampire-gorillas with beaks for sucking human blood. The three races of hnaus (intelligent creatures) described in Lewis's *Out of the Silent Planet* are similarly grotesque, but individually more coherent. The Sorns are thin-legged, large-chested caricatures of men; the Hrossa are barrel-shaped creatures that combine the qualities of the penguin, the otter, the seal, and the stoat; the Pfifltriggs combine the qualities of the frog and the grasshopper to look "rather like a little, old taxidermist whom Ransom knew in London."

And yet other animated creatures inhabit the strange worlds of scientific fiction, such as animated plants, plant-animals, and plant-men. Bradshaw's *The Goddess of Atvatabar* contains a variety of animated plants, such as the Lillipoutum, a bird that feeds through roots on its feet and tail; for dinner, it selects a river-bank, inserts its roots into the ooze, and dines. Similar creatures appear in later fiction. On one planet visited in Smith and Garby's "The Skylark of Space," a motionless "tree" becomes animated and attacks two great animals: "It ripped at them with the long branches, which were veritable spears. The broad leaves, armed with revolting sucking disks, closed about the two animals." Stapledon's *Star Maker,* of course, includes plant men, among the several varieties trees with manipulative limbs, eyes, and feet that are also mouths to draw sap from the detachable roots (which remain planted) or foreign matter of any kind. By day these beings "sleep" on their roots as trees; by night, they prowl as animals.

Sometimes the inhabitants of other worlds are spirits. The traveller of Lucian of Samosata's *Icaromenippus* finds spirits on the moon; so does the traveller of Cyrano de Bergerac's *The Moon.* In later fiction, Astor's *A Journey in Other Worlds* describes Saturn as a spirit-world; spirits from Old Testament narrative are encountered. The traveller Ransom finds that the planet Malacandra (Mars), described in Lewis's *Out of the Silent Planet,* is ruled by Oyarsa, tutelary spirit of that planet; over Oyarsa rules Maledil, apparently God or the Spirit of the Universe; under Oyarsa are the eldila, or messenger-spirits. These spirits are described as made of forces or energies like that of light, "so fast that it is at rest, so truly body that it has ceased being body at all." To the eldila "what we call firm things—flesh and earth" seem "more like clouds, and nearly nothing. . . . These things are not strange, . . . though they are beyond our senses."

The senses of the eldila are, of course, different from those of men. This idea that other creatures may have other senses than the five known on earth is an old one. In Voltaire's "Micromegas," for instance, the visitor from Saturn has seventy-two senses, but Micromegas, from Sirius, says that "in our globe . . . we have nearly a thousand senses." Just how these senses perceive and what they perceive—beyond colors not seen on earth— is not specified. Frequently, however, pieces of scientific fiction describe creatures that perceive electric rays, radio waves, thought waves, cosmic rays, colors beyond the visible spectrum, sounds beyond hearing, and the influences of events, even future ones. The various aliens of Stapledon's *Star Maker* perceive in many ways unknown on earth. In the first world visited by the narrator, for instance, beings taste not only with their mouths, "but with their moist black hands and with their feet," experiencing their planet intimately in tastes of metals and woods, earths and rocks and plants crushed underfoot.

The favorite clothing for strange worlds, especially utopias, is a loose-flowing garment or a tunic suggestive of Greek and Roman dress. The travellers in yet other worlds find other kinds of clothing. In Mercier's *Memoirs of the Year Two Thousand Five Hundred*, the sleeper at once discards his ungainly clothing for the cloak, gown, and sash of the world of the future. Under such a garb, his host "had none of those garters that bind the hams and restrain the circulation," but instead "wore a long stocking, that reached from the foot to the waist; and an easy shoe, in the form of a buskin." Similarly, the first thing that happens to Graham, in Wells's *When the Sleeper Wakes,* is that a tailor comes to measure him and clothe him properly— like Mercier's sleeper, in trunk hose, with puffs and slashes, and flowing robe. "The fashions of the days of Leo the Tenth were perhaps the prevailing influence, but the aesthetic conceptions of the far East were also patent." A dandy of this world is more elaborately described in Wells's "A Story of the Days to Come": "His legs he encased in pleasant pink and amber garments of an air-tight material, which with the help of an ingenious little pump he distended so as to suggest enormous muscles. Above this he also wore pneumatic garments beneath an amber silk tunic, so that he was clothed in air. . . . Over this he flung a scarlet cloak with its edge fantastically curved. On his head, which had been skilfully deprived of every scrap of hair, he adjusted a pleasant little cap of bright scarlet, held on by suction and inflated with hydrogen, and curiously like the comb of a cock."

It was conventional in the imaginary voyage of the sixteenth and seventeenth centuries that the inhabitants of strange lands go naked, even when civilized. In fact, some civilized peoples are shocked that the traveller should wear clothing. This tradition persists in many pieces of scientific fiction. In Wright's *The World Below,* for instance, the Amphibian is horrified at the traveller's clothing; the traveller says that "the wearing of clothing confessed me to be an inferior, even among my own kind, as a Leader naturally would not enter into such a competition" in adornment. In Herrick's *Sometime,* people wear light garments for ornament, but bathe naked in public; when they undress they touch matches to their clothes, as they never wear the same garment twice. In Kearney's *Erone,* Earthly is embarrassed when Doreece suggests that they go swimming, for he has no bathing suit. Doreece laughs at him, strips, plunges in, and invites him to do the same.

At any rate, inhabitants of strange worlds are never ashamed to display their bodies, which are nearly always superior to those of men in health and natural beauty (even when the beauty is grotesque.) As well as having superb health, the people of Utopia and other worlds remain young for a long time, seldom show signs of senility (or even middle age), and live to great ages. Smith, in Hudson's *A Crystal Age,* for instance, supposes that Yoletta is sixteen or eighteen and is shocked to find that she is in her thirties; her father is 198 years old and hale. The inhabitants of the world inside the earth in Emerson's *The Smoky God* go to school from twenty to fifty, marry at a hundred, and live to six or eight hundred years of age. In Von Hanstein's "Utopia Island" scientists who were old before they reached the island are getting younger every day, at least in appearance, because their mode of life is based on the studies in rejuvenation made by the scientist Weigand; no drugs are given or operations performed; they are simply happy, healthy, and hopeful. When a woman of fifty disrobes in Herrick's *Sometime,* the author comments: "Her limbs were young and rounded,—the body of a mature middle-aged woman about fifty years of age, still fit and pleasing. . . . (The naked body of an average middle-aged woman of the late Christian era would have been considered a disgrace in modern Khartoum!)" Superb health of this kind, beauty of body, and longevity reach a climax in Stapledon's *Last and First Men.* The Eighteenth Men spend a thousand years in adolescence and live for a quarter of a million years.

Before a traveller to a strange world can learn much about it, he must be able to understand its language. The simplest expedient is to have the people of the strange world speak English. In Bradshaw's *The Goddess of Atvatabar* the inhabitants speak an archaic and transposed English; no explanation is offered. Similarly, in Griffith's *A Honeymoon in Space* the inhabitants of Mars speak English; the explanation is that the Martians have evolved in the same way as the English. Martians speak English in Wicks's *To Mars Via the Moon* because they are, unknown to people on earth, in spiritual communication with the earth. The Eronians, in Kearney's utopian romance, speak English, as "thought influence" has helped to shape the English language.

Almost equally absurd is communication in some universal language. In Cyrano de Bergerac's *The Moon,* people of the moon speak in music; they speak also in gestures: "For example, the movement of a finger, of a hand, or an ear, of a lip, or an arm, of a cheek, will make singly a discourse or a sentence." For ease in talking, they go naked. In the same author's *The Sun* inhabitants of a small planet near the sun discourse in a mother-tongue in which every word declares its own essence. Griffith's *A Honeymoon in Space* describes the people of Venus as speaking in song; Zaidie, the bride, breaks into song, and the Venusians understand her. Trapped by the apes of Pellucidar, in Burrough's *Tarzan at the Earths' Core,* Tarzan is scarcely surprised to hear the apes speak in a language he understands, for Tarzan has long "understood the language of the great apes as the primitive root language of created things."

But travellers through space in intellectually better disciplined books have to learn the language. In Godwin's *The Man in the Moone,* Domingo Gonsales finds the language a sort of singing, like the Chinese, but he has to learn it before he can communicate in it. The traveller in Bulwer-Lytton's *The Coming Race* is aided by hypnotism, but he has, none the less to learn a difficult language; the system of the language, including declensions of various nouns, is set forth in the romance. The traveller to Mars in Greg's *Across the Zodiac* is taught the language; it is a difficult, logical language artificially constructed as Esperanto is. The philologist Ransom, in Lewis's *Out of the Silent Planet,* both learns the language from a hross and teaches this creature:

" 'Hross,' it said, 'Hross,' and flapped itself.

" 'Hross,' repeated Ransom, and pointed at it; then 'Man,' and struck his own chest.

" 'Hma—hma—hman,' imitated the *hross.*"

The quickest way out of the difficulty that is still a reasonable way is to have the aliens exceptionally brilliant in learning language. In many books, as in Seaborn's *Symzonia* and Wells's *The First Men in the Moon,* specialists are assigned to learn the stranger's language, and they do so with amazing speed. In *Symzonia,* for instance, "At the end of the first week I was astonished and delighted to find my instructors addressing me in very good English." And in Wells's romance, two Selenites, a philologist and a rememberer, are assigned to Cavor. The philologist understands at once, and the rememberer never forgets.

In some worlds, however, there is no difficulty about language, for telepathy has been developed. Something like telepathy made its appearance in scientific fiction as early as Cyrano de Bergerac's *The Sun.* In that book the traveller meets a man who is able to read his thoughts by the simple process of arranging all parts of his body in the same order as those of the traveller: "I excite in myself by this disposal of my matter the same thought that is produced in you by this same disposal of your

matter." In Lloyd's *Etidorhpa,* I-Am-the-Man learns gradually
to converse with his host by "thought-contact." When the
traveller first speaks, and then attempts to use sign language, in
Bellamy's "To Whom This May Come," his hosts burst into
laughter; "The small boys now rolled on the ground in convulsions of mirth," for they read every thought in his mind.
Mr. Three in Stribling's "The Green Splotches" speaks English
because, he says: "I take your language forms right out of your
own minds and use them." In Wells's *Men Like Gods* the people
of earth can understand the wave-projected thought of the
Utopians, but they translate this thought into their own words;
they must have, therefore, some basic concepts to match those
of the Utopians, or they do not comprehend. For instance, when
Urthred (or Adam, as his name seems to some of the company)
describes his occupation: "He called himself something that Mr.
Barnstaple could not catch. First it sounded like 'atomic mechani-
cian,' and then oddly enough it sounded like 'molecular chemist.'
And then Mr. Barnstaple heard Mr. Burleigh say to Mr. Mush,
'He said "Physio-chemist," didn't he?'
" 'I thought he just called himself a materialist,' said Mr.
Mush.
" 'I thought he said he weighed things,' said Lady Stella."
When the narrator of Wright's *The World Below* speaks to the
Amphibian, she recoils in revulsion, for speech is an animal
characteristic; they communicate finally by telepathy, but to
do so the "receiver's" mind must be receptive and the "sender's"
must concentrate. The Fifth Men of Stapledon's *Last and First
Men* are enabled to reach their utopian culture because they
master telepathy, which conveys thought exactly where words
convey only inexact symbols. In Stapledon's *Star Maker* the
narrator enters at once into the mind of a host and sees everything through both his own mind and his host's mind; then
they go together to a third host, and so on, until they comprise
a cosmic mind. The advanced "peoples" of this book learn to
link whole planets, and finally whole galaxies, into one telepathic
union, so that "to be a conscious individual was to enjoy immediately all the united sensory impressions of all the races inhabiting a system of worlds."
Frequently natural telepathy is replaced by some mechanical
device that enables the thought of one mind to be transferred
to another. In Binder's "Adam Link's Vengeance," the automaton
Eve Link is fitted with a charged helmet; "Kay Link is fitted with a
similar helmet. "Kay's thoughts then set up an electro-vibration that
modulated the electron flow of Eve's metal brain" and "Kay's
mind poured over into the receptive Eve's."

The traveller to a strange world is nearly always taken in hand by a host, who entertains him, cares for him, and instructs him. When the sleeper of Mercier's *Memoirs of the Year Two Thousand Five Hundred* wakes into a strange Paris, a man approaches at once and offers to be his guide and teacher. When the traveller of Greg's *Across the Zodiac* arrives in Mars, Martialists (Martians) set upon him to beat him, but a kindly man of authority arrives to rescue him and receive him into his home to instruct him in Martial ways. The social propaganda in Bellamy's *Looking Backward* is enunciated through the questions of Julian West and the answers of his host, Dr. Leete. Before I-Am-the-Man of Lloyd's *Etidorhpa* goes underground, a host arrives at the cavern-mouth to escort him; the crustacean that finds the narrator of Verrill's "Beyond the Pole" becomes his custodian-host. In fact, John Earthly is brought to the planet Erone, in Kearney's romance, in order that his scientist-host can explain to him the economics and social organization of that utopian world.

The host nearly always has a lovely daughter, and the traveller promptly falls in love with her. Gulliver, in Swift's *Gulliver's Travels*, escapes falling in love, but he becomes the pet of the daughter of his host in Brobdingnag, and when Gulliver is sold to the queen, this girl becomes his nurse. The narrator in Bulwer-Lytton's *The Coming Race* falls in love with his host's daughter. In Butler's *Erewhon*, Higgs is entertained by two hosts in turn; he falls in love with Yram, daughter of the first one, but neglects her when he meets Arowhena, the daughter of his second host, with whom, finally, he elopes in a balloon. The traveller in Greg's *Across the Zodiac* saves the life of Eveena, the daughter of his host, and then marries her; he is somewhat embarrassed when the Prince gives him an apartment at court and a bevy of wives, but Eveena is willing to remain as favorite. In Hudson's *A Crystal Age*, Smith falls hopelessly in love with Yoletta, the daughter of his host, but she cannot return his love, as she is not eligible to be a Mother. Julian West, in Bellamy's *Looking Backward*, discovers that the daughter of his host, Edith Leete, is a direct descendant of his nineteenth-century sweetheart, Edith Bartlett; of course he falls in love with her. The traveller from the twenty-fifth century, in Allen's *The British Barbarians*, falls in love with the daughter of his host, who is also a married woman; the husband finally shoots the traveller back into his own century. In Wicks's *To Mars Via the Moon*, John Claxton falls in love with the daughter of one of his hosts, but cannot decide to propose to her, as he thinks it unwise to bring back to London a wife over seven feet in height.

Headley, in Doyle's *The Maracot Deep,* is unaccountably attracted to Mona, daughter of his host; they discover later that they are reincarnations of lovers in ancient Atlantis. In Kearney's *Erone,* Doreece, the daughter of Earthly's host, sets out to conduct Earthly on a sightseeing tour, and they return engaged to be married.

Shortly after his arrival in a strange world, the traveller is usually taken on a visit to the ruler. When Gonsales arrives on the moon, in Godwin's *The Man in the Moone,* he is led at once to the Prince. Klimius in Holberg's *A Journey to the World Under-Ground* is first instructed in the language of the strange planet and then sent to court. Seaborn, in Seaborn's *Symzonia,* is taken to the Great Council to meet the Best Man (ruler). In Tucker's *A Voyage to the Moon,* Atterley and the Brahmin are promptly taken to see the Governor. Cavor, in Wells's *The First Men in the Moon,* is granted an elaborate formal audience with the Grand Lunar. In Emerson's *The Smoky God,* an envoy is sent to Olaf to invite him to court and to give him the freedom of the kingdom. In Smith and Garby's "The Skylark of Space" the whole party is given lavish entertainment at the court of the Emperor. Sometimes—less frequently—the traveller's entertainment at the court arouses the jealousy of the spiritual rulers, usually a priestcraft, and a covert struggle ensues between traveller and priest, as in Greg's *Across the Zodiac.*

A tour through the World-University is important in most of the utopian romances. It is described, and its rôle as fountain of wisdom for the state is discussed. Detailed description of the University occupies a great deal of space in Campanella's *The City of the Sun.* The civilization of Bacon's *The New Atlantis* is based upon the researches conducted in Salomon's House. Klimius's visit to the University is an important part of Holberg's *A Journey to the World Under-Ground.* The traveller in Greg's *Across the Zodiac* is conducted through the University. Von Hanstein's "Utopia Island" is simply a story of how a University-of-the-World was founded on a secret island, where its researches might proceed unmolested. Yeldir, Earthly's host in Kearney's *Erone,* is a professor in the University of Astroradio Scientific Research, situated at the center of the planet's largest metropolitan area. In these stories and others, the University is the basis on which progress rests. The stimulation of scientific research is an item of first importance. Besides local research, the University sends agents everywhere to seek knowledge, somewhat as newspaper correspondents seek news; and in recent novels, new knowledge, reports on experiments, etc. are spread around the world by telegraph and radio with the speed of sports-news. Councils of state, of course, seek guidance from the University. Though Wells's *Men Like Gods* does not present a tour through a University, the entire world of this future is a kind of University; co-ordinated intellectual interests are a part of daily life.*

A number of the worlds visited are described as the original Garden of Eden. The traveller in Cyrano de Bergerac's *The Moon* arrives on the moon by falling upon the Tree of Life; he finds various Biblical characters in the Garden of Eden. The narrators of Beale's *The Secret of the Earth* and of Emerson's *The Smoky God* find that the Garden of Eden described in the Bible is located in the center of the earth. Sometimes the races found are surmised to be the Lost Tribes of Israel. There is evidence that Poe intended to have Pym discover the Lost Tribes in the interior of the earth, in the unfinished *Narrative of Arthur Gordon Pym*. The narrator of Butler's *Erewhon* surmises that the Erewhonians may be the Lost Tribes, though he cannot be sure. Sometimes Atlantis is discovered. In Verne's *Twenty Thousand Leagues Under the Sea,* the voyagers come to a dead city on the bottom of he sea; it is Atlantis. The city discovered under the sea in Doyle's *The Maracot Deep* is Atlantis.

The strange worlds are usually so idealized that few unpleasant aspects of life are described, except, of course, in the satires. But death must be dealt with. Most often, especially in recent utopias and satires, death is voluntary when a person feels his physique beginning to break down. It is accomplished by some form of euthanasia. In Wells's *When the Sleeper Wakes,* the person about to die goes first to a Pleasure City for a final good time, and, when exhausted, has euthanasia administered. In Huxley's *Brave New World* people are kept young by glandular extracts until there is some indication that death is near; then they are taken to "something between a first-class hotel and a feely-palace," given a soma-induced trip to the gorgeous East, and allowed to die; bodies are cremated in a furnace that recovers all the phosphorus. To remove fear of death, children are brought in to see how happily people pass away. In Herrick's *Sometime,* a Lethal Temple stands in the center of a square; candidates for death are examined by an elderly physician, who discourages suicide but not to the point of forbidding it; a cheerful chamber is prepared, and the candidate is put to sleep, gassed, and removed to a crematorium.

---

* It is interesting to observe that Mr. Wells's most recent, non-fictional suggestion for solving the ills of the world is simply this idea of a World-University, conventional in the scientific fiction he used to write. He elaborates the suggestion in his *The World Brain* and elsewhere.

2.   The Cities of a Strange World

In describing cities of a strange world or of the future, writers of scientific fiction have generally sought to realize either the ideal of the mammoth city or that of the beautifully planned small town. The influence of recent city-planning is manifest in later romances that combine the two in metropolitan areas of gigantic pylons separated by cultivated parklands. In Wells's "A Story of the Days to Come," the countryside has disappeared as a habitation for man. Many-laned highways stretch out from London; people motor to their engineering-agriculture in the country, but no one lives there. London is a city of massive architecture, with buildings like cliffs. As Graham looks out on this same London in *When the Sleeper Wakes,* he sees across the street an "opposite facade . . . grey and dim and broken by great archings, circular perforations, balconies, buttresses, turret projections, myriads of vast windows, and an intricate scheme of architectural relief." The public ways between the blocks of architecture are moving lanes of seats. A glass roof extends over the entire city; wind-vanes furnish ventilation; the temperature of the city is kept constant. In *A Modern Utopia,* likewise, Wells describes "great arches and domes of glass" above the wider spaces of London, and the "slender beauty of the perfect metal-work far overhead." The city described in Coblentz's "After 12,000 Years," and in many other stories from the magazines, simply magnifies the London that Wells describes; windowless buildings of steel present walls of cliffs rising for "unthinkable hundreds" of feet; far above, "edifice was joined to edifice by blindingly bright sheets of a silvery metal, which formed a roof over the streets." The "people" of Allos, in Hansen's "The Prince of Liars," live in similar cities under roofs of glass, but their buildings of luminous metal spiral upward in a twisted-cane effect. In Balmer and Wylie's *After Worlds Collide,* the plastic-covered cities of Bronson Beta stand on a plain like gigantic bubbles; buildings of plastic substances are half a mile in height and are connected by a tracery of suspended bridges.

The opposite ideal is represented in various romances. For instance, Seaborn's *Symzonia* describes a lovely city of small, white stone buildings individually designed and set in pleasant gardens. Cities of mammoth architecture are satirized in Herrick's *Sometime;* the ideal city of Khartoum is laid out in a maze of irregular design, and each section is treated by itself: "A square here, a small park there, a broad strip of greensward would be broken by color plantings," and "the bright pots of colored

plants harmonized with the frescoed walls, the vine-covered
roof lines, the rivulets of flowing water."

The effort to combine these two ideals in terms of recent
city-planning is evident in the city (or metropolitan area) of
Newlon, in Kearney's *Erone*. It is a city of widely-spaced
tower-groups set in gardens around a Civic Center. To describe
the effect, Kearney asks the reader to imagine "the finest pieces
of architecture the world over, increase their size and height
by several times, and place them at intervals round a circle
some two miles in circumference . . . then plant in the space
between, the choicest of the world's gardens." Other circles of
towers lie beyond. Each tower-group is a complete small-city
of apartment-dwellings, restaurants, stores, theatres, etc. Pleasant roadways and covered pathways connect the tower-groups,
and all connect to the Civic Center by roads like the spokes of
a wheel. Underground monorailways offer rapid transportation
to all parts of the metropolitan area. This idea is developed on
a gigantic scale in Stapledon's *Last and First Men;* as civilization reaches its apex, the whole earth becomes covered with
cruciform pylons rising several miles into the air; each pylon
is a city, separated from similar cities by twenty miles or more
of cultivated parkland.

The direction in actual city-growth, of course, has been toward
the mammoth city, in spite of the development of means of
transportation to make the great city unnecessary. But if worst
comes to worst in our Atomic Age, and bombs do fall upon
our cities, they may be rebuilt in none of the patterns suggested
above. When atomic bombs destroy the great cities in Wells's
The World Set Free, men leave the smoking craters and go to
live in towns of neighborly size. After all, a city like New York
might be more pleasant, and just as efficient, if it were broken
into five hundred towns of 20,000 each and spread over a
metropolitan area from Connecticut to mid-Pennsylvania and indefinitely up the Hudson. An alternative suggestion is offered
in Tardé's *Underground Man*. After the great collapse in that
book, men carve spacious cities from the solid granite of the
earth. But suppose the Devil himself discovers that one can
deliver an atomic bomb in a suitcase, as well as from an airplane?

A subsidiary feature of the cities of scientific fiction is worth
notice. Many of them have museums to preserve relics of the
past. Andreae's *Christianapolis* and Campanella's *The Ciity of
the Sun* describe museums. The traveller in Butler's *Erewhon*
finds that all machinery has been destroyed except that preserved in museums; in Wells's *The Time Machine,* the traveller goes to a palace of green porcelain that he discovers to be

a long-neglected museum. In Verrill's "Beyond the Pole," the crustaceans have a museum that illustrates the progress of their science.

3. The History of a Strange World

Nearly every piece of scientific fiction that describes an alien world, especially of the future, contains a synopsis of its history. This synopsis may be narrated to the traveller by his host or someone else, such as the old man of the public ways in Wells's *When the Sleeper Wakes;* it is sometimes given to him while he lies in hypnotic sleep; he sometimes gathers it from records carved on the walls, from books he is instructed to read, or from phonograph records.

These historical synopses fall into several patterns. In worlds that are simply exaggerated versions of our Machine Age, the synopsis is a record of more and more invention. In Wells's "A Story of the Days to Come," for instance, the invention of Eadhamite and of airplanes and automobiles did most to revolutionize the world; the old railways became weedy ridges and ditches; country towns disappeared; automatic machinery multiplied; technological unemployment was solved by the Labour Company whose charter compels it to feed and house any person making application—and then to put him to work in the blue canvas of the Company to pay for his sustenance. The Company has eliminated destitution, but has enslaved most of the population of the world at subsistence wages.

This problem of the Machine Age has been solved in a number of other books. In Bulwer-Lytton's *The Coming Race,* the first acceleration of invention among the Vril-ya brought about a Machine Age of "envy and hate, of fierce passions, of constant social changes more or less violent, of strife between classes, of war between state and state." But as more and more latent powers in vril were discovered, the scientific intelligence gradually asserted itself, and this power came to be used for the benefit of all classes. Similarly, in Howell's *A Traveler from Altruria,* the Altrurian describes a period when "Machines to save labor multiplied themselves as if they had been procreative forces" until it was seen that "machines for saving labor were monsters that devoured women and children." Then the people voted peacefully to discard the capitalistic system and to establish a kind of communism that employs machines for the benefit of all the people, with utopian results. Wells's *A Modern Utopia* describes the acceleration of a Machine Age to the point where there seemed no way out of the Age of Confusion except descent into a new series of dark ages. But all along the social sciences were building up data, making plans, and pointing the way toward Utopia. Gradually "the foundations of the new state were laid by a growing multitude of inquirers and workers . . . brought into unconscious co-operation by a common impulse to service and a common lucidity and veracity of mind." The result was a gradual progress that gained momentum as its benefits were seen, until finally Utopia is reached. On the planet One, as Mr. Three describes it in Stribling's "The Green Splotches," a similar adjustment took place as the planet passed through the prehistoric Steel Age into the Aluminum Age and finally into the Radium Age, employing atomic disintegration as a source of unlimited power.

Frequently in scientific fiction destructive wars and the collapse of social order precede reorganization of society. In Boisgilbert's *Caesar's Column,* after destructive wars break society into fragments, a utopian remnant flees to Africa, to organize and re-establish world-order. Astor's *A Journey in Other Worlds* describes the wars of the twentieth century, brought to an end only when weapons became so destructive that wars were suicidal; the Americas are united in one government, and Britain controls the rest of the world. The twentieth century is filled with wars in Tardé's *Underground Man;* following them, and the descent of a new ice age, a utopian remnant reorganizes underground. The Controller explains to his students, in Huxley's *Brave New World,* that the present system is the result of many wars, and finally the "Nine Years' War, the great Economic Collapse" that left a choice between "World control and destruction." Stapledon's *Last and First Men,* which is nearly all a synopsis of history from now until the Eighteenth men, describes destructive wars in the twentieth century, leading finally to a World State for some thousands of years, but ultimately to a Dark Age—and so on for many repetitions. The Utopia of Herrick's *Sometime* was founded after a series of wars had disorganized society and then a new Ice Age completed the collapse—except for an intelligent remnant who took affairs in hand.

Still other histories describe climatic changes that affect the social system. The sleeper in Hudson's *A Crystal Age* never finds out exactly what happened, but something climatic happened to bring about "a sort of mighty Savonarola bonfire" that consumed "politics, religions, systems of philosophy . . . schools, churches, prisons, poorhouses . . . kings and parliaments . . . history, the press, vice, political economy, money, and a million things more" and left man without a rag to hide his nakedness, figuratively and literally. With this opportunity, man built a pastoral, matriarchal Utopia. Doyle's *The Maracot Deep* describes the chaos when Atlantis sank into the sea, carrying, however, its utopian remnant to construct a happy society in its glass city on the ocean floor.

There is something like a utopian remnant toward the end of Best's *The Twenty-Fifth Hour*. This feature may be the most unlikely item in the book. The novel recounts the history of the immediate future as it might have been from 1940 on. The history of what brings about the collapse explains the desolation when World War II comes to a futile stalemate. Placed alongside what did happen, the record differs only in the direction taken by the lucky breaks. This and other histories in scientific fiction intend to be a warning.

H. P. Lovecraft narrates history for an entirely different purpose, to evoke wonder and terror. Many of his stories, especially the two I have selected, expound his ghastly myth of the Elder Ones who dwelt on earth in the unimaginable epoch before pre-history. From the records on the walls of the stone Antarctic city, the narrator in "At the Mountains of Madness" learns the history of the Old Ones and their dominion till the great cold came to drive them underground. Professor Peaslee, in Lovecraft's *The Shadow Out of Time,* spends his time in the library of the Great Race adding a chapter to the history of all past and future time, and his companions are historians from all times and places. He pieces together scraps about the Great Race and its origins in a transgalactic world, its journey to the earth, and its warfare with the nameless horrors underground, and with the "winged, star-headed Old Ones who centered in the antarctic." This history is both a striking piece of quasi-scientific mythology and the basis for many gruesome yarns.

4. Customs and Ideals of a Strange World

One of the oldest traditions of scientific fiction is that the traveller boastfully describes to his host the customs and ideals of his world and expects his host's admiration. But instead the host is horrified; he finds the ways of the traveller's world barbarous; he counsels him not to speak of these things in any public place. A good example of this traditional device is the chapter in Swift's *Gulliver's Travels* in which Gulliver describes English customs and ideals to the King of Brobdingnag and is rebuked with the conclusion that the English are "the most pernicious race of little odious vermin that nature ever suffered to crawl upon the surface of the earth." A similar scene occurs in Holberg's *A Journey to the World Under-Ground;* when

Klimius describes the customs of his world, the king at first yawns, and then is filled with disgust. The narrator in Bulwer-Lytton's *The Coming Race* describes America to his host; his host falls into a musing study and then extracts from him a solemn promise not to repeat a word of this description to anyone among the Vril-ya. The Professor describes customs on earth to his host in Wick's *To Mars Via the Moon*, who likewise says that he personally is willing to "make every allowance for the present state of development of the terrestrials," but these things must not be made public. In a somewhat similar way, Stapledon's *Star Maker* throws earthly customs and prejudices against a background of similar ones in the first Other World; for instance, there is no color-prejudice in the Other World, but instead an odor-prejudice. People of the "sweet" races detest the "salt"; the "sour" races detest both, and so on.

The customs and ideals of the strange world, then, are different from those of earth. The features in which they differ form a fairly consistent pattern.

Frequently, among the superbly healthy races of men found in the strange worlds, ill-health is considered to be criminal and subject to punishment, and moral obliquity is considered a sickness to be treated by a physician. In Butler's *Erewhon,* for instance, a man who becomes ill before he is seventy years old is given a trial by jury, and if he is convicted, he is held up to public scorn and perhaps sentenced to prison. Such a minor defect as failure of the eyesight in a man over sixty-five may be excused with a fine, if it is a first offense. In Square's *Flatland,* to be born with an irregular figure subjects one to the scorn of his fellows and the punishment of the law. Smith, in Hudson's *A Crystal Age,* becomes sick with love for Yoletta, but instead of finding pity for his state, he is threatened with imprisonment. In the same worlds, crime is usually regarded as a disease. In Holberg's *A Journey to the World Under-Ground* Klimius is accused of the crime of assaulting a virgin because, frightened by a bull, he climbs an animated tree. His trial for this crime consists of a blood-test to determine by what operation he can be cured. In Butler's *Erewhon,* if a man forges a check, commits robbery or violence, or suffers from any sort of immorality, physicians called Straighteners tend him, and his friends come daily to his house to inquire with solicitude whether he is recovering.

In somewhat the same way, inhabitants of many strange worlds do not fear death, but look forward to it with pleasure. In Godwin's *The Man in the Moone,* a man about to die prepares a feast and invites his friends to rejoice with him that he is soon to leave the counterfeit pleasures of the world. In DeMille's *A Strange Manuscript Found in a Copper Cylinder*, people of the strange world wish not only for death, but to be eaten afterward; they struggle for the honor of being sacrificed in the annual cannibalistic feast. His host cannot understand why More, the traveller, should fear death; it seemed to him an absurd idea. In some of the utopias or worlds of the future where euthanasia is a standard feature, suicide is encouraged.

Frequently, poverty and self-sacrifice are held to be practical virtues. This conception is given extreme development in De-Mille's *A Strange Manuscript Found in a Copper Cylinder*. More is loaded with riches, feasted, honored, and indulged; citizens scramble to make themselves his slaves. He is flattered till he learns that he is being used as scapegoat for people who wish to get rid of wealth and that only people in rags are respected. This creed from Christianity, Buddhism, and Islam alike reappears, of all places, among the utopian remnant of Best's *The Twenty-Fifth Hour*, where it is given a practical explanation. When Fitzharding and Ann arrive, a man gives them his house and loads them with vegetables and fruit. As they demur, Fitzharding's Oxford friend, clothed in rags and authority, explains that the man "isn't likely to get such another chance for 'meritorious gift' as they call it, in his lifetime." He goes on to explain why the state joins Islam in encouraging this attitude: "public services benefit, knowing neither the honor of poverty, nor the shame of wealth. Schools and colleges will flourish. . . . Gifts to public charities, including all the departments of government, have allowed us gradually to wipe out taxation with its wasteful overhead . . . crime becomes rare, if not impossible. There's . . . so little motive for theft, for murder, for fraud." Laws and regulations, chiefly concerned with property-rights, wither away: "We're on our way to being a moderately free people, for the first time in civilized history."

Many kinds of social structure are described in scientific fiction. Underlying them is nearly always some ideal of freedom, often manifested in something like anarchism. In Kiplng's "With the Night Mail," for instance, the world is ruled by the A. B. C. (Aerial Board of Control); the only laws in the world are those that concern traffic and all that it implies; that is, a man is free to conduct his personal life as he pleases, to be moral or immoral, so long as he does not interfere with the affairs of other people. This sort of anarchism prevails in the Utopia of Wells's *A Modern Utopia*. The priest among the travellers from our world, Father Amerton, objects strenuously to the Utopian habit of going naked now and then; he is shocked to learn that the in-

stitution of marriage has disappeared. "In Utopia there was
no compulsion for men and women to go about in inseparable
pairs. For most Utopians that would be inconvenient. Very often
men and women, whose work brought them closely together,
were lovers and kept very much together, as Arden and Green-
lake had done. But they were not obliged to do that." Similarly,
in Coblentz's "After 12,000 Years," marriage has been abolished.
But in this, as in nearly every other utopistic society, marriage
and procreation are separate things. Lovers may love whom they
will, but they may not have children except with the permission
of the state and according to the principles of eugenics and the
population-needs of the state. Allen's *The Child of the Phalanstery*," for instance, is concerned entirely with the state-killing
of a deformed child—in spite of the parents' affection for it.

In some scientific fiction advanced peoples have discarded faith
in feeling, especially the feelings of sentimental love and mystic
religion. In Greg's *Across the Zodiac*, for instance, the Martialists (Martians) rely entirely upon ruthless and dispassionate
mental processes for guidance. The Martians in Griffith's *Olga
Romanoff* "have no passions and they make no mistakes. What
we call love they call sexual suitability." The Martians of Wells's
The War of the Worlds are "minds that are to our minds as
ours are to those of the beasts that perish, intellects vast and
cool and unsympathetic." In Smith and Garby's "The Skylark
of Space," the religion of Kondal is "partly Darwinism, or at
least, making a fetish of evolution, and partly pure economic
determinism," though there is also a rational belief in a First
Cause. In Huxley's *Brave New World*, love is only sexuality,
and religion is a sensual orgy stimulated by the narcotic soma.

Dozens of customs appear again and again. Some worlds have
abolished machinery; worlds having a socialistic organization have
abolished money; the duodecimal system of counting, a revised
calendar, weights and measures reduced to a single pattern, and
so on, occur again and again. The Erewhonians of Butler's
Erewhon have abolished machinery; the utopians of Morris's
News from Nowhere have abolished it. Credit cards take the
place of money in Bellamy's *Looking Backward*, Kearney's
Erone, and a number of other socialistic romances. The people
of Mars, in Greg's *Across the Zodiac*, have not only a duodecimal system of counting, but a non-Arabic method of writing
figures; figures are written on paper squared like graph paper,
and the relation to a central square determines the value of a
figure, that is, whether the figure standing for 1 means 1 or 12
or 144 or 1/12, or so on.

These features are found in various romances over and over again.

5. Science in a Strange World

In many of the worlds described in scientific fiction, science has reached a state of development far beyond that of the earth. Mars, in Greg's *Across the Zodiac*, for example looks back to a period of development like our own as a dark age; the world of Wells's *Men Like Gods* strongly contrasts our sporadic science a hundred years or so old with three thousand years of organized, directed, and co-ordinated research; Stapledon's *Last and First Men* describes civilization after civilization of the future based upon the progress of science beyond any horizons now seen on earth.

Some of these worlds, especially the utopias found in uncharted places on the earth, not only develop their own science, but keep abreast of the science of the rest of the world by sending scouts on regular expeditions over the earth. The inhabitants of Utopia described in More's *Utopia*, Campanella's *The City of the Sun*, and Bacon's *The New Atlantis* regularly send out such scouts. In *The New Atlantis*, for instance, members of Salomon's House go every twelve years to various parts of the world to learn "especially of the sciences, arts, manufactures, and inventions of all the world." The Altrurian of Howells's *A Traveler from Altruria* is such a scout; the Altrurians are farther advanced than men elsewhere, "But," he says, "we profit, now and then, by the advances you make in science." The expeditions to earth in Stribling's "The Green Splotches" and in Hansen's "The Prince of Liars" are for the purpose of learning our science.

In general, the attitude toward science in scientific fiction is that it is a new magic and a new expression of beauty. Over and over again, pieces of scientific fiction assert that to science all magic is simple possibility. McLociard's "Television Hill," for instance, derides the idea that anything is impossible to science. "Impossible? . . . What may be apparently beyond the power of human intelligence to conquer today, may be . . . ridiculously simple tomorrow." Even such satires as Huxley's *Brave New World*, though they may find the machines of science brutalizing, do not find them sooty, smoky, grimy, or ugly; the machines of science are things of gleaming beauty. The attitude, in general, resembles that of Azuma-zi in Wells's "The Lord of the Dynamos": this heathen from somewhere east of Suez worships his dynamo as a god, "Greater and calmer even than the Buddhas he had seen at Rangoon, and yet not motionless, but living!" In Wells's *A Modern Utopia*, the railways, dams, and bridges are dreams of architectural perfection for "There is nothing in machinery, there is nothing in embankments and railways and iron bridges and engineering devices to oblige them to be ugly."

A great deal of scientific fiction has the avowed purpose of inculcating a love for science and, indeed, of teaching science. Prefaces and authors' Introductions declare this purpose. The anonymous author of *A Fantastical Excursion into the Planets* hopes to "excite in some young people a desire for more real and proper instruction in astronomy." Waterloo says, in his Introduction to *The Story of Ab*, that the book is based upon the work of the "ablest searchers of two continents," and he makes clear his purpose to illustrate the theory of evolution so that anyone can understand it. Wicks, in the Preface of *To Mars Via the Moon*, says that in his experience as astronomical lecturer he has found many who are interested in astronomy whenever it can be explained in "untechnical language which they can readily grasp and understand," and his romance is planned to satisfy this interest. Even in the stories found in *Weird Tales* and similar magazines, authors' forewords often state their purpose to explain some theory in science.

Even when this purpose is not expressed, it may be evident in the contents of the romance. Jules Verne wrote to explain to young people (and anyone else) such science as they might find dull in textbooks, but would find thrilling in his romances. He presents chapter after chapter of exactly the same material one would find—where Verne probably found it—in encyclopedias and textbooks, but he presents it in the midst of exciting action. Besides the story, to hold the reader's interest, Verne's *Journey to the Center of the Earth* is simply an animated and illustrated lecture on the formation of the earth, its geological periods with their flora and fauna, and the theory of evolution. His *From the Earth to the Moon and Round the Moon* is a similar lecture on the formation of the moon, its topography, and scientific research about it; his *Twenty Thousand Leagues Under the Sea* presents lectures on diving, submarines, ocean depths and ocean pressures, the flora and fauna of the sea, oysters, pearls, the mass of earth covered by the seas, geological changes in earth-and-sea masses, the formation of dry land, coral islands, the prices and values of coral, the Sargasso Sea, ocean streams, and dozens of other topics that come to mind in the course of twenty thousand leagues.

Often the author's aim is to present or defend a recently advanced scientific theory. Godwin's *The Man in the Moone* inserts into the story a fairly elaborate discussion of the new Corpernican astronomy. Cyrano de Bergerac's *The Moon* similarly explains and defends Copernican astronomy, and *The Sun,* continuing this explanation, illustrates it in the traveller's observations of the heavenly bodies and their motions. In Tucker's *A Voyage to the Moon* the narrator and the Brahmin, on their way to the moon, discuss, among other astronomical topics, the various theories to account for the formation of the moon and its composition. Greg's *Across the Zodiac* presents, in the guise of an elaborate moving picture, a panorama of the development of life on Mars—a development admirably illustrating the theory of evolution. In *Flatland,* Square's explanation of a third dimension to a two-dimensional creature by implication explains to his readers what is meant by four-dimensional space. London's *Before Adam* presents an illustration of the theory of evolution; and somewhat similarly, Doyle's *The Lost World* and Taine's *Before the Dawn* describe the pterodactyls, iguanodons, and similar creatures that lived on earth in prehistoric ages.

Frequently, of course, the science is only quasi-science. Cyrano de Bergerac's *The Moon,* for instance, explains that water rises in a pump not because Nature abhors a vacuum, but because "it is joined with the air by an imperceptible link and so is lifted up when we lift the air which holds it." The same book offers an explanation for the turning of the earth: sunbeams striking upon it turn it as one turns a globe by striking it with the hand. Perhaps Cyrano believed these theories in 1657. Perhaps, likewise, Seaborn believed (as Symmes and others did) that the earth is hollow and habitable within, as it is described in *Symzonia.* A great deal of the fiction recently published in magazines presents quasi-science. An elementary knowledge of atomic structure, for instance, would discredit the idea that atoms may be inhabited, as they are supposed to be in Cummings's *The Girl in the Golden Atom.*

6. The Crisis in a Strange World

The foregoing features, found everywhere through scientific fiction, tell no story, and there must be a story. To tell a story in which something happens authors of scientific fiction invent a conflict of some kind. For this reason, the traveller to a strange world usually arrives at a moment of crisis in the life of that world. This crisis is not found in all the earliest pieces, such as the utopias of More and Bacon, or the early imaginary voyages, such as Godwin's *The Man in the Moone* and Paltock's *John Daniel.* It is, however, found in the satires of Swift and Holberg; for instance, in Swift's *Gulliver's Travels,* Gulliver arrives in Lilliput as that country is threatened by Blefuscu, and he per-

forms the service of capturing the Blefuscan fleet. Verne achieves
narrative interest in the conflict of the individual inventor—such
as Captain Nemo or Robur the Conqueror—with a hostile world.
But Greg, in *Across the Zodiac,* describes a Mars-wide conflict
between the followers of the Star and the materialists, during
his narrator's visit to Mars. The historic romances of the period
1895-1914 describe tremendous wars of the future; and Wells,
writing chiefly in this period, describes crises in the present
world (as in *The War of the Worlds* and in *The War in the Air*)
and periods of crisis in other worlds, as in *When the Sleeper
Wakes.* Graham's awakening is a signal for the outbreak of
civil war, in which Graham takes part and loses his life.

In recent scientific fiction, especially in the magazines, the
traveller to a strange world nearly always arrives at the outbreak
of some critical struggle. In Cummings's *The Girl in the Golden Atom,* for instance, the Chemist arrives at court just as
a hostile race from the other side of the atomic planet is about
to attack, and he performs the service of a modern Gulliver by
enlarging his size and trampling the hostile army to extinction.
Wells's *The Time Machine* tells of no crisis in the life of the
Eloi except the somewhat permanent threat of the Morlocks,
but Cummings, retelling that story in *The Man Who Mastered
Time,* has his traveller take part in a destructive war. In
Verrill's "Beyond the Pole," the narrator arrives just when the
enslaved ants revolt, escape, and advance to battle. In Smith
and Garby's "The Skylark of Space," the travellers arrive on
a strange planet when the armies of two great nations, Mardondale and Kondal, are preparing for deadly combat; the men
of earth play a critical rôle in the war that breaks out. In magazine fiction, men of earth, no matter how far behind Martians
or Venusians in civilization, science, or technical equipment,
manage to play critical rôles in the worlds they visit.

The foregoing features are found in all kinds of scientific fiction with enough frequency to be called traditional patterns.
Other patterns are found in special kinds of scientific fiction.

B. *Patterns in Adventures on a Strange Planet*

1. The Voyage Through Space

The voyage through space on the way to a strange planet
falls into a fairly consistent pattern. If the space-flier is a projectile that starts with a sudden impact, the traveller is stunned
at the start, but he wakens to consciousness within a short time,
as the travellers do in Verne's *From the Earth to the Moon.*

His first observation then is a view of the earth that seems spread out like a map below him; he may keep a diary, recording his views of earth, as Hans does in Poe's "Hans Pfaal"; he may observe closely to see whether the polar areas show any such opening as Symmes declared to exist in his theory of the hollow earth. Atterley and the Brahmin, in Tucker's *A Voyage to the Moon,* fail to see such an opening, but suppose that it may exist. Hans in Poe's "Hans Pfaal" does see a great depression and a black space surrounded by ice; he supposes that Symmes's theory may be correct. Finally, as the spaceship recedes, the earth becomes a vast moon, seeming from the moon itself ten to thirteen times as large as the moon seems from the earth; its markings of light and shadow outline earthly geography as on a map.

Then the traveller turns his attention to the planet he is approaching. He imagines, perhaps with fear in his heart, as Hans Pfaal does, what he may find there. A typical approach to the moon is that in Wells's *The First Men in the Moon.* Bedford and Cavor talk of the extinct volcanoes, lava wildernesses, and wastes of frozen air they may find; they talk of the length of the lunar day and the blaze of sunlight that falls upon the moon. The moon grows larger as they approach it, till finally, "The whole area was moon, a stupendous scimitar of white dawn with its edge hacked out by notches of darkness, the crescent shore of an ebbing tide of darkness, out of which peaks and pinnacles came climbing into the blaze of the sun." Then, in spite of using the gravitation of the sun as a brake, they crash on the moon into a "snow" bank of frozen air that, as the sun touches it, becomes a mist, and then thins into an air that, when they leave the car, pinches the lungs.

In Verne's *Round the Moon* and Wicks's *To Mars Via the Moon,* the observation of lunar topography is an important part of the fiction. Verne lectures on the moon in detail; the Professor of Wicks's book devotes chapters to discussion of lunar geography, and includes astronomers' maps of various areas. Sometimes the trip through space affords magnificent spectacles. In Balmer and Wylie's *When Worlds Collide,* for instance, the travellers see not only the geography of the earth as it turns beneath them, but the approach of the destructive star, Bronson Alpha. They watch the earth bulge out toward the star, crack, become plastic before their eyes, and finally grind into it in a sun-burst of flame. "The magnitude of the disaster was veiled by hot gases and stupendous flames."

In less-exciting voyages, the phenomena of gravity beyond the influence of the earth attract the traveller's attention. In Verne's

From the Earth to the Moon, for instance, the travellers find themselves very light; they enjoy jumping to the top of their cylinder; later they weigh nothing at all and can float in the air of the cylinder; when Captain Nicholl "drops" a glass of water it remains suspended just where it leaves his hand. The dog dies, and it is ejected from the car; internal pressure spreads it to a shapeless mass, but it is attracted by the gravitational pull of the space-ship and accompanies the travellers just outside the window. Greg, in *Across the Zodiac,* offers elaborate observations on the phenomena of interplanetary gravitation; he weighs something, but is able to suspend himself from the ceiling by his little finger for a quarter of an hour without fatigue; he upsets a cup of coffee, but picks up the cup and catches the liquid before it completes its feather-like fall to the floor; he stands on his head without effort and without congestion of blood. In Wells's *The First Men in the Moon,* the loose bundles and blankets on the floor float into the center of the car and form a rough sphere, the center of gravity for the car. In Pseudoman's *Zero to Eighty* the travellers try to draw water from a water-cooler, but have to compress the air above it to make it flow through the spigot; when it gets into a glass, it assumes a spherical shape, and to drink it, the travellers have to toss the ball of water into their mouths. They enjoy blowing spheres of water around the car as children blow bubbles.

Holberg's *A Journey to the World Under-Ground* involves Klimius's travel from planet to planet inside the earth; for a time he is a satellite of one planet, until a bird takes him to the planet; while he is in this predicament, crumbs of bread and cheese from his lunch circle around him like satellites. The same thing is true in Bradshaw's *The Goddess of Atvatabar;* Starbottle and Flathootly go up to a point of equilibrium between the ground and the sun inside the earth and there dine with their dishes floating in the air. Weston of Lewis's *Out of the Silent Planet* builds a tremendous sphere, and in its center places a smaller sphere; the inner sphere is packed full of all the goods to be taken to Mars; then around it, the outer sphere is arched into a number of pleasant rooms with curving floors—the surface of the inner sphere. In space, therefore, the loaded central sphere draws everything downward to it as a gravitational center.

At the point of gravitational equilibrium between the earth and another planet any car that is weighted at the bottom turns over. This *bouleversement* is, in earlier scientific fiction, a surprise to the traveller. In Paltock's *John Daniel,* the travellers do not know they are going to the moon; they are simply flying in an airplane. Then something happens; the machine joggles and seems to overset; after they descend quickly to the "earth," find everything strange, and re-ascend, the same thing happens again. In Tucker's *A Voyage to the Moon,* Atterley is asleep during the *bouleversement;* he wakens to find himself lying not on the floor, but on the ceiling; the Brahmin explains to him what happened. Similarly, Hans is asleep in Poe's "Hans Pfaal" when the *bouleversement* occurs; when he wakes he looks up toward the "moon" and is amazed at its vast expanse, but looking downward toward the "earth" and seeing it to be really the moon, he is able to understand what happened. Verne's *From the Earth to the Moon* contains a similar *bouleversement,* and it occurs or is accounted for in more recent scientific fiction.

Travellers to other planets in recent fiction anticipate and prepare for not only the *bouleversement,* but other eventualities. Poe supposed air between the earth and the moon, but found it very thin indeed; a condenser supplies Hans of "Hans Pfaal" with breathable air. Recent fiction supposes no air in interplanetary space, and but thin air on the moon—heavy air, perhaps, on other planets. Some preparation must be made for entering this air. The traveller in Greg's *Across the Zodiac* lets the air of Mars gradually into his space-car through a valve, testing it carefully. Likewise Cavor and Bedord, in Wells's *The First Men in the Moon,* spend a long time letting air out of their car through a valve and becoming accustomed to the thin lunar air. Other travellers prepare themselves for thin (or heavy) air while flying through space; for instance, the Professor in Wicks's *To Mars Via the Moon* has a special compartment in the car filled with a thin air and a little of the nitrous oxide they expect to find on Mars. Each traveller spends eight hours a day in this compartment in "training" for the atmosphere of Mars.

Sometimes the voyage through space has curious mental effects; the traveller feels cut off from reality; he doubts his own identity. Bedford, in Wells's *The First Men in the Moon,* for instance, "became, if I may so express it, dissociate from Bedford. . . . I saw him . . . very much as one might review the proceedings of an ant in the sand." Ransom, in Lewis's *Out of the Silent Planet,* feels himself curiously vitalized while travelling through space; rays that do not penetrate the earth's atmosphere immerse him in a bath of energy and of lucidity of thought.

Convincing descriptions of the voyage through space are found chiefly in book-length romances. In many magazine stories a trip to Venus is too commonplace for description—let's get on with the action! Some stories of the magazines have space-ships that travel faster than light. Space-fliers in Smith and Garby's "The Skylark of Space" click off 236 light-years in two days!

2. Features of a Strange Planet

Arrived on a strange planet, the travellers may discover a world that is, for the most part, like the earth. The moon in Tucker's *A Voyage to the Moon,* for instance, offers no strange features. The vegetation of Mars is more orange than green in Greg's *Across the Zodiac,* and of course seas and land-masses are different from ours, but the physical features of the planet are not very different. Sometimes the traveller arrives in a "prehistoric" world of great beasts, birds, and serpents, such as are described on Jupiter in Astor's *A Journey in Other Worlds,* but this grotesqueness belongs to the epoch of the arrival, rather than to anything strange in the planet.

Strangeness appears, however, in many of the trips to the moon. Kepler's *Somnium* describes a moon divided into zones, one of which is bathed in burning heat and light, another in eternal cold and darkness. Mountains and valleys are rugged and gigantic; fissures extend for miles into the moon. All life is conditioned by the fortnightly visit of the sunlight; life springs up, plants grow apace, and then everything withers. A similar moon is described in Paltock's *John Daniel;* mountains are precipitous, valleys perpendicular; tunnels lead into the moon. The travellers of Verne's *Round the Moon* do not land, but they observe a similar volcanic desolation—though indeed, at one point on the dark side of the moon, they think they see the ruins of some great fortress. The newlyweds of Griffith's *A Honeymoon in Space* likewise find the moon a dead and desolate world, though at the bottom of a valley they do come upon ruins of cities; they find something like a cross between an octopus and a smooth-skinned gray ape living at the bottom of a crater in the mountain Newton. Wells's *The First Men in the Moon* describes a similar moon on the surface, but inside it is a honeycomb of caverns and galleries around a central sea.

Saturn is sometimes found to be, as in Griffith's *A Honeymoon In Space,* a planet with a soupy atmosphere in which strange creatures swim, as large as whales but as formless as jellyfish. Sometimes Saturn is described, as in Astor's *A Journey in Other Worlds,* as a world of spirits. Sometimes a planet is so strange that the traveller can make no sense of anything until he has been there for some time. When Ransom steps onto Mars, in Lewis's *Out of the Silent Planet,* he sees colors and shapes, but he is able to form no coherent images of the planet until he learns more about it. Even the water of a lake, for instance, behaves in a queer way; instead of rippling, it rises into sharp-pointed peaks; mountains are steep cones. These phenomena, he finds later, are due to the slight gravitational pull of the planet that enables any upward force to thrust higher and a weight to rest on a more slender foundation than on earth.

Strange worlds, especially the planets, often have an abundance of precious stones and precious metals, some of them not found on earth at all. In Godwin's *The Man in the Moone,* the Prince makes Gonsales a present of three jewels, a Poleastis stone that, put in fire, remains hot until cooled in liquid, a Machrus stone that gives off light like a lamp, and an Ebelus stone that, clapped to a man's skin, takes away weight or, reversed, increases weight. Atterley, in Tucker's *A Voyage to the Moon,* brings back a stone that takes away weight. Bedford, in Wells's *The First Men in the Moon,* finds that chains with which he is bound are solid gold; he and Cavor find gold everywhere. In one of the worlds of Smith and Garby's "The Skylark of Space," platinum, gold, and silver are more plentiful than such metals as copper. The worlds inside the earth likewise contain precious stones and metals. Seaborn's *Symzonia* describes an abundance of gold and pearls; in Beale's *The Secret of the Earth,* the domes of buildings are made of green gold, columns of lapis lazuli, and archways of malachite; in Emerson's *The Smoky God,* tables of the inner world are veneered with gold.

Naturally, weight on a strange planet varies from that on earth; on small planets, men weigh little and leap about with a minimum of effort; on large planets, such as Neptune, they are so pressed · to the ground they can scarcely lift one foot above another. In Godwin's *The Man in the Moone,* for instance, Gonsales is able to leap fifty or sixty feet into the air; Lunarians often travel by leaping into the air and fanning themselves along with fans. The traveller is usually aware of this diminution of weight as a theory, but the fact takes him by surprise. In Tucker's *A Voyage to the Moon,* for instance, Atterley meets a dog in the street, intends to leap across a gutter, and lands on the opposite side of the street. In Verne's *Hector Servadac,* Ben Zoof intends to leap a ditch, but bounds forty feet into the air. The traveller in Greg's *Across the Zodiac* is well aware that his weight is diminished on Mars, but he forgets this fact when he comes to jump a ditch and naturally lands some distance beyond the other side. The thin air of the moon exhilarates Bedford in Wells's *The First Men in the Moon;* he jumps from one crag to another and lands beyond it, clutching to the side; he and Cavor then spend some time practising leaps till they can gauge their distance properly.

3. The Invasion from a Strange Planet

The idea is very old in scientific fiction that men from earth may invade a planet or that creatures living on a planet may invade the earth. Cyrano de Bergerac's traveller in *The Moon* meets a man on the moon who came originally from the sun with a party that invaded the earth in ancient times. In Tucker's *A Voyage to the Moon,* an official on the moon wishes to detain Atterley and the Brahmin because he fears that they will show other people on earth the route to the moon and the moon will be invaded. The Prince, in Greg's *Across the Zodiac,* seeks to buy the secret of apergy so that he may send an invading party to the earth; the narrator, of course, refuses to sell. Wells's *The War of the Worlds* is the story of an invasion from Mars. In later fiction, this invasion of the earth—or threat of it—is a standard feature. According to the myth underlying Lovecraft's stories, life did not originate on earth at all, but invaded it, filtering down from the stars, or grasping eagerly at earth from dying older worlds, and waging gigantic war for earth incredible millions of years before the beginning of man. The molecular entities of Mars invade the earth in clouds in Stapledon's *Last and First Men,* and, in turn, the Fifth Men invade and conquer Venus; later species of men invade and conquer Neptune.

So far as I know, Greg's *Across the Zodiac* is the first book to suggest that an invasion may be repelled through the use of bacteria. The suggestion is an oblique one. Rose cuttings taken to Mars by the traveller evidently are infected with a Turkish disease; one of the narrator's wives on Mars, Eunane, tends the roses, becomes infected, and, without any resistance to this disease, dies. Other inhabitants of Mars take the greatest precautions to stamp out this disease, deadly to them. Apparently Wells made use of this suggestion for the "surprise" climax of his *The War of the Worlds;* in the midst of their conquest of the earth, all the Martians die, victims of man's diseases to which they have no resistance. Since Wells's use of this feature, it has become a standard one. Wells makes use of it again, for instance, in *Men Like Gods.* The Utopians of that book have stamped out diseases, and when men from earth enter their world bringing bacteria, several epidemics break out, so that the men of earth have to be isolated on a crag, and the Utopians fill their hospitals with people desperately diseased. Likewise, in Balmer and Wylie's *After Worlds Collide,* people who reach Bronson Beta safely and there work on a particular "automobile" that they discover contract a disease unknown on earth and die of it. According to scientific fiction, then, as long as man is diseased he has a powerful weapon against invasion from any strange planet.

C. *Patterns in Adventures in the Future*

1. The Sleeper

Traditionally, a traveller gets into a world of the future by going to sleep and waking into the future world. The earliest sleepers re-awakened into their own world and found that the adventure was a dream.

The earliest utopias are utopias in hidden places; modern utopias are generally in future times. To get to them, as well as to get to other worlds of the future, a man falls into a sleep like a trance that lasts any number of years. Mercier's *Memoirs of the Year Two Thousand Five Hundred* is frankly a dream, for the narrator awakens in the opening chapter and then proceeds to tell how he went to sleep after a discourse on Reason and then dreamed that he awakened as an old man, in the Paris of 2500. Mrs. Griffith's "Three Hundred Years Hence" is also a dream, but the reader does not know it is a dream until the end of the story. Aside from this final awakening, the narrator goes to sleep, an avalanche covers his house, and he is dug out in the excavation for a new street three hundred years later. Stories not concerned with utopian material prepared the way for the later sleepers who do not merely dream, in employing suspended animation for other purposes. For instance, About's *The Man with the Broken Ear* is the fantasy of a man who is desiccated and preserved for half a century, to come to life when moistened; Russell's *The Frozen Pirate* describes a man who comes to life after being frozen for half a century. Then Hudson's *A Crystal Age* describes a man who loses consciousness in a cave during a landslide and awakens in a distant future. Bellamy makes the long sleep of Julian West reasonable by describing his insomnia, the underground sound-proof room in which he sleeps, and the fact that a hypnotist has to put him to sleep; when the hypnotist leaves town, others neglect to waken the sleeper, and he is found during excavations two hundred years later. Wells's sleeper in *When the Sleeper Wakes* falls into a cataleptic trance after drugs, exercise, and other devices have failed to give him a normal sleep; he remains in this trance for two hundred years. In Coblentz's "After 12,000 Years" a man is made the subject of an experiment in suspended animation, but an explosion of chemicals kills the experimenter, doctors declare the sleeper dead, and he awakens from his grave during a landslide twelve thousand years later.

The amazement with which the sleeper discovers the date of his awakening is a conventional feature. In Mercier's *Memoirs of the Year Two Thousand Five Hundred,* the sleeper goes to sleep a young man, but awakens in the future a white-bearded old man; he stares into the mirror; he finally goes out into a strangely splendid street and looks at the date on a new-looking statue; he puzzles over the "MMD" on it, but finally accepts the fact that the year is 2500. When the resuscitated pirate of Russell's *The Frozen Pirate* is informed that the year is 1801 instead of 1753, he believes his informant is either crazy or a trickster. When Julian West awakens in Bellamy's *Looking Backward* and is informed of the date, he becomes nauseated; Dr. Leete gives him a draught that puts him into a natural slumber for twelve more hours. The Catholic priest in Benson's *The Dawn of All* is so shocked at his sleep of more than half a century that he breaks one of the commandments: "Good God! Father, am I mad? . . . Oh, for God's sake!"

2.   Other Time-Travellers

Three other means of travelling through time are employed in scientific fiction. In *The Time Machine,* Wells carefully rationalized time as a fourth dimension and described a machine for travelling through it at any speed, as an airplane travels through space. This time-machine becomes a vague device in Wright's *The World Below* and a time-airplane in Cummings's *The Man Who Mastered Time;* it has appeared in a great variety of forms in the magazines. It is simple: one adjusts a dial and moves forward or backward through time at any speed, to any destination.

This rationalization of time as a fourth dimension suggests that present and future (or past) may be co-existent. In Allen's *The British Barbarians,* the traveller from the twenty-fifth century comes into the present and departs into his own world by fading into the proper dimension. In Wells's *Men Like Gods,* scientists in a world of the future revolve a dimension, and Barnstaple, riding along an English road in an automobile, finds himself suddenly on a similar road in this future.

Another method of time-travel assumes the co-existence of past, present, and future, but supposes that three-dimensional bodies cannot move about at will along the time dimension. The mind, however, may do so. The time-traveller goes into a trance and projects his mind into the desired past or future where it enters a selected body, either to oust the mind already inhabiting it or simply to dwell within this mind, occasionally influencing it. This is the method of time-travel employed in Stapledon's *Last and First Men.* A member of the eighteenth species of man dictates the book through a man living in the present. In *Last Men in London,* the mind from the future is content to look through the eyes of his host and occasionally to influence him. In Lovecraft's *The Shadow Out of Time,* this process of mental time-travel is aided by a vaguely-described machine, and a double-transfer takes place. The mind from the Great Race enters Peaslee's body, and Peaslee's captured mind goes back through time to dwell in the body of his captor.

Other methods of explaining a present picture of the past or future do not involve time-travel. For example, in John Taine's *Before the Dawn* pictures of the past are mechanically released from light stored up in atoms; and in Hunting's *The Vicarion* pictures of both the past and the future are materialized from impressions in the ether.

Many writers, however, tell a story of the past or future without time-travel. Huxley's *Brave New World,* Forster's "The Machine Stops," and many others simply have a setting in the future.

3. The Marvel of Compound Interest

The inheritance or discovery of a vast fortune plays some part in scientific fiction. Verne's *The Five Hundred Millions of the Begum* and Chamberlain's *6000 Tons of Gold* are based upon such a fortune. In About's *The Man with the Broken Ear,* the wealth of the desiccated man grows by compound interest during his period of suspended animation, and part of the story concerns his attempts to lay hands on this money. Wells used the device of cumulative interest in *When the Sleeper Wakes.* Graham, the sleeper, is willed a fortune by a cousin, and the fortune is administered by a Board of Trustees. These men invest the money wisely; other people, marvelling at the sleeper's continued trance, leave more money to him. When Graham awakes, he discovers that he owns half the world and that his Trustees are, in fact, masters of the world, "Because they are the paying power—just as the old English Parliament used to be."

D. *Patterns in Adventures in Still Other Worlds*

1. The World Within the Earth

Adventures into a world inside the earth fall into two patterns. One pattern is based upon Symmes's theory that the earth is a hollow shell, open at the poles, and habitable within. Among the pieces of fiction that are more or less based on this theory are Seaborn's *Symzonia,* Poe's "MS. Found in a Bottle" and *The Narrative of Arthur Gordon Pym,* Bradshaw's *The Goddess of Atvatabar,* Beale's *The Secret of the Earth,* and Emerson's *The Smoky God.* A second pattern, by no means so consistent in details, is not based upon Symmes's theory. It is illustrated in such pieces of fiction as Holberg's *A Journey to the World Under-Ground,* Verne's *A Journey to the Center of the Earth,* Bulwer-Lytton's *The Coming Race,* Harben's *The Land of the Changing Sun,* Lloyd's *Etidorhpa,* and Tardé's *Underground Man.*

a. Symmes's hollow earth

In Symmes's theory, strong ocean currents near the poles flow toward the poles and then through them into the internal world. The traveller coming close to either pole is caught in an irresistible current and borne across the "rim" into the earth. In Seaborn's *Symzonia* the current draws the ship into a region where "The compass was now no manner of use," and Captain Seaborn is sure that he is going over the rim, as later events prove to be the case. The southward currents are, of course, found in Poe's *The Narrative of Arthur Gordon Pym* and other pieces based upon Symmes's theory. In Poe's *Narrative* the current becomes gradually faster, a mile an hour, and finally a "cataract." In Beale's *The Secret of the Earth,* though the travellers enter the earth through the North Polar opening, they are carried by similar currents.

Symmes's theory explains that the flattening of the earth at the poles and the refraction of sunlight there cause the climate to be warm. Seaborn's *Symzonia* describes a rim of ice beyond which the air gradually warms to a temperature of spring-like warmth; Poe's *Narrative* exaggerates this feature and includes heat of volcanic origin, so that both air and water are hot; the water is finally so hot that Pym cannot bear to hold his hand in it.

In Symmes's theory, the polar ocean simply merges, without break or cataract, into the ocean of the internal world. Except for the strange position of the sun and the queer behavior of the compass, there would be, according to Symmes, no strange phenomena at the rim or in the inner ocean. Seaborn's *Symzonia* follows this pattern; the sailors do not know that the ship is inside the earth, but suppose it proceeding northward toward the outer equator. In Poe's "MS. Found in a Bottle" and *The Narrative of Arthur Gordon Pym,* however, a cataract is suggested; both stories break off just as the travellers reach the cataract. Other pieces based upon Symmes's theory follow it somewhat more faithfully. In Bradshaw's *The Goddess of Atvatabar,* the ship sinks into a "vortex," but it amounts to only an acceleration in the current.

On the rim itself, Seaborn's *Symzonia* describes volcanic islands inhabited by friendly, black natives. Poe's *Narrative* heightens this picture by describing active volcanoes and natives that seem friendly, but turn out to be treacherously hostile. The other books following Symmes's theory omit this detail. *Symzonia* also describes the discovery of "mammoth bones" on an island; Poe's *Narrative* describes the discovery of strange bones; Emerson's *The Smoky God* discusses the factual discovery of mammoth bones by scientists exploring the North Polar regions.

Seaborn, in *Symzonia,* conjectures that the original habitation of man was inside the earth; men outside the earth may be, he supposes, "indeed descendants of this exiled race; some of whom, penetrating the 'icy hoop' near the continent of Asia or America, might have peopled the external world." What Poe's *Narrative* would have found, if it had continued, is not clear, but suggestions in the story indicate that the Lost Tribes of Israel people the inner world. The travellers in Beale's *The Secret of the Earth* surmise that the Garden of Eden was located inside the earth; those compelled to leave it, "from whatever cause, naturally looked back to it as the hailing place of their race, and taught that fact to their children." In Emerson's *The Smoky God,* "Beyond question, this new land 'within' is the home, the cradle, of the human race."

b.   Other hollow earths

Bradshaw's *The Goddess of Atvatabar* and Emerson's *The Smoky God,* though following Symmes's theory in general outline, depart from it in describing a sun at the center of the earth. About it, in *The Smoky God,* clouds rotate regularly to leave it a brilliant white during the "day," but a smoky red in the evening. This central sun may have been suggested by journeys to the world underground that have no relation to Symmes's theory. In Holberg's *A Journey to the World Under-Ground,* the hollow earth contains a solar system; around a central sun, various planets move in regular orbits; this sun lights also the inner surface of the earth.

Still other worlds inside the earth are not set in an earth entirely hollow, but in vast caverns. This is true in Verne's *A Journey to the Center of the Earth,* lighted by volcanic fires and constantly flickering electrical flashes; Bulwer-Lytton's *The Coming Race,* lighted by vril; Harben's *The Land of the Changing Sun,* lighted by an artificial electric sun; Lloyd's *Etidorhpa,* lighted by a sort of osmosis of light through the shell of the earth; and Tardé's *Underground Man,* set in artificially made and artificially lighted caverns. All these worlds describe the use of volcanic fires as a source of warmth and power.

Verne's *A Journey to the Center of the Earth* finds a lake at the bottom of the cavern; Wells's *The First Men in the Moon* describes the honeycombed galleries of the moon to lead toward a sea in the center of the moon. Lovecraft's "At the Mountains of Madness" supposes that the Elder Ones live about a sea in the center of the earth. Lloyd's *Etidorhpa* describes the center of the earth as something like a power-charged vacuum, where, perhaps—for the story breaks off—spirits dwell. The phenomena of gravitational change, similar to that in voyages to the planets, are found in descents into the earth in Holberg's *A Journey to the World Under-Ground* and Lloyd's *Etidorhpa.*

2. The World in the Atom

To illustrate the play of forces within the atom, physicists have drawn pictures that resemble diagrams of the solar system. The nucleus bears some analogy to a sun, and the electrons to planets. From this hint, writers of scientific fiction, neglecting the difference between force and matter, have discussed relativity of size and told stories of adventures on "planets" within the atom.

The basis for such a story was laid long ago (1858) in O'Brien's "The Diamond Lens." This story went no further than the narrator's discovery, through a powerful lens, of a beautiful girl dwelling within an atom of a drop of water, his falling in love with her, and his despair when the water dried up and the girl died. But in the later pattern of adventure within the atom, illustrated in Cummings's *The Girl in the Golden Atom,* the narrator takes an elixir that reduces him in size so radically that he can enter the atom, join the beautiful girl, and engage in various adventures. Essentially these adventures, narrated in a number of stories in the magazines, do not differ from those on any alien planet.

E. *Patterns in the Adventures of a World-Catastrophe*

1. Cometary Collision

Poe's "The Conversation of Eiros and Charmion" narrates the story of the end of the world; a comet swinging close to the earth increases the proportion of oxygen of the atmosphere to the point where, at first, people are singularly exhilarated, and then the earth itself bursts into flame.

The pattern of world-catastrophe outlined by Poe is very frequent. Verne toys with the idea in *Hector Servadac*, but the idea must have seemed to him too grim for serious treatment. At the climax of Griffith's *Olga Romanoff*, as the Aërians battle Olga's Russian hordes, word comes from astronomers on Mars that in September of 2037 a comet, the fragment of a collision near Andromeda in the year 1920, will pass close enough to the earth for its incandescent gases to destroy terrestrial life. It comes as a "Fire-Cloud," growing from a minute "star" to a flaming mist, and then disappearing from view as the earth is clothed in a mantle of steam. The Aërians have given up the battle, hollowed a cavern deep in the earth, and retreated into it. When they emerge after a long time, the star has passed, but every combustible thing on the earth has been burned to cinders. Wells's "The Star" describes the storms, upheavals, tidal waves, volcanic eruptions, and slipping of whole continents on their bases, as a wandering star comes from outer space, swings close to the earth, and plunges into the sun. There is vast destruction, but men are able to move closer to the poles and to build there a better civilization, for the star greatly increases the heat of the sun.

Balmer and Wylie's *When Worlds Collide* and *After Worlds Collide* tell the story of the destruction of the earth by the star Bronson Alpha, while a remnant of men escape to its planet, Bronson Beta, now become a satellite of the sun. In Stapledon's *Last and First Men*, the Eighth Men, at the height of their glorious career on Venus, discover a luminous cloud on its way to the solar system and calmly observe that it will strike the earth and Venus; they migrate to Neptune, and from that planet observe it as it catches earth and Venus "in its blazing hair" and leaps at the sun. The sun now becomes, of course, a star nearly as wide as the old orbit of Mercury.

In Sherriff's *The Hopkins Manuscript*, scientists have nearly a year's warning that the moon is falling toward the earth, with a daily acceleration of eight miles. They suppose that the moon may either crash upon the earth and explode it, or graze the earth and bounce off into space. It does neither, but grazes Europe, rolls into the Atlantic, and there collapses. Geologic and meteoric disturbances are tremendous while they last, but they soon subside.

2. Destructive Warfare

In most scientific fiction, however, world-catastrophe is brought
about by means of desperate wars, usually about the middle of
the twentieth century. Complete collapse follows the invention of
a means of destruction against which there is no defense; when
both sides get hold of this weapon, the antagonists batter one
another to pieces, and warfare ends only with mutual collapse.
This is the general pattern of Boisgilbert's *Caesar's Column*,
Griffith's *Olga Romanoff*, Wells's *The War in the Air*, and many
others. The collapse is especially detailed in Wells's *The World
Set Free* and Best's *The Twenty-Fifth Hour*.

In *The World Set Free*, a means is discovered for causing the
rapid disintegration of bismuth. Disintegration can be controlled,
and at first it is used as a means of power, with a promise that
it will free man at last from drudgery. But use of this new
power without careful planning leads to unemployment, strikes,
and economic confusion—especially as capital invested in coal and
oil becomes worthless. Foreseeing war, military men prepare the
old conscriptions, intrenchments, and strategies, laughable to the
men of the scientific corps. Suddenly the first atomic bomb falls
on Paris. To retaliate, a Frenchman drops an atomic bomb on
Berlin, and the whole world flares into "a monstrous phase of
destruction. Power after power about the armed globe sought to
anticipate attack by aggression. They went to war in a delirium
of panic, in order to use their bombs first." By the spring of
1959, the "flimsy fabric of the world's credit had vanished, industry was completely disorganised and every city . . . trembled
on the verge of starvation. Most of the capital cities of the world
were burning; millions of people had already perished, and over
great areas governments was at an end." The only way out, a way
men see in time and accept, is the abdication of all national sovereignties and the establishment of a world state, slowly to rebuild.

Best's *The Twenty-Fifth Hour* does not describe the use of the
atomic bomb, but the same effect is achieved, toward the end of
World War II, by the increased destructiveness of bombs that
batter cities to pieces and by the use at last of virulent bacteria.

The principle is the same: when weapons so powerful that there
is no defense against them are used, governments vanish, and
fragments of armies are left to pillage and kill, till the world is a
wasteland. It is clear that in the actual world of the Atomic Age,
we have just attained, in this twenty-fourth hour, the means for
the mutual destruction described in these books. It is still possible
that the way out suggested in *The World Set Free* may forestall
warfare like that described in *The Twenty-Fifth Hour*.

3. The Collapse of Social Order

Writers of scientific fiction emphasize the idea that civilization rests upon a precarious base. Neglecting the possibility of cometary collision and even the idea of a weapon against which there is no defense, book after book describes the collapse of society.

The historian of Jefferies's *After London* is not certain what happened to destroy civilization; there were wars, no doubt; there were also climatic and geologic changes such as have visited the earth in the past. But finally men have become savages again and lost all memory of how machines, still rusting and falling to pieces, were used. In Hudson's *A Crystal Age,* no doubt there were wars fought to an end with armies that became guerrilla bands, and then there were changes in climate. Men who speak English do not know where England is, and they have never heard of Shakespeare or anything else that establishes connection with the past. In Wells's *The War in the Air,* the chaos of confused world wars eradicates central governments; autonomous village-governments spring up, and society is again in the Dark Ages. In Stapledon's *Last and First Men,* the First Men fight their way to dark age after dark age, until finally atomic explosions set off in Patagonia ignite the surface of the earth and destroy all the First Men except a remnant in the Arctic.

4. The Utopian Remnant

One remnant of world-catastrophe is the "last man." His story is told in a number of books, including Mary Shelley's *The Last Man,* Shiel's *The Purple Cloud,* and Moxley's *Red Snow.*

Other books, more hopefully perhaps than warranted by the assumed fact of warfare to the death among men reduced to savagery, describe a utopian remnant banded together to rebuild society. The Aërians in Griffith's *Olga Romanoff* retire to Africa and shoulder the responsibility of rebuilding the world. A remnant flees to central Africa in Boisgilbert's *Caesar's Column* to prepare for the same task. The High Lama of Hilton's *Lost Horizon* foresees a war that will wipe out civilization, but a utopian remnant will remain in Shangri-La; the treasures of the world will be hoarded in the valley of the Blue Moon "as by miracle for a new Renaissance." Even in *The Twenty-Fifth Hour,* Captain Fitzharding and Ann, fleeing from a Europe reduced to cannibalism, come at last to a Moslem civilization along the valley of the Nile.

F. *Patterns in Adventures in a Prehistoric World*

1. The Prehistoric Survivor in the Modern World

One pattern of the romance concerned with prehistoric times describes the discovery of prehistoric creatures in some out-of-the-way corner of the modern world. In those journeys inside the earth that follow Symmes's theory, the travellers usually find bones of mammoth creatures. In Verne's *A Journey to the Center of the Earth,* however, the debt is not to Symmes, but to Darwin. The explorers find a giant prehistoric man guarding a flock of mastodons. Some of the creatures on Mars, in Greg's *Across the Zodiac,* are undoubtedly inspired by the theory of evolution, for "creatures of a type long since supposed to be extinct on Earth still haunt the depths of the Martial seas." The narrator goes on a hunting expedition to capture a sea serpent of prehistoric kind. In DeMille's *A Strange Manuscript Found in a Copper Cylinder,* More goes on a "sacred hunt" to kill one of the sea serpents that still inhabit waters around the warm South Pole. Astor's *A Journey in Other Worlds* describes prehistoric monsters of the Devonian period on Jupiter: mastodons, dinosaurs, glyptodons, and pterodactyls. Wells's "Æpyornis Island" describes the hatching of eggs, long preserved in a creosote swamp, into supposedly long-extinct æpyornis birds; Wells's "In the Avu Observatory" describes the attack of some unknown flying monster upon an observatory. Doyle's *The Lost World* supposes an isolated plateau in central South America; on it Professor Challenger and his group find not only iguanodons and pterodactyls, but also ape-like sub-men.

2. The Racial Crisis

The romance that tells a story in the life of prehistoric men always describes some crisis in man's evolution. Bierbower's *From Monkey to Man* is concerned with two species of apes and their quarrels just before one species perishes in the advancing Ice Age, and the other flees to the southward to develop into the first true men. During the course of the story, the apes make phenomenal progress. For instance, because of a plague of snakes, they make themselves houses into which snakes cannot come, and so make the first beginning, says the author, in architecture. One bold ape attacks volcanic fire with a stick, finds that it stays on the stick and warms his hands, and so discovers the use of fire; another ape accidentally warms his frozen food and so thaws it out; continuing to warm it, he improves the flavor by cooking it. By the end of the book, the apes of the Ammi tribe are well on the way toward becoming men. Likewise, in Wells's "A Story of the Stone Age," Ugh-lomi, playing with a piece of flint and a stick, accidentally makes a weapon like a hatchet; to catch a horse, he drops on the back of one from a tree, and to save his life, hangs on during the gallop. Consequently, he learns to ride horseback. Ab, in Waterloo's *The Story of Ab*, discovers the bow and arrow quite by accident when a stick caught in a bent twig flies off and hurts his sister. Marrow-Bone, in London's *Before Adam*, discovers how to carry water in a gourd and thereafter is able to have water without going always to the river.

There are no men in Taine's *Before the Dawn*, but the chapter called "Revolution" describes the passage of the races of reptiles through a crisis as they flee to the southward across a land-bridge when the great cold comes. Though intelligence dawns in the reptile called Belshazzar, as he works out for practical purposes the principle of the lever, thinks out the law of falling bodies, and employs some of the principles that govern floating bodies, it is the beginning of the end for the reptiles and their armored prey.

G. *Patterns of the Imaginary Invention*

Since the imaginary inventions of scientific fiction are of many kinds, romances of invention fall into general patterns at the point where their effect upon society is discussed. Nearly every invention or discovery may be either good or bad, according to how it is used. Many romances say, therefore, that the invention is to be kept secret, at least until man is ready for it, for fear that it may be used to do irreparable damage; a powerful weapon in a warring world may bring about suicidal destruction, especially in the hands of an unscrupulous man. A final pattern concerns the biological discovery that makes its possessor a misfit in society.

In Verne's *Robur the Conqueror*, aviation develops on Robur's hidden X island; mankind at large is not ready for the airplane and the power it might give to unscrupulous men. All in good time, Robur promises, when men are ready to use the airplane properly, it will be given to them. In Griffith's *Olga Romanoff*, Richard Arnold does not dare to give his airplane to the world; it is kept for the Terrorists, who use it to become the Aërians and to establish a beneficent world-control. They keep the secret of the airplane for a hundred years. Holsten, discoverer of a means for releasing atomic energy in Wells's *The World Set Free*, debates for a long time whether he should give this power to the world; perhaps "some secret association of wise men should take care of his work and hand it on from generation to generation until the world was riper for its practical application." The Chinese physicist who discovers the secret of atomic energy in Stapledon's *Last and First Men* uses this energy to wreck a hostile air-fleet, and then destroys his formulas and commits suicide.

Nearly every major invention in scientific fiction is described as something that may radically alter the course of history. This claim for such inventions as that of the airplane scarcely needs illustration. But the claim is made for even minor inventions. In McLociard's "Television Hill," for instance, it is stated that "Once television is commercialized, the entire social life of man will have to undergo a decided and sudden change." Here and there, however, there is a realistic protest against this attitude. The many inventions of Wells's "A Story of the Days to Come," for instance, change the physical conditions of life radically, but they do not affect human nature, at least in any good way. Hugo Danner, in Wylie's *The Gladiator,* dreams of changing the world, but he is everywhere frustrated; he comes to the conclusion that "so mean and inalterable is the gauge of man that his races topple before his soul expands," and the most any man can do is "inculcate an idea in a few and live to see its gradual spreading."

Weapons of destruction are nearly always described as world-altering in their effects. Tanks determine the outcome of warfare in Wells's "The Land Ironclads"; airplanes wreck civilization in Wells's *The War in the Air;* and atomic bombs force a choice between suicide and peace in Wells's *The World Set Free.*

Naturally inventions, especially dangerous ones, give their inventors a sense of power and, perhaps, the ambition to dictate to the world. "I hold control of the entire world," says Robur in Verne's *The Master of the World.* Griffin in Wells's *The Invisible Man* intends to terrorize the world and dictate to it. Storm in England's *The Golden Blight* refuses vast wealth for his invention; he wishes to shape world-destiny with it. In Leinster's "The Storm that Had To Be Stopped," Preston demands the submission of all the nations of the earth; the nations bow to the islands of steel in Shiel's *The Lord of the Sea.* Perhaps more frequently in romances than in life, persons or forces arise to arrest these mad ambitions.

*   *   *   *   *

The patterns outlined in this chapter are chiefly those found in book-length romances over a period of time. Naturally, recent books that follow a pattern invented long ago develop the original in many ways. The cometary collision in Poe's "The Conversation of Eiros and Charmion," for instance, is only sketched; the idea is made into a much more complex story in Balmer and Wylie's *When Worlds Collide.* The wars and breakdown of society in *Olga Romanoff* are more remote than the realistic pictures of *The Twenty-Fifth Hour.*

The patterns of stories in the magazines exaggerate the grotesqueness of life on other worlds, the powers of the imaginary inventions, or the magnitudes of the wars. The magazines contain romances of interplanetary wars fought between space-fliers in space, thinking machines that outdo humanity, and so on. It is difficult to form a just opinion of these stories, there are so many thousands of them, each seeking to be "different" and more colossal than its predecessors. "Fans" have reiterated that the magazine stories have value as prophecy and science-teaching. Mr. H. C. Koenig, a lifelong reader of scientific fiction in both books and magazines, sharply challenges this point of view in an article, "Little Men, What Now?" (*Fantasy Commentator,* I, 85-86 and 90). His contention that the science in the magazines is thin and that the stories have value chiefly as entertainment seems to me just. The best I have seen in the magazines has been such work as that of Lovecraft, construction from the materials of science of a consistent and wonder-laden mythology.

A marked tendency in fiction of all kinds toward the close of World War II was revolt against materialism and toward discussion of mystical, semi-religious ideas. This tendency is observable, for instance, in the work of formerly realistic writers—in Somerset Maugham's *The Razor's Edge* and in the later novels of Aldous Huxley. In scientific fiction, the tendency has appeared in Lewis's *Out of the Silent Planet* and in the work of Stapledon. An article by Margaret Curtis Walters, "Space-Time in Literary Form" (*Fantasy Commentator,* I, 92-97), analyzes a number of recent romances of reincarnation, spiritual experiences, and experiences in coalesced space, time, or space-time. I have not treated these pieces, because their interest is not in science or in what science means to human life. On the other hand, some future attempt to outline the development of scientific fiction may find here an important junction with a new type.

Suggestions toward new patterns are found in Stapledon's *Odd John* and *Sirius.* Perhaps the most fruitful further development of scientific fiction will lie in similar psychological and ethical studies, efforts to discover the right adjustment to the Machine Age and Atomic Age and to see guidingly into the future of the race, in the best light of science. The confused aftermath of

World War II and our many unsolved problems suggest that it is worth while to take thought for the future. Many pieces of scientific fiction have proved fruitful in prophecy and suggestion. No doubt this older attempt to foresee man's adjustments to a Machine Age will continue along with whatever other trends may develop.

CHAPTER NINE

Inventions and Discoveries

Long before the century of invention that has given us the radio and the airplane, dreamers believed that one way toward Utopia lies in the development of machinery. Sir Thomas More, chiefly concerned with social polity, described an imaginary machine, the incubator. The cluster of utopias about the time of Bacon's *The New Atlantis* is filled with imaginary mechanical devices.

Writers of satires have supposed invention to be bad; it leads to chaos, destructive wars, or a mechanical kind of life. The "projectors" of Swift's *Gulliver's Travels* are busy with absurdities while practical concerns fall into neglect. The Erewhonians of Butler's *Erewhon* have destroyed machinery for fear it might enslave mankind. Machinery has enslaved and brutalized man in Wells's "A Story of the Days to Come"; and the weapons of science are used to destroy society in Wells's *The War in the Air*. Because invention means change and so menaces stability, the Controller in Huxley's *Brave New World* says that science must be treated as an enemy; the state jealously controls invention and estops most mechanisms in the patent office.

Both these attitudes toward invention are illustrated in stories of what happens when an imaginary machine is invented.

It would be interesting to know whether any important invention has been inspired by an imaginary invention in fiction. Imaginary inventions belong to the period of experimentation. Many people were working on the problem of heavier-than-air flight when Jules Verne described it and discussed its principles in

Robur the Conqueror. Imaginary inventions to disintegrate the atom and imaginary rocket-propulsion of airplanes and space-fliers have been found in scientific fiction for some years, while scientists have been building up a fabric of knowledge to support these inventions.

Even though a direct influence of imaginary invention upon actual invention can hardly be demonstrated, the course of important inventions and discoveries in scientific fiction is worth record.

A. *Inventions in General*

In some fiction, a single invention is the core of the story. In other pieces, inventions appear by dozens, sometimes as only incidental features of the story. Hertzka's *Freeland,* for instance, like More's *Utopia,* could have omitted mechanical inventions without disturbing the central story; but, as usual, incidental inventions appear. Horses are groomed by "enormous cylindrical brushes set in rotation by mechanism"; there are scouring machines and machines for giving the horses fodder and even water.

Other books describing societies of the future, even when a principal invention is fully described, present lists of incidental inventions. Labor-saving devices, from electric razors to radio-controlled tractors, are characteristic of scientific fiction. Verne's *Floating Island,* for instance, describes a hotel room fitted with taps for hot and cold water, basins emptying automatically, hot baths, hot irons, sprays of perfume, ventilators, mechanical brushes for the head, the clothes, and the boots, and numerous bells and buttons for communication. Bradshaw's *The Goddess of Atvatabar* lists pneumatic tubes, telegraphs, telephones, phonographs, electric lights, rain makers, seaboots, marine railroads, flying machines, megaphones, velocipedes without wheels, aerophers, machines for sowing, reaping, sewing, bootblacking, knitting, printing, and weaving. Some of the machines are not described at all. None are described in Forster's "The Machine Stops," but it is asserted that a woman sitting in a room studded with electric buttons may touch the proper ones to secure food, music, clothing, baths of any temperature, literature, and any kind of communication.

B. *Inventions Based Upon New Principles*

Nearly every important mechanism of the Machine Age was described in fiction before it was invented, though not necessarily before inventors began experimentation. In the same way, scientific fiction anticipated a number of principles and laws before scientists were ready to demonstrate them. For instance, hints of evolution are found in descriptions of the "Chain of Being" in eighteenth-century fiction, as in Mercier's *Memoirs of the Year Two Thousand Five Hundred. Abbott's Flatland* anticipates some aspects of relativity.

Machines for doing the work of our engines and motors are found very early in scientific fiction. Before the invention of the steam engine, they are operated by either vague principles or powerful springs. The triremes of Campanella's *The City of the Sun* are moved by a "marvelous contrivance." Similar vessels in Holberg's *A Journey to the World Under-Ground* are operated by "Machines like our Clock-work," but the narrator, "being not well vers'd in Mechanicks," cannot describe them in detail. "Elastic springs" wound by steam power propel both the automobiles and the "gondolas" of Hertzka's *Freeland.*

Internal combustion engines operated by various kinds of explosives and pressures are found in scientific fiction both before and after the invention of the gasoline engine. The "agency of a curious engine" is used in Seaborn's *Symzonia* to propel ships by forcing compressed air through tubes that "perforated the after part of the vessel under water"; air pressure against the water propels the ships with "amazing rapidity." "Curious vehicles that moved by some Internal machinery" are described in Mrs. Griffith's "Three Hundred Years Hence"; this machinery, which is not steam-power, operates implements of the kind now operated by gasoline engines. In Tucker's *A Voyage to the Moon,* the narrator observes a "large grist and saw mill" operated by the explosion of gunpower within cylinders to drive pistons; the principle is that of the gasoline engine except for the kind of fuel used.

By the 1890's the gasoline engine had been invented, and the improvement upon it described in Chamberlain's *6000 Tons of Gold* is merely one of fuel. Liquefied carbonic acid gas under a pressure of two thousand pounds to the inch is released into cylinders to drive pistons like those of the gasoline engine. The key to the invention is a valve that lets the gas into the cylinders with the proper expansion. The automatic boring projectile of Stockton's *The Great Stone of Sardis* is operated by an internal explosive that increases its pressure as it encounters greater obstacles, so that the projectile bores through stone with great speed. Ships described in Shiel's *The Purple Cloud* are driven by internal combustion engines using liquid air. A combination of turbines, vacuum-suction, and gaseous expansion has superseded gasoline to drive the engine of Kipling's "With the Night Mail."

A source of energy described in scientific fiction but not yet widely used is the concentrated heat of the sun. In Astor's *A Journey in Other Worlds,* for instance, boilers placed at the foci of concave mirrors generate steam from the heat of the sun. The internal heat of the earth is likewise used as a source of energy in scientific fiction. Temperatures "hot enough to liquefy granite" and the extreme cold of the earth's surface furnish the "mining physicists" of Tardé's *Underground Man* with "thermic cataracts by the side of which all the cataracts of Abyssinia and Niagara were only toys." The scientists of Von Hanstein's "Utopia Island" tap the sources of heat lying underneath a volcano. Steam power from the internal heat of the earth and tidal power are frequent in scientific fiction.

Heat from the reaction of chemical substances warms the space-flier of Tucker's *A Voyage to the Moon* on its flight through space. Newcomb in *His Wisdom* describes a substance called therms that acts like a permanently charged electric battery to furnish light, heat, and power. The crustaceans of Verrill's "Beyond the Pole" have something like a radioactive substance that drives airships, operates machinery, and gives off light. These substances are not immediately burned up in the process of giving off energy.

Chemical reactions are even more frequently used as sources of power. In Poe's "Hans Pfaal," a metallic substance and a "common acid" are used to generate a gas with density thirty-seven times less than that of hydrogen; it is used in the balloon that takes Hans to the moon. Captain Nemo, in Verne's *Twenty Thousand Leagues Under the Sea,* generates all-purpose electricity from the disintegration of sea-water. Olga, in Griffith's *Olga Romanoff,* derives electrical energy from "atomised carbon and vaporised petroleum." "Proper proportions of air and water" furnish all the fuel needed in Beale's *The Secret of the Earth;* a generator, using chemical catalytics, causes air and water to give off energy to drive the airplane.

In recent fiction atomic disintegration is a standard source of inexhaustible power. Holsten in the year 1933, according to Wells's *The World Set Free,* succeeds in setting up and controlling atomic disintegration; bismuth explodes into a radioactive gas that gives off tremendous energy and degenerates into gold. By 1953, radioactive engines operate industrial plants and even replace the clumsy automobiles of the previous era. Atomic energy propels the rockets of Balmer and Wylie's *When Worlds Collide* to Bronson Beta; in *After Worlds Collide,* men discover that the scientists of Bronson Beta had used a combination of electricity and radioactivity to operate their machinery.

Stapledon's *Odd John* describes a curious way of controlling atomic power by psychic means: "What I do, then, is to hypnotize the little devils [protons and electrons] so that they go limp for a moment and loosen their grip on one another. Then when they wake up they barge about in hilarious freedom, and all you have to do is to see that their barging drives your machinery." On the island of the supernormals, Ng-Gunko prepares all-purpose power by hypnotizing pinches of radioactive elements and laying them on wafers to sleep till needed. In Stapledon's *Star Maker*, sub-atomic power enables scientists to drive whole worlds across space. Atomic power is everywhere in the stories of the magazines. The intra-atomic energy of copper drives a space-ship in Smith and Garby's "The Skylark of Space"; and in Lovecraft's *The Shadow Out of Time*, members of the elder Great Race travel on "huge, boat-like atomic-engined vehicles."

The atomic bomb is a natural next step. In Wells's *The World Set Free*, the first atomic bomb wrecks Paris; then Berlin and two hundred other cities are bombed to craters. The terrible danger in atomic power is recognized in Stapledon's *Last and First Men;* a Chinese physicist manufactures an atomic bomb, observes the effects of an explosion, destroys his formula, and kills himself. When atomic power is rediscovered, it gets out of hand in Patagonia and sets the whole surface of the earth ablaze.

A fantastic source of energy is described in Lloyd's *Etidorhpa.* The etheric current said to be flowing through all matter is interrupted by a molecular arrangement; it is an "endless source of power" that drives a boat across a lake at nine hundred miles an hour.

This force resembles the anti-gravitational force that is a standard feature of scientific fiction from its use to sustain the island of Laputa in Swift's *Gulliver's Travels* to the present. Tucker's *A Voyage to the Moon* discusses the "principle of repulsion as well as gravitation in the earth" and describes a metallic substance, found united with a heavy earth, that tends to fly upward; it is used to propel Atterley and the Brahmin to the moon. It is not a substance, but a force called apergy, in Greg's *Across the Zodiac;* apergy is a repulsive energy generated by electrical means; it acts in a straight line upon objects at any distance. The same apergy is used in Astor's *A Journey in Other Worlds.* The etherine of Newcomb's *His Wisdom* resembles it, though its repulsive action is said to be a reaction against the ether. The R. Force of Griffith's *A Honeymoon in Space* seems to be the same force, though it may be generated in various strengths from electric motors. Wells, in *The First Men in the Moon,* describes a substance, Cavorite, that is opaque to gravita-

tion; "roller blinds" of this substance around a space-car enable
it to be drawn to the moon and slowed down before it strikes
the moon; a "blind" toward the sun is rolled up, and the attraction of the sun serves as a brake. Recent fiction returns, in
general, to the use of a controllable anti-gravitational force.
Hansen's "The Prince of Liars" uses a mechanism that acts
against gravity itself, as an airplane might fly into a head wind.

Still another force, resembling a cross between telepathy and
electricity, is frequent in scientific fiction. In Bulwer-Lytton's
The Coming Race it is vril, "akin to . . . mesmerism, electro-
biology, odic force, &c.," collected apparently from the air and
applied through wands; it runs machinery, enables men to fly,
controls the weather, and affects "minds, and bodies animal and
vegetable." It is described as telekinesis in Kline's *The Planet
of Peril;* it operates various machines, including airplanes. In
Wright's *The World Below* the narrator becomes exhausted, but
touching the finger of an Amphibian causes a psychic force to
flow into him and fill him with energy; the Amphibians wage
war on the Killers by trapping them in mind-force, against which
the Killers struggle like swimmers in a lake of syrup. In *Star
Maker,* Stapledon describes interplanetary wars fought by telepathic thought-control.

Strange rays are, of course, frequent in scientific fiction.
Stockton's *The Great Stone of Sardis* describes an "artesian
ray" that penetrates any substance, as X-ray does, to any desired depth and reflects whatever surfaces lie at the controlled
termination of the ray.

Bodies transparent to rays of light are frequent in scientific
fiction. O'Brien's "What Was It?" De Maupassant's "The Horla,"
and Bierce's "The Damned Thing" all describe invisible living
creatures; they are explained to be transparent, as air and
certain forms of marine life are transparent, or they are said
to be of colors beyond the range of sight. Wells's *The Invisible
Man* tells the story of a method that Griffin discovers for making
his body invisible. The reverse of this idea is made use of in
Leinster's "The Man Who Put Out the Sun"; Preston discovers
a ray that causes the air above the earth to become opaque
and therefore to insulate the earth from the sun's rays.

Machines and methods for travelling into or through a fourth
dimension, often considered to be time, are common. The explosion of a green powder in Wells's "The Plattner Story" sends
Plattner into a spatial fourth dimension that interpenetrates
the other three dimensions; another explosion sends him back
into the everyday world, but with his anatomy reversed. In
Wells's *The Time Machine,* the fourth dimension is time, and

the Time Traveller invents a machine for riding about in it as one rides an airplane through space; something like the gravitation of events holds men to a slow pace through time, but the machine annuls this gravitation. In Burkholder's "Dimensional Fate" the fourth dimension is a space entered when the rate of travel through space exceeds that of light; as length diminishes toward zero (according to Einsteinian physics), an object "spreads" into the fourth dimension.

Many inventions of scientific fiction do not employ new principles, but known principles in a multitude of imaginary uses.

C. *Inventions Concerned with Electricity*

Electricity, appearing in scientific fiction as magnetism, odic force, and vril, before Edison's inventions in the 1870's and 1880's, is perhaps the most important single wonder-worker. Nearly every application of electricity is anticipated just a few years before the actual invention.

In fiction from 1870 through the 1890's, many twentieth-century applications of electricity are anticipated. In Verne's *Twenty Thousand Leagues Under the Sea* the submarine *Nautilus* and everything on it are operated by electricity. Batteries are charged in the heart of Captain Nemo's volcano; then motors drive the submarine; electricity lights it, cooks the food, operates the nautical instruments, and does everything that it would do in a twentieth-century submarine. In Verne's *Floating Island*, electricity moves the island, lights and heats the hotels, operates the telegraphs and telephones, cooks, and lights the streets. On the Mars of Greg's *Across the Zodiac* electricity is a similar all-purpose energy. In Astor's *A Journey in Other Worlds* electricity has "superseded animal and manual labour in everything"; drawn from waterfalls, tides, and winds, electric power is very cheap.

The fact that incandescent electric lights are described in fiction before Edison invented them does not mean that fiction inspired Edison; no doubt many inventors were working toward the invention. Verne described portable electric lights, "Ruhmkorff coils," in *A Journey to the Center of the Earth* (1864). By the time of Griffith's *The Angel of the Revolution* (1893), cities were already being lighted by electricity; the book reflects this fact in magnifying street lights into "huge electric suns"; Harben's *The Land of the Changing Sun* describes an artificial electric sun to give "daylight" to a cavern a hundred miles in diameter. Fluorescent lighting, commercially developed in the 1930's, is anticipated in Doyle's *The Maracot Deep*. Verne's

Floating Island describes flashing electric billboards; the advertisements of Wells's *When the Sleeper Wakes* resemble those
of Times Square today; electric placards spell out the news
in the London of Benson's *Lord of the World.*

The use of electricity for transportation is common in scientific fiction. The ships of Poe's "Mellonta Tauta" are called
"magnetic propellers"; apparently they are driven by electricity.
In Verne's *Floating Island,* the musicians are carried to the island
on an electric "ferry"; the island-harbor is filled with electrically
driven fishing smacks; an electric train carries the musicians
to the town at "nine to twelve miles an hour"; the island itself
is propelled by electricity. Ships on Mars in Greg's *Across the
Zodiac* are electrically driven. Electric monocycles and trains
move noiselessly through the world of Tardé's *Underground
Man.* All the transportation of Altruria, as described in Howells's
A Traveler from Altruria, is electrically driven. Trains, in Astor's
A Journey in Other Worlds, are driven by electric magnets
placed fifty miles apart to attract the oncoming train and repel
it when it has passed. In the same book, electric "phaetons"
have replaced automobiles.

In Greg's *Across the Zodiac,* the Martians print by electricity;
characters are written on a sheet of gold leaf; then chemically
coated sheets of "difra" (a linen paper) are stacked under it.
When an electric current is passed through the gold leaf and
difra, the writing intercepts the current and so "prints" the
message on all the sheets. Verne's *Twenty Thousand Leagues
Under the Sea* describes electric clocks, speedometers, and guns.
In Griffith's *Olga Romanoff,* a pale electric flame that paralyzes
leaps from the point of a sword when a button is touched. In
Greg's *Across the Zodiac,* Martians use the "electric rack" for
torturing criminals and sometimes for electrocuting them. In
Von Hanstein's "Utopia Island" electric waves "abduct" ships
at a distance, drawing them to the island; electric currents
liberate enough hydrogen under water to calm the surface of
the sea during a storm. In Smith and Garby's "The Skylark of
Space" electrodes clamped onto the heads of two persons affect
convolutions of the brain so that one person knows everything
that is in the other's mind.

The use of electricity for hypnotism and for vitalizing the
human spirit goes back to the odic force and vril of Bulwer-
Lytton's fiction. In Bradshow's *The Goddess of Atvatabar,* a
vital fluid, something like electricity, generated from the yearning
of ten thousand hopeless lovers, brings the dead Lyone back to
life; the electrically surcharged air of Emerson's *The Smoky
God* fills the traveller with exuberance.

To these examples might be added nearly all actual applications of electricity, such as electrically operated elevators, as in Verne's *Floating Island,* and electric dumbwaiters to serve food at the pressure of a button, as in Boisgilbert's *Caesar's Column.*

D. *Inventions Concerned with Transportation*

1. Land Traffic

Railway trains operated by steam are old-fashioned for most scientific fiction. Poe, however, in "Mellonta Tauta," describes transcontinental trains as elaborate as hotels—with ballrooms for dancing—moving on rails set fifty feet apart. Wells, in *A Modern Utopia,* develops this idea in describing trains with libraries, billiard rooms, bathrooms, barbers, and the like. Verne makes use of steam power to propel a mechanical elephant drawing a luxurious house across the plains and hills of India, in *The Steam House.*

Many trains of the future are monorail trains. Stockton's *The Great Stone of Sardis* describes electric trains suspended from wheels that run on a single rail twenty feet above the ground. Wells's *The War in the Air* describes monorail trains balanced by gyroscopes; "great iron Eiffel Tower pillars" carry the monorail cables a hundred and fifty feet above the English Channel. Kearney's *Erone* provides a detailed description of "monoways" (electrically driven, monorail subway trains). The book advocates their adoption, and indeed they do seem to have practical advantages. Their stations are on the surface, but the trains run about a hundred feet underground. From each station, a train departs down a fifteen per cent gradient, which gives it acceleration, and on arriving, runs up the same gradient, slowing down without the excessive use of brakes. The romance also advocates the use of monoway tubes a hundred feet underground as air-raid shelters, an appropriate suggestion in a book published in London in 1943.

The automobiles of Wells's *The War in the Air* use gyroscopes and run on two wheels. In general, however, the automobiles of scientific fiction are less spectacular. The wagons of Campanella's *The City of the Sun,* propelled by the wind by a marvellous contrivance of wheels within wheels, suggest the automobile. Verne's *Floating Island* is filled with electrically driven automobiles. Three-wheeled automobiles operated by electricity amaze the traveller in Greg's *Across the Zodiac;* they travel at a speed "far greater than that of the swiftest mail coach," from fifteen to thirty miles an hour. The Martians also have semi-automatic tractors; a man stands at each end of a field to jump upon the tractor and turn it, but it proceeds straight across the field of its own accord. Hertzka's *Freeland* describes automobiles operated by steel springs wound up by steam-power at winding stations along the principal roads. The professor in Newcomb's *His Wisdom* manufactures an automobile to run "almost any speed, even forty miles an hour, with a thermic engine supplied with therm by a little petroleum lamp." The newlyweds of Griffith's *A Honeymoon in Space* discover that the people of Ganymede have automobiles. In more recent fiction, Kline's *Planet of Peril* describes one-wheeled automobiles on Venus: the car is supported by a gyroscope on an "idling wheel" inside a wheel twenty feet in diameter. In Von Hanstein's "Utopia Island," Bob White—like Robur in Verne's *Master of the World*—demonstrates a combination automobile, motor-boat, and airplane. In Kipling's "As Easy as A. B. C." a girl stands at an "old-fashioned Controller" to operate an "obedient cultivator" half a mile away.

Automobiles require paved roads, and many-laned highways belt the continent in recent fiction. A cheap plastic, Eadhamite, is used to build the highways of Wells's "A Story of the Days to Come" and *When the Sleeper Wakes.* In Von Hanstein's "Utopia Island" cars travel on either land or sea in a sealed "tube road" that lies on land or floats a hundred meters below sea level; cars are propelled through it by a combination of compressed air and magnetism.

In cities of the future moving sidewalks carry people for short distances, and express "ways" carry seated passengers. Only the larger streets of Verne's *Floating Island* are provided with moving pavements "worked by an endless chain"; people in a hurry may walk "as if on a travelling train." Similar "moving platforms," going in opposite directions, are described in Stockton's *The Great Stone of Sardis.* In Wells's *When the Sleeper Wakes* a main "way," three hundred feet wide, is broken into lanes; the lanes on one side of the way move in one direction, those on the other side in the opposite direction. The inner lanes move slowly; the outer lanes move faster, till the outermost lane moves with the speed of an express train. Speeds are so graduated that one may step from lane to lane and finally take a seat on the fastest lane.

2. Submarines

Bacon's *The New Atlantis* mentions "ships and boats for going under water," but does not describe their operation. Besides such mention, the submarine of scientific fiction cannot be said to anticipate experimentation, for Verne's *Nautilus* of *Twenty*

Thousand Leagues Under the Sea is named for the submarine *Nautilus* purchased by Napoleon from Robert Fulton in 1797. But Verne's submarine is far superior to any actual submarine of the nineteenth century. This most popular of Verne's romances naturally stimulated the imaginary invention of submarines, and they are everywhere in recent fiction. Ordinary ships on Mars, in Greg's *Across the Zodiac,* are convertible into submarines by a process of closing the hatches and descending. Gigantic submarines of the metal azurine, "which would cut and pierce steel as a diamond cuts glass," are used in the warfare of Griffith's *Olga Romanoff;* they carry both guns for surface fighting and torpedo tubes. Kipling's "With the Night Mail" describes undersea freighters that, along with the airships, have taken most of the world's commerce away from surface craft.

3. Flying Machines

The balloon of the Montgolfier brothers in 1783 rose because it was filled with heated air. This principle was at least surmised in scientific fiction more than a hundred years before this date. Among the various devices for flying (many of them absurd) described in Cyrano de Bergerac's *The Moon* is the device by which Enoch flies to the moon; he fills large vessels with smoke from a sacrificial fire and because the smoke "had a tendency to rise straight up to God," Enoch, attaching the vessels under his arm-pits, is lifted to the moon. Immediately after the Montgolfiers' invention, the anonymous *Aerostatic Spy* (1785) described a balloon that is lifted first by heated air, and later by a mysterious gas that is lighter than air. Balloons of this period, however, were at the mercy of the wind; a means of steering them was something to dream about. In the world inside the earth, as Seaborn's *Symzonia* describes it, the dirigible balloon has been invented. It is a cylindrical bag, with a rudder like the tail of a fish; people in the car beneath it drive it forward with sail-like oars. Mary Shelley's *The Last Man* describes a dirigible balloon with "feathered vans cleaving the unopposing atmosphere" and a "plumed steerage"; nothing is said of motive power. Poe's "Mellonta Tauta" describes dirigible balloons that travel at a speed of a hundred and fifty miles an hour, though, curiously enough, the method of guiding them is to raise or lower them into a favorable air current. Verne seized upon this method for guiding the balloon described in *Five Weeks in a Balloon;* the bag, filled with hydrogen, may be inflated or deflated until it floats in an air current travelling in the desired direction. The balloons of Mars, in Greg's *Across the Zodiac,* are fish-shaped dirigibles; in Boisgilbert's *Caesar's Column,* fish-shaped balloons of aluminum are driven by electric motors from New York to London in thirty-six hours. In Kipling's "With the Night Mail" the air is filled with thousands of dirigible balloons, so that various "lanes" must be used for traffic at various speeds.

A step closer to the airplane is a mechanism that enables man to fly with such movable wings as those of birds. Bacon's *The New Atlantis* offers no details, but the host says, "We imitate also flights of birds; we have some degree of flying in the air." The airship described in Paltock's *John Daniel* resembles a cross between bird's wings and an airplane; planes like those of an airplane are flapped up and down by means of a pump like that of a railway handcar; the description of the apparatus is detailed and exact in measurements. Just before the airplane was invented, Monson, in Wells's "The Argonauts of the Air," follows photographic studies of the flight of birds to construct an airplane shaped like a bird, with wings fluttered by gasoline engines.

Detachable wings are standard equipment in the world of Bulwer-Lytton's *The Coming Race;* children swoop in aerial sport; men at rest fold their wings as pictured angels do. In some way the force vril is connected with flying, but the explanation is not detailed. The wayleals of Bradshaw's *The Goddess of Atvatabar* are winged with oar-like blades attached to crimson jackets; portable dynamos use "magnicity" to turn the blades. Greer's *A Modern Daedalus* keeps secret the principle of flight, but it describes wings strapped to the shoulders, operated by "an apparatus in the highest degree simple, portable, and inexpensive," and guided by throwing the weight of the body to one side or the other. In Stapledon's *Last Men in London,* the Eighteenth Men put on flying suits like overalls, studded with sub-atomic generators on the soles of the feet and the palms of the hands; they fly as easily as birds.

That the airplane as we know it would some day be invented is the most persistent single item of faith in scientific fiction before 1903; that it will develop enormously and affect all conditions of life has been a persistent feature since that date. Bishop Wilkins stated in 1641 that "amongst all other possible conveyances through the Air, imagination itself cannot conceive any one more useful, than the invention of a flying Chariot." This "flying Chariot" appears in many forms in scientific fiction, but gradually the preferred form came to be the airplane.

Before the successful principle of heavier-than-air flight had been worked out, pieces of scientific fiction commonly described airplanes built like the decks of ships and operated by two sets of propellers, one set to lift the car and the other to drive it forward. The airplanes of Mars, described in Griffith's *A Honeymoon in Space,* have vertical masts with "revolving helices" on their tops; the same author's airships in *The Angel of the Revolution* and *Olga Romanoff* employ a principle somewhat like that of the helicopter to raise the ships. "Steel rotoscopes" lift Frank's airplane in Noname's *Young Frank Reade and His Electric Airship.*

Robur's airships in Verne's *Robur the Conqueror* and *Master of the World* are lifted by propellers on vertical masts; they are driven by electricity drawn from powerful "accumulators." No doubt the problem of flight would have been solved much earlier than the twentieth century if a suitable motor had been available. In fact, Verne's *Robur the Conqueror* pauses to discuss for several pages the various experimental advances toward flight in heavier-than-air craft. The merits of "helicopters or spiralifers," "orthopters" (mechanical birds), and "aeroplanes" are carefully compared. The principle that will finally be successful says Verne, is that of "Aeroplanes, which are merely inclined planes like kites, but towed or driven by screws." The motive power, says Verne, will be electrical—as no doubt it would be if "accumulators" as powerful as Robur's were available. Astor's *A Journey in Other Worlds* says that the airplane "came when we devised a suitable motive power," and this book describes an airplane operated by light electric batteries of great power. Richard Arnold, in Griffith's *The Angel of the Revolution,* invents the airplane at once when he discovers "the true motive power at last," the internal combustion engine.

Among airplanes described just before their invention, a propelling apparatus of wheels "having numerous aerial fans . . . supplemented by aeroplanes . . . inclined at an angle, so that their forward rush upon the air supported the ship" is described in Bradshaw's *The Goddess of Atvatabar.* The sleeper of Wells's *When the Sleeper Wakes* finds many varieties of airplanes in the future London, the two chief ones the commercial airplane with a wing-spread of six hundred feet or more and cabins for a large number of passengers, and the individual "aëropile" or monoplane—both driven by gasoline motors.

The date on which Richard Arnold, in Griffith's *The Angel of the Revolution* (1893), invents the airplane is September 3, 1903—a prophecy that missed the date of the Wrights' first power-driven flight by a little over two months. Wells's *The War in the Air* was written after 1903, but it describes several new types of heavier-than-air machines. The one allegedly invented by Butteridge has planes and propellers, but it is shaped like a wasp; the new Japanese planes described in the same book have planes like bent butterfly's wings; they are made of a plastic like celluloid. Airplanes in Huxley's *Brave New World* go from America to Europe in six hours, flying through the stratosphere; the airliners of Herrick's *Sometime* circle the earth in twenty-four hours.

An improvement upon the airplane that is constantly suggested in scientific fiction is the rocket-driven airship. Pseudoman's *Zero to Eighty,* for instance, describes rocket ships that fly through the stratosphere from New York to Paris on a five-hour schedule; propellers lift the ship (with sealed cabin) into the thin air of the stratosphere, and there rockets drive it forward at nearly seven hundred miles an hour. More fantastic suggestions include the idea that airships may be suspended by an anti-gravitational principle, as in Beale's *The Secret of the Earth.*

It is prophesied that the development of the airplane will influence human life in many ways, especially in the new terror that the airplane adds to warfare. As soon as the principle of heavier-than-air flight is learned, Wells said in *Anticipations* (1901), "the new invention will be most assuredly applied to war." Wells's *The War in the Air* is simply a fictional development of this belief; German dirigible balloons, attended by swarms of *Drachenflieger,* destroy the United States Navy and then New York; the Japanese enter the conflict with a new type of airplane, the *Niaio,* and the result is the collapse of civilization.

4. Space-Fliers

The earliest flights through interplanetary space were made in fantastic ways. Gonsales, in Godwin's *The Man in the Moone,* flew to the moon on a raft drawn by gansas. The narrator of Cyrano de Bergerac's *The Moon* starts to the moon on a rocket-driven machine, but when his machine falls in Canada, he is drawn to the moon because beef-marrow is rubbed on his wounds; in *The Sun* the narrator is drawn to the sun by heated air that rises through a box when the sun's rays focus upon it. In Paltock's *John Daniel,* John and Jacob get to the moon on an airplane; Hans, in Poe's "Hans Pfaal," goes to the moon in a balloon.

Perhaps the use of an anti-gravitational force or substance opaque to gravitation is scarcely more reasonable, but it is better rationalized. It is the propulsive power in Tucker's *A Voyage to the Moon,* Greg's *Across the Zodiac,* Wells's *The First Men in the Moon,* Serviss's *A Columbus of Space,* and numerous other voyages. Verne's travellers to the moon in *From the Earth to the Moon* are shot from a gigantic gun; apparently the

Martians of Wells's *The War of the Worlds* are shot to the earth from a gun on Mars; an electric gun, plus rockets, furnishes motive power in Pseudoman's *Zero to Eighty*. Rockets emitting streams of blasted atoms drive the space-ships of Balmer and Wylie's *When Worlds Collide* from earth to Bronson Beta; the Eighteenth Men of Stapledon's *Last and First Men* send space-ships three thousand feet long—and five miles long in Stapledon's *Last Men in London*—on regular trips among the planets. The motive power is atomic energy released through rockets. In Stapledon's *Star Maker* planets, sometimes accompanied by a real or artificial suns, are sent on journeys across interstellar space, spending thousand of years en route. The motive power is sub-atomic.

By the time of Tucker's *A Voyage to the Moon*, it was realized that a trip across space could scarcely be undertaken in an open carriage and (with some exceptions, such as Poe's "Hans Pfaal") interplanetary voyages since this time have been taken in sealed cylinders or cars. The car of Tucker's *Voyage* is a hollow copper cube six feet in diameter with an opening closed by sliding panels; windows of thick glass are fitted into each side. A mechanism in the car supplies air from a condenser. The car is provided with various instruments, such as telescopes, thermometers, and lamps, and with "light refreshments" for some days. Verne's cylinder in *From the Earth to the Moon* adds shock absorbers. The car in Greg's *Across the Zodiac* is larger and more elaborate; it is insulated by a layer of cement between metal walls; it is carpeted with layers of cork and cloth, and it includes elaborate equipment and furnishings—even a five-foot square of garden with soil three feet deep. Ayrault's *Callisto*, in Astor's *A Journey in Other Worlds*, is insulated with mineral wool; it is large enough to have two storeys. The space-ship of Lewis's *Out of the Silent Planet* is a tremendous globe divided into many rooms whose floors are a central globe. Other cars vary in details of shape, size, and equipment, but they resemble one another in the foregoing fundamental features.

E. *Inventions Concerned with Communication*

1. Telegraphs and Telephones

The host in Bacon's *The New Atlantis* says that "We have all means to convey sounds in trunks and pipes, in strange lines and distances." These "means" have been described in scientific fiction ever since that time. Bishop Wilkins's *Mercury* suggests a code for communicating at a distance, by "Muskets, Cannons,

Horns, Drums, &c.," alternating loud and soft notes to form something like the dot-and-dash alphabet of the Morse code. Indeed Bishop Wilkins, considering all means for communicating at a distance, states the principle of the telegraph; prisoners may communicate silently through walls "two or three foot or thereabouts" by using "magnetical vertues." (The use of a wire to convey these "vertues" would have yielded the telegraph.) The Prefect in Tiphaigne de la Roche's *Giphantia* communicates with all points on the earth through minute vibrations in "imperceptible pipes"; a globe in some way amplifies these vibrations coming from any desired point.

The telegraph was in use when Poe wrote "Mellonta Tauta"; but he describes a "magnetic cutter" that guards "floating telegraph wires" across the Atlantic. The millionaires of Verne's *Floating Island* first hear the musicians as they play in Boston; the music comes to the floating island by cable. In Greg's *Across the Zodiac* the Martians sit in their homes and listen to music sent out over electric wires; householders may turn on one program or another, as one turns a dial on a radio. The wires are also used for ordinary telephonic purposes; "almost every house of any pretension possesses such a wire." In Bellamy's *Looking Backward,* Julian West listens to a sermon in a modern way; Mr. Barton "preaches only by telephone, and to audiences often reaching 150,000." He listens to music in the same way. The telephone wires in Astor's *A Journey in Other Worlds* convey not only the voice, but an image of the speaker's face, as in television.

2. Telautographs

Pictures are today sent by radio. In scientific fiction, pictures, handwriting, and moving scenes have been sent by wires for a good many years. In Greg's *Across the Zodiac,* for instance, the postoffice does not convey letters from place to place; instead, it furnishes a wire from one town to another. A person desiring to send a message places the message in a small box—a transmitting instrument—and the message is exactly reproduced, "with every peculiarity, blot, or erasure," in the selected receiving station; from there it is delivered as a letter is on earth; pictures also may be sent; secrecy may be secured through the use of ciphers or codes. In Benson's *The Dawn of All* the Prime Minister's speech is printed on tickers in individuals' homes by means of the telautograph. Such tickers, used to replace newspapers, are frequent in scientific action, as in Grant's *The King's Men.*

3. Radio and Radar

Wireless communication appeared in scientific fiction by the early 1890's. In Griffith's *Olga Romanoff* the Aërians and the scientists of Mars communicate regularly by "photo-telegraphy, in which the rays of light passing between the earth and Mars . . . perform the functions of the electric wires in modern telegraphy." News and programs of all kinds are received on machines like radios in the London of Wells's *When the Sleeper Wakes,* though Wells is not explicit about whether the machines are wireless. In Emerson's *The Smoky God,* inhabitants of the land inside the earth "hold communion with one another between the most distant parts of the country, on air currents." In Wells's *Men Like Gods,* written after radio had passed the earliest stages of experiment, the boy Crystal sends and receives messages on a portable wireless set. In Kipling's "As Easy as A. B. C." distant machinery is controlled by radio.

Various other developments of something like radio for controlling distant mechanisms, guiding bombs or torpedoes, locating an approaching enemy, or deflecting a distant compass are frequent in recent stories. In Stapledon's *Odd John,* the super-normals set up a device to deflect the compass of any ship that comes within fifty miles of their island. In Smith's "Identity," Cal is guided to Murdoch's hoard, even though it is on Venus, when he has the key for operating a "cavity resonator and antenna system"; and his brother Benj, waiting in ambush for Cal in the Venusian fog-country, is guided by his own "detector."

4. Television

Perhaps radio was developed too quickly after it was first prophesied, or it would have been more widely exploited in scientific fiction. Television is being widely exploited.

In the earliest television sets, the trick is done with mirrors. The host in Tiphaigne de la Roche's *Giphantia,* for instance, shows the traveller events going on in all parts of the world and explains that images are constantly "remitted" to his mirror from mirrors on the "several parts of the earth's surface." Successive scenes are viewed if "the Mirrour is placed successively in all possible aspects." The idea then rested till late in the nineteenth century, when Harben's *Land of the Changing Sun* described a similar mirror in the king's palace; by pressing various buttons to adjust it, the king is able to see the landscape pass "like a panorama." It is done, he says, "Through a telescopic invention, aided by electricity" to pick up views "reflected to this point from various observatories throughout the land." A similar use of mirrors appears in Wells's *When the Sleeper Wakes;* in a darkened room, Ostrog shows Graham views of events all over London. "He judged that this mirror was some modern replacement of the camera obscura, but that matter was not explained to him." Something like television that requires no sending apparatus, but is "plugged into" telephone lines is described in England's *The Golden Blight;* but Storm rages because, "Damn this visualizer, it's far from perfect, yet! The best it can do for me is to follow the telephone-system!" True television, that is, images thrown on a glass plate by an apparatus like that of radio, is described in later fiction, such as Forster's "The Machine Stops." When a dial is turned, a round plate glows, lights shoot across it, and then a woman can see "the image of her son, who lived on the other side of the earth, and he could see her."

Fiction, of course, goes beyond this actual television. Mc-Lociard's "Television Hill" describes an apparatus that can be focused on any point; it penetrates walls and sends back a minutely detailed image of whatever it is focused upon. The principle is that of rays whose length, or projection, is controlled; whatever they are focused upon at their extremity is reflected to the sending-receiving station along the outgoing rays. There the rays are translated into scenes on a screen; the scenes are so detailed that Tom McManus is able to make news-reels of events in any part of the world as they occur. A device providing "radio-touch, -taste, -odour, and -sound" is described in Stapledon's *Star Maker;* it operates by direct stimulation of brain-centers, so that a person may go to bed with a "specially constructed skull-cap" on his head and there experience every sensation that is broadcast from the sending station.

Hunting's *The Vicarion* describes a device that is hardly television, but has the same effect. The apparatus reproduces scenes from the past in every sensory detail, "sound, scent, color, depth, heat." Waves of the ether, says the book, retain impressions of all events; when the proper wave-length of an event is found upon the vicarion, the phantasm of the event may be condensed into a "bomb" and then released, reproduced, and released again and again. The "televisor" or "electronic analyser" of Taine's *Before the Dawn* operates in the same way, though it yields only light. According to the theory stated, light slightly modifies the atoms of a substance until a shell is formed; when the needle of light from the televisor plays upon these atoms, scenes locked into them are reproduced. The device is used to explore fossils, and thereby to present prehistoric scenes.

F. *Discoveries Concerned with Biological Improvement*

1. Biological Discoveries

Many discoveries for controlling the processes of life appear in scientific fiction. The simplest are methods for improving varieties of plants and breeds of animals. In Verne's *Floating Island* beautiful gardens and majestic trees are produced with the aid of "electro-culture." Proper electric currents accelerate growth to produce, for instance, "radishes eighteen inches long and carrots weighing seven pounds apiece." In Kearney's *Erone,* the parklands between the tower-groups of Newlon are bright with flowers and green with vegetables; electrical means stimulate plant-growth so much that these gardens within the city provide most of the food needed there.

In Mercier's *Memoirs of the Year Two Thousand Five Hundred* careful breeding has increased animals to twice the normal size. It is apparent that Tucker's *A Voyage to the Moon* intends to satirize the "Glonglim" farmer who improves the size of his cattle by selective breeding; none the less, this farmer has a buffalo as large as three of the ordinary size. His method is to kill all the young animals that are not "uncommonly large and thrifty" and then to feed the others an abundance of carefully prepared foods.

Many discoveries in surgery are described in scientific fiction. Dr. Moreau, in Wells's *The Island of Dr. Moreau,* studies to find the extreme limit of plasticity in a living form, and his results are "men" carved from living panthers, monkeys, pigs, and the like; the change is not merely in the outward form, but, to a large extent, in physiology, "chemical rhythms," and even emotional attitudes. But when Dr. Moreau is killed, the old "rhythms" assert themselves, and the "men" revert toward the beast. In Von Hanstein's "Utopia Island" Dr. Frank learns to preserve alive portions of the bodies of people who have died and to use these parts in replacing broken or worn-out parts of living people; altruistic citizens sound in body volunteer to have portions of their bodies revitalized and used for the health of others. Renard's *New Bodies for Old* describes the inter-grafting of plants and animals; Klotz kills Lerne, but somehow manages to transfer himself to Lerne's body; a surgical operation exchanges Nicolas's brain and that of a bull; and finally, Klotz even transfers his life-principle to the body of an automobile.

Advances in medical science include the elimination of diseases and bacteria. Mercier, of course, did not dream of bacteria as a source for disease, but in his *Memoirs of the Year Two Thousand*

Five Hundred physicians have discovered the "secret of dissolving the stone without burning the entrails," a cure for phthisis, and a "happy specific" for syphilis. In Astor's *A Journey in Other Worlds* disease bacteria are used to destroy insect pests and animal pests; people are inoculated against all bacteria-borne diseases. Apparently the inhabitants of Mars, in Wells's *The War of the Worlds,* eliminated disease bacteria from their planet so long ago that they did not foresee attack by the bacteria of earth; this attack destroys them. The "last microbes" are discovered and eliminated in Tardé's *Underground Man,* where a sick man would be as strange "as a double-headed monster formerly was, or an honest publican."

These discoveries account in part for the longevity found everywhere in scientific fiction. In Greg's *Across the Zodiac,* for instance, discoveries in the "chemistry of life" and remedies for the hardening of bones and the weakening of muscles have been found; hair does not whiten, teeth do not decay, and eyes do not dim; death comes at an advanced age. In nearly all the Utopias, men live from a hundred years onward to many centuries. Swift, however, had ridiculed the supposed blessing of longevity in *Gulliver's Travels,* and Huxley follows Swift in *After Many a Summer Dies the Swan.* Dr. Obispo discovers that the transfer of the intestinal flora of the carp to the human colon extends life indefinitely, but nothing halts senility; the Fifth Earl, two hundred years old, has degenerated into something more stupid and repulsive than an ape.

Other physiological discoveries concern the glands, the alteration of bodily processes, and the strengthening of tissues. Rays from the element "asterium," described in Taine's *The Iron Star,* change the chemical composition of glands, whose new secretions cause men to degenerate into ape-like creatures. The Chemist in Cumming's *The Girl in the Golden Atom* has a drug that enables him to shrink the cells of his body enough that he can enter the world in an atom. Professor Gibberne's drug in Wells's "The New Accelerator" stimulates bodily processes several thousand times, so that one taking the "accelerator" seems to live for half an hour in a few seconds. Wylie's *The Gladiator* is based upon the discovery of a medicine to give flesh and muscles the strength of steel. Thomas Trelone in Stapledon's *Sirius* discovers a hormone that, injected into a mother's blood, increases the bulk of the cerebral cortices and refines the nerve fibers in the unborn young, so that finally a dog is born with the intelligence of a brilliant man.

The Third Men of Stapledon's *Last and First Men* achieve an even greater biological control first through manipulation of the germ-plasm and later through "manipulation of hereditary factors in germ-cells (cultivated in the laboratory), manipulation of the fertilized ovum (cultivated also in the laboratory), and manipulation of the growing body." After attempts that produce various monsters, the Third Men finally create the Fourth Men, the bodiless Great Brains lodged in ferro-concrete turrets who finally destroy the Third Men and create a better type, the Fifth Men. But even these manipulations are not creation of life from dead matter. Other romances, however, describe the creation of life. In the future visited in Cummings's *The Man Who Mastered Time*, scientists find a workshop containing the artificially made organs of a man, joined together by a network of vessels, and though apparently not conscious, alive. It is the process of *Frankenstein* brought up to date.

2.   Psychological Discoveries

Bellamy's *Dr. Heidenhoff's Process* describes a mechanism that eradicates any unpleasant memory. More "practical applications of psychology," that is, hypnotism and hypnopaedia, eradicate all undesirable thoughts and instill socially valuable learning in Wells's *When the Sleeper Wakes* and Huxley's *Brave New World*. In *When the Sleeper Wakes*, any set of facts, however complex, may be learned in a few trances; children of the laboring classes are hypnotized to enjoy being "beautifully punctual and trustworthy machine minders." It is a "psychic surgery," able to graft the logarithm tables onto the mind or to obliterate the memory of a previous husband. In *Brave New World*, the process is more complex and more thorough. "Conditioning" begins with the embryo, which struggles toward birth in a bottle. An excised ovary is fertilized under controlled temperature, salinity, and viscosity; drugs determine the intelligence of Alphas, Betas, and on down to semi-moron Epsilons; bokanovskification checks the normal growth and causes the egg to bud again and again and so to produce identical twins to the number of several thousand. When the children are "decanted," hypnopaedia—soft mechanical voices under their pillows, electric shocks, baths of hot and cold—continues to predestine them for their rôle in a stable society.

To these discoveries in psychology may be added the nearly universal idea that races of the future will develop telepathy. It is simple, wordless communication in some books, as in Wells's *Men Like Gods;* it is the ranging of the mind through time and space to seek out other minds and influence them in Stapledon's *Last and First Men* and Lovecraft's *The Shadow Out of Time;* and it is a union of thousands of minds in a mutual meditation in Stapledon's *Star Maker.*

3. Marvellous Foods

Scientific romances offer an improvement upon nature in the continual forecast of synthetic foods. Cyrano de Bergerac's traveller in *The Moon* finds that the people of the moon do not eat food, but breathe its fumes; the fumes, however, arise from pots of boiling meats. But Captain Nemo, in Verne's *Twenty Thousand Leagues Under the Sea,* is able to make delicious foods, and even cigars, from seaweed and other products of the sea. A still further step toward synthetic food is prophesied in Boisgilbert's *Caesar's Column;* chemistry and electricity will enable men to turn mountain ranges into bread without the "slow processes of agriculture." In *When the Sleeper Wakes* and "A Story of the Days to Come," Wells describes chemical wine and cakes and pastries that, though originally derived from plants and animals, have no "suggestion in colour or form of the unfortunate animals from which their substance and juices were derived." In Tardé's *Underground Man,* chemists are able to manufacture food from rocks, and "butter, albumen, and milk from no matter what!" This use of synthetic food is a standard feature in recent scientific fiction. Sometimes a dinner is served as a few tiny pills, to the amazement (and the disgust) of the hungry traveller from the past, as in Coblentz's "After 12,000 Years."

In the romances that picture the future satirically, synthetic food always angers the traveller. In Huxley's *Brave New World,* for instance, Mr. Savage storms at the merchant from whom he tries to buy some food: "No, *not* synthetic starch and cotton-waste flour-substitute!" But he accepts pan-glandular biscuits and vitamized beef-surrogate.

The problem of reconciling the advantages of natural foods and those of synthetic foods is solved by the Eighteenth Men of Stapledon's *Last Men in London.* The Eighteenth Man and his sweetheart, Panther, eat a picnic-meal of "rich sun-products," some prepared in the photo-synthesis stations on Jupiter and some from the farms on Uranus, "but we ourselves had gathered the delicacies in our own gardens and orchards."

Perhaps the most marvellous food of scientific romance is the Boomfood of Wells's *The Food of the Gods,* an ingredient in food that supplies to the body a chemical needed for constant growth—as opposed to the intermittent growth said to produce animals and plants of normal size. Boomfood simply makes every plant, animal, or person that eats it grow to giant size.

G. *Discoveries and Inventions Concerned with Economy and Convenience*

1. Alchemistic Discoveries

Medieval alchemists were interested in the transmutation of base metals into gold, and this interest is carried over into scientific fiction in such a story as Poe's "Von Kempelen and His Discovery." Using a laboratory process, Von Kempelen manufactures gold, "absolutely pure, virgin, without the slightest appreciable alloy," from lead and a mixture of antimony and some unknown substance; scientists are unable to discover what the unknown substance is. This idea is reversed in England's *The Golden Blight,* for Storm discovers a ray that causes gold to disintegrate into a worthless powder, though the powder later reverts into gold of its own accord.

2. Photography

About seventy years before photography was developed, it was described in Tiphaigne de la Roche's *Giphantia.* The principle of operation is stated in some detail, from the coating of a piece of canvas with a "most subtle matter, very viscous, and proper to harden and dry," to the development of the canvas in "some dark place," where the subtle matter "dries." The use of a lens to limit and focus the light falling upon the light-sensitive substance is not described; formulas, of course, are not given, but are left "to the naturalists of our days, and . . . their sagacity." In more recent fiction, color photography is described, as in Astor's *A Journey in Other Worlds.*

3. Automatons

The automations of scientific fiction occur in many forms, from that of complex machinery to that of robot men or animals having life and even the power to reproduce themselves. In Bulwer-Lytton's *The Coming Race,* the traveller discovers that the men he takes to be servants are really vril-operated labor-saving machines, without separate intelligence. In Bierce's "Moxon's Master," however, an automaton chessplayer—a piece of machinery —not only has the intelligence to play chess but, when checkmated, flies into a passion and kills Moxon. In Hamilton's *The Metal Giants,* the scientist Detmold creates a metallic brain-stuff and actuates it with vibrations that cause it to become conscious; he then appends mechanical limbs to be controlled by this brain. When Detmold is absent for a while, this metallic brain constructs a number of gigantic metal automatons to be operated by radio from the metal brain. Adam and Eve Link, in Binder's "Adam Link's Vengeance," are automatons with iridium-sponge brains and electric-battery hearts, but their brains are impressed with all the knowledge of their human makers, and they possess every human feeling, including that of passionate love.

Not exactly automatons, but something like them, are the intelligent trained animals frequent in scientific fiction. In Greg's *Across the Zodiac* the Martians use domestic animals for nearly all manual labor. Large birds called "tyrees" follow simple instructions to do agricultural work; other animals called "ambaus" gather fruit. Birds are similarly used for agriculture in Wright's *The Island of Captain Sparrow*. In Bradshaw's *The Goddess of Atvatabar* mechanical birds, "bockhockids," built like ostriches, but forty feet in height, serve as cavalry; their legs are moved by a "powerful magnic motor."

H. *Inventions Concerned with Entertainment*

1. Phonographs and Theatrophones

Bishop Wilkins's *Mercury* speaks of an invention mentioned by Walchius, "so to contrive a trunk or hollow pipe, that it shall preserve the voice entirely for certain hours or days, so that a man may send his *words* to a friend instead of his *writing*," but Wilkins himself thinks this invention may be impossible. In Cyrano de Bergerac's *The Moon,* however, writing is performed by a box "almost similar to our clocks, filled with an infinite number of little springs and imperceptible machines." To "read" this writing, one winds up the machine and then listens to it as it "gives out all the distinct and different sounds which serve as the expression of speech" on the moon. A somewhat similar machine is observed by the sleeper in Mercier's *Memoirs of the Year Two Thousand Five Hundred;* it imitates "all the articulations of the human voice, of the cries of animals, and the various notes of birds." The millionaires of Verne's *Floating Island* have phonographs and a library of phonographic books—"all you had to do was to press a button and you heard the voice of some excellent reader aloud."

Inhabitants of Mars, in Greg's *Across the Zodiac,* have a machine that takes dictation and translates it into "handwriting"— that is, it prints sound as written letters; each person's "phonogram" is individual, as his handwriting is. Each character is "a true physical type, a visual image, of the spoken sound." In Wells's *When the Sleeper Wakes,* Graham finds a library of

cylinders that he supposes may be phonographic books, but when
he presses a button on a machine he finds that it is a theatro-
phone; colored moving pictures appear on a small screen, and
the figures converse in "clear small voices." When Earthly awakes
in Kearney's *Erone,* he finds himself looking on the stage of a
tiny theatre just like that in Wells's book. In Von Hanstein's
"Utopia Island," printed books are read aloud by "a machine which
converts written or printed characters into light rays and then
into sound." Libraries of phonograph records are found everywhere in recent scientific fiction, as in Herrick's *Sometime.* In
Stapledon's *Last and First Men* these records do not produce
sound, but ethereal vibrations that affect the mind of the "reader"
directly—that is, they record telepathic vibrations and, when set
in motion, reproduce them.

2. Moving Pictures

Painted pictures so arranged on the walls of the city that
they tell a story are found in Campanella's *The City of the
Sun;* in Mercier's *Memoirs of the Year Two Thousand Five
Hundred,* pictures of this kind are assembled in an "optical
cabinet," and some mechanism presents the pictures: "They
caused to pass before my eyes landscapes, prospects, palaces,
rainbows, meteors, luminous cyphers, imaginary seas." On Mars,
the traveller in Greg's *Across the Zodiac* finds "most complicated magic lanterns" that present upon a stage "a truly living
and moving picture" whose characters speak by means of "a
gigantic hidden phonograph." By means of this instrument, the
traveller is shown the evolutionary history of Mars. In Griffith's
A Honeymoon in Space, the travellers find on Ganymede "an
immeasurable development of what is called the cinematograph
process on Earth," and they witness the evolutionary history of
Ganymede. In Huxley's *Brave New World,* moving pictures
have developed into "feelies." A feature-picture is advertised
as "Three Weeks in a Helicopter. An All-Super-Singing, Syn-
thetic-Talking, Coloured, Stereoscopic Feely, with Synchronized
Scent-Organ Accompaniment." When the spectator lays his hands
upon knobs at his seat, he feels the emotions broadcast from
the feely; as "stereoscopic lips" come together, "the facial erogen-
ous zones of the six thousand spectators in the Alhambra tingled
with almost intolerable galvanic pleasure."

I. *Inventions Concerned with Warfare*

Warfare in the Machine Age becomes increasingly horrible

through the use of scientific weapons of destruction. The weapons of scientific fiction were sheer imaginations when they were described; some of them have recently been given pet names by G. I. Joe. Altogether, both those that have been used, like the atomic bomb, and others yet in the laboratory make it clear that we have to choose now between world-peace and suicide.

1. Guns

The guns of scientific fiction become ever more and more destructive. Guns firing electric charges are described in Greg's *Across the Zodiac;* the Martians fire flashes of lightning. In Grant's *The King's Men,* guns fire charged bullets that electrocute whomever they hit. Professor Schultz in Verne's *The Five Hundred Millions of the Begum* invents a gun whose shells are themselves guns, "fitted one into the other, like the parts of a telescope"; as a shell reaches the peak of its trajectory, a smaller shell is fired from it, another in turn from it, and so on, the last one to "vomit forth little shells loaded with incendiary matter . . . a whole battery hurled through space." Very often, especially in the magazines, guns are simply tubes for rockets. Aim becomes deadly when it is managed from a dial. In Wells's "The Land Ironclads," scientific instruments enable soldiers to aim by looking into a camera and touching "a little push like an electric bellpush." Mechanisms adjust for every variation of conditions due to atmospheric pressure or movement.

2. Explosives

Ordinary gunpowder was obsolete in scientific fiction before 1900. Professor Schultz in Verne's *The Five Hundred Millions of the Begum* uses guncotton that has an "expansive power . . . four times that of ordinary powder," and treated with "eight tenths of its weight of nitrate of potash" is fivefold more powerful than when untreated. The bombs of scientific fiction increase in power from the dynamite bombs of Greer's *A Modern Daedalus* to the atomic bomb of Wells's *The World Set Free.* Possessing the atomic bomb, the handful of colonists in Stapledon's *Odd John* feel sure they could defeat the rest of the world, but they desist because the slaughter would make them mentally unfit for their work. The intra-atomic forces set loose in Stapledon's *Last and First Men* destroy the first species of mankind and leave the world a steaming cinder.

3. Battleships

The battleships of scientific fiction are larger, faster, and more powerful than actual ships. Sometimes a new design is described. In Parabellum's *Banzai!* for instance, Japanese attack a fort with cruisers that present to the enemy only revolving gun turrets; the rest of each ship is under water. The ships run so close to the fort that the guns, set for long-range battle, cannot aim low enough to hit them. One recalls that the British guns at Singapore could not be turned to fire upon the Japanese.

4. Tanks

Many varieties of tanks appear in fiction after Wells's "The Land Ironclads." Wells's tanks advance across trenches, hillocks, and depressions on eight pairs of wheels set with caterpillar feet; that is, they are remarkably like the tanks in actual use since 1916. The tanks of Newcomb's *His Wisdom* are gigantic mechanical men, controlled by soldiers inside them to stride across obstacles and into enemy lines.

5. Balloons

Dirigible war-balloons of every kind appear in scientific fiction. In Wells's *The War in the Air,* for instance, a fleet of airplane-carrying German balloons flies across the Atlantic, pauses en route to destroy the American Navy, and then descends upon New York. In Tardé's *Underground Man* balloons are iron-clad; they carry aërial torpedoes.

6. Airplanes

But in Griffith's *The Angel of the Revolution,* the gigantic war-balloons of the Tsar are no match for the faster, more maneuverable airplanes of the Aërians. The Germans open the war, in Wells's *The War in the Air,* with balloons, but these balloons are airplane carriers, swarming with deadly *Drachenflieger,* swift little planes that machine-gun the decks of the American Navy and then drop bombs straight into the funnels of the ships in the "final fight of those strangest things in the whole history of war: the ironclad battleships"—destroyed by "cheap things of gas and basketwork . . . smiting out of the sky!" In this book, airplanes can destroy, but not garrison; the Japanese appear with other airplanes, and destruction ceases only when civilization topples into barbarism.

7. Gases and Poisons

The Martians of Greg's *Across the Zodiac* possess guns to shoot bullets of compressed gas that asphyxiates all life for an area of several yards. A gas that rolls along the ground and spreads into hollows is used in Boisgilbert's *Caesar's Column*; it brings "sudden death to those that breathe it." In Wells's *The War of the Worlds,* the Martians wipe out whole cities with a few rockets of a "Black Smoke." "Tiny capsules containing a gas capable of killing billions" are described in Moxley's *Red Snow;* a gas that sinks into the body and dissolves the bones "like sugar in water" to produce "instant collapse and death" is described in Hamilton's "The Metal Giants."

8. Flame-Throwers and Rays

Flame-throwers appear as early as Seaborn's *Symzonia;* tubes projecting from balloons eject burning gases for half a mile. Weapons to eject electricity of varying intensity, to paralyze or to kill, are described in Bulwer-Lytton's *The Coming Race,* Griffith's *Olga Romanoff,* and Cumming's *The Man Who Mastered Time.* The Martians of Wells's *The War of the Worlds* employ a heat-ray, an "invisible sword of heat" that flashes whatever it impinges upon into white flame: "lead runs like water, it softens iron, cracks and melts glass, and when it falls upon water, incontinently that explodes into steam." A ray that disintegrates whatever it touches destroys 360,000 workers in Farrère's *Useless Hands.* Recently, rays are jets of atomic energy. Ng-Gunko, in Stapledon's *Odd John,* develops "a destructive ray, derived from atomic distintegration" that would annihilate a battleship at forty miles. Whole planetary systems are annihilated by such rays in the galactic wars of Stapledon's *Star Maker.*

9. Insects and Bacteria

Cultivated insects—ants, beetles, termites, and disease-bearing mosquitoes—are used in the warfare described in Coblentz's "After 12,000 Years." When World War II becomes desperate, in Best's *The Twenty-Fifth Hour,* America is laid waste by specially bred disease germs. In Stapledon's *Last and First Men,* the great war between the West and the East is brought to a climax when American bacteriologists develop bacteria to "disintegrate the highest levels of the nervous system." Spread through China, these bacteria turn Chinese cities into bedlams. When Martians invade the earth in Stapledon's *Last and First Men,* the only weapon effective against them is a virus; though it is suicidal to use it, men are desperate enough to destroy themselves along with their enemies.

10. Miscellaneous Weapons

The ingenuity of writers of scientific fiction is reflected in an arsenal of miscellaneous weapons, from sword-points heated white-hot by electricity to light and sound that shatter the nerves. Among specimens from this arsenal are the magnetized shells that are attracted to enemy ironwork, in Stockton's *The Great Stone of Sardis;* the whirling knives magnetized to seek out human prey and the magnetic machines that pull airplanes from the air in Cummings's *The Man Who Mastered Time.* Shells charged with liquid carbonic acid to explode and freeze a large area with "cold of a hundred degrees below zero" are described in Verne's *The Five Hundred Millions of the Begum.* Leinster's "The Man Who Put Out the Sun" describes fluorescent waves that cause whatever they touch to radiate away "whatever energy it possesses" and to sink in temperature to absolute zero. Searing light and nerve-wracking sound are used in Kipling's "As Easy As A. B. C." to reduce a population to grovelling terror; the new siren "can break an iceberg in half, if you find the proper pitch." In Smith and Garby's "The Skylark of Space," the Mardondalians attack with sound-vibrations that "racked the joints and tortured the nerves as though the whole body were disintegrating."

11. Psychological Weapons

The final weapon, superseding all weapons of mere destruction, is psychological control. When the world first hears of the island of supernormals in Stapledon's *Odd John,* the British send a ship to capture the islanders. Odd John and his fellows confuse the minds of the British; they cannot erase all memory from the visitors' minds, but when the captain returns home empty handed and reports, his account seems to make no sense. Ship after ship reports in the same way, till finally a ship is sent to bombard the island without landing. In worlds used to telepathy, psychological control is even more powerful. In Wright's *The World Below,* the Amphibians bind the Killers in psychic chains; in Stapledon's *Star Maker,* inhabitants of sane worlds defend themselves against fanatic attackers by psychological penetration; telepathic mind-force disintegrates the will to attack.

J. *Miscellaneous Inventions and Discoveries*

A complete list of the inventions and discoveries described in scientific fiction would sound like a list of headings in the files of a patent office.

Innumerable devices for the preparation of food are found. In Tucker's *A Voyage to the Moon*, for instance, the traveller finds that a farmer uses steam for cooking, with results none too satisfactory; the process is ridiculed. In Pseudoman's *Zero to Eighty* food is cooked by the "direct passage of electric rays" through it, a process that preserves all the vitamin-content. Clothing is likewise machine made. When Graham wakes, in Wells's *When the Sleeper Wakes*, he is naked; a tailor arrives with a complex machine, stands Graham in front of it to be measured, allows him to select colors, pushes a few buttons, and turns out a perfectly tailored suit in a few minutes.

Mechanical luxuries of all kinds, such as the vibro-vacuum machines of Huxley's *Brave New World* and the electric hair-root removers of Wells's "A Story of the Days to Come," are plentiful in scientific fiction. The automobiles of Greg's *Across the Zodiac* are provided with heaters; "motion itself was made to supply a certain warmth through the tubular open-work of the carriage." The typewriters of Von Hanstein's "Utopia Island" are automatic from dictation to finished typescript; "we just dictate into a tube and by the use of selenium cells the speech is changed into writing." The "complicated fabrics that have since been called handling machines," used by the Martians in Wells's *The War of the Worlds*, perform all sorts of automatic actions; for instance, they scoop up clay, extract aluminum from it in some swift process, and deposit bars of metal in a pile.

Enclosed cities are often ventilated and heated or cooled to a constant temperature, as London is in Wells's *When the Sleeper Wakes*. In his *A Modern Utopia* isolated houses are warmed by electrical currents in the floors and walls; even the mattress of a bed is warmed; a noiseless fan keeps the air constantly fresh. In some utopias, the air of cities is perfumed, perhaps distributed from a "central atmosphere station," as it is in Herrick's *Sometime*. Colored flames in rhythms are "made to synchronise" with corresponding musical notes in Greg's *Across the Zodiac*.

Plentiful aluminum, synthetic substances, and useful plastics are common in scientific fiction. Most airplanes are made of aluminum and its alloys. Even the buildings are made of aluminum, "seven times as light as iron, the metal of the future," in Verne's *Floating Island*. In Newcomb's *His Wisdom*, a process is described for refining aluminum cheaply and in great quantities.

In Greg's *Across the Zodiac*, the buildings of Mars are constructed of plastics with a "jewel-like lustre and brilliancy," molded and hardened by the "simultaneous action of cold, electricity, and pressure." "Still plastic blocks of mineral paste" are swung into position by machines in Wells's *When the Sleeper Wakes*, and a building rises quickly; roads are made of Eadhamite, a plastic "resembling toughened glass." In Kipling's "As Easy as A. B. C." a road-surfacing machine melts down and fuses the stone of the old Chicago City Hall to make a road: the "stone wreckage crumbled, slid forward, and presently spread out into white-hot pools of sticky slag, which the leveling-rods smoothed." The lovely buildings of Herrick's *Sometime* are made of a "colored viscous substance that was poured and molded into any desired shape with incredible ease and rapidity, offering a great variety of design and color." The entire civilization of Verrill's "Beyond the Pole" is based upon a plastic that "can be made opaque, transparent or translucent; as hard as steel or as soft and plastic as putty; as brittle as glass or as flexible as rubber."

Pneumatic tubes are frequent in fiction. In Bellamy's *Looking Backward*, people do not go to various shops to order goods, but to a central distributing point; orders are transmitted to the proper parts of a vast warehouse, and in a few minutes the packages arrive by pneumatic tube. In Wells's *When the Sleeper Wakes*, Graham would like to have a cigar; there are none in London, as smoking has almost vanished. But by the time he completes his dinner, cigars have been ordered from Florida and have arrived by pneumatic dispatch. Huge pneumatic tubes are used for transportation in Von Hanstein's "Utopia Island."

In many romances, the inhabitants of strange worlds are able to control the weather. In Bradshaw's *The Goddess of Atvatabar*, rain is regularly produced by "firing into the air balls of solid gas so intensely cold that in turning to the gaseous form they condense in rain the invisible vapor in the air." The process is more complex in Astor's *A Journey in Other Worlds;* surface air is forced by blowers up mountain sides or towers and there discharged to cool the surrounding air and start a rain. The Altrurians of Howells's *A Traveler from Altruria* secure an equable climate by cutting a peninsula to change an ocean current. In Kearney's *Erone*, life is made possible on a planet very far from the sun because the Eronians know how to bend the rays of the sun and relay them to desirable parts of the planet's surface.

Drugs or mechanisms to affect the brain, read the mind, or alter the course of thought are common in scientific fiction. In Griffith's *Olga Romanoff* a drug so hypnotizes the will that a captured Aërians reveals to his enemies every secret of the Aërians. A physician in Benson's *The Dawn of All* examines the contents of a patient's mind by means of an electrical instrument. A machine that reflects thought in pictures is described in Doyle's *The Maracot Deep*, "a combination of such telepathy and television as we dimly comprehend upon the earth." A thought-recorder in Smith and Garby's "The Skylark of Space" takes evidence that will not lie. The matter-duplicator in Smith's "Identity" duplicates people, including the contents of their minds.

Magnetic needles that trace criminals through the mazes of the underworld, marvellous gyroscopes, bomb-sights, petroleum furnaces, black light, shaving creams that remove hair when they are wiped off, and uncounted thousands of other devices are found in scientific romances. Future times described in scientific fiction belong, as Farrère says in *Useless Hands*, to the "MACHINE: for there is mathematically only one, while appearing to be legion." The legion making up this entity more or less anticipates every important modern invention and many that have not appeared.

CHAPTER TEN

Creeds

SOCIAL ADJUSTMENTS for a hundred years have been sharply diverted from older courses by the presence of more and more machines. As gunpowder and the printing press helped put an end to the Middle Ages, steam power, electricity, the internal combustion engine, and the machine gun helped put an end to the designs for living that seemed, to some men in the eighteenth century, to have reached a reasonable perfection. The rôle that humanism played in disrupting medieval stability has been played by Darwinism and relativity in disrupting whatever sense of stability men felt in the eighteenth century. Every adjustment has been disturbed into maladjustment, until finally, as evolution and relativity have influenced thought, the theory has been widely stated that life is dynamic, never adjusted, but always in the process of becoming adjusted.

The old-fashioned utopia described a perfect place, a static society, and progress that amounted to accumulation. Bacon's *The New Atlantis* describes no revolution; Bellamy's *Looking Backward*—enough later to know better—describes a revolution accomplished and the attainment of a static perfection. But Wells's *A Modern Utopia,* aware of the pace of progress and its uncertain direction, speaks of relative perfection in a dynamic society; Huxley's *Brave New World* describes a society held stable only because Controllers both manipulate the human embryo to remove unrest and clamp a desperate prohibition on all science. Stapledon's *Last and First Men* presents utopia after utopia, each in turn corroded and collapsed by the forces of change.

There can be no doubt that scientific romances, including utopias and satires, have helped to shape modern attitudes, if not the official ones of philosophers, spokesmen, and political leaders, the more numerous ones of college boys, merchants, laborers, and housewives, whose will the leaders must, in the long run, represent and reflect. For one thoughtful man who reads *The Origin of Species, Capital,* and *The Theory of the Leisure Class* and forms his own philosophy, several pass the time with *Twenty Thousand Leagues Under the Sea, The Time Machine,* and *Amazing Stories* and absorb from this reading conceptions of the world they live in, the rôle of science in changing it, and desirable and undesirable routes of change. The recent multiplication of scientific fiction is a mass-phenomenon; so in the long run, in one way or another, is every political or social system, democratic or dictatorial, that has a chance to survive in the modern world.

The historian of literature must recognize as perhaps the most striking feature of fiction between 1840 and 1940 its increasing concern with social protest, humanitarian in the mid-Victorian era, utopian and semi-socialistic around the turn of the century, and proletarian in the 1920's and 1930's. Most of this fiction of social protest, ranging from Dickens's *Oliver Twist* to Dos Passos's *U. S. A.,* is concerned simply with protest; here and there doctrinaire, its major purpose has been the realistic illumination of social evils. Insofar as the realistic fiction of social protest is only descriptive, it attacks evils without showing how they can be eliminated; wherever it is doctrinaire, offering remedies, it is abstract. It cannot present a concrete realistic picture of a completely satisfactory adjustment; it cannot illustrate its doctrines, for the evils attacked prevail—the doctrine suggested is a theory. The protest against slums, for instance, may stir in the reader some will to abolish them; it has difficulty in showing him how. Lately realistic fiction has presented the way to do so in the words of reformers, often radicals. But realistic writers dealing with the American scene are often faced with the problem that faces Dos Passos in *U. S. A.*: a college boy writes to inquire why it is that radicals, so right in theory, are so often stinkers in their private lives.

Like this college boy, the masses who read fiction for entertainment are inclined to be impatient of theory; the generalization, heavy with meaning for the philosopher, has little weight for people—certainly most of the people of the world—who do not think abstractly.

No doubt most scientific romances are written for entertainment, just as most love stories are. But many pieces of scientific fiction, not merely the utopia and satires, but also stories of inventions and adjustments to them, of future history, and of trips to other planets, are serious efforts to give specific, concrete illustration of general principles in science and society. Where realistic fiction concerned with social adjustment must stop with protest about what is, and generalization about what may be, the scientific romance presents the concrete example of what may be. The example may be highly fantastic—it is necessarily imaginary—but at least it is concrete. The reader may think of social adjustment not in terms of what stinkers the reformers are in their private lives, but in terms of the visible reform.

The validity of such a scientific romance as blue-print for adjustment must depend, of course, upon the extent to which the fiction is faithful in extending scientific and social laws into an imagined situation, the validity of the laws themselves, and the course of unforseen events. Bellamy's *Looking Backward* is, no doubt, an honest book, but the social laws applied in it have been modified by Marxian theory, actual invention has already outstripped most of the inventions prophesied, and the course of events since 1888 has made unlikely any such peaceful establishment of socialism as the book describes. But even so that book, among others, influenced the many thousands who read it; for instance Eugene Debs, standing on the platform outlined in *Looking Backward,* in 1912 received nine hundred thousand votes for president of the United States.

The realistic view is often a short view; views influenced by geology and astronomy, for instance, look farther ahead. Scientific fiction serves the purpose, for the most part, of encouraging the longest possible range of vision. Its failure perhaps is that it is not sufficiently realistic; the telescope and the microscope can hardly serve the same purpose.

On the other hand, as we enter the Atomic Age, facing for the first time in history the mandatory choice between Permanent World Peace I and a World War III that might easily blackout civilization, we need now the long view. We need all the light any telescope trained upon the future can provide.

Because the telescope is trained upon a cosmic process in which a great deal is dim, the reports of scientific fiction are not unanimous. They differ sharply in their views of the future. The social philosophies of this fiction constitute a debate concerning the destiny of man in the present Machine Age and in the Atomic Age of more powerful, more ubiquitous machines. Some romances are optimistic, seeing in science and invention the means for realizing Utopia; others are pessimistic, seeing in science and invention premonition of life mechanized, brutalized, and even destroyed altogether.

A. *Optimistic Ideas*

1. Science Is to Develop Tremendously

A hundred years of progress in science and invention proceeding at an accelerated pace toward horizons that are constantly receding leaves little room for doubt that science and invention will continue toward some development now undreamed of. At least no such doubt appears in scientific fiction, except in a few pieces in which men wilfully halt invention when it becomes dangerous. During the past hundred years, no one invention has completely altered human life, but all the inventions together have obviously made civilized life in the twentieth century far different from that in the eighteenth. It is possible that the latest major product of science, the atomic bomb and the probable development of atomic power, will prove to be the long-predicted agent of revolutionary change.

Scientific fiction constantly predicts that invention will revolutionize the world. In Greer's *A Modern Daedalus,* for instance, the ability to fly, it is said, will enable man to master the poles, "the snowy peaks of earth's mightiest mountains ... the swarming life of tropic forests," and to civilize the "wildness of the Australian or New Zealand bush." The power to fly, says Newcomb's *His Wisdom,* "will revolutionize the world, and make those who are instrumental in that revolution the greatest benefactors the world has ever seen." Single inventions of other kinds will likewise revolutionize the world; the disintegration of water, in Verne's *The Mysterious Island,* is predicted as a motive-power for the utopian future. The disintegration of the atom, a constant prediction, will revolutionize the world.

In Tardé's *Underground Man,* technology in general has advanced to the point where factories supply all men's wants by running only three hours a day; the goods of the world are so abundant that even a three-hour working day is nearly voluntary. Many inventions, plus political, social, and moral adjustment to the new conditions, eliminate altogether the necessity for labor, in Wells's *A Modern Utopia;* people work at such art and science as they please. During their "high noon," the First Men of Stapledon's *Last and First Men* think of science as a religion, not merely because "it was through science that men had gained some insight into the nature of the physical world, but rather because the application of scientific principles had revolutionized their material circumstances."

As inventions revolutionize man's material circumstances, the principles of science furnish him a new philosophy. To achieve utopia, men looked first to reason, which is itself guided by discovery of scientific principles; Mercier's *Memoirs of the Year Two Thousand Five Hundred* calls upon Reason to bring about utopia. Reason, in this eighteenth-century sense, was idealistic and theoretical. The nineteenth and twentieth centuries have destroyed some abstractions and modified others; that is, science has informed reason with knowledge. Utopia today is less abstract, less perfect, but utopian fiction describes still a rational way of life based upon a tremendously developed, and infinitely developing, science. In Wells's *Men Like Gods,* "competition has not gone from our world." No principle of rest, but a principle of evolution rules. Through guiding evolution—a blind law of nature, as willing to take one direction as another—men guide themselves; everyone labors, without drudgery but without indolence; they do not seek to master and exploit one another, but themselves and the ever-mastered, every-mysterious universe.

2. Science Is to Improve the Race

An important suggestion in the theory of evolution is that the human race may improve itself. Reformers have always stumbled upon the empty cranium, the indolent body, and mass passions. No one would question the worth of democracy if every citizen were alert, intelligent, and responsible; government could wither away into law-abiding anarchy. Scientific fiction has dealt with the problem of securing intelligent citizens from the time of More's *Utopia* onward, and the principle of evolution has suggested to many people that the human race may gradually eliminate its unfortunates and reach utopia by selective birth control.

More's *Utopia* described empirical eugenics. The Utopians know nothing of the laws of heredity, but they wish to be sure that only healthy and sound men and women are united in marriage. For this reason, "Before marriage some grave matron presents the bride naked, whether she is a virgin or a widow, to the bridegroom, and after that some grave man presents the bridegroom naked to the bride." In Campanella's *City of the Sun,* one of the chief magistrates is in "charge of the race. He sees that men and women are so joined together, that they bring forth the best offspring. Indeed, they laugh at us who exhibit a studious care for our breed of horses and dogs, but neglect the breeding of human beings."

The theory of evolution stimulated this feature of utopian life and based it upon science rather than upon impressions and the judgment of a magistrate. In Hudson's *A Crystal Age,* for instance, the society is matriarchal, each family organized around a specially selected Mother. No woman thinks of becoming a mother who is not selected for that high office; the narrator falls in love with the beautiful, perfect-looking Yoletta, but his judgment is not enough; as she has not been selected for motherhood, she laughs at his protestations. In Tardé's *Underground Man,* the people selected to continue the race are the hardiest, handsomest, and most talented; weaklings are put into the army to be used for cannon fodder. But health and strength are not enough: "The right to have children is the monopoly and supreme recompense of genius," and it is "unheard of and unexampled in our day for a woman in love to abandon herself to her lover before the latter has under her inspiration produced a masterpiece which is adjudged and proclaimed as such by his rivals."

Drastic limitation of births is a feature of recent scientific fiction. The population of the world of Wells's *Men Like Gods* is far less than that of the earth today and every citizen "would have ranked as an energetic creative spirit in former days . . . the idle strains, the people of lethargic dispositions or weak imaginations, have mostly died out; the melancholic type has taken its dismissal and gone; spiteful and malignant characters are disappearing." People may marry or make love as they choose in the world of Herrick's *Sometime,* but having children is another matter. Only a few men and a few women, entitled to wear a thread of gold in the hem of their garments, are allowed to have children; they normally share their children with families not allowed to have children but eager to bring them up. This control of births is the greatest single factor in producing the healthy citizens of Utopia.

Another factor is the development of medical science and especially its mergence with the social and psychological sciences. It is a serious suggestion in Bellamy's *Looking Backward* that criminals be treated in hospitals as cases of atavism rather than in prisons. In the world of Wells's *A Modern Utopia,* medical science has enabled men to "put off the years of decay" through scientific care of the health. "They keep their teeth, they keep their digestions, they ward off gout and rheumatism, neuralgia and influenza and all those cognate decays that bend and wrinkle men in the middle years of existence." The same situation exists in all the recent utopias, and even the utopistic satires—for whatever the attitude toward science, it has demonstrated that it can control decay. Frequently any person born unsound or crippled is chloroformed, like the pitiful child of Clarence and Olive in Allen's "The Child of the Phalanstery."

The application of the principles of science to control births and to keep men healthy answers the age-old objection to utopian dreams, that human beings cannot be changed. Evolution shows that they are changed and changing, and the task ahead of the world is to change them wisely in accordance with the knowledge furnished by science.

3. Science Is to End War

Another stumbling block on the way to utopia is war. It runs like a perpetual motif through human history; so far, the effect of science upon war has been chiefly to furnish the nations with weapons that are constantly more destructive.

Yet in the very destructiveness of these weapons, many writers see a hope for peace. Science may finally furnish weapons so frightful that either (1) human nature will revolt against their use or (2) the choice for the human race will lie between peace and suicide. The flame-throwing dirigible balloon of Seaborn's *Symzonia* was used to drive the selfish members of society out of the internal world and after this to establish permanent peace. The inventor says of it: "I would show my abhorrence of war by rendering it too horrible to be encountered. I would abolish war by ensuring inevitable destruction to all who engaged in it." In this statement, the inventor sums up a faith running through scientific fiction that science can abolish war through destructive invention.

Even the historic romances whose central story concerns a destructive war express this faith. The inventor of a flying machine that bombs England in Greer's *A Modern Daedalus* speaks of the "irony of fate" that his labors for the "general good of mankind, and the promotion, as I fondly dreamed, of peace and goodwill and universal amity among nations" introduce an "unprecedentedly destructive method of warfare." But after the Irish win their independence, there is to be no more war; flying will be used for commerce and exploration. In Newcomb's *His Wisdom*, the Professor finds it unnecessary to fight the last great war; under the shadow of his airplanes, his menlike tanks simply stride among the assembled armies of the world, take the guns from the soldiers' hands, and bring an end to armies. People considered as national masses are too stupid, in Wells's *The World Set Free*, to see that "war was becoming impossible. . . . They did not see it until the atomic bombs burst in their fumbling hands." But when "the flimsy fabric of the world's credit had vanished, industry was completely disorganised and every city, every thickly populated area was starving or trembled on the verge of starvation . . . the capital cities of the world were burning . . . and over great areas government was at end," a few clear-headed leaders gather in the Alps, abolish the old-fashioned national state, and establish the new era.

The new weapons of science are different from previous weapons in effect upon the decisiveness of war. Older weapons enabled an army to win, but the new weapons enable it only to destroy. In *The War in the Air,* Wells points out that "The special peculiarities of aerial warfare were of such a nature as to trend . . . almost inevitably towards social disorganisation." First, from the air a city can be destroyed, but not garrisoned—therefore not conquered. Second, airplanes are effective in destroying what lies below, but risk suicide in attacking one another. Third, aerial warfare, enormously destructive, is indecisive, without victor or vanquished. It becomes guerrilla warfare till society collapses, then piracy, and finally dies out as society sinks into barbarism. Wells's reasoning has not proven entirely sound when applied to the airplane alone; old-fashioned "blockbusters" are not destructive enough. But the same logic sounds convincing when various nations have the atomic bomb. It does not seem possible that warfare can end in victory for anybody.

Furthermore, writers of scientific romances often point out the incompatibility between use of the weapons of science and the age-old traditions of war. This incompatibility is a constant theme in Wells's romances. Old-fashioned strategy in "The Land Ironclads" has stalled a war; soldiers waiting in the trenches are proud to hold their lines, and about the contest there is something like football rivalry. This is war as it ought to be, as the manuals of strategy describe it. Then the "ironmongery" appears, tanks that anger the defeated general because they are not according to the rules. The old general storms while a "half-dozen comparatively slender young men in blue pyjamas" stand about their tank laughing and drinking coffee; but the game is up. This idea is best expressed in one of Wells's books not otherwise treated in this study because not primarily scientific fiction, *The Autocracy of Mr. Parham.* Dictator Parham wants to fight an old-fashioned heroic war, but events move against his armies. He appeals to scientists for new weapons, but they oppose him. He may have his war if he wants to play that silly game, but "Why drag in modern science? Use historical armies and fleets for historical destinies and leave gas and tanks and submarines out of it. If you must still play about with flags and frontiers, go back to Brown Bess and foot-slogging. . . . Chemistry doesn't belong to your world. . . . It's new. It's out-size."

In the new point of view of science, war is ridiculous. This attitude is expressed as early as Voltaire's "Micromegas." When a philosopher explains to the visitor from Sirius that men are cutting one another's throats, some for a Sultan and some for a Caesar, whom the men fighting have never seen, about a lump of clay no bigger than the Sirian's heel, the Sirian looks upon the spectacle as one looks upon fighting ants. The world belongs to mankind, not to nations. Force may be required to make this point of view acceptable, as it is in Griffith's *The Angel of the Revolution,* but once accepted, internationalism replaces nationalism, as it does under the Aërians, and all the world, of which nations are co-operative parts, makes as a unit the progress that no nation alone can make. Like Voltaire's Sirian, the Eighteenth Men of Stapledon's *Last Men in London* find the World War of 1914-18 an absurdity. As an Eighteenth Man (a symbol for the new point of view of science) influences the mind of Paul, Paul is torn in an agony of conflicts; the old catch-words, flag-waving, and ideas of patriotism, as well as reluctance to be thought a coward, urge him to fight; the Eighteenth Man makes him see that mankind is the body and the nations are only parts of it, and favoring one side against another is like favoring the right arm against the left. This parable reflects, no doubt, an attitude that has been spreading for some time. It is, on the one hand, the Christian doctrine of the brotherhood of man; and, on the other, part of the long-range view of man's destiny suggested by science. In World War II, armies on all sides had to care for the morale of soldiers who found it difficult to hate. Many soldiers, no doubt, suffered from the inability to reconcile warfare with the view of man's destiny suggested by science.

4.   Science Is to Be Socialized

In the long-range view suggested by science, old-fashioned individual invention or isolated discovery must yield to some form of socialized and international science. Science, in both its inventions and its principles, belongs to mankind; invention and discovery are ceasing to be individual exploits, and are becoming more and more contributions to a world-wide possession of machinery and structure of knowledge; and finally, this structure will rise with accelerated speed as fast as it is made the possession of not only a nation, but the world.

Scientific fiction argues that individual invention places in one man's control power too great for any one individual. Science and invention, controlled by individuals or nations, can threaten all society; co-operatively developed for the good of the world, they immeasurably benefit all the world. In Bacon's *The New Atlantis*, science and invention are the business of the state; in Von Hanstein's "Utopia Island," they are the business of the world, and the scientists of Santa Scientia appeal to the League of Nations for guarantees: "For it is necessary that this world university, which is never to be involved in two things, politics and war, shall not belong to any existing nation, but be an organic whole of itself."

The individual inventor, typical of science in the eighteenth and nineteenth centuries, worked, no doubt, partly for patents and profits; the research-worker was the true type of scientist, for his discoveries were often their own reward. Scientific work in the twentieth century has been less individual, more the piecemeal contributions of many scientists working together in universities and the laboratories of great corporations. A twentieth-century discovery is usually developed, as the airplane, the automobile, and the radio have been developed, by workers all over the world, rather than brought to perfection by any one man. The twentieth-century scientist is a salaried man like Steinmetz, rather than a free-lance inventor like Edison. When comfortably salaried, his spurs to work are those of curiosity and perhaps fame, rather than the hope of profits. The equipment that he can work with is not just what he can make or buy himself; it is provided by a corporation, of business or of the state.

This drift, according to scientific fiction, must lead toward the complete socialization and internationalization of science. Mercier dreamed of this state of affairs as long ago as the eighteenth century; in *Memoirs of the Year Two Thousand Five Hundred*, the narrator learns that "we have united the force of each individual . . . the one finished what the other began . . . and this chain of ideas and of successive labour may one day surround and embrace the universe. It is not merely a personal glory, but the interest of the human race." A central theme in Wells's romances is that science must be socialized, and that when it is, it will be tremendously accelerated. In *A Modern Utopia*, for instance, more than a million scientists are engaged in world-wide, state-salaried research; when desirable, salaries are supplemented by "All sorts of grants in the hands of committees of the most varied constitution." In Wells's *The World Set Free*, research engages the attention of "a thousand thinking hard, observing, experimenting, for one who did so in 1900." A vast indexing system keeps every worker constantly abreast of accomplishments all over the world; thousands catalog up-to-the-minute records, and "every week sheets are taken out and replaced by fresh sheets that are brought to us by the aeroplanes of the Research Department." Science is both "the awakening mind of the race" and the world-wide co-operative application of its discoveries; uninhabited wildernesses are opened up, swamps are drained, and roads are laced about the whole earth. The acceleration does not lessen. In Wells's *Men Like Gods,* after a "hundred million good brains have been put like grapes into the wine-press of science" for three thousand years, Sungold says, "we know to-day—how little we know."

Naturally these ideas are constantly reflected in the fiction of the magazines. Nearly every picture of a world in the future or on another planet describes a tremendously developed science planet-wide in organization.

5.   Science Is to Compel World Planning

This socialization of science so clearly implies economic and political planning that writers in the magazines of the 1920's and 1930's, stimulated by wide-spread interest in the various brands of centralized social control in Russia, Italy, and Germany, used scientific fiction for propaganda of all kinds, sometimes thoughtful and sincere, sometimes merely conventional in the tradition of older historic romances. But whatever the -ism favored in this or that story, scientific fiction is almost unanimous in including some discussion of social control and in foreseeing, as either good or bad, approach to some form of world planning in the present trend of history.

The progress of science will bring about some form of social control because science offers only two alternatives. The weapons of science offer means for the destruction of a civilization that pursues counter-purposes that lead through aggression inevitably to war; on the other hand, science offers in labor-saving machinery and in discovery of the laws of life the means for founding a planned state that may be utopian or, the satirists say, inhumanly mechanical. Acceptance of the first alternative, continued individualism, leads to social suicide, that is, return through war to barbarism. Acceptance of the second, some form of world planning, is necessary if society is to continue.

Bellamy's *Looking Backward* is largely doctrinaire, but it sees utopian socialism as inevitable in the trend of history in an age of science. Bellamy's future world is the "result of a process of industrial evolution which could not have terminated otherwise." Wells presents the future satirically in *When the Sleeper Wakes,* but the future he foresees is a socialistic dictatorship, and the socialistic feature of it, at least, is inevitable.

Graham "perceived at once how necessarily this state of affairs
had developed from the Victorian city." The advancement of
science and invention, as they are presented everywhere in scientific
fiction, compels men to adopt a planned economy in which the
individual is unimportant, and society as a whole is important.

This planned economy is manifested in various political forms.
Nearly always little nations disappear; sometimes three or four
great nations—no small ones—remain in the world; sometimes
the whole world is organized as a single political unit. In Stockton's *The Great Stone of Sardis,* for instance, North America
is a single nation: "Greenland, Norland (formerly British America,
British Columbia, and Alaska), Canada, The United States,
Mexico, Central America, and West Indies were united under
one confederated government." In Kipling's "As Easy as A. B. C."
the only government in the world is the Aerial Board of Control.

Traditional utopian socialism is found in a good many pieces
of scientific fiction. It succeeds so well in the experimental state
of Hertzka's *Freeland* that the nations of the world adopt it;
the consequences are world-peace and prosperity The survivors,
a utopian remnant, flee from world-catastrophe in Boisgilbert's
Caesar's Column to set up a socialistic government in Africa,
embodying universal suffrage, compulsory education, state
ownership of natural resources, state regulation of all industry
(to set wage scales and determine the number employed and
conditions of labor), and a governing body called "The People"
made up of three branches containing representatives of workers,
merchants, and professional men. In Griffith's *The Angel of the
Revolution,* the Aërians dictate a benevolent socialism to the
world; all armies are disbanded, land becomes public property,
and the state is supported by land-rents (and the rents of buildings in the cities) instead of by taxation. The World State
founded in Wells's *The World Set Free* acquires all utilities and
public services—heating, lighting, power, communications—and
of course, the land of the world, administered by municipalities,
"holding, as it were, feudally under it as landlords." The State
pays individuals for healthy birds, maintains public health, and
subsidizes research and even literature. It spreads a single language
over the earth as the standard language; a simplified form of
English supersedes all other languages.

The ultimate goal of socialism, as it is described in scientific
fiction, is self-disciplined anarchism. Perhaps there should remain
some scaffolding of government, a world-congress that meets
now and then to debate policies that something like a self-
sustaining civil-service puts into execution. In Wells's *The World
Set Free,* for instance, after the World State has been in opera-

tion for some time, "government gathers now for a day or so in each year under the sunshine of Brissago when Saint Bruno's lilies are in flower, and does little more than bless the work of its committees." In the socialism of Wells's *Men Like Gods,* even money has been abolished, a credit system takes its place: "People ceased to draw coin for their work; the various departments of service, and of economic, educational and scientific activity would credit the individual with his earnings in the public bank and debit him with his customary charges for all the normal services of life." Passes issued for ten years are good in all means of conveyance; a fixed annual charge furnishes everyone with matches, stationery, newspapers, food, clothing, and housing. Meanwhile, government loses its functions of political control; everyone is a servant of the state, for all activities are a part of the state, but everyone chooses what he wishes to do. Some plan and build houses where they are needed. "Others pursue pure science. Others . . . are artists. Others again teach." They do these things without a central executive or legislature.

This is essentially the system described in the latest important English utopia, Kearney's *Erone.* The state provides each citizen his annual share of the national dividend, usually about $5,000. The state owns all public services, including transportation systems and restaurants, and even meals away from home are free to everyone. In return, every citizen may be called upon to work for the state, "ready to do anything that might be necessary in the service of the state." Usually a person gets his choice of work; Doreece, for instance, enjoys her work as an engineer on the Eronian monoways.

Perhaps the drift toward utopian socialism described almost everywhere in scientific fiction is best summed up in Stapledon's *Star Maker.* The narrator, exploring the entire universe, finds intelligent life everywhere struggling toward some form of socialism, but he finds the political forms that embody it extremely varied. "For instance, in the loosest possible sense, all were communistic; for in all of them the means of production were communally owned . . . . Again, in a sense all these world-orders were democratic. . . . But in many cases there was no democratic machinery." The political form is sometimes a "highly specialized bureaucracy, or even a world-dictator." In worlds that reach stability, laws wither away and become something like "the canons of an art," with no penalty beyond that of public disapproval.

Frequently socialization implies that older moralities, especially the credit-making virtues of a capitalist economy, are scrapped; sometimes, as in Kipling's "With the Night Mail," the only legal restraint on individual behavior is that no one shall interfere with the traffic and all that it implies. Marriage is often a free association without legal restraint; as in Herrick's *Sometime,* sexual pruriency has vanished. Women work beside men and at the same kind of work—usually work involving no drudgery; men and women bathe together without clothing. Racial prejudice has vanished. In general, the socialization of the world brought about through the development of science liberates the human mind from every pruriency and prejudice and leaves it able to apply to every problem the free play of reason.

The satires find a socialized world dull and mechanical, but the utopias insist socialism does not mean dullness. Everyone develops a hobby, an art, or a scientific interest; a baker's hobby, for instance, is statistical work. In Wells's *The World Set Free,* "Men study and save and strive that they may leave behind them a series of panels in some public arcade. . . . Or they give themselves to the penetration of some still opaque riddle in phenomena as men once gave themselves to the accumulation of riches." The Fifth Men of Stapledon's *Last and First Men* spend "scores of millions of years not wholly, not even chiefly, on industrial advancement, but almost entirely on art, science and philosophy" without ever "falling into ennui."

Perhaps we may wisely quarrel with many details in the utopian socialism of these books. But since the development of the atomic bomb, many thoughtful people who would not like to be branded Socialists have come to the same essential conclusion: that science has now brought us to the place where we must have a planned world. An editorial of November 26, 1945, in *Life* magazine, for instance, comments that Mr. Harold Stassen's "scheme for an international air force, armed with a monopoly of the bomb, is of course a proposal for world government." *Life,* certainly no Socialist organ, then agrees: "Some kind of world government is certainly an ultimate necessity and we are lucky to have men like Stassen to keep that necessity before our eyes." For a good many years, scientific fiction has foreseen both atomic power and the ultimate necessity for a world government and has kept that necessity before the eyes of a great many readers.

B. *Pessimistic Ideas*

1. The Machine Age Weakens Man

To the argument that science is to develop at an accelerated pace, the pessimists oppose the conclusion that the Machine

Age weakens man in body, mind, and spirit, and, therefore, an accelerated development of it will result in degeneration of the species.

Butler's *Erewhon* presents in the form of a parable the idea that extensive use of machinery will enslave man to it; already, says the Erewhonian philosopher, men are so dependent on machines that they would become extinct in six weeks if stranded on a desert island, and if any survived "even these in a year or two would become worse than monkeys." This slavery, which affects "Man's very soul," grows more abject as machines multiply; the only solution is the destruction of machinery. After this destruction, Higgs finds the Erewhonians a healthy, handsome, and self-reliant race, taller, stronger, and longer-lived than the people of Europe. Forster's "The Machine Stops" presents a picture of the future in which the Machine has completely enslaved mankind: "Humanity, in its desire for comfort. . . . Quietly and complacently . . . was sinking into decadence, and progress had come to mean the progress of the Machine." While the Machine runs, men live lives of bleached and flabby comfort, exerting themselves only to press buttons; when the Machine stops, they perish like flies in a trap.

The first stage in this complete enslavement of man to the machine is the destruction of individuality, the stereotyping of people themselves through mechanical elimination of the forces that differentiate man from man. Mass-production tends to stereotype such products as shirts, workers' houses in factory districts, and college graduates. As the Machine Age advances, increased mass-production may stereotype everyone. In Wells's *When the Sleeper Wakes*, the old-fashioned home has disappeared; children are born in public crèches and are brought up in them (while their mothers work); babies are suckled by "mechanical figures, with arms, shoulders and breast of astonishingly realistic modelling, articulation, and texture, but mere brass tripods below, and having in the place of features a flat disc bearing advertisements likely to be of interest to mothers." When they grow up, these children live in identical rooms in more or less identical hotels—varied in size and luxury, but alike in pattern—and dine in public dining halls on food produced by mass-production methods. Children themselves are products of mass-production in Huxley's *Brave New World;* and because the human body occasionally needs the tonic of passion, men and women are given "Violent Passion Surrogate. Regularly once a month. . . . All the tonic effects of murdering Desdemona and being murdered by Othello, without any of the inconveniences." This tendency of the Machine Age to reduce men to a dead level corrodes the semi-utopian society of the First Men in Stapledon's *Last and First Men*. America, the most highly mechanized nation, drenches the planet with canned foods, canned art, and canned thought, till "the whole world, and with it the nobler parts of America herself, were irrevocably corrupted."

The Machine Age weakens man's body. When the world war of Wells's *The War in the Air* breaks out, only the aggressor nations are hard; peaceful populations have become soft with an urbanized gentleness, "peculiar to the crowded townsmen of that time" who "never saw anything killed, never encountered . . . the fact of lethal violence that underlies all life." When war destroys the mass-products on which men had lived, they are helpless to create anything—for instance, to hunt and kill animals for food, to make clothes, and to bake bread—and simply slide into a state more helpless than that of primitive society. Machinery makes it unnecessary for men to use their hands, and so, as the dog Sirius observes in Stapledon's book, the "regressive human types" of the upper classes are ashamed to use their hands. The consequent lack of manual dexterity and the "poor teeth and eye-sight and digestions of civilization" are largely responsible for the swift collapse into barbarism, once the cities are destroyed, in Best's *The Twenty-Fifth Hour*. Advances in medical science soften men so that they cannot resist disease; when the virulent bacteria of London's *The Scarlet Plague* get a start, human beings have no resistance and perish by the millions. In Forster's "The Machine Stops," it is "a demerit to be muscular." Strong children are killed at birth, for an athlete "would never have been happy in that state of life to which the Machine had called him," and the weak survive, only to perish when the Machine breaks down.

The Machine Age weakens man's mind. The Eloi of Wells's *The Time Machine*, products of ages of machine-supported luxury, are childish in mind, without the capacity for concentrated attention or thought of any kind. The people of Wells's "A Story of the Days to Come" are harder, but almost equally without individuality; hypnotism takes the place of education; braying machines vend ready-made news; public taste in literature is jaded to the point where a lecturer is advertised because he "has six toes, dresses in red, and never cleans his teeth"; the public street-ways blare gaudy advertisements of a kind to attract only morons: "'ets" (hats) in letters of flame projected on one's body or on a bald head— and everywhere a deafening blare. In Wells's *When the Sleeper Wakes*, the highest culture of the period is represented in "At this moment . . . nearly five hundred phonographs are lecturing . . . on the influence exercised by Plato and Swift on the love affairs of Shelley, Hazlitt, and Burns." Effective propaganda in time of war comes from the General Intelligence broadcast: "Haha! Galloop, Galloop! They are lively fellows. Lively brave fellows. Let this be a lesson to the disorderly banderlog of this city. Yah! Banderlog! Filth of the earth! Galloop, Galloop!" The historian of the future in Tardé's *Underground Man* reflects that "pre-salvationist" man possessed machines "to stereotype without the slightest trouble on rags of paper without the slightest value, all his ideas, idle or serious, piled indiscriminately one on the other." In the world of Forster's "The Machine Stops," an advanced philosopher rails against originality: "Beware of first-hand ideas!" Instead of going to first-hand documents to study the French Revolution, "Learn instead what I think that Enicharmon thought Urizen thought Gutch thought Ho-Yung thought Chi-Bo-Sing thought Lafcadio Hearn thought Carlyle thought Mirabeau said about the French Revolution." In Huxley's *Brave New World*, Mr. Savage manages to stir up a riot among workers; police arrive to quell the riot by playing Anti-Riot Speech Number Two on a Synthetic Music Box. "I do so want you to be good. Please, please," says the music box, and the workmen are satisfied with an extra ration of soma. From childhood, indeed, the minds of people in this society are conditioned by phonographically repeated suggestions, until "at last the child's mind *is* these suggestions. . . . The adult's mind too—all his life long. The mind that judges and desires and decides—made up of these suggestions."

The Machine Age weakens character and morale; it fosters scepticism, materialism, and spiritual decay. The Martians of Greg's *Across the Zodiac* are atheists; they send to prison anyone who suggests any theory not demonstrable in the laboratory; the "Christians," that is, the few men who are not complete materialists, are forced to keep their organization of the Star a secret order. A "terrible moral degeneration" accompanies this materialism. In Wells's *When the Sleeper Wakes*, religion is something between big business and a racket; religious advertisements in glaring electric signs seem to Graham "almost incredible blasphemy." Naive Gabriel, in Boisgilbert's *Caesar's Column*, is amazed at the material splendor of New York, but when he looks at the faces of successful men in a fashionable restaurant, he sees cunning, ruthlessness, and cynicism. He listens to a sermon in a church adorned with "splendid representations of naked human figures"; the minister preaches about the presence of spirits in air, as proved by a California scientist, and ends with a rhapsody on "Love! Entrancing, enrapturing Love! With its glowing cheeks—its burning eyes—its hot lips—its wreathing arms —its showering kisses—its palpitating bosoms." Science suggests that sexual continence builds up complexes of frustration and inhibition, and for this reason even the children of Huxley's *Brave New World* are taught erotic play, and the adults run about from one pneumatic assignation to another; religious service is a combination of worship of Ford, soma-induced trance, and sexual orgy. On another level, science fosters a moral code based upon the power of the ruthless to survive.

The Machine Age destroys personality and makes man a machine, or a cog in a machine. Laborers in Wells's *When the Sleeper Wakes* are no longer burly, muscular fellows; "The latter-day labourer, male as well as female, was essentially a machine-minder and feeder, a servant and attendant." All day long he pulls a lever or regulates a screw; in the evenings, he eats synthetic food, drinks synthetic wine, listens to synthetic entertainment, and goes to sleep in a cell in a block of cells. But, though he has lost personality, he is still human. If specialization goes on, perhaps a society like that of Wells's *The First Men in the Moon* will result; Selenites are specialists in a vast ant-hill; they master one field each, and think nothing, know nothing, and care nothing about anything outside it. In Forster's "The Machine Stops," the individual is taken from his mother at birth and placed in the public nurseries; when he grows up, he is assigned a room, and he has no need ever to leave it all the days of his life. In Coblentz's "After 12,000 Years," the social ideal is that of the ant hill; every citizen is born into an occupational caste from which he may not depart.

The conditions of the Machine Age severely punish any attempt to escape from this standardization, weakening of body, mind, and morale, and destruction of personality. In Wells's "A Story of the Days to Come," Benton and his sweetheart dream of the free and independent life of that far away and long ago time of Queen Victoria; they flee from London to live all alone in an abandoned little town, but use and wont have softened and weakened them, so that old-fashioned chairs and beds and vegetables, thunder storms and prowling dogs, fill them with agony and terror; they return to London even though doing so means enlisting in the Labour Company, for the "world is too civilized. Ours is the age of cities . . . . To each generation the life of its time." When workers revolt against the brutalizing monotony of their work in Farrère's *Useless Hands,* the captain of industry decides that the fittest should survive; as the Machine is fittest, he turns a disintegrating ray upon 360,000 workers. The Controller, in Huxley's *Brave New World,* carefully explains to Mr. Savage that, in a Machine Age, man must choose between standardization on a low level of intelligence, or self-destruction with the weapons of science.

2. Man Is a Limited Animal

Man may escape the standardization of the Machine Age if, as the utopian writers suggest, he controls machinery and uses it to supply his wants without bending to its pressure for a mechanical pattern of life. The pessimists reply that man is himself too limited for any sane adjustment. To the contention that human nature may be changed and the race improved, they reply that man is basically an animal who will always be ruled more by passion than by reason.

The idea that man is essentially an animal is very old in satire. It is found in Cyrano de Bergerac's *The Sun* as well as in the Yahoos of Swift's *Gulliver's Travels.* In *The Sun,* the traveller is tried before a tribunal of birds on charges of being a man; to escape, he pretends to be a monkey, but the birds decide that he is a man because they feel revulsion toward him, he "laughs like a madman . . . weeps like a fool . . . blows his nose like a vagabond" and "is plucked of feathers like one that is mangy." This satire calls attention to man's bestial qualities without scientific evidence to support the contention. The theory of evolution furnished this evidence. Then Allen's *The British Barbarians* described man as "a development from a particular type of monkey-like animal—the Andropithecus of the Upper Uganda Eocene," much addicted to chattering, bickering, and irrational behavior. Wells's *The Island of Dr. Moreau* suggests that the differences between man and the beasts are so slight that surgery can eliminate most of them. Man's intelligence is viewed as a psychological pattern of taboos like the "mad litany" that the Sayer of the Law intones in the huts of the Beast-Folk. For this reason, says Wells in *The War in the Air,* when the materials for developing a high civilization lie at hand in science and machinery, man uses them only for warfare that leads to barbarism. Such a cosmic disaster as the fall of the moon does not destroy society in Sherriff's *The Hopkins Manuscript;* governments and individuals meet the disaster with foresight and sanity. But the discovery of gold on the moon sets off old national rivalries; common sense disappears, fanatic leaders arise to whip up national pride, and Western civilization disappears in a meaningless war.

Odd John, in Stapledon's book, believes that men behave this way because human nature is dominated by sub-human traits. John sees in men everywhere "the need to hate something . . . to find something to unload your own sins onto, and then smash it." This need to hate becomes an "exalted sort of excitement" if the victim is nationally or racially foreign. Man has muddled along so far, without complete disaster, because his knowledge of science and his machines have not been too large for his limited intelligence. Now, however, science and mechanism are outsize; the present state of affairs "cannot be dealt with properly save by capacity which is much more developed than his." In *Last and First Men,* Stapledon illustrates this fear that man does not have the capacity to cope with his opportunities. The First Men—our species—muddle through a semi-utopian Machine Age, destroy it senselessly at its peak, and descend into dark age after dark age, until finally atomic explosions wipe the species out, and eons of slow advance prepare the finer Second Men.

Perhaps man is not the end and aim of creation. His opposable thumb and his intelligence have enabled him temporarily to become master. But, as Taine's *Before the Dawn* points out, there have been other masters. Various species became masters and ruled the earth for long ages because they developed claws, or powerful legs, or armor-plate, relied upon the fortunate factor, overdeveloped it, and perished. Perhaps "intelligence . . . is the subtle weapon which nature has reserved for our undoing." It may be so, for intelligence has enabled us to create enormously destructive weapons.

Or perhaps man will be conquered by some other species. De Maupassant's "The Horla," for instance, supposes some strange, intelligent creature developed in the Brazilian jungles and asks: "Why should not another variation arise after the completion of the period, which separates the successive appearances of the various species?" In Wells's "The Empire of the Ants," intelligent, poison-bearing ants attack men in the Amazon valley, and soldiers are helpless against them. Holroyd wonders: "Suppose presently the ants began to store knowledge, just as men had done by means of books and records, use weapons, form great empires, sustain a planned and organized war?" In some romances of the very distant future, other creatures have supplanted man; in Wright's *The World Below,* for instance, the Amphibians are furred sea-creatures who communicate by telepathy and are in other ways superior to man, and the Dwellers, though man-like, are another species; they look back upon the present era as the "False Skin Age," too brief and confused to be worth attention.

3. Science Is To Destroy Civilization

Because man is a limited animal, he will not be sane enough, the pessimists say, to end war, but will fight with the destructive weapons of science until civilization is destroyed.

The development of science will bring about warfare for two

reasons. First, it does not permit the world to attain stability, but heralds an era of incessant change and hence maladjustment; and second, it provides ambitious rulers with machines for conquest, especially if they develop weapons more effective than the rest of the world possesses. The world is at peace when Wells's *The War in the Air* opens, but aimless and uncontrolled invention has brought about haphazard development, planless cities, and the necessary fruits of feudal traditions in an industrial world. Social maladjustment while the world is yet at peace is even more emphasized in Wells's *The World Set Free;* the development of atomic power has brought about unprecedented unemployment: "gold was undergoing headlong depreciation . . . banks were tottering, the stock exchanges were scenes of feverish panic— . . . these were the black and monstrous underconsequences of the Leap into the Air." In *The War in the Air,* the German rulers seize the opportunity to develop aviation for world-conquest; in *The World Set Free,* they develop atomic bombs for the same purpose.

The special feature of each of these weapons is that it can destroy, but not garrison and conquer. Once the destructive weapon is used, it passes into the hands of the enemy, who likewise can only destroy. The result is indiscriminate destruction that cannot be stopped, for it strikes across frontiers at the political nerve-centers; social disorganization follows; and the chaos is so great that when the exhaustion of mechanical resources brings the actual fighting to an end, the resources of science for combatting pestilence and famine are likewise exhausted. The result is anarchy, land-piracy, and barbarism.

Barbarism described in scientific fiction is not a return to the simple life, a locally self-sufficient "pioneer economy," or any other sort of Golden Age—at least for a long time. Men softened by the Machine Age are too helpless to till the soil without machines. The barbarism is savagery. Best's *The Twenty-Fifth Hour* fills in details suggested in many books. An illustrative detail is that ex-Captain Fitzharding ranges over Europe stalking men (and being stalked), and when he kills it would be dangerous to build a fire; he eats the flesh raw.

4. Progress Is Cyclic

Optimistic writers interpret the theory of evolution hopefully in terms of continued progress toward finer human types in possession of ever-widening knowledge and control of their universe. But other writers believe that evolution is blind and without any sense of values to correspond with man's moral or ethical conceptions. As Wells says in *Mr. Blettsworthy on Rampole Island,* "far from Evolution being necessarily a strenuous upward progress to more life and yet more life, it could . . . become a graceless drift towards a dead end."

The examples of history suggest that civilizations, like those of Egypt or Assyria, rise and fall. Even when intelligent guidance of development according to the principles of evolution may enable men to construct a utopian society, this perfection may last but a little moment of geologic time; in all nature, ripeness is the forerunner of decay.

Reasoning in these ways, writers of scientific fiction assert that progress is cyclic, or a rhythm of rise and inevitable fall. In the world of Hudson's *A Crystal Age,* the sleeper awakes into Utopia, but it is not a development from our present civilization; in some dark age that follows our period all memory of the present has vanished. In Mitchell's *The Last American,* Persian explorers, intrigued by old legends, repeat Columbus's voyage to discover America and its forest-covered ruins of ancient cities. Granser, in London's *The Scarlet Plague,* foresees that a new civilization will rise, as the old one rose, and crumble in its turn: "It may take fifty thousand years to build," he mumbles, "but it will pass. All things pass. Only remain cosmic force and matter, ever acting and reacting." In Wright's *The World Below,* countless civilizations have risen and fallen before the era of the Dwellers, who, aware of flux as a basic law, are struggling to insure that their civilization too will not pass away. Stapledon's *Last and First Men,* recording man's career through eighteen species that rise and fall through 2,000,000,000 years, tells the story of the slow struggle to Utopia, the rise of forces of decay, the descent of a great dark age, barbarism, and again the slow struggle upward, over and over; even the greatest species of men, the Second Men, the Fifth Men, and the almost superhuman Eighteenth Men, are powerless to arrest the inevitable drift that destroys each in turn. For always, as Stapledon says in *Star Maker,* when utopia has been achieved, "Presently a general loosening of fibre would set in. The golden age would be followed by a silver age. Living on the achievements of the past, the leaders of thought would lose themselves in a jungle of subtlety," and finally after many stages of decay, "would come sheer barbarism, followed by the trough of almost sub-human savagery."

Yet these are long views, very long ones in Stapledon's books; they predict the course of Fate, which our knowledge is powerless to alter. They do not deny that it is possible for us to sign a pact with Fate for progress in our time.

5.   The End of Life Is Fated

An even longer view suggests that life is ultimately doomed, because the universe itself is running down. Swift, in *Gulliver's Travels*, ridicules the Laputans who concern themselves lest the sun shall fail to rise, and doubtless no practical application, even in the twentieth century, can be made of the knowledge that the sun will some time cool to a cinder. On the other hand, Olaf Stapledon has won some reputation as a writer on ethical questions, and it is his belief, expressed in the Preface to *Star Maker*, that the longest possible range of view may have some bearing upon men's sense of values.

At any rate, prophecies of doom are frequent in scientific fiction. Even Verne's *Twenty Thousand Leagues Under the Sea* contains the reflection that "the earth will one day be that cold corpse . . . uninhabitable and uninhabited like the moon." The Time Traveller in Wells's *The Time Machine* discovers among the Eloi "how brief the dream of the human intellect had been," and finally he advances through time to view the desolation of a dying world, thirty million years hence. In *Last and First Men*, Stapledon supposes that 2,000,000,000 years may yet remain in the life of man, especially if cometary visitations like those that formed the planetary system enlarge the sun and increase its waning heat. But life in our solar system must finally die out, and finally all life in all the universes, Stapledon says in *Star Maker*, must retire to the interiors of burnt-out stars to perish there.

*   *   *   *   *

Shorter views of man's destiny are of more practical importance to us in the twentieth century. Some of these creeds of scientific fiction suggest the way for us now.

World War II, still smouldering, was not inevitable. Everybody saw it coming, and now, when it is too late, we see how it could have been forestalled. There were Have and Have-not nations; frustrated peoples ripe for any Fuehrer; a powerless League; and in America and Britain especially, isolationism more suitable to horse-and-buggy days than under the wings of ocean-spanning 'planes. Perhaps this isolationism in the teeth of the Machine Age was the fundamental factor, general cause of all the other causes. That is what scientific fiction says.

Statesmen have now another chance to readjust our society to a world of new machines, brief distances, and new powers. These new machines and new powers are on a level different from that of historical dominion, boundary line, naval power, empire over palm and pine, and all the other creeds of a world of isolated, predatory nations. New machines and new powers demand that the world has to be One World, and surely statesmen, with atomic power in their laps, will gradually see the idea.

Different as the optimists and pessimists in scientific fiction are, they are unanimous that we have to advance into the Atomic Age as a human race.

CHAPTER ELEVEN

Journey's End

In retrospect, it is well to look at values.

I have not applied esthetic criteria to scientific fiction; I have only presented its chronological development in a number of major or typical pieces, and the patterns of form and substance found in them. But as scientific romances form a kind of literature, the question naturally arises, whether these stories have value as art.

In the first place, they are romances. Though serious fiction of the twentieth century is generally realistic in mood, most popular books for pastime reading are romances. Our millions like escape into detective stories and love stories, and into the far-away and battles long ago of novels like *Gone With the Wind*. The stories of the magazines, *Amazing Stories* and *Weird Tales,* for example, are likewise romances of escape. They portray incredibly fantastic discoveries and elaborate action; they seldom limit invention to a probable future and ponder the meaning of new machines and new powers in man's psychological, social, and political adjustments. Probably the most zealous "science-fiction" fans entertain few illusions that escapist literature of this kind has noteworthy esthetic value.

Yet some of it has the esthetic value of the myth. The modern Hercules, Thor, King Arthur, and Jack-the-Giant-Killer, the twentieth-century Paul Bunyan, is a creature of scientific fiction. He appears as Stapledon's Odd John; on another level, from the magazines on through the movies and the comic books, he is Superman; in a series of world-wide best-sellers, he is Tarzan. His space-ships, death-rays, and invasions from Mars are Machine Age equivalents of thunderbolts, magic carpets, and the sword

Excalibur. Perhaps the most stirring, consciously created single myth in scientific fiction is the story of the Elder Ones, the Great Race of the time before prehistory, worked out in a logical, consistent pattern in the stories by Lovecraft. This myth undertakes, like ancient folk-myths, to explain the beginnings of things, the races before man, the races that threaten man from a nether world, and the doom yet to descend.

Aside from these pieces of the magazines, the best examples of scientific fiction have other claims to esthetic value. Scientific fiction has opened to the imagination a sizable area not widely available to artists before the nineteenth century. Tales of imaginary voyages, from the *Odyssey* to *Robinson Crusoe,* exhausted Hades and the still-vex'd Bermoothes; Sir Walter Scott and his followers mined the ore of history. Writers of scientific fiction have extended the travelogue beyond the confines of earth, and the historical romance into the future. A widening knowledge of science in the nineteenth century and a deepening faith in it as wonder worker have prepared men's mind to include these realms of space and time within the area of imaginative art.

Whether scientific romances are considered art depends upon, first, the definition of art, and second, which of many romances are judged. If art is only the impassioned expression of powerful feeling, or if it is limited to the interpretation of mankind on the stage of the actual world, past or present, it does not include scientific fiction. But if art may include in its subject-matter the adventures of man's mind, scientific fiction may be art whenever it is thoughtful and well written. Wordsworth's sonnets are, no doubt, art in any definition; fourteen-line verses published as "Today's Poem" in a newspaper are often art by courtesy only. Pieces of scientific fiction vary as widely in literary quality. Fielding, Austen, Thackeray, Eliot, and Hardy did not write scientific fiction; Poe, Verne, Bierce, Wells, Kipling, Huxley, and Stapledon did, and they are not without reputation as artists. Canons of criticism are necessarily based on traditional conceptions and the continued appreciation of succeeding generations; in large volume, scientific fiction is relatively new. As our Machine Age becomes better understood, the extent to which scientific fiction offers an artistic expression of it can be more definitely stated.

Though most scientific romances are romances of escape, even the stories of the magazines are often something more. They reflect many ideas from more serious scientific fiction and express them over and over. For example, an editorial in *Astounding Science Fiction* for November, 1945, develops the theme that: "Civilization —the civilization of Big Power balances, of war and peace and bad international manners, of intolerance and hates, of grinding poverty and useless luxury—is dead. We are in the interregnum now, the chaos of moving our effects, our ideas and our hopes from a blasted edifice into a new structure." This editorial expresses ideas that have been a part of the pattern of stories in this magazine. Concern with civilization in a changing time gives these stories some importance as vehicles for conveying ideas to a wide audience.

The seriously written utopias, utopistic satires, historic romances, and attempts to see man from a viewpoint outside man, spring from the desire not only to escape the world as it is, but to change it. In this respect they differ from other literary avenues of escape. Sharing the social purpose of much realistic fiction, they would like to make the world a better place to live in. Their value as blue-prints for change is dependent upon the solidity of their thought. Often this thought, an effort to portray trends graphically in terms of their long-range results, is informed and is carefully pondered.

Therefore another criterion, more practical than esthetic, for judging the worth of this fiction is the extent to which it influences life and thought. Hertzler, in *The History of Utopian Thought,* traces the influence of Bacon's *The New Atlantis.* He offers the testimony of the founders as evidence that the institution of the Royal Society "was due to the prophetic scheme of 'Salomon's House' in 'The New Atlantis.'" He traces the widespread influence of this book in Italy and in France, where it was "one of the inspiring causes of . . . The French 'Encyclopedie.'" Bellamy's *Looking Backward* not only aroused a storm of "answers" from people who feared that it would have influence, but it became a standard hand-out at Socialist meetings. Mr. Orson Welles's fake news-broadcast of an invasion from Mars aroused widespread panic because thousands of people had been softened up for this invasion by a literature in which they must have placed some faith. On May 10, 1940, the German army was able to gain entry into Belgium by taking the strong fortress of Eben Emael. The swift, mysterious fall of this fortress gave rise to newspaper and magazine speculation about a "secret weapon," a nerve-gas, a paralytic, a death-ray, or something even more fantastic. People credited these fantasies, all of them the stock-in-trade of scientific fiction. Beyond such examples, specific instances of the influence of scientific romances upon social attitudes would be as difficult to demonstrate as instances of the effect of the *Spectator* in shaping eighteenth-century morality. Yet this influence cannot be doubted. The masses of people in America in 1900 did not accept the theory of evolution, a fact reflected in state legislation; the teaching of biology in the public schools has been, no doubt, the major factor in gaining its acceptance; but at the same time, thousands of the generation just reaching manhood in 1900 had been reading the romances of Verne and Wells.

Perhaps an equally important and equally imponderable influence of scientific fiction upon thought lies in the way it has presented anticipations of the future, utopian idealizations, in romances that stimulate the emotions of purpose and desire. It has presented them largely to the young and impressionable. The world is now in process of unsettled, piecemeal, radical change, and many scientific romances have sought with honesty and seriousness to see change in relation to results, especially as scientific principles suggest the probable shape of the future that grows out of the present.

Values change. Scientific fiction suggests a sense of values based not so much upon traditions from the past or practical expedients of the present, as upon the extension of present trends into the future. For instance, racial feeling in the Southern United States rests upon a tradition that guards white supremacy; though racial feeling is changing, practical expedients continue the Jim Crow laws. Where scientific fiction touches this problem of racial prejudice—as in Herrick's *Sometime*—the problem has been solved by the elimination of prejudice; people dine together, or marry, because of temperamental or intellectual affinity, without regard to pigmentation. The result does not seem horrible as it is described in Herrick's romance. Similar values based upon long-range results (as best science and reason can foresee them) are set up in all social, political, economic, and even ethical fields.

In Wells's *When the Sleeper Wakes*, Graham remarks: "We were making the future . . . and hardly any of us troubled to think what future we were making. And here it is!" Scientific fiction is more concerned than any other literature that men in a changing age, a Machine Age that is becoming an Atomic Age, shall trouble to think what future they are making. Naturally not all pieces of scientific fiction carry the same message; the long-range view is many views of many writers. No one can be sure where to turn when hot for certainties about the future, and no doubt the prophecy laid out in any one historic romance is wrong in many details. And yet, where the science in a romance is science and the author is intellectually honest and informed, as Wells and Stapledon are, the recommendations are more to be trusted than most of the political -isms characteristic of our age. The basis is sounder: scientific principle. The leverage is longer: the point of view of biology or geology. When one has read Wells, or perhaps mused for a while upon Stapledon's imaginations of 2,000,000,000 years, one is inclined to feel a little detached from a too-partisan enthusiasm. To be troubled about what future we are making, to see the social and political arena in a long-range perspective, is a good thing. Scientific fiction suggests, as clearly as Matthew Arnold's *Culture and Anarchy* and to a vastly larger audience, that it is important not merely to act, but to act with detached intelligence.

In 1946 it would seem—certainly it would seem to an intelligent observer from the moon—that the Machine Age is drifting into a phase of self-destruction. The Atomic Age provides the lethal weapon. That men should not behave as they behaved in World War II, and are behaving in its aftermath, has been a theme for many years, in literature of all kinds, whether sermons, poetry, essays, or fiction. That men launch a war of conquest with tanks and airplanes and conclude it with reduction of cities to dust and grease is not merely immoral; it is not merely stupid. It is dangerous, not just to a few million soldiers in the old-fashioned way, but to the whole fabric of civilization. Scientific fiction has said over and over again that it is dangerous, and this fiction is obviously and tragically right.

Scientific fiction has pointed out why warfare becomes increasingly dangerous, and finally suicidal, as man progresses through a Machine Age into an Atomic Age. As recently as Napoleon's time, wars were determined by manpower, the strategy of generals, and the courage of soldiers. To some extent, even the War Between the States was determined by these factors, but there were other factors that "Stonewall" Jackson's genius and Confederate courage could not overcome. The North had machinery, organized industry, and superior natural resources behind its armies. To a large extent, the outcome of World War I was determined by industrial power. Industrial power was the determining factor in World War II. What could the millions of brave farmers of China do against the industrial machine of Japan? Or Japan's industrial piece-work against American mass-production? What chance did Germany have if the Germans could not knock out Pittsburgh and Detroit? Then a new factor entered the war at its close. It was the atomic bomb.

Manpower and military strategy decided old-fashioned wars; machines and industry decided recent ones. Science will decide the outcome of any wars from now until the blackout. It may be blackout, because the latest weapon of science is the fundamental discreative force of the universe.

This fact, argued fully and logically in scientific fiction, is obvious to millions now. They understand also the alternatives stressed and re-stressed in this fiction: we must have One World and no foolishness about national sovereignties, or else war until,

Journey's End

as Wells says, man's career on earth, begun over a little fire behind a windbreak, will end in the smoking ruins of a slum.

Perhaps through tragic experience, through the teachings of wise men, and to some extent through the constant dinning of this theme that peace is necessary for survival in an Atomic Age, the people of the world may be led to insist that statesmen scrap backward-looking legalisms, establish a just and strong World Government, and put an end to war. Perhaps other agencies for the spread of knowledge disseminate this theme better than scientific fiction. None presents it more constantly.

None proceeds more constantly upon the premise that the proper interest of man is all mankind, especially in relation to the machines and powers of science.

Bibliography

A. Scientific Romances

The following is a list of romances to which reference is made in this book. When first editions are not easily available, a later edition is cited in parenthesis. Titles first printed in foreign languages are cited in parenthesis.

ABOUT, EDMOND FRANCOIS VALENTIN. *The Man With the Broken Ear.* New York: Leypold & Holt, 1867. (*L'homme à l'oreille cassée.* Paris: Hachette et Cie., 1862.)

Aerostatic Spy, The; or Excursions With an Air Balloon. By an Aerial Traveller. London: E. Fawcett, 1785. 2 vols.

ALLEN, GRANT. *The British Barbarians.* New York and London: G. P. Putnam's Sons, 1895.

——. "The Child of the Phalanstery" in *Twelve Tales.* London: Grant Richards, 1899.

ANDREAE, JOHANN VALENTIN. *Christianopolis.* New York: Oxford University Press, 1916. (*Reipublicae Christianopolitanae Descriptio.* 1619.)

ARATUS (*pseud.?*). *A Voyage to the Moon.* London: privately printed, 1793.

ARIOSTO, LUDOVICO. *Orlando Furioso.* London: George Bell and Sons, 1876. (Translated into English during the reign of Elizabeth.)

ASTOR, JOHN JACOB. *A Journey in Other Worlds.* New York: D. Appleton & Co., 1894.

ATTERLEY, JOSEPH (*pseud.* for George Tucker). *A Voyage to the Moon.* New York: Elam Bliss, 1827.

BACON, *Sir* FRANCIS. *The New Atlantis.* London: 1627.

BALMER, EDWIN, and PHILIP WYLIE. *After Worlds Collide.* New York: Frederick A. Stokes Company, 1934. —— and ——. *When Worlds Collide.* New York: Frederick A. Stokes Company, 1932.

BALZAC, HONORE DE. *Elixir of Life.* New York: The Macmillan Co., 1901. (*L'elixir de longue vie.* 1830.)

——. *The Quest of the Absolute.* New York: The Macmillan Co., 1901. (*La recherche de l'absolu.* 1834.)

BEALE, CHARLES WILLING. *The Secret of the Earth.* London and New York: F. Tennyson Neely, 1899.

BECKFORD, WILLIAM. *Vathek.* London: 1782.

BELLAMY, EDWARD. *Dr. Heidenhoff's Process.* New York: D. Appleton and Co., 1880.

——. *Looking Backward.* Boston: Ticknor, 1888.

——. "To Whom This May Come" in *The Blindman's World.* Boston and New York: Houghton Mifflin and Company, 1898.

——. "With the Eyes Shut" in *The Blindman's World.*

BENSON, ROBERT HUGH. *The Dawn of All.* London: Hutchinson & Co., and St. Louis: B. Herder, 1911.

——. *Lord of the World.* London: Pitman, 1907, and New York: Dodd, Mead & Co., 1908.

BEST, HERBERT. *The Twenty-Fifth Hour.* New York: Random House, 1940.

BIERBOWER, AUSTIN. *From Monkey to Man.* Chicago: Dibble Publishing Co., 1894.

BIERCE, AMBROSE. "Charles Ashmore's Trail" in *Can Such Things Be?* New York: Cassell Publishing Co., 1893.

——. "The Damned Thing" in *Can Such Things Be?*

——. "Moxon's Master" in *Can Such Things Be?*

BINDER, EANDO. "Adam Link's Vengeance" in Phil Stong, *ed., The Other Worlds, q. v.*

BOISGILBERT, EDMUND (*pseud.* for Ignatius Donnelly). *Caesar's Column.* Chicago: F. J. Schulte & Co., 1890.

BRADSHAW, WILLIAM RICHARD. *The Goddess of Atvatabar.* New York: J. F. Douthitt, 1892.

BURKHOLDER, A. L. "Dimensional Fate," *Wonder Stories,* VI (August, 1934), 262-269 and 366.

BURROUGHS, EDGAR RICE. *Tarzan at the Earth's Core.* New York: Grosset and Dunlap, 1929.

BUTLER, SAMUEL. *Erewhon.* London: Trübner, 1872.

CAMPANELLA, TOMMASO. *City of the Sun.* Washington and London: Walter Dunne, 1901. (*Civitas Solis.* Written, 1623; published, Paris: 1637.)

CAMPBELL, CLYDE CRANE. "The Avatar," *Astounding Stories,* XV (July, 1935), 128-149.

CAPEK, KAREL. *The Absolute at Large.* London and New York: Macmillan, 1927.

CHAMBERLAIN, HENRY RICHARDSON. *6000 Tons of Gold.* Meadville, Pa.: Flood and Vincent, 1894.

CHESNEY, Sir GEORGE TOMPKYNS. "The Battle of Dorking," *Blackwood's Edinburgh Magazine,* CIX (May, 1871), 539-572.

CHILDERS, ERSKINE. *The Riddle of the Sands.* 1903. (New York: Pocket Books, Inc., 1940.)

COBLENTZ, STANTON A. "After 12,-000 Years," *Amazing Stories Quarterly,* II (Spring, 1929), 148-221.

COLLINS, WILLIAM WILKIE. *The Moonstone.* London: Tinsley Brothers, 1868.

CUMMINGS, RAY. *The Girl in the Golden Atom.* London: Methuen, 1922.

————. *The Man Who Mastered Time.* Chicago: A. C. McClurg & Co., 1929.

CYRANO DE BERGERAC. *Voyages to the Moon and the Sun.* London: George Routledge & Sons, 1923. (*Histoire comique des états et empires de la lune et du soliel.*

Paris: Charles de Sercy, 1657, and Lyons, Christopher Fourmy, 1662.)

DACRE, Mrs. CHARLOTTE. *Zofloya.* London: 1806. (London: The Fortune Press, 1928.)

DANIEL GABRIEL. *A Voyage to the World of Cartesius.* London: T. Bennet, 1694. (*Voiage du monde de Descartes.* Paris: S. Bernard, 1691.)

[DEMILLE, JAMES.] *A Strange Manuscript Found in a Copper Cylinder.* New York: Harper and Brothers, 1888.

DOYLE, Sir ARTHUR CONAN. "The Disintegration Machine" in *The Maracot Deep.*

————. "The Horror of the Heights," *Everybody's Magazine,* XXIX (November, 1913), 578-590.

————. "The Los Amigos Fiasco" in *Round the Red Lamp.* 1894.

————. *The Lost World.* New York: Hodder & Stoughton; George H. Doran Co., 1912.

————. *The Maracot Deep.* London: John Murray, 1929.

DU MAURIER, GEORGE LOUIS PAMELLA BUSSON. *The Martian.* New York: Harper & Brothers, 1896.

EDWARDS, GAWAIN. *The Earth Tube.* New York: D. Appleton & Co., 1929.

[ERSKINE, THOMAS.] *Armata.* London: John Murray, Pt. 1, 1816; Pt. 2, 1817.

EMERSON, WILLIS GEORGE. *The Smoky God.* Chicago: Forbes & Co., 1908.

ENGLAND, GEORGE ALLAN. *The Golden Blight.* New York: H. K. Fly Co., 1916.

Fantastical Excursion Into the Planets, A. London: Saunders and Otley, 1839.

FARRERE, CLAUDE (*pseud.* for Charles Bargone). *Useless Hands.* New York: E. P. Dutton & Co., 1926.

FEARN, JOHN RUSSELL. "The Blue Infinity," *Astounding Stories,* XVI (September, 1935), 70-104.

FORSTER, EDWARD MORGAN. "The Machine Stops" in *The Eternal Moment.* New York: Harcourt, Brace, 1928.

FOWLER, GEORGE. *A Flight to the Moon.* Baltimore: A. Miltenberger, 1813.

FREEMAN, RICHARD AUSTIN. *The Mystery of 31, New Inn.* Philadelphia: The John C. Winston Co., 1913.

GARBY. See Smith, Edward Elmer.

GARDNER, ERLE STANLEY. "A Year in a Day," *Argosy* (July 19, 1930), pp. 740-775.

GONSALES, DOMINGO (*pseud.* for Bishop Francis Godwin). *The Man in the Moone.* London: Ioshua Kirton and Thomas Warren, 1638. (In *Smith College Studies in Modern Languages,* XIX (October, 1937), 1-48.)

GRANT, ROBERT, JOHN BOYLE O'REILLY, J. S. OF DALE, and JOHN T. WHEELWRIGHT. *The King's Men.* New York: C. Scribner's Sons, 1884.

GREER, TOM (*pseud.?*). *A Modern Daedalus.* New York: E. P. Dutton & Co., and London: Griffith, Farran, Okeden & Welsh, 1885.

GREG, PERCY. *Across the Zodiac.* London: Trübner & Co., 1880. 2 vols.

GRIFFITH, GEORGE. *The Angel of the Revolution.* London: Tower Publishing Co., 1893.

———. *A Honeymoon in Space.* London: C. Arthur Pearson, 1901.

———. *Olga Romanoff.* London: Tower Publishing Co., 1894.

[GRIFFITH, Mrs. MARY.] "Three Hundred Years Hence" in *Camperdown.* Philadelphia: Carey, Lea & Blanchard, 1836.

HAGGARD, Sir HENRY RIDER. *Allan Quatermain.* 1887. (London, New York, etc.: Longmans, Green & Co., 1922.)

———. *She.* New York: Harper & Brothers, 1886.

HALE, EDWARD EVERETT. "The Brick Moon," *Atlantic Monthly* (1870-71). (*The Brick Moon.* Boston: Little, Brown & Co., 1899.)

HAMILTON, EDMOND. "The Metal Giants," *Weird Tales* (December, 1926), pp. 724-738, 860-861, and 863.

HANSEN, L. TAYLOR. "The Prince of Liars," *Amazing Stories,* V (October, 1930), 582-599.

HARBEN, WILLIAM NATHANIEL. *The Land of the Changing Sun.* New York: The Merriam Co., 1894.

HARDY, THOMAS. *Two on a Tower.* New York: G. Munro, 1882.

HARROWER, JACK. "The Brain Blight," *All-Story,* XXX (March, 1913), 481-509.

HAWTHORNE, NATHANIEL. "The Birth Mark." 1843. (In *Mosses from an Old Manse.* 1846.)

———. "Dr. Heidegger's Experiment" in *Twice-Told Tales.* 1837.

HERRICK, ROBERT. *Sometime.* New York: Farrar & Rinehart, 1933.

HERTZKA, Dr. THEODOR. *Freeland.* London: Chatto & Windus, 1891. (*Freiland.* Vienna: 1889.)

HILTON, JAMES. *Lost Horizon.* New York: William Morrow, 1933.

HOLBERG, Baron LUDVIG. *A Journey to the World Under-Ground.* London: T. Astley and B. Collins, 1742. (*Nicolai Klimii iter subterraneum* . . . Hafniae & Lipsiae: Iacobi Preussii, 1741.)

HOLMES, OLIVER WENDELL. *Elsie Venner.* New York: 1861. (Serial with the title "The Proftssor's Story," *Atlantic Monthly,* beginning December, 1859.)

HOWELLS, WILLIAM DEAN. *A Traveler from Altruria.* New York: Harper & Brothers, 1894.

HUDSON, WILLIAM HENRY. *A Crystal Age.* 1887.

HUNTING, GARDNER. *The Vicarion.* Kansas City, Mo.: Unity School of Christianity, 1926.

HUXLEY, ALDOUS. *After Many a Summer Dies the Swan.* New York and London: Harper and Brothers, 1939.

———. *Brave New World.* Garden City: Doubleday, Doran & Co., 1932.

J. S. OF DALE. See Grant.

JEFFERIES, JOHN RICHARD. *After London.* London, Paris, New York, and Melbourne: Cassell & Co., 1885.

JESSEL, JOHN. "The Adaptive Ultimate" in Phil Stong, *ed., The Other Worlds, q.v.*

KEARNEY, CHALMERS. *Erone.* Guildford, England: Biddles, 1943.

KELLERMANN, BERNHARD. *The Tunnel.* New York: The Macaulay Co., 1915. (*Der Tunnel.* Berlin: S. Fischer, 1913.)

KEPLER, JOHANN. *Somnium.* Available in the Smith College Library. (*Joh. Keppleri Mathematici Olim Imperatorii Somnium . . .* Frankfurt: 1634.)

KIPLING, RUDYARD. "As Easy as A. B. C.," *London Magazine* (March and April, 1912).

———. "Wireless," *Scribner's Magazine* (August, 1902).

———. "With the Night Mail," *Windsor Magazine* (December, 1905).

KLINE, OTIS ADELBERT. *The Planet of Peril, Argosy All-Story,* Vol. 205, No. 2 (July 20, 1929) through Vol. 206, No. 1 (August 24, 1929).

LAING, ALEXANDER. *The Cadaver of Gideon Wyck.* New York: Farrar & Rinehart, 1934.

LEINSTER, MURRAY. "The Man Who Put Out the Sun," *Argosy* (June 14, 1930), pp. 24-58.

———. "The Storm that Had to be Stopped," *Argosy* (March 1, 1930), pp. 454-489.

LEWIS, CLIVE STAPLES. *Out of the Silent Planet.* London: John Lane, 1938.

LLOYD, JOHN URI. *Etidorhpa.* Cincinnati: The Robert Clarke Co., 1895.

[LOCKE, RICHARD ADAMS.] "Discoveries in the Moon Lately Made at the Cape of Good Hope . . .," *New York Sun* (August and September, 1835). (Later published as *The Moon Hoax.* New York: William Gowans, 1859.)

LONDON, JACK. *Before Adam.* New York and London: The Macmillan Co., 1907.

———. *The Scarlet Plague.* New York: The Macmillan Co., 1912.

LOVECRAFT, HOWARD PHILLIPS. "At the Mountains of Madness," *Astounding Stories* (February, March, April, 1936).

———. *The Shadow Out of Time, Astounding Stories* (June, 1936). (In Wollheim, *ed., The Portable Novels of Science.*)

LUCIANUS, SAMOSATENSIS. *Icaromenippus.* Second century. (In *The Works of Lucian of Samosata.* Oxford: Clarendon Press, 1905. Vol. II.)

———. *The True History.* Second century. (*Alethes Historia.* In *The Works . . .*)

LYTTON, Sir EDWARD GEORGE EARLE BULWER—. *The Coming Race.* 1871. (Knebworth edition, London and New York: George Routledge and Sons, 1874.)

———. *A Strange Story.* 1861. (Knebworth edition.)

———. *Zanoni.* 1842. (Knebworth edition.)

[MADDEN, SAMUEL (?).] *The Reign of George VI. 1900-1925.* London: W. Nicoll, 1763. (London: Rivington, 1899.)

McLOCIARD, GEORGE (*pseud.* for George F. Locke). "Television Hill," *Amazing Stories,* V (February and March, 1931), 967-987 and 1090-1114.

MAUPASSANT, GUY DE. "The Horla," in *The Works of . . .* New York: Brentano's, n. d., Vol. VIII. ("Le horla." 1887.)

MAUROIS, ANDRE. "The Weigher of Souls," *Scribner's Magazine,* LXXXIX (March, 1931), 235-250 and 334-349.

[MERCIER, LOUIS SEBASTIEN.] *Memoirs of the Year Two Thousand Five Hundred.* London: 1771, and Philadelphia: Thomas Dobson, 1795. (*L'an deux mille quatre cent quarante. Rêve s'il fût jamais.* Amsterdam: 1770.)

MICHAELIS, RICHARD C. *Looking Further Forward.* Chicago and New York: Rand, McNally & Co., 1890.

MITCHELL, JOHN AMES. *The Last American.* 1889. (New York: F. A. Stokes Co., 1902.)

MORE, Sir THOMAS. *Utopia.* 1516; in English, 1551.

MORRIS, WILLIAM. *News from Nowhere, The Commonweal* (January-October, 1890). (In *The Collected Works of* . . . London, New York, etc.: Longmans, Green and Co., 1912. Vol. XVI.)

MOXLEY, F. WRIGHT. *Red Snow.* New York: Simon and Schuster, 1930.

NEWCOMB, SIMON. *His Wisdom, the Defender.* New York and London: Harper & Brothers, 1900.

NONAME (*pseud.* for Lu Senarens). "Young Frank Reade and His Electric Air Ship," *Happy Days,* XI, No. 261 (October 14, 1899).

O'BRIEN, FITZ-JAMES. "The Diamond Lens." 1858. (In *Short Story Classics.* New York: P. F. Collier & Son, 1905.)

———. "What Was It? A Mystery." 1859. (In *The Best American Tales.* New York: Thomas Y. Crowell & Co., 1907.)

O'REILLY. See Grant.

[PALTOCK, ROBERT.] *The Life and Adventures of Peter Wilkins.* London: J. Robinson and R. Dodsley, 1751. (London: J. Harris, 1804.)

[———. (?)] *A Narrative of the Life . . . of John Daniel.* London: M. Cooper, 1751. (In *The Library of Impostors.* London: Robert Holden & Co., 1926.)

PARABELLUM (*pseud.* for Ferdinand Heinrich Grautoff). *Banzai!* New York: The Baker and Taylor Co., 1909. (*Bansai!* Leipzig: T. Weicher, 1908.)

POE, EDGAR ALLAN. "The Balloon-Hoax," title usually given to "Astounding News by Express," New York *Sun* (April 13, 1844). (This and the following stories by Poe may be found in *The Complete Works of* . . . New York: Thomas Y. Crowell & Co., 1902.)

———. "The Conversation of Eiros and Charmion," Burton's *Gentleman's Magazine* (December, 1839).

———. "The Facts in the Case of M. Valdemar," *American Whig Review* (December, 1845).

———. "The Gold Bug," Philadelphia *Dollar Newspaper* (June 21-28, 1845).

———. "Maelzel's Chess Player," *Southern Literary Messenger* (April, 1836).

———. "Mellonta Tauta," Godey's *Lady's Book* (February, 1849).

———. "MS. Found in a Bottle," Baltimore *Saturday Visiter* (October 12, 1833).

———. *The Narrative of Arthur Gordon Pym.* New York: Harper & Brothers, 1838.

———. "Some Words with a Mummy," *American Whig Review* (April, 1845).

———. "The Thousand-and-Second Tale of Scheherazade," Godey's *Lady's Book* (February, 1845).

———. "The Unparalleled Adventure of One Hans Pfaal," *Southern Literary Messenger* (June, 1835).

———. "Von Kempelen and His Discovery." 1848.

PSEUDOMAN, AKKAD (*pseud.* for E. F. Northrup). *Zero to Eighty.* Princeton, N. J.: Scientific Publishing Co., 1937.

REEVE, ARTHUR BENJAMIN. "The Poisoned Pen," in *The Poisoned Pen.* New York and London: Harper & Brothers, 1911.

RENARD, MAURICE. *New Bodies for Old.* New York: The Macaulay Co., 1923.

RUSSELL, WILLIAM CLARK. *The Frozen Pirate.* New York: Harper & Brothers, 1887.

RUSSEN, DAVID. *Iter Lunare: or, A Voyage to the Moon.* London: J. Nutt, 1703.

SEABORN, Captain ADAM (*pseud.* for John Cleves Symmes?). *Symzonia.* New York: J. Seymour, 1820.

SERVISS, GARRETT PUTNAM. *A Columbus of Space.* 1909. (New York and London: D. Appleton and Co., 1911.)

SHELLEY, MARY WOLLSTONECRAFT. *Frankenstein.* 1817. (London: H. Colburn and R. Bentley, 1831.)

———. *The Last Man.* 1825. (Philadelphia: Lea & Blanchard, 1833.)

SHERRIFF, R. C. *The Hopkins Manuscript*. New York: The Macmillan Co., 1939.

SHIEL, MATTHEW PHIPPS. *The Lord of the Sea*. New York: F. A. Stokes Co., 1901.

———. *The Purple Cloud*. London: V. Gollancz, 1901.

SIMAK, CLIFFORD D. "The Creator," *Marvel Tales*, I (March-April, 1935), 128-156.

SKENE, ANTHONY. "The Man Who Stole Life," *Detective Weekly* (British), No. 17 (June 17, 1933), pp. 3-11, 14-20, and 23-24.

SMITH, EDWARD ELMER, and LEE HAWKINS GARBY. "The Skylark of Space," *Amazing Stories*, III (August, September, and October, 1928), 390-417, 528-559, 610-636, and 641.

SMITH, GEORGE O. "Identity," *Astounding Science-Fiction*, XXXVI (November, 1945), 145-178.

SQUARE, A. (*pseud.* for Edwin Abbott Abbott). *Flatland*. Boston: Roberts Brothers, 1885.

STAPLEDON, W. OLAF. *Last and First Men*. London: Methuen & Co., 1930.

———. *Last Men in London*. London: Methuen & Co., 1932.

———. *Odd John*. New York: E. P. Dutton & Co., 1936.

———. *Sirius A Fantasy of Love and Discord*. London: Secker & Warburg, 1944.

———. *Star Maker*. London: Methuen & Co., 1937.

STEVENSON, ROBERT LOUIS. *The Strange Case of Dr. Jekyll and Mr. Hyde*. 1886.

STOCKTON, FRANCIS RICHARD. *The Great Stone of Sardis*. New York and London: Harper and Brothers, 1897.

———. "A Tale of Negative Gravity," copyrighted 1884, in *A Chosen Few*. New York: Scribner's, 1895.

STONG, PHIL, ed. *The Other Worlds*. New York: Wilfred Funk, 1941.

STRIBLING, T. S. "The Green Splotches," *Adventure Magazine* (January 3, 1920).

SWIFT, JONATHAN. *Gulliver's Travels*. 1726.

TAINE, JOHN (*pseud.* for Eric Temple Bell). *Before the Dawn*. Baltimore: The Williams and Wilkins Company, 1934.

———. *The Iron Star*. New York: E. P. Dutton & Co., 1930.

TARDE, GABRIEL DE. *Underground Man*. London: Duckworth & Co., 1905.

THORPE, FRED. *The Silent City*. New York: Street and Smith, n. d.

TIPHAIGNE DE LA ROCHE, CHARLES FRANCOIS. *Giphantia*. London: R. Horsfield, 1760-61. (*Giphantie*. Babylone (*pseud.* for Paris): 1760.)

VERNE, JULES. *Around the World in Eighty Days*. Paris: Hetzel, 1872. *Note*: The romances of Jules Verne are so well known in English that the French titles are not given here. The date of first publication is given, whether in French or in English. The publications are innumerable. All the stories cited here may be found in *Novels by* . . . London: Victor Gollancz, 1929; or *Works of* . . . , ed. by Horne. New York and London: Vincent Parke and Company, n. d.

———. *Captain Hatteras*. Paris: Hetzel, 1865.

———. *The Castle of the Carpathians*. First publication? Akron, Ohio: Saalfield Publishing Company, 1900.

———. *Dr. Ox's Experiment*. Paris: Hetzel, 1874.

———. "A Drama in the Air," *Musée des familles, c.* 1850.

———. *The Five Hundred Millions of the Begum*. Paris: 1879.

———. *Five Weeks in a Balloon*. Paris: Hetzel, 1863.

———. *Floating Island*. 1876(?).

———. *From the Earth to the Moon and Round the Moon*. Paris: Hetzel, 1865 and 1870.

———. *Hector Servadac*. Paris, 1877.

———. *In Search of the Castaways*. Paris: Hetzel, 1870.

———. *A Journey to the Center of the Earth*. Paris: Hetzel, 1864.

———. *The Master of the World.* Paris: Hetzel, 1905.

———. *The Mysterious Island.* Paris: Hetzel, 1870 and 1875.

———. *The Purchase of the North Pole.* 1889(?).

———. *Robur the Conqueror.* Paris: Hetzel, 1886.

———. *The Sphinx of Ice.* 1897.

———. *The Star of the South.* Paris: Hetzel, 1884.

———. *The Steam House.* Paris: Hetzel, 1880.

———. *Twenty Thousand Leagues Under the Sea.* Paris: Hetzel, 1870.

———. *The Underground City* (also published as *The Black Indies*). 1877.

VERRILL, A. HYATT. "Beyond the Pole," *Amazing Stories,* I (October and November, 1926), 580-595 and 725-735.

VOLTAIRE, FRANCOIS DE (*pseud.* for François Marie Arouet). "Micromegas." 1752. (London: George Bell and Sons, 1891.)

VON HANSTEIN, OTFRID. "Utopia Island," *Wonder Stories,* II (May, 1931), 1352-1397 and 1471, and II (June, 1931), 76-128.

WANDREI, DONALD. "The Red Brain," *Weird Tales,* X (October, 1927), 531-536.

WATERLOO, STANLEY. *The Story of Ab.* Chicago: Way and Williams, 1897.

WELLS, HERBERT GEORGE. "Æpyornis Island," *The Pall Mall Budget* (Christmas Number. 1894). *Note:* Wells's romances have been published in so many editions that only the first publication is noted here. The short stories are collected in *The Short Stories of* . . . London: Ernest Benn, 1927, and other collections. The full-length romances are found in various publications, including the Atlantic Edition of *The Works of* . . . London: T. Fisher Unwin, 1927.

———. "The Argonauts of the Air," *Phil May's Annual* magazine (1895).

———. *The Autocracy of Mr. Parham.* Garden City: Doubleday, Doran and Co., 1930.

———. "The Country of the Blind," *The Strand Magazine* (April, 1904).

———. "The Crystal Egg," *New Review* (1897).

———. "The Diamond Maker," *The Pall Mall Budget* (about 1894).

———. "A Dream of Armageddon," *Black and White Magazine* (1901).

———. "The Empire of the Ants," *The Strand Magazine* (December, 1905).

———. *The First Men in the Moon.* London: George Newnes, 1901.

———. "The Flowering of the Strange Orchid," *The Pall Mall Budget* (August 2, 1894).

———. *The Food of the Gods.* London: Macmillan & Co., 1904.

———. "The Grisly Folk," *Storyteller Magazine* (April, 1921).

———. "In the Abyss," *Pearson's Magazine* (August, 1896).

———. "In the Avu Observatory," *The Pall Mall Budget* (August 9, 1894).

———. *The Invisible Man.* London: C. Arthur Pearson, 1897.

———. *The Island of Dr. Moreau.* London: William Heinemann, 1896.

———. "The Land Ironclads," *The Strand Magazine* (December, 1903).

———. "The Lord of the Dynamos," *The Pall Mall Budget* (September 6, 1894).

———. "The Man Who Could Work Miracles," *The Illustrated London News* (July, 1898).

———. *Men Like Gods.* London, New York, etc.: Cassell and Company, 1923.

———. *Mr. Blettsworthy on Rampole Island.* London: E. Benn, 1928.

———. *A Modern Utopia.* London: Chapman and Hall, 1905.

———. "The New Accelerator," *The Strand Magazine* (December, 1901).

———. "The Plattner Story," *The New Review* (April, 1896).

———. "The Sea Raiders," *The Weekly Sun Literary Supplement* (December 6, 1896).

———. "The Star," *The Graphic* (Christmas Number, 1897).

———. *Star-Begotten.* New York: The Viking Press, 1937.

———. "The Stolen Bacillus," *The Pall Mall Budget* (June 21, 1894).

———. "The Story of Davidson's Eyes," *The Pall Mall Budget* (March 28, 1895).

———. "A Story of the Days to Come," *Pall Mall Gazette* (1897).

———. "The Story of the Late Mr. Elvesham," *The Idler* (May, 1896).

———. "A Story of the Stone Age," *The Idler* (May-September, 1897).

———. *The Time Machine.* London: William Heinemann, 1895.

———. "The Valley of the Spiders," *Pearson's Magazine* (March, 1903).

———. *The War in the Air.* London: George Bell and Sons, 1908.

———. *The War of the Worlds.* London: William Heinemann, 1898.

———. *When the Sleeper Wakes.* New York and London: Harper and Brothers, 1899.

———. *The World Set Free.* London: Macmillan and Co., 1914.

WESTALL, WILLIAM, *A Queer Race.* New York and London: Cassell & Co., 1887.

WICKS, MARK. *To Mars Via the Moon.* London: Seeley and Co., and Philadelphia: J. B. Lippincott Co., 1911.

[WILKINS, JOHN.] *A Discourse Concerning a New World and Another Planet.* Book I, 1638. Book II, 1640. London: John Norton for John Maynard, 1640 (third impression, first complete edition).

[———.] *Mercury: or the Secret and Swift Messenger.* London: John Maynard and Timothy Wilkins, 1641. (London: Rich. Baldwin, 1694.)

WOLLHEIM, DONALD A., ed. *The Portable Novels of Science.* New York: The Viking Press, 1945. (Contains Wells's *The First Men in the Moon,* Taine's *Before the Dawn,* Lovecraft's *The Shadow Out of Time,* and Stapledon's *Odd John.*)

WRIGHT, SYDNEY FOWLER. *The Island of Captain Sparrow.* New York: Cosmopolitan Book Corporation, 1928.

———. *The World Below.* London: W. Collins & Sons Co., 1929.

WYLIE, PHILIP. *The Gladiator.* New York: Alfred A. Knopf, 1930.

———. See Balmer.

B. *Critical Works*

ADKINS, NELSON F. "An Early American Story of Utopia," *Colophon,* New Series, I, No. 1, pp. 123-132.

BAILEY, J. O. "An Early American Utopian Fiction," *American Literature,* XIV (November, 1942), 285-293.

———. "Sources for Poe's *Arthur Gordon Pym,* 'Hans Pfaal,' and Other Pieces," *Publications of the Modern Language Association,* LVII (June, 1942), 513-535.

BIRKHEAD, EDITH. *The Tale of Terror.* London: Constable & Co., 1921.

BLODGETT, ELEANOR DICKINSON. "Bacon's *New Atlantis* and Campanella's *Civitas Solis*: A Study in Relationships," *Publications of the Modern Language Association,* XLVI (September, 1931).

CAZAMIAN, MADELEINE L. *Le roman et les idées en Angleterre L'influence de la science (1860-1890).* London: Oxford University Press, 1923.

DEISCH, NOEL. "The Navigation of Space in Early Speculation and in Modern Research," *Popular Astronomy,* XXXVIII (February, 1930).

DERLETH, AUGUST. *H. P. L. A Memoir.* (A biography of Lovecraft.) New York: Ben Abramson, 1945.

GOVE, PHILIP BABCOCK. *The Imaginary Voyage in Prose Fiction. A History of Its Criticism and a Guide for Its Study, with an Annotated Check List of 215 Imaginary Voyages from 1700 to 1800.*

New York: Columbia University Press, 1941.

HERTZLER, JOYCE ORAMEL. *The History of Utopian Thought*. New York: Macmillan, 1923.

LAWTON, H. W. "Bishop Godwin's *Man in the Moone*," *Review of English Studies*, VII (1930), 23-55.

MUMFORD, LEWIS. *The Story of Utopias*. New York: Boni and Liveright, 1922.

NICOLSON, MARJORIE. "Cosmic Voyages," *ELH A Journal of English Literary History*, VII (June, 1940), 83-107.

———. "Kepler, The *Somnium*, and John Donne," *Journal of the History of Ideas*, I (June, 1940), 259-280.

———. "A World in the Moon," *Smith College Studies in Modern Languages*, XVII (1936), 12-13.

PECK, JOHN WELLS. "Symmes' Theory," *Ohio Archaeological and Historical Publications*, XVIII (1909), 28-42.

RAILO, EINO. *The Haunted Castle*. London: Routledge, 1927.

RUSSELL, FRANCES THERESA. *Touring Utopia*. New York: Lincoln MacVeagh, 1932.

SCARBOROUGH, DOROTHY. *The Supernatural in Modern English Fiction*. New York and London, 1917.

Index

The Index lists titles of pieces of scientific fiction under each author's name. Additional references to an author on a page that mentions a piece of his fiction are indexed under the title of the fiction. Selected general terms are indexed; they are usually inclusive, as "Eugenics" may include "Selective parentage," "Birth control," and Population control." Other general terms, like "Science," "Invention," Machine Age," and "Warfare," so constantly used that they occur on nearly every page, are not indexed. Names of characters in pieces of fiction are not indexed. Passing references to authors and titles of general works are not indexed.